# THE
# KINGDOM
# OF
# ZYDECO

*Crowley, Louisiana, 1938.*

# THE

# KINGDOM

## OF

# ZYDECO

MICHAEL TISSERAND

ARCADE PUBLISHING · NEW YORK

to **Tami and Cecilia**
*for the house dances*

Rounder Records has released the companion CD to this book. Also called *The Kingdom of Zydeco,* it features recordings by major zydeco musicians and is available at fine record stores everywhere, or via mail order at 1-800-443-4727.

FIRST EDITION

*Library of Congress Catologing-in-Publication Data*

Tisserand, Michael, 1963–
        The kingdom of zydeco / by Michael Tisserand. —1st ed.
                p.      cm.
        Includes bibliographic references.
        ISBN 1-55970-418-7
        1. Zydeco music—History and criticism.  I. Title.
    ML3560.C25T57  1998
    781.62'410763—dc21                                                    98-6640

Published in the United States by Arcade Publishing, Inc., New York
Distributed by Little, Brown and Company

10 9 8 7 6 5 4 3 2 1

Designed by API

PRINTED IN THE UNITED STATES OF AMERICA

# CONTENTS

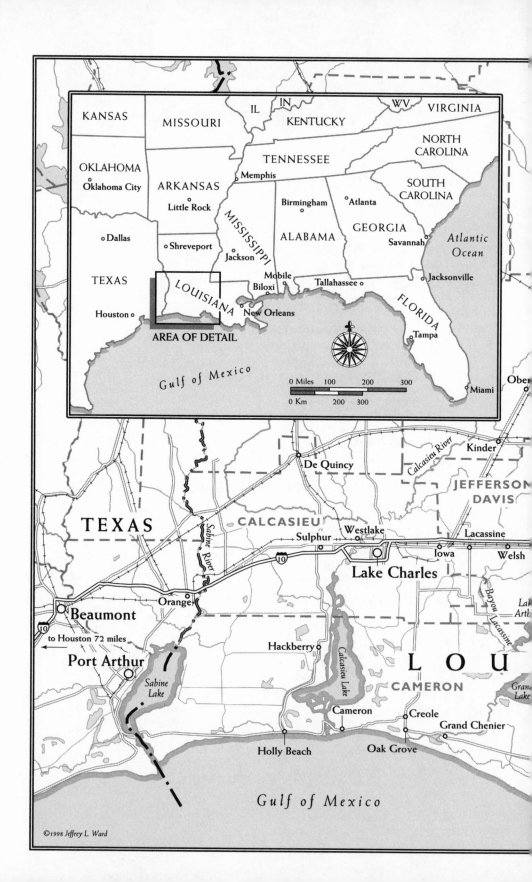

KANSAS
MISSOURI
IL
IN
KENTUCKY
WV VIRGINIA

OKLAHOMA
○Oklahoma City

ARKANSAS
○Little Rock

TENNESSEE
○Memphis

NORTH
CAROLINA

SOUTH
CAROLINA

○Dallas
○Shreveport

MISSISSIPPI

Birmingham
○

Atlanta
○

GEORGIA

ALABAMA

Savannah
○

Atlantic
Ocean

TEXAS

LOUISIANA

Jackson
○

Mobile
○
Biloxi ○

Tallahassee ○

○ Jacksonville

Houston ○

New Orleans
○

FLORIDA

AREA OF DETAIL

○ Tampa

Gulf of Mexico

0 Miles  100      200      300
0 Km        200    300

Ober

○ Miami

Calcasieu River

Kinder

De Quincy ○

JEFFERSON
DAVIS

TEXAS

CALCASIEU

Sabine River

Sulphur

Westlake
○

Lacassine

Iowa
○

Welsh
○

Bayou

10

Lake Charles

Orange ○

Beaumont

10

to Houston 72 miles

Port Arthur

Hackberry ○

Sabine
Lake

Calcasieu Lake

Lac
Arth

L  O  U

CAMERON

Gran
Lake

Cameron ○

Creole ○

Grand Chenier ○

Holly Beach ○

Oak Grove ○

Gulf of Mexico

©1998 Jeffrey L. Ward

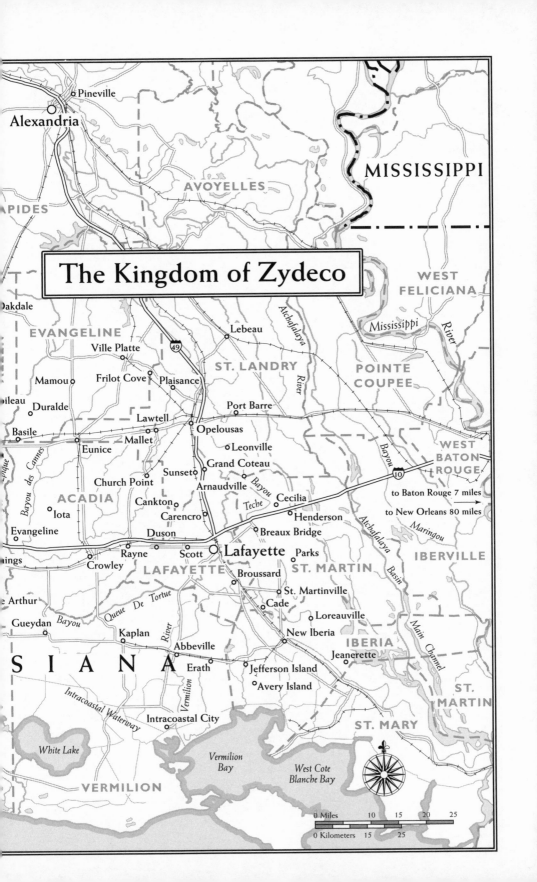

# The Kingdom of Zydeco

MISSISSIPPI

WEST FELICIANA

Pineville

Alexandria

APIDES

AVOYELLES

Oakdale

EVANGELINE

POINTE COUPEE

Mississippi River

Atchafalaya River

Lebeau

Ville Platte

ST. LANDRY

Mamou

Frilot Cove

Plaisance

Duralde

Port Barre

Basile

Lawtell

Opelousas

Eunice

Mallet

Leonville

Grand Coteau

WEST BATON ROUGE

Bayou

Sunset

Church Point

Arnaudville

Cecilia

to Baton Rouge 7 miles

ACADIA

Cankton

Teche

Bayou

Henderson

to New Orleans 80 miles

Iota

Carencro

Maringou

Evangeline

Duson

Breaux Bridge

IBERVILLE

Rayne

Scott

Lafayette

Parks

Atchafalaya Basin

Crowley

LAFAYETTE

Broussard

ST. MARTIN

Arthur

Queue De Tortue

St. Martinville

Gueydan

Bayou

Cade

Loreauville

Main Channel

Kaplan

River

Abbeville

New Iberia

IBERIA

Jeanerette

SIANA

Erath

Jefferson Island

ST. MARTIN

Vermilion

Avery Island

Intracoastal Waterway

Intracoastal City

ST. MARY

White Lake

Vermilion Bay

West Cote Blanche Bay

VERMILION

0 Miles    10    15    20    25

0 Kilometers    15    25

# ACKNOWLEDGMENTS

"THE WORD 'BOOK,' it means that you got to roam around," zydeco saxophonist John Hart once told me. This particular book represents several years of roaming through zydeco communities in Southwest Louisiana, East Texas, and California. I owe the greatest debt of gratitude to the musicians, families, and others who warmly invited me into their homes and trusted me with their stories. Special thanks to Warren Ceasar, Leona Chavis, JoAnn Delafose, Al and Alice Lewis, and Cynthia Simien, for culinary kindnesses. It was always a good sign when the interviewing had to wait until gumbo was served.

Thanks to Keith Spera for first procuring me directions to Dog Hill, and for much help through the years. Thanks to Jan Ramsey and everyone else at *OffBeat* magazine, under whose auspices I first ventured out on the zydeco trail. Portions of this book also initially appeared in the pages of *Living Blues*, *Louisiana Cultural Vistas*, *The Oxford American*, and the *Times of Acadiana*. I am grateful to everyone at these publications for their interest and support.

For many favors, thanks to Charles Adcock, Lawrence Ardoin, Shane Bernard, Jason Berry, Scott Billington, Les Blank, Willie Davis, Glenn Dicker, Ted Fox, Herman Fusilier, David Gaar, Matt Goldman, Peter Guralnick, Gary Hayman, Stuart Klipper, Dicky Landry, Mike Levier, Marc Lipkin, Tina Mayfield, Judith Meriwether, Francis Pavy, Tom Piazza, Jack Reich, Paul Senegal, Floyd Soileau, Chris Strachwitz, John Ullman, and Carolyn Ware; to Bob Kehew for drawing the map; to Ben Sandmel for sound advice and assistance over the years; to Lisa Richardson for ethnomusicological navigations; to Carolyn Dural for Creole and French transcriptions and translations; to Paul Hefti and Georgie Richard for helping to uncover new information about Amédé Ardoin; to Philip Gould for photos, suggestions, and breakfasts at Dwyer's.

I owe my initial education in zydeco and Creole culture to the work of Barry Ancelet, Carl Brasseaux, John Broven, Michael Doucet, Ann Savoy, and Nick Spitzer, all of whom considerately answered my many queries. Thanks to Jared Snyder, for sharing both published and unpublished research concerning the life of Amédé Ardoin and the history of the accordion; D'Jalma Garnier for his interview tape of Canray Fontenot; Junior Thomas and Frank Malbrough for the introduction to the world of trail rides; Wilbert Guillory, Liz Savoy, and Paul Scott of the Zydeco Festival; Kermon Richard at Richard's Club; Sid Williams at El Sid O's; Tony Gradney at Slim's Y-Ki-Ki; John Blancher at Mid-City Lanes; and Don Cravins of the Zydeco Extravaganza.

For help with photographs thanks to: Johnny Allan, Brett Bonner, Claude Boudreaux, Josie Breger, Tim Cape, JoAnn Delafose, Andrus and Michelle Espre, Philip Foster, Jean Hangarter, Cilla Huggins, Linda Keenan, Michael Kieffer, David Kurtz, Al Lewis, Alice Lewis, Hazel Lewis, Robin May, Barbara Roberds, Joseph A. Rosen, Scott Saltzman, Ann Savoy, Michael P. Smith, Jack Vartoogian, Linda Vartoogian, and Brian Ashley White.

Many thanks to everyone at the Louisiana Endowment for the Humanities, which funded part of my research. I am especially grateful to the endowment's director, Michael Sartisky, for encouraging me to request an interview from Canray Fontenot. Thanks also to the staffs at the Archive of Folk Song at the Library of Congress, the Louisiana State Museum, and the Lafayette Convention and Visitors' Center.

The benevolent Bob Mugge shared his interview tapes from his movie *The Kingdom of Zydeco* — and if that wasn't enough, he even let me make off with his title. Thanks to Richard McDonough, whose redoubled efforts brought this book to the dance. And many thanks to the good folks at Arcade. My editor, Tim Bent, was always there with help and direction. Ann Marlowe and her purple pencil also made this a better book.

Thanks to my mother and father, who first taught me to read and write, and then took me on family trips to New Orleans; to Tami, for encouraging a career in writing and then riding out the consequences; to Cecilia, for her inestimable contributions to the final weeks of editing.

Lastly, during the course of my work zydeco lost some of its truest friends and practitioners, each of whom generously gave of their time to this project. Thank you to John Delafose, Canray Fontenot, Lee Lavergne, Anderson Moss, Rockin' Sidney Simien, Doris McClendon, and Beth Verret. Your lives and contributions are remembered.

# FOREWORD

---

**M**Y FIRST ANCESTOR to come to America was named Jean-Baptiste Tisserand. When he disembarked in New Orleans, it was 1840, and the city was infested with yellow fever. Jean-Baptiste stayed for several years, finding work burying the dead in trenches. Then he moved north.

I was born in Indiana — not a kingdom of rubboards and French accordions. It was 1983 when I first moved to New Orleans. I was twenty years old and I wanted to see Mardi Gras. Then one Thursday night, I followed a French Quarter musician's hand-drawn map to the Maple Leaf Bar, where John Delafose and the Eunice Playboys were holding court.

Walking into the Maple Leaf was like being transported to another place and time. The music glanced along the tin roof and crashed against my confused ears: Delafose was singing in French and playing accordion, his son Geno was on drums, and a nephew named Jermaine Jack was loudly striking a metal washboard that hung from his shoulders. Before that night I had always associated the accordion with Lawrence Welk, washboards with washing, and French with . . . France. While my ears took in the new sounds, my eyes were dazzled by the sight of couples whirling under ceiling fans, turning in graceful waltzes and intricate two-steps. It was my introduction to the kingdom of zydeco.

Though I didn't know it then, this was a significant time in zydeco. The music was beginning to be regularly heard in dance venues outside its home communities in rural Louisiana (about a two-hour drive west of New Orleans), East Texas, and California. The scene in the Maple Leaf demonstrated how popular a sturdy, dance-oriented zydeco band — no strobe lights or fancy choreography for John Delafose — could be with a new crowd. I watched the dancers and practiced my first steps in an empty corner on the tiled dance floor.

Soon I began to discover events like the New Orleans Jazz and Heritage Festival, the Festivals Acadiens in Lafayette, and the Zydeco Festival in Plaisance. During Jazz Fest, at the late Allison Miner's magical Music Heritage Stage, I first had the opportunity to listen to musicians speaking about their life and art. When I later started writing as a profession, one of my first thoughts was to explore the world of zydeco.

I suspect that much of my early interest in zydeco followed a typical pattern for new fans. Dancing draws listeners into the music, and today new converts are joining the flock at a pace any evangelist would envy. Out-of-towners make zydeco pilgrimages to Southwest Louisiana dance clubs like Richard's and Slim's Y-Ki-Ki. Touring bands attract large crowds from Seattle to Washington, D.C. Zydeco is becoming the latest rage in couple dancing: instructors fly in with musicians, teaching the latest steps to students who sew boot soles to the bottoms of their tennis shoes. Internet correspondents excitedly report hearing zydeco in Zagreb. As for me, I am, at this writing, beginning to pack my bags for my fourth move back to Louisiana.

But in the past decade, thanks to a confluence of events in American pop culture, it has no longer become necessary to go to Louisiana to find zydeco. During my first weeks in New Orleans, I took a short-lived job washing dishes at K-Paul's Louisiana Kitchen, where Opelousas-born chef Paul Prudhomme was busy igniting a worldwide craze for Cajun cooking. At the same time, Rockin' Sidney's song "My Toot-Toot" became an international novelty hit; a Mexican version sold over a million copies. Also in the 1980s, zydeco enjoyed newfound critical acceptance as Queen Ida, Clifton Chenier, and Rockin' Sidney all won Grammies. The watershed year for the popularization of zydeco was 1987, when the Hollywood movie *The Big Easy* featured a Cajun detective and a Louisiana soundtrack, and musician Rockin' Dopsie had a song on Paul Simon's *Graceland*.

Today, zydeco continues to claim new territory. In 1996 both presidential candidates appeared with zydeco bands during their swings through Louisiana, and Buckwheat Zydeco played before a television audience of billions during the closing ceremonies of the Summer Olympics. Hundreds of national television commercials are harnessing zydeco rhythms to peddle everything from breakfast cereal to lottery tickets. The children and grand-children of players who performed at rural house dances have taken their music into halls named Carnegie and Royal Albert.

Yet what most intrigues newcomers about zydeco — why I am most drawn to its sound — is that it also remains deeply embedded in its home on the Louisiana prairies. Here it defines a way of life that is both rooted in tradition and as contemporary as next weekend. Few traditional American music cultures enjoy the vitality of the zydeco scene. Every weekend, young fans meet at the clubs and outdoor "trail rides," as do older couples who still speak French at home. In this way, zydeco is created in the collaboration be-tween another generation of dancers and musicians. Explains Sean Ardoin, drummer for the band Double Clutchin': "We can't all sing together, we can't all pray together, we can't all speak the same language, but we can all dance."

# AUTHOR'S NOTE

**M**OST OF THIS BOOK — like the lives of most black Creoles today — is conducted in English. It is not uncommon, however, for a conversation in Southwest Louisiana to also move fluidly into French. This fact is represented in the French transcriptions and translations here.

Although not "standard" French, both Creole and Cajun French have distinct rules of structure and syntax. Such usages (the singular personal pronoun "mo" for "I," for example) correspond with Creole-speaking cultures around the world. Other words and rules seem to have originated in Louisiana. And as C. J. Chenier observes, language in this region changes from town to town, street to street, even house to house. The French used in these pages, therefore, may look different from that seen elsewhere.

Song titles pose another problem. When speaking of a song in general, I employ standard French. When referring to specific recordings, I use original names and spellings. Some of these — such as Clifton Chenier's "Ay-Tete Fee" and "Tu Le Ton Son Ton" — clearly result from newly invented spellings for French phrases such as *eh 'tite fille* ("hey, little girl") and *tous les temps en temps* ("every now and then"). These titles often reflect the language barriers between French-speaking musicians and English-speaking producers. Nonetheless, these words become the new standard when they are used as names of bands (Zolo Go) or dance clubs (Bon Ton Rouley).

Complicating things even further is the fact that different spellings have been used in various recordings of the same song. For example, Clifton Chenier's 1965 "Zydeco Et Pas Salé" roughly translates to "Snap Beans and No Salt." When the song was later reissued, the line was modified to "Zydeco Sont Pas Salé," meaning "The Snap Beans Aren't Salty." This has more or less become the standard transcription and translation of this song for other artists, as well; it is the one used here.

# THE
# KINGDOM
# OF
# ZYDECO

The kingdom of heaven is like unto treasure hid in a field; the which when a man hath found, he hideth, and for joy thereof goeth and selleth all that he hath, and buyeth that field.

—MATTHEW 13:44

That crown wasn't make-believe to my daddy, man. It was real.

—C. J. CHENIER,
*talking about legendary zydeco accordionist Clifton Chenier*

# INTRODUCTION

## CREOLES AND CAJUNS

---

THE LOUISIANA FLATLAND reaches across a half dozen parish lines on its way from brown basin marshes to the sunset gateway of Texas, drops southward into sugarcane fields and sandy cheniers, and rises northward to prairie lawns of rice and cotton and cattle. It is the wettest state on the continent; clouds of steam roll in from the Gulf, there's an annual wash of five feet of rain, and it thunders every five days.

In both open country and busy cities, weekends bring other sounds, sounds that rise from wood-frame buildings bordering dark pastures, and come clattering from cinderblock clubs on street corners. Inside, musicians wielding gilded accordions and sculpted metal vests are accompanied by the staccato clap of dancers' boot soles. Floor joists shake, stoic faces drip sweat, and the damp air fills with musical complaints:

> "I got a paper in my shoe."
> "Give him cornbread."
> *"Zydeco sont pas salés!"*

At the start of each song, a new crowd fills the floor, and another zydeco is under way.

1

Zydeco is the traditional dance music — and the dance — of the black Creoles of Southwest Louisiana. Today its syncopated rhythms and spirited joie de vivre translate to audiences around the world. Yet wherever zydeco goes, it is followed by misunderstandings about both the music and its culture.

Confusion usually starts with a confusing word: "Creole." Derived from the Latin *creare*, which means "to create," "Creole" has created new meanings for itself around the world. It has been applied to all colonial-born persons, and its meaning is entangled in the briars of class and race. For the Portuguese, a *crioulo* meant a slave of African descent born in the New World; this meaning was used in Louisiana as well. Paradoxically, it was also used to designate society members of European descent. Not surprisingly, the ambiguous word is currently falling out of favor in New Orleans. But on the other side of the Atchafalaya Basin, in the rural parishes, it is enjoying a renaissance. Here it is used by many — though not all — blacks to describe their heritage and values. When people in Southwest Louisiana describe themselves as "black Creole," they usually mean that they prefer a way of life that expresses itself in traditional food, the French language, and zydeco.

In Southwest Louisiana, it is not unusual to hear someone describe himself as both an African-American and a true Frenchman. Creoles acknowledge — indeed celebrate — such a mixed ancestry. Among their forebears are slaves brought directly from Africa, as well as through Haiti and other Caribbean islands. They arrived to discover a rural society that included free blacks who had established themselves long before the Civil War. The character of the state's African-American population changed again after 1791, when *gens libres de couleur* — free persons of color — moved here following the Haitian revolution. The heritage of modern Creoles is a blending of these diverse black groups, as well as American Indians and Europeans, especially French and Spanish. Zydeco, with its mix of European- and African-Caribbean-derived song traditions, is the musical voice of this experience.

Yet the meeting of these groups also resulted in some discordance. Following the Civil War, poor whites and most free blacks occupied precarious ground defined by a system of laws that seems as odd now as it was hidebound then. A free black could sue a white in court, but the two races couldn't legally share a church pew. Blacks were forbidden to copy white clothing styles. Discrimination also became a way of life within the black communities, as some former free blacks struggled to hold on to their slipping social status.

There is a story told by musicians in Louisiana that helps explain the personal impact of this history. The central figure is an accordion player. The details usually change according to the storyteller, but the setting is usually a country house dance. It begins one evening, when a black Creole is hired to play accordion. He arrives at the house to find that the dancers are lighter-skinned Creoles. The patrons are shocked to see the musician's skin. They have him put on a pair of white gloves and stand outside a window. He is told to reach his hands through the window and play the accordion inside the room. There, in the lamp-lit darkness, the only thing the dancers can see is a pair of white hands making their music.

"Isaie Blasa used to tell me about that," musician Herbert Sam recalls. "He'd tell me that. He's a real dark fellow, and not far back here, not far — I'd say about eight or ten miles — he'd play for them people, and they wouldn't let him in there. They'd set him on a tub or box to the window with white gloves on and play. Oh yeah! And he used to tell me and he'd say, 'I make my money. That's all I got to do is make my money.'"

Blasa is also the man credited with giving Clifton Chenier his first accordion. Because Chenier is the most influential musician in zydeco history, the story is often recounted with him as the central figure. Musician Hiram Sampy also heard that it happened to his father. Occasionally the patrons are remembered as whites, but more often they are light-skinned Creoles. The story bespeaks the strangeness of the day, and the shades and degrees that racism can take. It also makes it clear that the accordion player has become a symbol of the black Creole community and its place in the world.

Perhaps the most widespread misunderstanding about Southwest Louisiana culture is that Creoles and Cajuns are the same people. They're not. In fact, for many Creoles, defining themselves apart from Cajun culture has become essential in asserting their own identity. The state legislature has officially named the Southwest Louisiana region Acadiana, and it is unofficially known as Cajun Country everywhere else. Some scholars and journalists have settled on the oxymoron "black Cajun" to refer to Creoles, and the national press has labeled zydeco as Cajun music's "younger cousin," and the like. Wilbert Guillory, founding director of the Southwest Louisiana Zydeco Festival, has led the fight against these misconceptions. "I don't use the phrase 'Acadiana,' I use 'Southwest Louisiana,'" he says. "I let people know up front. I also let them know that the Cajuns have done a good job of promoting their culture. But I'm not a Cajun. I'm Afro-American Creole, black Creole — whatever you want to call me other than a Cajun, you can."

However, arguably the single most important cultural and musical influence on the Creoles has been from their neighbors the Cajuns. Their histories, like their music, are interlocked. Coming from Acadia — the region in Canada now covered by Nova Scotia — the French-speaking Acadians had been expelled from their homes in the 1755 Grand Dérangement after refusing to take a loyalty oath to the English king. At the time, Spain governed Louisiana, and saw the Acadians as ideal settlers: Catholic, farmers, productive, and anti-British. They settled in close-knit communities on bayous and prairies. They primarily worked as trappers, fishers, and *petits habitants*, or small-scale farmers.

Now a proud marker of identity, "Cajun" originated as an ethnic slur. The new arrivals were quickly shunned by other whites. Their reputation in the rest of the country wasn't very high, either. A cover story in an 1866 edition of *Harper's Weekly* indicates the degree of contempt endured by both Cajuns and poor blacks. The Cajuns, it proclaimed, are "behind the age in every thing. . . . So little are they thought of — that the niggers, when they want to express contempt for one of their own race, call him an Acadian nigger." Into the twentieth century, young Cajuns and Creoles continued to face ridicule and punishment when they tried to speak French in school. "When I was coming up, my first words were in French," recalls zydeco accordionist Rosie Ledet. "But my parents thought it wouldn't be good for school, so they stopped me. Now I wish I would have just kept talking." Their music was also ridiculed. When Cajun and Creole musicians set out to play the Newport Folk Festival in the 1960s, the local papers derided them as cultural embarrassments.

It is not surprising, then, that white Cajuns and black Creoles have often found themselves with much in common. When the Cajuns arrived in Louisiana, they worked side by side with the Creoles, sharecropping the same fields. This close contact resulted in an intense period of cultural exchanges. Regional foods such as gumbo and crawfish etouffee combined French, African, and American cooking styles and ingredients. Musical partnerships also blossomed across the fence. African-Caribbean polyrhythms and call-and-response forms blended with European-derived dances such as the waltz and the two-step. The most celebrated pairing was the Creole accordionist Amédé Ardoin and the Cajun fiddler Dennis McGee. Many of their tunes, such as the landmark 1929 recording "Eunice Two-Step," are now considered common property.

But if music was free-flowing, society was trying to build a dam. Dances became the most segregated events in Southwest Louisiana. "They played ball against one another in the pasture, but they decided to go dancing among themselves," recalls Creole accordionist Walter Polite. "That was about 'twenty-six or 'twenty-seven, before the high water." If these lines were crossed, the result could be quick violence. In the Opelousas newspaper of April 9, 1926, there is an account of thirteen blacks entering a white dance in Basile. They were from out of state, working on what is now Highway 190, and apparently had been told they could go and watch the dance. But the moment they entered, the white dancers became furious. The city marshal hurried the strangers into a local jail for their own safety, but some in the dance hall picked up a battering ram and a rope. City fathers pleaded with them to turn back, and the mob eventually relented.

By the middle of the twentieth century, the Cajuns and Creoles started to take their music on divergent paths. Cajuns began to listen to country western, with musicians such as Jimmy C. Newman striking off for Nashville. Creole artists were more interested in blues and R&B, and Clifton Chenier was packaged in tours with the Cadillacs and Lowell Fulson. Today the most obvious difference between the two sounds is in the instrumentation: the fiddle shares the lead in Cajun music but is rarely heard in zydeco. The rubboard is predominantly a zydeco instrument. Zydeco bands are also more likely to include a horn section. Cajuns have more lyrics in French. Yet the spirit of both a zydeco dance and Cajun *fais do-do* continues to reflect the music's common origin. Both can be best described in the words writer Albert Murray once used to define the blues: "Not only is its express purpose to make people feel good . . . [but] . . . to generate a disposition that is both elegantly playful and heroic in its nonchalance."


Yet the story of the gloved accordion player outside the window would continue to resonate in the twentieth century. Within the black Creole community today, even young musicians recall instances of overt racism. "I used to play with my dad at the Triangle Club in Frilot Cove," remembers Jeffery Broussard. "It was a real nice place, real huge. It would stay packed just about every weekend. There was only one thing that was different with it, and excuse me for saying this, but I felt that it was wrong. If you would go to the Triangle, it was like all the blacks were on the left-hand side, and the lighter people — they called them mulattos — were on the right-hand side. And I never could understand why. Because they were all part of the same community. I mean, everybody knew each other. Well, the young generation blew that out of the water."

A series of events in the 1990s would reveal that dance-hall discrimination still continues, however. Recently, time-honored practices have begun to undergo closer scrutiny because of a new factor in rural Louisiana life: tourism. A decade earlier, oil prices plummeted at the same time that interest in Louisiana culture soared. The economy began turning to what writer Octavio Paz called "the industry without smokestacks." And before long, black tourists began to encounter the unwritten laws that still hold sway at some Louisiana dances.

The most publicized event occurred on a weekend night in 1994, when a Cajun dance club called La Poussière allegedly refused entrance to a black patron. According to case documents, a club employee told a black tourist that the traditional Saturday dance was a private party, and turned her away. But the tourist, Zaldwaynaka Scott, was a federal prosecutor from Chicago. Another member of her party, a white civil rights prosecutor, later returned to the club. She would report that an employee told her that Scott was kept out because she was black.

The FBI sent in black and white agents to pose as potential patrons, to determine if the club was in violation of the Federal Civil Rights Act of 1964, which prohibits discrimination in public places. The matter was quietly settled two years later when the owners of La Poussière signed a consent decree that required posting a sign stating that the club welcomed all visitors. But the question at the center of debate didn't go away: the problem of music, dance, and identity. "All the coloreds got their own clubs, and the whites got their own clubs," explained one white patron of La Poussière to the *New York Times*. "And the coloreds don't dance the way the whites do."

The events at La Poussière were not isolated. Writer and radio deejay Herman Fuselier covers all sides of Louisiana music in his "Bayou Boogie" column in the *Opelousas Daily World*. He recalls a situation that developed after a jam session at a local music store. When Fuselier told one of the musicians that he'd like to hear him play at a club, the musician advised against it. "He was saying, 'I'd invite you to come with me, but the manager doesn't like blacks there, and some of the people would get mad about it.' And you know, I didn't make anything of it. I said, 'Yeah, I understand.' But it always hurts."

Yet since the partnership of Ardoin and McGee in the 1920s, musicians have also led the way in crossing the color line. Zydeco accordionist and club owner Roy Carrier recalls the Creole dances when he was growing up near Lawtell. "They had a few white people where we was at that got along with us," he remembers. "We even had Aldus Roger, the Cajun musician. And he heard about Canray Fontenot, and they got together and talked French, you know. When you're in the country, hell, there's nothing to do but be friends."

That attitude is shared by nearly all musicians today. There are many examples of important collaborations between Cajuns and Creoles: Cajun fiddler Dewey Balfa and zydeco accordionist Rockin' Dopsie demonstrating their craft in public schools; Clifton Chenier and Cajun swamp-pop star Rod Bernard having a rocking meeting of the minds on their record *Boogie in*

*Black & White.* Cajun fiddler Michael Doucet performing with Delton Broussard and the Lawtell Playboys and recording with Canray Fontenot and Nathan Williams. C. J. Chenier recording with Steve Riley. Riley with Geno Delafose. Delafose with Christine Balfa. Balfa with Bois Sec Ardoin. Today, such collaborations are the rule, not the exception.

Not all attempts to meet at the dance have been successful, however. In 1997 a newcomer to the town of Sunset planned to open a club and hire both Cajun and zydeco bands. One afternoon some young local whites came in to tell him that if he wanted to have a zydeco band, they might be returning in sheets. But most young musicians in Louisiana today share the views of Cajun bandleader Christine Balfa, which she expressed in letters to local newspapers after she encountered difficulty bringing a zydeco musician into a Cajun club. "White and black musicians playing together is nothing new," she wrote. "One can look back to Amédé Ardoin and Dennis McGee, some of the first to record 'French Music' from the area. Have you ever heard old 'Acadian' music and compared it to 'Cajun' music? I can tell you, a large part of what we consider Cajun music came from the influence of the Creoles. It is something we should be proud of."

# 1

# WHAT'S IN A NAME

---

O N A JUNE EVENING IN 1934, as the day's lingering heat drifts
through a pale-board Baptist church in Lake Arthur, Louisiana,
a thundering music resounds off wooden walls and into a microphone; it is sent in lines of cable through the door to a
parked Model A Ford with its backseat removed and replaced with five hundred pounds of recording equipment. In the car, powered by two giant Edison batteries, a weighted needle sculpts a groove in a spinning aluminum
disc. The machine is recording a song about snap beans.

Engineering the recording is a Texas college student named Alan
Lomax who, with his father, John Lomax, is braving the punishing heat of a
Southern summer to increase the holdings of the new Archive of Folk Song
in the Library of Congress. By this time, the elder Lomax has already made
his name as a folklorist: his 1910 book *Cowboy Songs and Other Frontier Ballads*
introduced such standards as "Home on the Range." In 1932, with support
from the Macmillan Company, the Library of Congress, and the American
Council of Learned Societies, he set out on a sweeping project of collecting
more than ten thousand recordings of folk songs, many performed by
Southern blacks. In 1934 alone, John estimated that they traveled thirty-two
thousand miles in nine Southern states and recorded about six hundred
songs.

Southwest Louisiana has not been an easy stretch, as John Lomax would admit in his annual report. The recording machine is always malfunctioning. Someone steals the tires from their car. Then they overturn their customized Model A and drench their clothes in battery acid. Alan Lomax would later recall that his father decided to stay in their hotel room in Jennings and work on his next book, allowing his son to test his fieldwork skills and college French among the Cajuns and Creoles of Louisiana.

But on this evening in Port Arthur, the church session is on the verge of completely derailing. The aluminum disc spinning, a group of young Creoles form couples and dance around in the church, and a man named Jimmy Peters sings a mournful tune about a woman whose man has not returned home before sundown — an ominous absence, considering the curfew that blacks once had to observe in the area. He wails, *"Mon nègre est pas arrivé"*— "my man is not home" — accenting the negative *pas*, heightening the sense of despair. It is a thrilling performance, but after Peters repeats that the *soleil après coucher*— "the sun is setting" — for the eighth time, the other singers in the church start to get restless and begin talking. One launches into a new song, and others soon join in. A nail is scraped across a rusty slice of metal, and the group launches into a giddy tune about wanting to marry but having no shoes and no money. Peters tries to finish his lament, then he gives up in disgust. Perhaps forgetting that the Library of Congress is recording his words, he starts yelling at his friends. "As it happened," Alan Lomax would later write in his notes for a reissue of the recordings, "a fight broke out at the peak of the session, and I had to pick up my machine and leave hastily, and thus was unable to find out more about this remarkable music at the time."

But before Lomax packs up and leaves the church, Peters manages to perform a song in an a cappella style today known as *juré* (from the French for "testify") or *bazar* (probably named for the church social where the music was often made). Against a fantastic background of howling vocals and sharp hand claps, he sings of a man who wanders the land with a ruined hat and a torn suit, too poor to see his woman. His lyrics date back to an old Acadian French folk song, but Peters adds a new phrase that will resonate for generations:

> *O mam, mais donnez-moi les haricots.*
> *O yé yaie, les haricots sont pas salés.*


> Oh Mom, give me the snap beans.
> O yé yaie, the snap beans are not salty.

Peters doesn't explain what he means, but the Lomaxes will learn a possible source when they hear the line again in New Iberia, where a worker named Wilfred Charles performs an unusual song about sick Italians, and concludes with:

> *Pas mis de la viande, pas mis à rien,*
> *Juste des haricots dans la chaudière,*
> *Les haricots sont pas salés.*
> *O! O nègre! Les haricots sont pas salés.*

> Put no meat, nor nothing else,
> Just snap beans in the pot,
> The snap beans are not salty.
> *O! O nègre!* The snap beans are not salty!

There is no salt meat to put in the pot with the snap beans. Like early blues musicians throughout the South, the Creoles in Louisiana are singing about poverty.

Many themes in contemporary zydeco lyrics are first heard in the remarkable performances recorded by the Lomaxes. On their journey in Louisiana they meet Paul Junius Malveaux and Ernest Lafitte, who play harmonica and sing "Bye-bye, bonsoir, mes parents" ("Good Night, My Parents") and imitate a dog in the song "Tous les samedis" ("Every Saturday"); today numerous zydeco songs include choruses of "bye-bye" or dog barks. Also in Jennings, Cleveland Benoit and Darby Hicks sing a haunting blues similar to the song Jimmy Peters couldn't get through, "Là-bas chez Moreau" ("Over at Moreau's"). Their voices cresting and falling, Benoit and Hicks trade parts as if completing each other's thoughts, singing lines about the setting sun and about going to Moreau's, a wonderful place that holds the promise of sweet candy and brown coffee. Both this song and Joseph Jones's "Blues de la prison" will be echoed years later in the music of Creole fiddler Canray Fontenot. But it's the phrase about snap beans — *les haricots sont pas salés* — that will be carried the furthest.

What's in a name? Defining "zydeco" is a matter of considerable contention; the remark that someone is or isn't playing "real zydeco" is today frequently heard at dances. In fact, it is likely that musicians will never agree on the borders of zydeco, because, in true improvisational spirit, they set out to redraw the map in every performance. In 1993 Thomas Fields asked a man in Lafayette named Paul "Papillon" Harris to teach him accordion. "The first

*Paul Junius Malveaux and Ernest Lafitte, Jennings, Louisiana, 1936.*

lesson this old man taught me," Fields recalls, "is that you're not a zydeco player if you can't make your own music." Nobody understood this philosophy better than Clifton Chenier.

It was on May 11, 1965, almost thirty-one years after Jimmy Peters sang about the snap beans, that Clifton and Cleveland Chenier entered the Gold Star studio in Houston. The tape rolling, the brothers shared a few words in Creole French:

CLIFTON: *Hé toi. Tout que'que chose est correcte?*

CLEVELAND: *C'est bon. C'est bon, boy.*

CLIFTON: *Tout que'que chose est magnifique?*

CLEVELAND: *O nèg', quittons amuser avec ça.*

CLIFTON: *Allons le zydeco!*

CLEVELAND: *Allons couri' à lé yé!*

(CLIFTON: Hey you. Everything's all right?

CLEVELAND: It's good. It's good, boy.

CLIFTON: Everything's magnificent?

CLEVELAND: Oh man, let's go have fun with that.

CLIFTON: Let's zydeco!

CLEVELAND: Let's go after it!)

Then the pair, backed by drummer Madison Guidry, launched into what would become Chenier's signature piece, "Zydeco Sont Pas Salé." On it, Chenier strips down his piano accordion and treats it like an old single-key button model, repeating notes of the same chord. Over this mighty rhythm he sings some lines about two mischievous dogs named Hip and Taïaut that date back to a 1934 Cajun record by Joseph and Cleoma Falcon, "Ils la volet mon trancas" ("They Stole My Sled"); Joe Falcon once explained that he heard the tune from a Creole accordionist named Babineaux. Chenier couples the old song with the lines about the snap beans:

> *O Mama! Quoi elle va faire avec le nègre?*
> *Zydeco est pas salé, zydeco est pas salé.*

*T'as volé mon traîneau, t'as volé mon traîneau.*
*Regarde Hip et Taïaut, regarde Hip et Taïaut.*


Oh Mama! What's she going to do with the man?
The snap beans aren't salty, the snap beans aren't salty.
You stole my sled, you stole my sled.
Look at Hip and Taïaut, look at Hip and Taïaut.


In Chenier's "Zydeco Sont Pas Salé" — today considered the anthem of zydeco — the lines about the snap beans are reunited with the same beat heard on the Lomax recordings. The result still sounds more like a *juré* performance than anything ever recorded on the accordion, before or since.

What did Chenier have in mind when he made the song? It is highly doubtful that he had heard the Lomax tapes, which were not commercially available at the time. More likely, he had direct experiences with *juré* when he was growing up in the town of Port Barre, Louisiana. "The beat came from the religion people," he once told writer Alan Govenar, clapping his hands to demonstrate.

Creole fiddler Canray Fontenot provided more details when he recalled a conversation between the two musicians.

"Clifton was the best on the accordion, and one day, me and Clifton was talking," Fontenot said. "He said, 'Say, Canray, a long time ago, they used to have some *juré*.' He said, 'Did you ever go at one of them things?' I said, 'No, Clifton, I never did.' Because they used to have that where they didn't have no musicians, but I was born where they had some musicians. What it was, them *juré*, they didn't have no music, but them old people would sit down, clap their hands, and make up a song. And they would dance on that, them people. Around Basile there, they didn't fool with nothing like that. I kept saying I wanted to go around Mamou and Ville Platte, where they used to have them *juré*.

"But Clifton's daddy was an accordion player, and he said that his daddy played one of them *juré* songs, and they called that 'Zydeco est pas salé.' Which means the snap beans don't have no salt in them. So Clifton says, 'That "Zydeco est pas salé" song is good, but the way Daddy played that, that's the wrong speed.' He says, 'I'm going to take that same song, and I'm going to put a different speed on it and them people are going to be able to dance that.' And he did, too. And when he started, everybody wanted to play the accordion, everybody wanted to play what Clifton played."


\*       \*       \*

By the time Chenier recorded the zydeco anthem, the lines about snap beans had been circulating in Houston's "Frenchtown" neighborhood, where people originally from Louisiana lived and danced. Four years earlier, Albert Chevalier and Sidney "Blind" Babineaux both recorded their own songs with this phrase. "That's the real zydeco," Babineaux, then in his eighties, told Arhoolie Records producer Chris Strachwitz. "That's been here since before I was born, too."

Yet before anybody made a record about snap beans, zydeco — or *les haricots* — was a vegetable grown by black Creole farmers.

Snap beans were a spring crop; the harvests started each year around mid-June, and these were often community events. "A lot of times there would be music with the snap bean harvesting," remembers Wilbert Guillory. "You know, a snap bean is one of the crops that it would take much more labor than any other crop that you put up in the jar, because you would have to break each end, and then you had to pull the little string off. It was very labor-intensive, because your parents wanted them snapped uniformly.

"So a lot of times the neighbors would go around each other's house and help," Guillory continues. "They would go to each other with a bucket, and harvest the snap bean, wash it, snap them, and can them. That was more in the later afternoon, mostly when you lay by your other crops. And in that case the music would be done when you were snapping the snap beans. In our community, it was my godfather, Willis Simien, Nolton Simien's daddy. And while he was playing, we were snapping snap beans and shaking — but not dancing, because you didn't have much time to dance."

The story of the snap beans next moves with the black Creoles to the Texas oil towns along the Gulf Coast. In 1901 the modern petroleum age in the United States began in a gusher of oil called Spindletop, near Beaumont, Texas. Starting almost immediately, and peaking through the years of World War II, black Creoles migrated to Texas in search of jobs, bringing along their accordions and French songs. In Houston the old spring crop was nostalgically evoked in music, and two songs recorded in Houston in the postwar era provide the first written documentation of the new sound's name. One, made sometime between 1947 and 1950, is a tune called "Zolo Go," recorded by famed blues guitarist Lightnin' Hopkins at Bill Quinn's Gold Star studio and released to area jukeboxes. Hopkins was cousin by marriage to Clifton Chenier, and Cleveland Chenier would regularly back him on rubboard; on "Zolo Go" Hopkins mimics Clifton's accordion with an electric organ, and introduces the song with a short explanation: "I'm going to zolo go a little while for you folks. You know, the young and old likes that."

The song is clearly a novelty for the guitarist, who never again attempted the style, and it would be quickly eclipsed by a lively R&B/rumba tune by a guitarist from Welsh, Louisiana, named Clarence Garlow. His now classic "Bon Ton Roula" landed in the R&B top-ten chart in February 1950. It recounted the story of "one smart Frenchman" who promises a tour of a "Creole town." Garlow points out the "church bazaar" and the "French la-la," then he finishes by making immortal these directions:

> You want to have fun, now you got to go
> Way out in the country to the zydeco.

Garlow continued to explore these themes in his follow-up songs "New Bon Ton Roulay" and "Hey Mr. Bon Ton," both recorded in New Orleans in 1953. Also that year, he provided vivid country details in "Jumping at the Zadacoe," which included a verse about butchering a sow and frying its skin into cracklin', a popular dish still served at zydeco events.

Hopkins's song was titled "Zolo Go," and Garlow used the word "zadacoe" for the big dance. But why did a word for music develop from "snap bean"? Popular etymologies often turn on a pun with the word "snap": the music is named after snap beans because it has a snappy beat. But the connection goes even deeper, and is found in Louisiana's position as a crossroads of French and African cultures.

Scholars generally agree that, during the years of slavery, more African music could be heard in the state of Louisiana than in any other part of the South. In the town center of New Orleans, now called Congo Square, African-Caribbean dances called the calenda and the bamboula began to seep into fertile musical soil, re-emerging in the modern flowering of Louisiana music: jazz, rhythm and blues, Mardi Gras Indian music, Cajun, swamp pop, and zydeco. Writers such as Elizabeth Brandon have demonstrated the link from Congo Square to zydeco (and other Louisiana music styles). In his book *Swamp Pop*, Shane Bernard traces the ritual calenda to the song "Colinda," still performed in dances today.

Language, too, kept alive an African influence. In his essay "Louisiana Creole among New World French Creoles," linguist Albert Valdman examines the Creole French interrogative *quoi faire* — literally "what to do," translated as "why." He explains that the construction is what linguists call a convergence, a blending of French and several West African languages, including Igbo and Yoruba. (*Quoi faire* is also an important phrase in Creole music and zydeco, showing up in song titles for both Amédé Ardoin and John Delafose.) For black Creoles in Louisiana, the word "zydeco" may have a similar blended history, resulting from the French *les haricots* converging with words from several languages of West African tribes, including the Yula, where *a zaré* means "I dance."

Support for this theory, which was put forth in 1986 by folklorist Nicholas Spitzer, and further developed by Barry Ancelet in his essay "Zydeco/Zarico: The Term and the Tradition," can be found in the remarkable existence of some musical cousins to zydeco located on a number of Indian Ocean islands, especially Rodrigues. Found here is a traditional musical culture that might be oddly familiar to zydeco fans: Creole French-speakers play a music called *zarico* or *cari zarico* on a goatskin drum, rattles, and an iron triangle. A dance called the *séga* includes a pantomime of the planting of beans. And in the *séga* is a step called *en bas en bas*, meaning "bend low" — suggestive of a Louisiana-born dance called the *baisse bas*.

That low bending in the *séga* and the *baisse bas* tested the limits of what was acceptable in polite dances. Ancelet reports that the traditional *séga* connects beans, fertility, and sex in a symbolic dance. Similarly, the phrase *"zydeco sont pas salés"* may be working as a double entendre, giving "zydeco" an origin similar to the word "jazz," which began as a term for sex in American black slang. Connections between food and sex are commonly made in African-American music, and while they usually involve sweets, such as jelly rolls and candy, there's also a palate for salt. Zydeco accordionist Willis Prudhomme provides an example when he explains how he wrote one of his biggest hits, "My Woman Is a Salty Dog."

"That's a little song we used to sing. We'd go behind the barn, and we'd laugh, we thought that was so funny, we'd just roll on the ground:

> My little woman is a salty dog,
> My little woman don't wear no drawers.
> She put it up in the dresser drawer.
> Santa Claus said it's against the law.

We couldn't say that in front of Mama. Mama would tear our butt up when she'd hear us. But here I am, about forty years after that, cutting a song about it — and everybody loves that little song."

For Willis Prudhomme, the salty expression started as a folk saying and resulted in a song. Perhaps "Zydeco sont pas salés" took a similar journey. Today the paths from snap beans to zydeco can only be reconstructed with much speculation. But the destination is more evident: all these unsalted snap beans finally came to a boil in 1950s Houston, in a dance that cultural historian Robert Burton "Mack" McCormick witnessed during visits to the

Frenchtown neighborhood bars. "Frenchtown was a little bit of a tourist attraction among blacks in Houston," he recalls. "There were always a lot of people teaching others the different dances, but particularly the thing with the breaking string beans." McCormick holds his hands in front of him, as if snapping beans. "People would always do this with their hands, simulating the effect, that's how it got its name, that's the basis of the whole thing. When somebody said, 'What is this?' somebody else must have said, 'Well, I'm breaking string beans, we call it zydeco.'"

Among McCormick's wide-ranging projects in the cultural arts was a two-volume album called *A Treasury of Field Recordings*, released in 1960 on the English label 77 Records. A showcase for the folk music of Houston, the album included one song by a concertina player named Dudley Alexander, who had moved to Houston from New Iberia during World War II. Backed by fiddle and rubboard, Alexander hops between French and English vocals in his version of the blues classic "Baby, Please Don't Go," which includes this introduction:

> I say Le Zydeco
> *Le Zydeco,* that means snap beans in English
> But in French — *on dit zydeco*
> 'Cause that means snap bean.

It was when he wrote out this transcription on the album notes to *A Treasury of Field Recordings* that McCormick himself played a pivotal role in transforming beans to music. He spelled the word.

McCormick's work began in his research for the project, when he had noticed that the signs and chalkboards outside Houston bars were advertising everything from "zodigos" to "zotticoes" to "zadicoes." He looked at the many ways people were spelling the music; he photographed them and studied the pictures, and he decided he didn't like any of them. So he wrote it out his own way: "zydeco." He had hoped for a popular word. He admits he's still amazed at what happened next. "It didn't occur to me that I was creating a cultural icon or whatever the hell — I'm not sure what the word is," he says. "If you coin a word, you coin a word, but what is it if you spell a word? What is the word for it? Have you coined it, or orthographically defined it? What have you done here?

"But there was a problem, because people were saying, 'We're going to the zydeco,' and I would ask them, 'What? What are you saying? Say it loud and clear.' 'Zydeco.' I went around and shot posters and signs, and came up with all these spellings. Interesting spellings. But I couldn't embrace any of them. One of them was z-o-r-d-i-c-o. Zordico. It's close but it wasn't right.

"Then there was the record Lightnin' Hopkins made — if you listen to what he says, it doesn't sound like the word they used. I reviewed all the photographs. I agonized over the thing, and would write it out and show it to people and ask them to pronounce it. 'Z-o-r' I saw, 'z-i,' but I never saw a 'z-y.' I debated for a long time whether I should deviate that far from the spellings I was seeing. And I debated about the letter to come after the 'd' — I worried about whether it should be 'd-i' or 'd-e,' and to this day I can even embrace an argument for the 'i.' But I did what I did. My objective was to get as close to the sound of the thing as possible."

But McCormick acknowledges other inspirations for his word, as well. "I must admit, as a kid, I was always fascinated with the end of the dictionary. I remember words like 'zymurgy' and 'zygote,' and that was slightly in my mind when the problem came up. With 'z-y,' I had in mind the typographer's view of this thing. With the 'z-y' flash, it has a Buck Rogers futuristic aspect, it suggests modernity. And it turned out to be a catchy kind of thing. There aren't too many words like it. 'Jazz' is an equally zippy-looking word and powerful — when it came around, you had the jazz age and jazz people, and I don't think all that would have happened if you couldn't start with that word. Look at Dean Martin and Bing Crosby. The crooners. See what a shitty word they got? What an awful word. I haven't seen that word in print for years, and I didn't want that to happen to the word 'zydeco.'"

He had no cause for alarm, for the new word soon hit the papers. When *A Treasury of Field Recordings* appeared, McCormick himself publicized it in articles for the *Houston Post* and the *Saturday Review of Literature*. Then a local printer began to use the new spelling on posters. "See, everybody loved the damn word, that's the problem with it," continues McCormick, not completely pleased with his success. "I've never had anything embraced this much. To this day, I keep thinking I should have just put a trademark on there and offered it to people, because they obviously liked it so well they would have given me a percentage to use it somewhere. If I figured out a distinctive way for the 'z' and the 'y' to be fitted together I'd have had a perfect trademark.

"But everybody just absolutely used it. I went back to Frenchtown about two years later and took some more photographs, and they all used the same spelling. Except one chalkboard that was outside of a building where somebody had gone out. They didn't know the new spelling. So I went in there and told them what it was, and they immediately wiped it out and put it down. I took pictures of that whole process, because to me it was like when you have a hit record. You've seen artists dazzled by how successful a record is that they've done. Well, it was the same thing. And it's one of the things that made me aware of how dangerous it is to go around screwing with people's way of doing things."

McCormick had intended the word to apply to the local alloy of Texas blues and French Creole music — the kind of sound you heard when a concertina player sang "Baby, Please Don't Go" in French and English — and he was horrified when the word was sucked back across the Louisiana border. "When I'm talking about zydeco, I'm talking about the music of Frenchtown, because I never fully accepted the second layer of the word," he says. "It jars me. And the people who usurped that and started it were the Louisiana tourist commissions. They had a massive publicity thing, so when they did it, it was done within a year's time. Louisiana's very big on tourists, so when they put out a map that says rice country, zydeco country, jazz country, and they send three million copies of the map out, it's over."

The word truly fell out of his hands when it was hitched to Clifton Chenier's star. In 1955 Chenier had recorded an accordion instrumental that Specialty Records titled "Zodico Stomp," but Chris Strachwitz was well aware of the new spelling when he went with Chenier into the Gold Star studio and recorded "Zydeco Sont Pas Salé." After that song, "zydeco" soon claimed the entire Gulf Coast, and Chenier himself took credit for naming the music. "See, the old people used to say, 'Let's go the zydeco,' meaning the dance," he once told writer Ann Savoy. "And I kept that in mind, and when I started playing music, I called my music 'zydeco.'" Chenier also once took credit for naming rock music, and in truth, the link from snap bean dances to zydeco music was probably made by hundreds of forgotten dancers and musicians throughout the bars of Frenchtown. But even if he didn't invent it, Chenier seemed to hold a natural right to the word, concedes McCormick. "When I think of Clifton, I remember him as flashing lights, because of all the chrome he had on his accordion under the spotlights," he says. "It was the spelling for Clifton."


Today, "zydeco" is accepted as the name of the music as well as of the event at which it is played, and it is also used to describe what people do when they get there — dancers are "two-nouns-and-a-verb" zydeco fans, as writer Susan Orlean puts it. The reign of the word "zydeco" would not prove absolute, however. The Texas-Louisiana confusion remains, and musicians still complain about people not playing "real" zydeco. And on signboards around Louisiana and Texas, spellings like "zodico" continue to show up from time to time.

Perhaps not surprisingly, more formal resistance has come from French-speakers who resisted the Americanized word, most notably Québecois filmmaker André Gladu, who titled his 1984 music documentary *Zarico*. "They may have a perfectly good point," McCormick replies to the charge. "Of course, every time you ask anybody what the origin was, they'd tell you back in the French, and *les haricots*, and all of that. But this is not a French-language enterprise. The signs for the dances all said 'Sunday afternoon' or 'Saturday night.' This was English, and I've always regarded it as an English word."

"Zydeco" like "jazz," is a word that continues to accrue new meanings. There is Cajun rocker Wayne Toups's term "zydecajun." A Kansas City–based soft drink company developed a highly caffeinated coffee-flavored drink called Zydecola. A Texas-based computer company enigmatically trademarked the name for a software program. When Louisiana musicians appear on national talk shows, they are frequently asked about the word's meaning, as on the night Zachary Richard went on *The Tonight Show* and host Jay Leno asked him: "Now, explain zy-DECO." Leno emphasized the last part, as in "art deco." "That's the New York pronunciation, Jay," Richard demurred.

But you're really taking your chances if you utter this word around older Creole musicians, who are at turns amused and chagrined when people apply it to their traditional, pre–Clifton Chenier sound. "Zydeco, zy-deco," said Canray Fontenot, starting out an interview for BBC. "I'm going to tell you one thing. There ain't no such thing. Because that's nothing but snap beans." Another Creole fiddler, Joseph "Bébé" Carrière, is even more scathing when I asked about the word. "They talk about the musicians, and say so-and-so is going to play a number about the zydeco, and I say, they ought to make some about the peas." He laughs. "Yeah, I'm going to get them to try to dance the peas. How about sweet potatoes? Yeah, if I'd have stayed playing, maybe I could have made one about that. . . . "

Long before dreams of zydeco software and cola and even professional recordings, these players remember when music came to life in dances every week in houses across Louisiana. Beginning in the late-nineteenth century, decades before Governor Huey Long would famously transform the state with seven thousand miles of new roads, most blacks were working as sharecroppers, living "on premises" in provided houses nestled in secluded coves, curtained by strips of woods, and connected mainly by bayous, railroads, and dirt tracks. They picked cotton, cut cane, and dug potatoes, providing the stoop labor for the farm holdings of mostly white Creole and Anglo planters. On weekends, these workers straightened their backs and cleared the chairs from the front room for the *bals de maison*, house dances.

*Louis Broussard, uncle to Queen Ida Guillory and Al Rapone, circa 1935.*

# 2

# SATURDAY NIGHTS DON'T COUNT

*There's people, they'll go to zydeco dances no matter how hard things are. I had an old aunt, she was sick all during the week. But Saturday, she'd forget the arthritis and the hurt knees, and she'd go to that dance — and believe me, she would dance. Now, that Sunday she would crawl in church, saying, "Oh, my knee hurts so much." And we'd say, "Yeah, but we saw you to that dance last night." "Yeah," she'd say, "but that was Saturday night. Saturday nights don't count!"*

*— Beau Jocque*

ONE OF THE FIRST RECORDED MENTIONS of a Louisiana house dance appears in a WPA interview of Catherine Cornelius, a former slave, who spoke of how people met to dance on Saturday nights in the slave cabins, and how they were left alone that night by the people in "the big house."

By the end of the nineteenth century, most black Creoles were living either in their own homes or in buildings provided by landowners, working in the crop lien system that defined farmlife in the South following the Civil War. It could be a difficult life, and social customs developed to help families survive through hard times. On Saturday mornings someone did the *boucherie*, slaughtering a cow or hog and passing out parts. Next week it was someone else's turn. If a neighbor fell behind in the fields, friends gave a *coup de main* (helping hand) and worked by moonlight to help bring in the crop. And on Saturday nights, houses filled with dancers. Young people met under their parents' supervision. Expectations of proper clothing, dancing, and behavior flourished. So did laughter, eating, drinks, gambling, gossip, and music. "It was all house dances," remembers Boozoo Chavis. "We ain't had no electricity, but man, that's where that music was."

What follows is a night at a house dance, from beginning to end, as recounted by twenty people who attended these grand events. Most of the people speaking are musicians. Others are promoters, including Wilbert Guillory; Wilbert Levier, who helped start the first zydeco festival; "Mama" Lena Pitre, who moved from Louisiana to the San Francisco area, where she has organized dances for the past thirty years; and William Hamilton, owner of Hamilton's Place in Lafayette, Louisiana. Interviews took place on front porches and in living rooms in Louisiana, Texas, and California. In concert, these stories recall those Louisiana Saturday nights when an accordion or a fiddle set the pace for an emerging culture.

## The House

MAMA LENA PITRE: You work sunup until the sundown. Go eat your dinner, and rest about a couple minutes under the tree, and go back to work.

ROY CARRIER: It was real hard stuff, things like pulling cotton, picking cotton by hand.

MAMA LENA PITRE: And I'm still there. That's why I say hard work don't kill, because if work have to kill, I've been dead, I think so.

ROY CARRIER: On weekends, after working six days a week in them days, sunup to sundown, on Saturday nights they'd go to this country house and have a dance. With a scrubboard and accordion.

FRANK ANDRUS: They had them old houses, you know. Two rooms, and the kitchen's behind, and a porch in front.

HIRAM SAMPY: And no electricity. We had a kerosene lamp, and you could pick up a pin down on the floor. Now we got light, now you can't see a pin. I guess we could see better during them days than right now.

ROY CARRIER: It was like a little prairie. You got ten houses around the area where you're working at. Tonight we go to his house. Next Saturday night we go to his house.

HIRAM SAMPY: They didn't have no fan. No air conditioning. All summer long. Looked like it wasn't hot like it is today. Well, maybe because we were used to it.

BÉBÉ CARRIÈRE: The young girls would go and meet the old people, and ask them, "Can we use your house tonight, for to make a dance?" Oh yeah, oh yeah. Said, "We're going to remove all your stuff in the house and put it somewhere on the porch, the bed and things, you know, then after the dance we're going to put it back." Yeah, they liked that, some of them old people.

WILLIS PRUDHOMME: When my sister got married, we were expecting so much people out there, we had to cut some blocks and put under the house, because we knew it was going to sag, that old house. You take forty people, that's a lot of people in just a regular house.

MAMA LENA PITRE: So they take out all the furniture in the front room, and they put some bench all around the wall, and they take some sheets and put on the bench, so everybody will sit down nice and clean and look good.

CANRAY FONTENOT: They would set some bench all around the house, they cut some block and throw one part away and one part was for the old ladies to sit. And them old men, they'd head to the barn and play cards and drink and talk, you know, while the young people was dancing.

ROY CARRIER: And about twenty or thirty people, they'd call that a packed house, then.

HERBERT SAM: You take a room like this here, sometimes the room wasn't no bigger than that. Wasn't no chairs to sit down. We'd be sitting down on the chair in the corner and playing the accordion and the washboard, and that'd be jam-packed. And boy, they'd say you had a nice time.


**I Ain't Coming Back**


MAMA LENA PITRE: Back then — you're going to laugh when I tell you this — two men were passing house to house with handkerchiefs tied in their necks, a real handkerchief. They jump on the horse and they go, they invite people, "I'm going to have the dance tomorrow, come on." "Okay, we be there." The next day the house was full of people.

HERBERT SAM: People would send somebody walking and tell you, "We got a dance tonight."

WILLIE DAVIS: The next person would tell the other person, the next person would tell the other person, the next thing that house would be full.

HERBERT SAM: The people all gather up, sometimes in a wagon, sometimes in a buggy, sometimes walking. And the closer you get there, you hear the music, you want to walk faster or run, to hurry up and get there.

CANRAY FONTENOT: In them times, I used to take the fiddle and hit the road. Whenever they see the fiddle, I was going to get a ride.

BÉBÉ CARRIÈRE: And when they knew it was me who was going to play there, oh they would be crowded up like that. They'd ask, "Well, who's going to play?" "Well, this Carrière man's going to play the dance." "Oh, we going, we going!"

HERBERT SAM: Now, at that time, I remember my daddy. I used to see him dressing up, put necktie and everything on, and grab his accordion. He had a horse and buggy, and when he'd leave to go and play, he'd tie his line up to the side of the buggy, and be rolling, playing, all the way to the dance. And he'd start singing, too, "I'm going away, baby, and I ain't coming back no more." He'd go on around Carencro, Arnaudville, up in there and play. And then if others had to pass by the road where we stayed, they'd be doing the same thing, and boy, you'd hear that music.

## Food and Drink

WILBERT GUILLORY: People would pay twenty-five cents to hear the band, fifteen cents for a plate of gumbo, and they would also gamble, they would also play for chip. You would win so many chip, you would be able to go back with a duck. You had the gumbo, gambling for the duck, and homemade beer.

FRANK ANDRUS: They would pour maybe two gallons of wine, and some candy, and sell that gumbo. But they'd make their money, though. I charge to play a dance. Every time I play a dance, six dollars.

BOIS SEC ARDOIN: That time, all the time you'd drink whiskey. Friday night, Saturday, and Sunday. Sometimes you get some free, sometime you have to buy.

HIRAM SAMPY: My father told me, if I wanted to play music, to make sure that I know what I'm going to do. Don't mess up the people, there, if you don't want to play, stay at the house. After you're drunk, you think you're playing good, but you ain't doing nothing. Said, "Whatever you do, give the people a satisfaction."

FRANK ANDRUS: My brother-in-law told me good, he said, "Andrus, don't quit dancing." "Dance all you can dance," he said, "and always drink." He said, "A good drink for you is good for you all times."

### What It Was Called

CANRAY FONTENOT: Now they're talking about zydeco music. They never had that. I never known that. They don't even know what it means. If you was black, you was playing Creole. If you was white you was playing Cajun.

MAMA LENA PITRE: They can call it la-la. We all going to la-la. Oh, are you going to the la-la tonight? Oh yeah, we're going to go to the la-la. They're going to the *la-la au soir. O, nous allons bal au soir.*

BOIS SEC ARDOIN: For me, I don't know much for the zydeco music, I never played that. I was born with Creole music, and I heard about Cajun music. But so far for me, Creole music is just blues music and Cajun music. Creole music is my music.

BOOZOO CHAVIS: I heard about la-la, but we never used that. In them days they'd call it a house dance. They didn't have no clubs, they'd go to a house dance. That's the name for it, right there, a house dance.

### The Players

ROY CARRIER: They had a lot of the old accordion players, you know, used to play them double-notes, from around Cecilia, back over there, Breaux Bridge. They had one they call Boulet, he could play accordion. He had a double-note. They used to come out there and stir that up.

WALTER POLITE: I was hearing some other older guys that used to play, and I tried to play like them, that's how I learned. Their name was Claude Faulk, Ernest Faulk, and Bidon, and Boulet. And I learned how to play just like they was playing, that's how I came up. Oh yeah, Boulet, that was another Cliff. I don't hear them play his songs.

WILLIAM HAMILTON: And there was my mama's brother too, they used to call him Machin, he was the rubbing board. And they had another, older guy, they used to call him Boulet. He had just one eye, and he played accordion. Oh, he was good.

FRANK ANDRUS: There's Jesse, there's Zo Zo, all brothers. Reynolds. I tell you one, living now, still playing, going strong. Boozoo Chavis.

BOOZOO CHAVIS: I was just a little rat. But in them days here Tee Ma Pet and Lenny P. and Henry Martin and Elridge Davis. Shit. God darn, Joe Jackson. That's the man I forgot. Sidney Babineaux is my grandmother's brother. And I didn't even know that. That little man could play.

THOMAS FIELDS: The music I heard was played mostly on triple-notes, music like Mr. Claude Faulk, Mr. Sidney Babineaux, and Mr. Paul Harris, we all called him Nonc Paul Papillon. We used to call Sidney "Blind," that was just a nickname. They drank a little bit and would tell them long tales because they was all music players.

AL RAPONE: My daddy and my uncles played them small accordions, then there came old Sidney Babineaux from Rayne, he had a triple-note accordion, him, and it was a different song. Joe Jackson played "Paper in My Shoe."

HERBERT SAM: My father was a single-note accordion. They were popular in their time, but it wasn't too many. They had Amédé, and they had Alfred Macy and Maurice Sam, and another guy by the name of Pierre Jolivette. That's all the accordion players that I knew in my daddy's time.

ANDERSON MOSS: They had a fellow named Bidon. That Mr. Bidon, he was tough, son. He played his music, and played it right. He played that music level. Anything he played you could dance on. I'd tell the world he's good. But Amédé was the king.

CANRAY FONTENOT: Oh yeah, they liked my daddy's music a whole lot better than Amédé. Amédé was good, and was a good singer. My daddy didn't sing good, him — but to dance to Amédé's music was kind of bad. His music was jumpy, and my daddy played smooth. He's the only accordion that I ever heard playing the "Arkansas Traveler."

**ANDERSON MOSS:** And then they had another one, they called him Sou-Pop. And they had one, his foot was long. His name was Belizaire Johnson. Big foot, tall man, but get out of the way, boy. He could play.

**FRANK ANDRUS:** I played when I was around eleven. Another guy used to play accordion, he's from Orange, Texas. I used to call him Slim. Slim Jordan, he's an old, slim guy. But he had an old, old double-note he used to play. After a while, he bought him a new one, and I bought the old one he had for five dollars. They were cheap this time, yeah. And I kept on trying, and I start playing dances.

**HERBERT SAM:** This Ledet guy, they had one by the name of Alphonse. They had Claude Faulk, they had one by the name of Sou-Pop. He was a fine fellow. He could play good. He lived in Lafayette. Now the accordion player that I admired, it was Ernest Faulk, Claude's brother. My daddy and them would go get him to play their dances, and he could play.

**HIRAM SAMPY:** The one called Sou-Pop used to play accordion, too. It was a nickname. When you're drunk, they call that *soûl.* He liked to drink, so they called him Sou-Pop.

**HERBERT SAM:** Another man could play, people don't know. Nanel Reynolds. People don't talk about them guys, but that guy there, Nanel Reynolds, could play some accordion. He was kind of a little brown-skin guy, he wore a big black hat. And let me tell you, he played a triple-note accordion, and he could play it. He could play that "Hold That Tiger." It was the way he would kick it off, and come in and play it, he had a good-sounding accordion. You don't hear nobody talk about that man. He's been dead years ago. Now he had other brothers that would play, they had Jesse Reynolds and Zo Zo Reynolds, but Nanel was the man.

### Accordions, Washboards, Fiddles

**HIRAM SAMPY:** It's not all houses that were big. And it was crowded, you were in a little corner there, you couldn't move. And we didn't have no fan in there, how you like that? Talk about hot, sweat from head to your shoes. The sweat'd be coming out your ear, and your nose. Oh yeah. Oh man, them accordion wouldn't last. You know that bellow, it would become soft.

**WALTER POLITE:** Without an amplifier, you had to pull it, sometimes you bust that old accordion. It's so hard to get that sound out of there, you just bust it, tear that old accordion in two. Boulet would have to pull hard. Sometimes they'd bust that strap that they have around their arm.

*Unidentified musicians, Crowley, Louisiana, 1938.*

BOOZOO CHAVIS: You know, I don't like to brag on myself. But them boys used to hit on the walls and them Coke bottles. They had them rubboard you wash clothes on, and me and the accordion. And there'd be a house full of dancers like that. Oh yeah, we didn't have no loudspeakers. We didn't have no drums.

FRANK ANDRUS: Them boys would put their accordions down and go and take a leak, and I'd keep at the washboard, and they would keep dancing, until they'd come back and get it going. That's behind a dry washboard. A dry board! That's right! I hit it best, you see.

HIRAM SAMPY: They had some on harmonica. But you had to have a lot of wind, because they didn't have no speaker, no microphone, yeah, for the people to hear you. Of course, people would hear better, I think, before them amplifiers.

FRANK ANDRUS: Them steel boards, you couldn't wear them out. Whatever you used to hit them with, them steel boards, you can't make the crack in them.

BÉBÉ CARRIÈRE: I'd pass some rosin on the bow on that thing good, good, and then when you pass that on them string, you could hear that a half a mile. Mostly at night, you know. At night music sounds more loud.

**Play Your Words**

CANRAY FONTENOT: You know, most of them songs, they got a story behind that. My daddy and grandpa had found some guy that knew how to find buried treasure. So they went in those woods down around Soileau, and they started digging until they hit a big box. Then they had a man coming in the buggy, and he was bringing that accordion and singing a waltz. The song was about somebody that was coming back from Basile. Boy, he was playing the accordion and singing that same tune there. And when he got by where they was, he started shooting. He didn't hit nobody, but they couldn't see nothing with the smoke. After that, you don't find that money there, and they say the man disappeared. And my daddy would play that waltz there. He would call it the "Ghost Waltz."

FRANK ANDRUS: "Bernadette, with your little bitty legs," we used to play that one, yeah. That's another crazy song that goes way back, yeah. Bernadette was an old woman, her legs were so damn little, you had to sing about her. "Can I dance with your little bitty legs?" Yeah, I knew her real good. Everybody sang about her. Oh, we caught hell about that. "Bernadette, with your little bitty legs, Bernadette with your little bitty legs." She'd be dancing, and she wouldn't think we were talking about her. And she was ugly like an old Mardi Gras, little bitty legs, big foot. And sassy. But oh, she had her hair down.

CANRAY FONTENOT: You see, that "Joe Pitre" is an old song. My daddy and them used to play that, they would call it "Joe Pitre." But they wouldn't sing it. So I said, "Well, I'm going to record 'Joe Pitre,' I'm going to put some words to it." And it all came about. Bois Sec's father-in-law, his name was Joe. So he was all the time telling us all kinds of stuff. Joking and teasing us about this and that. He had a habit sometimes he used to cook some stuff outside, and he'd say, "You must have ate the bone and all, I don't see much bone on the table." Well, I said, "I'm going to get you one of these days, here." So that's when I got the idea of talking about Joe Pitre had two wives. He didn't have no wife at all in them time. "Ahh," he said, "you went and used my name. You know damn well that's not the truth about the two wives." I said, "I told you I was going to get you one of these days!"

BÉBÉ CARRIÈRE: "Madame Faeille," that was a kind of fast number. Her husband was named Faeille, they was living not far from Lawtell. She had some beautiful girls, you know, Madame Faeille. In the song I say, "Give me one of your daughters." You know, when you're a musician, you got to play your words. She'd laugh. She had two nice girls. I had some of my friends that would fool around with them. But we were close friends, you know, and I didn't want to contrary them.

FRANK ANDRUS: I had to go to Pecaniere to play that song about "Hey, Zalee, where you left your drawers? I left my drawers at Mr. Polen's cotton gin." Oh that's right! We used to play that song, man, you would see the people dance, boy. And then the more you talked about them old ladies, in those days, they would hit you! Zalee, she lived in Pecaniere, she was going to be in that man's cotton gin at night, and forget her clothes in there, you see. They were using the cotton gin for a motel or something. Mr. Polen didn't know about that. If he'd known that, something would have happened, because that was a mean man and he had money. His grandpa told my father-in-law — they was big buddies, you know — he used to go in that man's house. That man would show him his clothes closet, he said, go look there. That man had dollar bills stacked from the floor to the top. Dollar bills, yeah. Had a stack of tens, a stack of twenties, a stack of hundreds, a stack of ones, a stack of fives. From the floor to the top. I wasn't married in them times there. I wouldn't play that song after I got married.

BOIS SEC ARDOIN: You got some songs that are sad, you know, you can cry when you sing, but some that can make you happy, too. That's one thing for sure.

## Your Feet Get to Do Something

FRANK ANDRUS: Oh, they'd dance like crazy. They'd swing out, they call that. They'd dance the slow drag. Back in Pecaniere, there, we'd ball till three and four in the morning. Then we had to walk back to Port Barre, see.

BÉBÉ CARRIÈRE: Oh Lord, I'd grab some of them girls, I didn't want to turn them loose. And they liked that too, yeah. I'd dance with them and talk with them, give them a little squeeze and all that, they'd go wild. And some of them girls could really dance kind of fast. And their parents were watching there. They'd keep their eyes open.

WILBERT LEVIER: They would dance differently to different music. They had one song the guy would play, and you would almost like tap-dance on it. It was almost like zydeco, they would play it with a violin, and you could hear their foot, tapping.

BÉBÉ CARRIÈRE: No, they wouldn't break too much noise with their shoe. Oh, some of them would tap-dance when they get excited, sometime tap their foot, and it would bring a loud sound.

FRANK ANDRUS: Oh, I was a good dancer, they wanted to pay me to dance, yeah. No joke, they thought I was the best there was in Port Barre. People, they can't follow me. But now my wife knows my steps. Every time I move, she knows it.

WILLIAM HAMILTON: My daddy was not a dancer hardly. When he was courting my mother, he used to stay outside and watch through the window. My mother used to love to dance. But not him. So he stay outside because he didn't know how to dance, you see, and when the dance was over, then he'd come in to take my mother back to the house.

MAMA LENA PITRE: The way they was dancing a long time ago, you could dance all night sundown to sunup. Because they was dancing the waltz different, the two-step different, you could dance all night. And now they jump a lot. When they jump, jump, jump, they get tired.

CANRAY FONTENOT: They didn't want no blues, because they would dance too close to one another, they didn't want that at all. You was out of business if you played blues. So we started to slip up on them with something like the "Prison Bars," where you could blues it or you could waltz it. Like "Bonsoir Moreau," they don't have too many people living that can do that no more. They would call that a *baisse bas*. That's a French name, that means "bend low." They would waltz it different from another waltz. You could play that all night if you want. It was okay, it wasn't the blues.

BOOZOO CHAVIS: A *baisse bas* is a pretty dance, but I never could learn it. It's the same thing as a waltz, you see, but it's more sad than that.

MAMA LENA PITRE: The *baisse bas*, yeah, my daddy used to dance that. Yeah, him and mama. You go side to the side, and your feet go side to side, and you come back on the side and you turn and *baisse bas*. Yeah, and make a circle and you make some step in the middle, and you invite a woman to go with you, so the woman go in the middle of the floor with you and make some two-step. But if she can't do what the song says, she'd go stand out, and another couple come and do it. One at a time. Make a circle, a lot of fun. Your feet get to do something.

BÉBÉ CARRIÈRE: *Baisse bas*, yeah, they had it. My poor old brother used to play that. I could play it on my fiddle, but I didn't keep up with that because I didn't like it too much, because you had to know how to dance it a certain way. The oldest ones knew how to dance it, but not too many.

## Manners

CANRAY FONTENOT: Oh, they had all kinds of rules that don't make no common sense at all. In the summer time, the young man, he'd go to the dance, he had to have two handkerchiefs. You had to wrap your right hand with a white handkerchief, so you wouldn't get her dress dirty in the summertime. You didn't have that, she wasn't going to dance with you. Oh, all kind of crazy rules.

HIRAM SAMPY: You had to hold your handkerchief out, the only way you invite her to dance. And then she would grab your handkerchief and you'd get on the floor. That was it. Oh yeah.

MAMA LENA PITRE: You got to respect a woman. A girl would never get up on the bench to go dance with a man if her man don't take his handkerchief out and invite a woman with the handkerchief. Now they just go grab a hand and go. A woman's not supposed to do that. When you see the handkerchief, you're going to get up and go dance. That's the way it was.

**WILBERT GUILLORY:** Now if this girl would decided that she didn't want to dance, if she refused you to dance that round, she was supposed to sit that round on that bench, until that tune was complete.

**MAMA LENA PITRE:** Women don't go outside. No, at that time, no. The girl, the woman, was sitting down on that bench.

**FRANK ANDRUS:** Them boys was so good them times, them boys was so respectful. If a girl would dance with them, they would take their hat off, and after the dance, they would get the girls a plate of gumbo, or pour some wine, if they wanted wine. And now them boys dance now, they give a girl nothing. No, they don't pull their hat off.

**MAMA LENA PITRE:** You couldn't be all over on yourself like they do right now, you have a distance to dance. And you have a place to put your arm behind the woman's back. You couldn't go low, you had to go high. Them old women, they go sit down and look at you. If you did a little bit of thing there, they go and tap on this boy, respect my daughter.

**CANRAY FONTENOT:** And them old ladies there! It was dancing, but you had to leave a gap. Oh! That's how come they didn't want no blues, because they would dance too close to one another. Oh, no common sense at all.

**MAMA LENA PITRE:** And sometimes, there was nothing to say, and they would still go and tell you, "Respect my daughter." Oh yeah. They would drink their moonshine and think the boy was doing something.

**FRANK ANDRUS:** The old-time boys, you have to have that coat. And now, shit, them boys go sometimes with a hot shirt on.

**CANRAY FONTENOT:** One Easter Sunday, they had just come out with short-sleeve shirts. Well, that old man was mad till it was pitiful: "They're going to put you right out of the house! Who ever seen that! The only way you got to have some short sleeve is when you go make a *boucherie!*" So his son was going, "Daddy daddy, that was in your time, things is changing!" Boy, he didn't like that, no, no.

**FRANK ANDRUS:** See, if her daddy sees you had your hat on, you couldn't dance with her. He wouldn't let you. Oh no.

**CANRAY FONTENOT:** I remember one time they had a dance over there in the community of Soileau. And it was an old guy, he's the one who was running the dance there. We got over there, and it ain't but one of them guys had a coat. "You all can't get in here and dance, no! Where's y'all coat?"

So in order for some of us to dance, we had to borrow the other fellow's coat when he come out, and go make a run in there.

MAMA LENA PITRE: When you go outside, the boy wants to walk you to the wagons, my mama and daddy never let me walk in the dark with a boy. I was in the front, they was in the back. Take me to the wagon, shake hands. You got to go. Now if he didn't talk enough, that was his fault.

## Memorable Nights

LEONA CHAVIS: Yeah, Boozoo had that billy goat. My mama give a house dance one night, and he turned that goat loose. That goat came to our house, we was living across the highway. And he was living right here. And he turned that goat loose, and that goat come to the house, and he walked in the house. That goat was something else. Johnnie Billy Goat. That's it. The lady said, "Get that goat out of here, y'all!" Boozoo's mama said, "Boozoo! Put that thing back home!" When they try to wrestle with him and get him home, he'd jump on top of the house so they couldn't catch him, and stay there till he was ready. That goat was something else.

BÉBÉ CARRIÈRE: Years back I was playing a dance, between Opelousas and Ville Platte. And a fellow shot another one, and it crossed in front of me, like that, and don't you know that smoke from that pistol, it kind of burned my face. That fellow that he shot there, he made a round, come outside the house, made around the house halfway and then he fell to the kitchen, and down he went, poor thing. I left, me. I took off, yeah. I'm pretty sure they stopped the man, caught the fellow and put him in the can.

HERBERT SAM: Now we have given the dances at our house, and there were so many people they broke the floor down. That's right there around Grand Coteau, back up in there. Well, we was living on another man's farm and that's what was the problem. So all the people around, they came and jacked it up and put braces, and fixed it back up. They had to do it a little at a time, because they were all people working in the field, you know.

FRANK ANDRUS: The last I played, that must have been 1954. My wife said, "Well, Frank, tonight will be the night." She said, "I'm going or the damn accordion." She said, "No, Frank, it's not dances you're playing, it's a woman you're playing." After that, I didn't play a dance.

## Coming Back Home

CANRAY FONTENOT: My daddy and them would play accordion, and anytime they played a house dance, that was the last tune, "Home Sweet Home."

BÉBÉ CARRIÈRE: That was the last number, "Home Sweet Home."

HERBERT SAM: Sometimes coming back at night, twelve, one o'clock, we'd hear my daddy, he'd be playing that music, coming back home. We're laying down, and they're playing going back home. We'd raise them windows up, listen at them. You see, the road passed right by our house. Oh yeah, it was some good time in them times, I remember that.

By the 1940s the house dances were starting to fall off. Clubs such as Slim's Y-Ki-Ki and Richard's Club began booking national R&B bands as well as zydeco acts like Clifton Chenier, who was quickly becoming a local star. "Every Saturday they had that Richard's Club there, so the people wouldn't hardly make no more house dances," remembers Bébé Carrière. "They'd go to the club. People came from different places and visit. That's how the thing went on there, until the house dance expired."

Social customs also changed with the move into the clubs. Men no longer held out their handkerchiefs for a dance. There were no more questions about playing the blues. And larger clubs could support bigger zydeco bands, with guitars, a bass, and drums. "I used to love house dances," Hiram Sampy says. "Then, after we start having clubs, well, I used to love clubs. Because you had more space." Not all agree. "I'd rather stay in my days where I was brought up than these days they got now," says Mama Lena Pitre. "Because when I was brought up, we were brought up poor, and we made it, and we enjoyed it."

A few of the old houses were literally broken down and converted to clubs. "I bought an old house, way on the other side, in the woods, and I had it moved over here," remembers Morris Ardoin. To move it, Morris and his family pulled the walls from the house and sliced the building in two. They borrowed a Caterpillar tractor from the parish and hauled the pieces to the new location next to Morris's home. There they reassembled it, with a bar and bandstand, into the new Cowboy Club.

Not all houses met such a symbolic fate, but by the 1950s the new era in zydeco was clearly beginning. Some house players moved to the clubs, including both Clifton Chenier and Boozoo Chavis. Others would never add a band behind their accordion, and their music fell out of step. "Take a hundred people and put them in this house here, he'd play for them," remembers Stanley "Buckwheat Zydeco" Dural Jr., about his father, Stanley Dural Sr., "but you take them out of here and take them to El Sid O's, he wouldn't touch it. He didn't believe in that. It's meant to be played for family entertainment." Today, some of the old songs can be heard from even the most contemporary zydeco musicians, such as Buckwheat Zydeco and Beau Jocque, whose father also played in the houses.

Older Creoles aren't fooled; they know that the era and its music are past. As they watch their children, grandchildren, and great-grandchildren play and dance zydeco, they can be heard lamenting that there aren't enough waltzes, that nobody can sing in French anymore, and that everyone jumps around too much when they dance. "They exercise," says Mama Lena Pitre. "I call that exercise. So I jump with them too. Because they do exercise, I do exercise too. That's why I say a lot of things change. People change, and the world stays the same."

# 3

# THE CREOLE CROSSROADS

THE SUNDAY AFTERNOON SUN BURNS DIMLY through the shaded windows of El Sid O's. The Lafayette zydeco club is cool and quiet, with bottles and debris of a successful weekend spilling over the tables. Nathan and Dennis Paul Williams are swapping stories with Cajun fiddler Michael Doucet, who has been collaborating with the Williams brothers on the album *Creole Crossroads*. For some reason the conversation moves toward the supernatural. Doucet talks about some unusual foot-size indentations in the floorboards of his attic. Nathan Williams counters with some advice he once heard from an old accordion player.

"I met this man one day at the store," he recalls. "He says, 'You get you a doggone little black cat, and tie it onto the chair, and start playing that accordion, and you're going to learn like that.' And I said, 'Well, I'll tell you what. If I got to sell my soul to the devil to play accordion, then I don't want that.'"

Nathan laughs. His brother Dennis nods. "You know they're very superstitious around here," he says.

"Now, you know one thing I believed in," Nathan continues, his voice dropping. "I had an oak tree behind the house. And the man told me, 'The best thing you can learn' — and I heard somebody say that about Clifton Chenier — 'best thing you can learn about playing the accordion, is to go

*Accordionist Raymond Latour at Mardi Gras in Iowa, Louisiana.*

there and sit under the oak tree, at about twelve o'clock at night, and you're going to see how you're going to learn fast.' Because when you're first playing the accordion, Dennis, it's hard for you to get your coordination. You understand what I'm saying?"

Dennis looks puzzled. "Oh yeah?"

"I used to go."

Dennis is astonished. "You did that?"

"I'd sit myself under the oak tree, man," Nathan repeats. "And that's how I was getting all kinds of keys, and I'm not lying. I didn't know a damn thing about keys. I'm not saying it made me learn, but I was playing better. I was feeling better."

Over the years, stories about playing music at the crossroads have been heard throughout the American South. In North Carolina the devil was a banjo player. He was a fiddler in Tennessee. In Louisiana he played accordion. But today's generation of zydeco players usually dismiss the tale. "I went to a livestock auction in Opelousas, and this one old man told me to take a black cat and boil him, and take the bones to the four corners at midnight," remembers Geno Delafose. "He said, 'Some man will come and meet you. Tell him what you want, and nobody is going to beat you.' And he meant that. I thought, 'This man must be crazy.'"

But if younger musicians scoff, their parents or grandparents believed in the story — or at least they knew someone who believed. "Some of them say Clifton Chenier had went to a four-cornered road with a black cat," Herbert Sam recalls. "That's what they said, but I knew Clifton Chenier pretty good, and he never did tell me nothing about that. But I know that Clifton Chenier was a hell of an accordion player."

Jumpin' Joe Morris heard similar tales when he played guitar with Eustis "Bidon" Hopkins. "Bidon told me that they used to want to catch some fresh air, so they opened the window, and while they're pulling their accordion like that, they get a hand catching them on the shoulder, pulling them back. He didn't know where the hand would come from. I said, 'Man, you must have been doing something dirty in your young days. The devil's catching up with you.'"

The matter comes up once again during a conversation with Mary Thomas, whose father, Elius Thomas, played for the house dances. Growing up on the outskirts of Lake Charles, Mary Thomas recalls, her home seemed to be a magnet for strange occurrences. She remembers a mysterious man in white — said to be the ghost of a country doctor — who would visit her family at night. And she heard from her father the popular legend that visiting ghosts were slaves who were killed and buried alongside treasure, ordered to stand as guards. If she saw a ghost, her father instructed her, she should ask him where the treasure was. One night, in fact, Elius Thomas dug a large hole in their backyard, looking for the bounty. "They had about fifteen men out there, and they dug up Mama's tree," Mary Thomas remembers. "She told my daddy to go gold-digging elsewhere or she was going to call the police."

But the story that made the biggest impression was the one about the crossroads. "There was a four-cornered road, out there in Marksville, and a man told my daddy, if you come here and you wait for twelve o'clock with this black cat, it was selling your soul to the devil. And he went, and he would tell us this story that would just scare the hell out of us. He said at twelve o'clock, there stood the tallest man that he had seen in his life, with red, red eyes, and every time his mouth opened, all he could see was red. And he didn't ask him anything — he just told him, 'Play a waltz.'

"Five minutes later the person was gone, and that cat had disappeared. He never found that cat till today. And the next morning, when he started up, he played the accordion, the violin, the harmonica, guitar, bass guitar. Anything he put his hands on, he could play.

"And as a result, he would not go to church," Thomas concludes. "My mom had more hell trying to get that man to go to church. And he would get fighting mad. But before he died, he joined a little Baptist church by our home, and they brought him over there to church and they baptized him. When they brought him back home, he stayed in bed. Every time we looked, there were snakes that kept coming, kept coming. I mean, you'd look out on the windowsill, and there would be one trying to figure out how to get in. But the preacher said his soul was saved. And after he got sick, he used to sit at home and he'd play for us. That's how I learned how to dance."

Where does the crossroads story come from? There is probably no single origin. Across the Atlantic, similar tales and possible antecedents are told in Senegal and the Gambia, where musicians are said to be possessed by spirits called *djinn* if they play the *kora* too late at night. In American blues, the most famous version of the myth concerns legendary Mississippi guitarist Robert Johnson, who recorded such evocative titles as "Me and the Devil Blues" and "Crossroads Blues."

Today few people seriously believe that Louisiana accordionists are under the sway of the devil. And despite zydeco's connections to African-Caribbean music and language, overt voodoo references are rare. There is the song "Colinda" or "Calinda," believed to derive from the calenda dance of the French West Indies. There are also a few instances of snake imagery.

In 1967 Clifton Chenier recorded a version of "Black Snake Blues" that probably owed its principal imagery to Texas bluesman Blind Lemon Jefferson's "That Black Snake Moan." In 1993 Beau Jocque introduced a new song, "Damballah"; William Ferris explains in the *Encyclopedia of Southern Culture* that Damballah is the chief deity in West African Dahomean *vodun* beliefs. Beau Jocque, however, reports that the inspiration for "Damballah" really came from a popular horror film.

Yet the crossroads story survives — in some form — because it is meaningful to the people who tell it. In fact, even the skeptics who dismiss the facts of the case accept its major tenet: a person who masters the accordion becomes a commanding figure. His ability is the result of either possession, inspiration, genetics, culture, or practice.

There is a second story-line that bespeaks the power attained by one who learns the accordion. Unlike the crossroads legend, the people who tell this tale acknowledge that it came from direct experience. The accordion, many zydeco musicians report, is first learned in secret. They recall how they would sneak the instrument away from their father, brother, mother, husband. By the time they were caught, they could prove their worth by being able to pull a song. For this Arthurian effort, they were rewarded with the accordion. "My daddy was a musician, Avery Sampy," remembers musician Hiram Sampy. "So he was playing a single-note, and I was too small, I guess, to be messing around with his accordion, because they didn't have no money. But every time he would turn his back, I'd get on that high-back chair and go catch that thing way on top of the armoire. I had to be about five years old, I guess. Then he would give me a whipping. Well, I'd leave that thing maybe for a week, then after that, I'd catch it again, until one day I was playing my little tune. Boy, when he appeared at the door, I stood up. I gave him my back. Because I had caught so many whippings and I never stopped, yeah. He said, 'No, you can keep on.'" Similar stories are told by Bois Sec Ardoin, Roy Carrier, and Rosie Ledet — among many others.

The next most important test for accordion players is making a personal statement with their music. "I began late in life, so I went to inquiring about somebody that played the old music," recalls Thomas Fields, who was in his forties when he started learning the instrument. "My wife Geneva's daddy told me about this old man, Mr. Paul Harris. He's about eighty years old and very stubborn, a short-patience man, but a real, real good accordion player. I found out where he stayed, and in a few days I went over there, and he was sitting outside waiting for me. And he said, 'You got an accordion?' And I said, 'Yes sir,' and he said, 'Go get it.' Paul taught me the old way. The first thing he said was that I had to play my own style."

Since the accordion's first arrival in Louisiana in the mid-1800s, Creoles have faced this task: to use the new instrument to make a personal statement. This leads to the third story-line about the accordion: its documented history in zydeco. It may have a few more exact dates and documentation than the other tales, but at times it involves no less speculation.

The accordion was first patented in 1829 by a piano and organ maker in Vienna named Cyrillus Demian. Almost immediately, the instrument went into commercial production and was being exported from Austria by 1840. It was quickly adopted by musical cultures around the world. In 1898 a traveler reported hearing it in every village in Madagascar, and the instrument also became popular in countries in Africa, Latin America, and Europe, as well as in the American South. The accordion owed this early success to several attributes. It was durable. It never went out of tune. And, in the words of historian Christoph Wagner, "it was much louder than all the older folk instruments put together."

The accordion, as folklorist Barry Ancelet has observed, first arrived in Southwest Louisiana without an operator's manual. It was adapted to the existing song traditions of the Creoles and Cajuns. Visual documentation of the instrument in the state is a daguerreotype titled *Accordion Player* in the collection of the Louisiana State Museum in New Orleans. The subject, wearing checkered pants with a waistcoat and tie, sits beside a vase of flowers. He rests the accordion on his leg, stretching his right hand across the buttons. The picture can't tell us if he is a freeman or a slave, or if the accordion is even his. But the positioning of his right hand indicates that he knows how to play. The museum dates the image circa 1850, which suggests that the accordion entered black Louisiana only twenty years after its invention.

By the end of that century, the instrument appears in Louisiana slave communities, marketed by traders who worked rural roads and waterways. Creole musician Canray Fontenot was born in 1922, but he remembers hearing tales of how the instrument was procured. "That was during the slavery, and some had learned how to play the accordion, some had learned how to play the fiddle," he says. "Whatever the big people had in the house. At least that's what they told me. And when they was going somewhere, them slaves was there and they'd slip up and play on them things."

The accordion is documented in a variety of settings in nineteenth-century Louisiana. One of the earliest is a black dance described by Virginia Newman, born in 1827 in St. Mary Parish. She told an interviewer for the WPA that when she was young, she would hear the accordion start to play and she would quit combing her hair, so as to be the first one at the dance. In his 1946 book *Voodoo in New Orleans*, Robert Tallant quotes one Raoul

*"Accordion Player," daguerreotype, circa 1850.*

Desfrene, "a 'French Negro' of 77," who remembered that "a Negro named Zizi played the accordion" at famed voodoo queen Marie Laveau's Monday night meetings at a house on Dumaine Street. In her short story "A Night in Acadie," the nineteenth-century writer Kate Chopin describes a circa-1897 white dance where the music is provided by a black trio — two fiddlers and an accordionist — who play all night and drink whiskey from a quart bottle.

And in north Louisiana, Huddie "Leadbelly" Ledbetter first heard accordions in local dances called "sukey jumps"; he later gained his fame as a blues guitarist, but would also continue to play accordion for the rest of his life.

By the turn of the century, accordions had begun to forever alter the musical landscape of South Louisiana. They were brought to the state by German immigrants and Midwestern farmers who moved to the region to grow rice, and were becoming widely available at general stores and through mail-order catalogues. According to Ann Savoy the Cajuns seem to have resisted the instrument through the late 1800s, largely because the early accordion keys (A and F) clashed with the open tuning of their fiddles. But by the 1920s, the availability of Monarch and Sterling brand accordions in the keys of C and D launched a new era of accordion-dominated Cajun music.

The early accordions also posed limitations for black Creole players interested in playing the blues. With these single-row, diatonic accordions, a musician could only squeeze the seven notes of a major scale. Unlike on a harmonica, notes on an accordion won't bend. As writer Jared Snyder has pointed out, when a musician such as Amédé Ardoin wished to play a song like "Les blues de Crowley," he solved the problem by shifting his hands down the buttons, playing his D accordion in the key of A, a move that allowed him to play the flattened seventh — a "blue note." The rest of the effect he accomplished with his powerful voice.

Despite the accordion's limitations, by the 1930s it had become the instrument of choice for Creole musicians. Its influence can be heard in several of John and Alan Lomax's field recordings, in which unaccompanied singers occasionally mimicked the instrument between lyrics. Ethnomusicologist Lisa Richardson has also speculated that the howls heard in Jimmy Peters's *juré* song may be imitations of wheezing accordion bellows.

Today, the accordion defines the zydeco sound. A blues band can be based around a harmonica, guitar, or piano. But there is simply no such thing as a zydeco band without an accordion. It is in fact possible to trace the changes in zydeco over the years by looking at just what kind of accordion was being played.

There are four types of accordions widely used in zydeco: single-row, double-row, triple-row, and piano. Each row adds one more key, which also allows skilled players to reach across the rows to play the blues. (In recent years, a few five-row styles have also begun to appear.) The fourth model, the piano-key, provides all the tonal options of a piano.

In the past, choice of instrument may have depended on where a player lived. Thomas Fields says that when he was growing up in the early 1950s, he could map out accordions by region. "The single-notes were up in the prairies, in the area of Eunice, Basile, Oberlin, Oakdale — back up there where Mr. Bois Sec Ardoin and them come from. The more you went east and towards the sugarcane, the more you went to the plantations. This was the part of Louisiana I was from, like Lafayette, Rayne, Crowley, Opelousas, Sunset, Grand Coteau, New Iberia. That's where the triple-note and the piano-notes were famous. It was still Creole, but it was more bluesy. I really think it was because they had a little more hard times, myself."

The accordions also differed in size, weight, and cost. A 1937 Sears catalogue distributed throughout the South priced piano accordions between twenty-eight and two hundred dollars, with button accordions selling for as little as $4.35. The larger styles also presented new challenges, as New Iberia musician Walter Polite once explained. "Exactly fifty pounds," he measured, lifting his triple-row. "I used to stand up four hours with that on my shoulders. I used to drink hard. Most of the musicians got to drink to hold up. That man standing up four hours, in one place there, with fifty pounds on that shoulder. That's a punishment, man." By contrast, a single-row presented a lighter opponent, weighing in at less than ten pounds.

If geography and alcohol consumption can be inferred by looking at an accordion, so can the approximate year. Each era in the development of zydeco has been marked by a change to a different style of instrument. Early Creole music is marked by the single-row, roughly dating from the advent of the first accordions in the nineteenth century to 1934, the last year in which Amédé Ardoin recorded. In the 1930s and 1940s, the double-row and triple-row began to emerge as musicians started to perform with drums and guitars; this early meeting of blues, R&B, and Creole music is frequently called "la-la."

In 1954, Clifton Chenier's first recordings marked the advent of the piano-key accordion. This instrument allowed Chenier to explore the full range of his talent, playing tunes by Louis Jordan and Ray Charles. But a close listen to his 1965 recording "Zydeco Sont Pas Salé" reveals that he could strip his piano-key accordion down to make it sound like the older single-row style as well. As he plays this zydeco anthem, he primarily stays in the key of G, favoring the higher registers, repeating notes to build tension. He holds on to the dominant as if to display his stamina, while the drums and rubboard create an undercurrent of tension. He sings in unison with his accordion, much in the style of a blues guitarist such as B. B. King. Then, at the end of his song, Chenier tosses in a flourish of jazz chords — perhaps as a reminder that all these old sounds are now being played by choice.

Thanks to Chenier's example, the piano-key would dominate zydeco for nearly thirty years. Then in 1980 John Delafose began to put the single-row in modern dress with his hit version of "Joe Pitre a deux femmes." The tune was first recorded by Bois Sec Ardoin and Canray Fontenot in 1971, with new lyrics based by Canray on a melody he heard from his father, Adam Fontenot. Delafose's innovation was to speed up the tempo and add a more contemporary-sounding arrangement. The impact on zydeco was immediate. "I started playing on an old white piano accordion because it was the kind of music that Clifton Chenier had," remembers Jeffery Broussard. "But when Delafose was playing that little single thing, they were going crazy over that. I started playing that, then I wouldn't give it up for nothing in the world. 'Joe Pitre,' that brought the single-note accordion back."

Delafose's success was also noticed by accordionist Boozoo Chavis, then about to embark on a comeback trail. When he first recorded in the 1950s, Chavis had played only triple-row accordions. But he used the single-row on his 1986 song "Dog Hill," establishing a new zydeco aesthetic: minimalist lyrics (Boozoo's son Poncho repeating the lines "We're going to Dog Hill / Where the pretty women at"); interlocking rhythms from the bass drum and rubboard; and a one-chord accordion riff that sounds for all the world like a cavalry charge. Like Chenier, Chavis built much of the tension in his music by holding the dominant and repeating notes on a sustained dominant, and his most influential song, "Zydeco Hee Haw," reworked many of the elements heard in "Zydeco Sont Pas Salé." Today Chavis's influence over modern zydeco extends to the current bumper crop of young single-row players who add hip-hop and reggae influences to Chavis's accordion style.

There is little agreement among musicians as to which accordion sounds best in zydeco. Single-row players prefer the choppy rhythms that can be squeezed out of the smaller boxes. Many piano-key players associate the single-row with Cajun music, arguing that real zydeco depends on the tonal possibilities represented in the music of Clifton Chenier. Still others like to keep their options open. "I have four single-notes, two triple-notes, three piano-notes, and a little double-note that I mess around with," explains Geno Delafose. "That little double-note sounds a little more Frenchier than the triple-note. The triple-note is bluesier, bigger, and a little bulkier. The little double-note is kind of stuck in between. You can get the blues, but you can also get that old chank-a-chank sound out of that thing, too."

The accordion is not the sole star in a zydeco band, however. The rubboard — also called the scrubboard, the washboard, or the *froittoir* — is a less complicated instrument, and there is less lore associated with learning it. But it is just as necessary to the zydeco sound as an accordion. "A year ago we had a family reunion, and there was an accordion there with no washboard," remembers Wilbert Guillory. "I was very disturbed the whole time."

The modern rubboard is a corrugated steel vest worn over the shoulders and played with bottle openers, spoons, or other adapted utensils. This board was probably designed in the mid-1950s in Port Arthur, Texas, by Clifton Chenier, from raw material widely available during the building boom on the Texas Gulf Coast. Its musical antecedents are found in a number of music traditions in West Africa, where scraping and scratching sounds are commonly drawn from such available objects as the notched gourd, or the metal *ferro* that accompanies the accordion on the Cape Verde Islands. In Louisiana, percussionists continued to use accessible materials: in his 1894 book *Louisiana Studies*, historian Alcée Fortier recalled his childhood on a sugar plantation where he watched slaves beat an oxhide-covered barrel and rattle the teeth of a mule jawbone.

Washboards were common in early jazz, Southern folk music, and "jug bands"; jazz musician Danny Barker remembers seeing them in New Orleans streetside "spasm" bands. Early models might be made of heavy glass or iron. They were held in the lap or hung from the neck with string, and played with anything from a coin to steel clips. In Southwest Louisiana, black Creole musicians searched around the house for objects that would make the right sound. "Them rubbing boards, you'd find that in the iceboxes," Herbert Sam recalls. "You'd buy your icebox, and they had that in there to set the ice to drip in a pan on the side. That's where the original washboard comes from. That's what we'd use."

In a 1978 interview for the French magazine *Jazz Hot*, Clifton and Cleveland Chenier described one of Cleveland's first instruments. "I learned with a can," Cleveland said, and Clifton explained further: "You put ice inside, a little piece of iron bar, and with the holes you pass a rope inside. He played with that." But as the name suggests, most washboards originally derived from boards used for washing clothes. "We'd have to sneak the boards away from Mother, and if she'd find us, we couldn't play," remembers Boozoo Chavis.

These early models were all eventually discarded after Clifton Chenier designed the modern rubboard. In an interview for the video *Clifton Chenier: The King of Zydeco*, Chenier once recalled the day he invented this original American instrument: "They used to have a rubboard, one of them old rubboards to wash clothes with, and they used to tie a string around it, you know? And it would fit right around your neck. So I went on to a white fellow down there, at the Gulf Oil Refinery. I told him, 'You got some tin?' He said, 'Yeah.' So I got down in the ground in the sand and I drew that rubboard and I said, 'Can you make one like that and put a collar to it?' He said, 'Sure, I can make one like that.' And he made one."

The new design also freed up the rubboard player to become a show-man. Among the famous players of the past was "Iron Jaw," who played with Rockin' Dopsie; he was famous for a performance that included picking up a chair with his teeth. Today's rubboard players might leap onto the dance floor or invite audience members onstage. The Dopsie tradition continues with David "Rockin' Dopsie Jr." Rubin. The only rubboard player currently leading a band, Rockin' Dopsie Jr. is known to include break dancing in his show.

Playing the rubboard well is a challenging task. Nevertheless, the instrument is often seen as the entry-level position in a zydeco band, covered by the youngest child in a musical family. It's also a favorite of band friends. "Guys who can't play anything, they get in the band by playing the scrub-board," Sean Ardoin says. "They can dance, so they know where the beat is supposed to be."

For all the rubboard's popularity, it is the mastering of the accordion that is seen as the task worthy of a king. Fittingly, the first Creole musician to dominate the landscape of Southwest Louisiana is also the first Creole accordionist to make a record: Amédé Ardoin. Together he and Dennis McGee created a single vein of music that is still tapped by both Cajun and zydeco players. The two were also good friends, known to sneak off to share a bottle of moonshine. But Amédé Ardoin is also remembered for a lonely night when he found himself on the tragic intersection of music and race. He never wore a crown, but he was the first Creole king of the accordion, and what happened to him is the other story that every zydeco musician knows.

# 4

# LE GRAND CHEMIN D'AMÉDÉ ARDOIN

*Loan me your handkerchief*
*I said, loan me your handkerchief*
*That I may dry your weeping eyes*

— *John Delafose*

AMÉDÉ ARDOIN SHUT HIS EYES until he couldn't see the two faces above him in the night. *Dead in the ditch*, he told himself. *You're dead, and that is why they will leave you alone.* He hadn't seen these two when he left the car to walk the rest of the way to Mr. Marcantel's farm. Ahead of him was a short path, covered by leaves from a recent storm. He was used to hitchhiking these roads with nothing but his accordion, which he carried in an old flour sack.

Celestin Marcantel hadn't hired five-foot-tall Ardoin to work on his farm — the musician was notorious for falling asleep in the fields. Mr. Marcantel, like so many in the area, was drawn to Ardoin's music. But he had told Ardoin he couldn't take him home in his horse and buggy that night, the way he often did when Ardoin played his accordion for the white people. "I can't stay for the dancing," he had said. "I'm sick. Somebody is going to bring you back." And when the car got to the road with the leaves, Ardoin told his driver to stop, not to drive over the leaves; he'd walk.

51

*Amédé Ardoin, circa 1915.*

The two men — had they followed him in a car or by horseback, or had they been waiting? — were at the dance, and they had been watching him all night. He was the little man who never worked in the fields. They had heard the high cry of his singing. They had heard his accordion. And they had seen him ask the man of the house for a rag to wipe his head, and then accept a handkerchief from the pale hand of one of Marcantel's own daughters.

After that, they could hear nothing else. There were rules about these things. A black Creole man can play accordion for dancing, but a hired musician is one thing and a tiny white hand on a small black face is something else — at least in Eunice on that Sunday night.

So nothing got in the way of the two men. Finally, they stood over the tiny, crumpled body, which they had beaten with their own hands until it had fallen into the ditch. Then one man broke the silence. "That damn nigger there, that white lady ain't going to never wipe his face," he said. Then they were gone.

And Amédé Ardoin half walked, half crawled down the road with the leaves, until he reached Mr. Marcantel's door.

That is how Creole fiddler Canray Fontenot heard the story, when he was a young boy, hanging on every word Ardoin told when he came to see his father, Adam Fontenot. Like Ardoin, Adam Fontenot was a popular accordionist, and the two men were close. In fact, remembers Canray, there was one night when you couldn't tell where one began and the other one stopped. Adam was playing a dance when Ardoin made a memorable entrance. "When he came back my daddy was playing, and he took his left hand off the accordion, and Amédé slapped his in there, then took his right hand, and the tune never stopped!" Fontenot laughs. "My daddy went in the kitchen, but the people never stopped dancing, they never noticed they had exchanged the accordion. How can that player do something like that?"

At this time Ardoin lived about a mile from the Fontenots, and Fontenot remembers that the two men would often go behind the house to repair a used accordion with a gas torch. Young Canray loved his father's and Amédé's music — he had already built himself a fiddle out of a wooden cigar box and wires from a screen door — and he listened closely when Ardoin told his father what had happened on the road to Mr. Marcantel's. "He says, 'They thought I was dead.' He says, 'I wasn't dead. . . .'

"So he got there and he said to his boss man, they had beat him so bad that he couldn't walk. The man got in his car and he brought him to see the doctor, and the doctor said, 'Well, they ruined his life, whoever done that

*Amédé Ardoin's draft cards.*

thing. They done hit him so hard he's not going to have his right mind.' And that's just what happened. He started losing his mind. Crazy, crazy."

Amédé's nephew Milton Ardoin also remembers when he heard about that night. Amédé was the seventh of seven sons; the sixth was Milton's father, Beaudoin. When Milton was a child, his uncle would put him on his knee and try to teach him accordion. "'A waltz is more easy for you to learn to play,' he used to say," Milton recalls. "But I didn't have that in my mind to learn, me. And when my daddy was working in the fields, Amédé would have his accordion, and he would sit down on the ground and play music. After that, they would go get that old 'white mule' moonshine and drink and have good time.

"Well, I was about sixteen years when it happened to him, when they beat him. We were staying by Basile. And I remember Daddy, he saddled his horse, he went to Eunice to see him, over there to Mr. Celestin Marcantel. And Amédé was in that little cabin, that little shack. I remember, Daddy told me, he was hurt so much that they tied a rope on the top of his bed, just to give him a chance to get up."

The story of Amédé Ardoin is well known to musicians throughout Southwest Louisiana, about how he took the handkerchief and was beaten, or how the men rolled a Model T over his throat so he'd never sing again. Not everyone has heard the same details, but the story fits a tragic pattern. There seems to be a decree in traditional American music that pioneers be touched by genius and then face a brutal end. So it was for Robert Johnson with the blues and Buddy Bolden with jazz, and so it is with Amédé Ardoin, the first and perhaps the finest Creole accordionist to make a record.

He was indeed a pioneer. "He laid the groundwork for Cajun music," writes Ann Savoy in her book *Cajun Music: A Reflection of a People*. He brought the blues into Cajun like nobody else before him. His impassioned vocals and syncopated accordion work defined the Creole style and pointed the way toward zydeco. And he showed just how popular an accordion man could become in Louisiana. "I knew Amédé when I was a little boy," remembers musician Anderson Moss. "He played his music and played it right. He had the people, man. Amédé was the king."

Amédé Ardoin was born on March 11, 1898, to Aurelia Clint and Thomas Ardoin. Thomas Ardoin's mother, Marie Tom, was a slave, and Thomas was also born into slavery. Yet by the time Amédé was born, Thomas had acquired 157 acres of land on Bayou Nezpiqué.

The tragedies that would mark Amédé's life started when he was in infancy. In October 1898 his father died. "My grandfather — his father — got killed when Amédé was small," Milton says. "He was on the road. They reached a bridge, and they had some beef to haul. It was old wood, and it broke, and my grandfather had his neck broken."

In 1918 Amédé reported to the draft board that he was working as a farmer in Eunice for a man named Eusebe Bertrand. At that time he was probably living alone with his mother, whom he listed as his nearest living relative. Soon after, Ardoin and his mother probably moved to the farm of Oscar Comeaux, near the town of Chataignier. In the 1920 United States census, Comeaux is listed just two names after Ardoin. The census also confirms that Amédé was single and his mother a widow. Both are listed as Louisiana-born French speakers, unable to read or write.

The census and the draft registration card list Amédé Ardoin as a farmer, but his family remembers otherwise. "Amédé's father died," recalls Amédé's cousin, Bois Sec Ardoin, "and Amédé's mother was poor and old, too. He tried to help a little bit after he was big enough, but after somebody found an accordion for him, he'd go and play. He didn't help his mama no more. He stayed with the white people." It is believed that Aurelia died when Amédé was in his twenties, and that Amédé moved into the home of his brother Austin; for the rest of his days he would sing of his life as an orphan.

His first accordion reportedly came from his older brother Beaudoin. "My daddy bought an accordion to start," Milton remembers. "He was not able to learn. Amédé, you know, he was the baby one, and he gave the accordion to him. When Amédé started to play, he was on a chair, and he was so small his foot was not touching to the floor. But he learned that over and over and over, until he caught it."

Amédé's brothers tried to get him to work in the cotton fields, but as Bois Sec puts it, "he didn't sweat much." Instead, he did something unheard of in that place and time: he turned to his music to provide food and shelter. "He never married, he didn't want to work," says Canray Fontenot. "Amédé would put his accordion in that sack and every day Amédé would get to the gravel road with his accordion, hitchhike, and he didn't give a damn which direction it was — he'd go somewhere where he could pick up a few nickels."

He was well aware of his talents. He carried a lemon in his pocket for his voice, and greased his throat with a mixture of oil and honey. He also kept his accordion near him in case inspiration hit. "I remember that he said that at night he would dream," Milton Ardoin remembers. "And he would take his accordion and play that dream, and then he was making a song with it." Among the many Cajun fiddlers who played with Ardoin was Arteman "Bijoux" Frugé, whose nephew Wade Frugé once recalled a night when the accordionist was challenged by a rival player from the town of

Breaux Bridge. Ardoin started the dance by listlessly covering a couple of tunes, and then went outside and drank a half bottle of whiskey and returned to the dance. "My uncle said he'd never forget that," Frugé told Ann Savoy. "When he and Amédé went back to play again, he took his accordion and opened the bellows up as far as they'd go. Then he'd make it tremble, holding it all the way down to the floor, before they started to play. Then, man, he said he got on that accordion! Nobody could play better than Amédé when he wanted."

Across Louisiana to the Texas border, crowds would flock to hear Ardoin. "Oh, that was some music," Milton Ardoin remembers. "And when he was playing over there to Mr. Quincy Davis's place, he had a song for when the dance closed up, you know? Every time he would play that, the fights would take place. I said, 'Uncle.' He said, 'What?' I said, 'Don't play that no more. It must be the devil what you play now, that little two-step.'"

Cajun fiddler Dennis McGee once recalled one of their nights performing together. "We brought so many people . . . that they climbed up on the little fence that they had put to protect the musicians from the crowd and they broke it," he told Barry Ancelet. "They came rolling in like balls. It was really funny to see. The people wanted to come to us. We were making good music in those days." In McGee, Ardoin had found a musician with the talent and personality to match his own, and the two became good friends. They met as sharecroppers, working the same patch of land; a few years later, McGee accompanied Ardoin for a series of landmark recording sessions.

It isn't clear just how Amédé Ardoin came to make a record. McGee recalls that it was after he had won an accordion contest. In September 1929, three months before the pair went to New Orleans to record six songs for Columbia Records, there was indeed a contest in the town of Opelousas. The sheriff and a local doctor, both Cajuns, built a platform in the center of town, and the weekend-long event attracted an estimated crowd of two thousand, including representatives from at least four record companies. But just what occurred in Opelousas is a bit of a mystery. The reported winner of the grand prize was a Cajun accordionist named Angeles Lejeune, with McGee accompanying, yet the local papers also noted that fifteen winners were chosen in all. It is likely that Ardoin attracted some attention that weekend — it is hard to imagine that he didn't. At any rate, on December 9, 1929, he was in a temporary recording studio in a New Orleans hotel, ready to sing his music in a new setting.

The recording industry had been launched right around the time Amédé Ardoin was born. Thomas Edison invented the phonograph in 1877. A decade later, a German immigrant named Emile Berliner built a gramophone that could play mass-producible flat disks. By the 1920s, record companies — hoping to compete with radio — were sending representatives in to communities around the country, banking that people would buy both the records of their favorites and the "talking machines" to play them on. Often the new machines were set up in the middle of a town's main street. When the records played, some older people were frightened by the disembodied voices.

Columbia Records engineered the first Cajun recording session when they brought Joe and Cleoma Falcon to New Orleans in April 1928 to record "Allons à Lafayette." With the recent influx of oil money in the region, the 78s were big sellers. Joe Falcon began to bill himself as the Famous Columbia Record King, and the company set up more sessions.

In 1929 Columbia returned to New Orleans primarily to record the gospel singer Blind Willie Johnson. Ardoin and McGee drove to the city, probably in McGee's car, perhaps staying in the hotel where the session was held. They recorded six tunes that day; Ardoin sang, and the accordion and the fiddle shared the lead. Many of these songs have since become traditional standards, including "Two Step de Eunice" and "Two Step de Prairie Soileau." The next year, Brunswick Records brought the duo back to New Orleans, where they recorded ten more songs in two days. In August 1934 they went to the Texas Hotel in San Antonio, recording six more songs for Bluebird/Victor records. By this time the dynamics between the two players had changed: McGee was now limited to playing a kind of rhythm fiddle behind Ardoin's accordion. Among the songs recorded in San Antonio is the "Crowley Blues," a one-chord tune that features a light shuffle beat and a bluesy vocal with improvised lyrics. On this song, suggests writer Jared Snyder, Ardoin is pointing the way to zydeco.

Ardoin would go into the studio one more time before the year was out, this time for Decca Records in New York City. His standing as a musician must have been at a new height, for only he and Joe and Cleoma Falcon made the incredible bus trip to New York, which would include a ride over the Hudson River on a ferry that nearly sank. On December 22, 1934, Ardoin recorded twelve more songs, playing solo for the first time. He sang, as he always did, of being alone on the big road, of being condemned for the rest of his days:

> O, jolie fille, rappelle toi, éou t'es t'assis, y yaie,
> Donc, aussi haut dans la porte de ta maison.
> O, t'après me garder, toi, quand moi, m'après passer
> Dans le grand chemin, toi, moi, c'est moi, tout seul.

Oh, pretty girl, remember where you were seated, *y yaie,*
Oh, just so high in the door of your house.
Oh, you were looking at me, you, when I was passing by
In the big road, me, all alone.

Then he and the Falcons boarded the bus and returned to Louisiana.

Ardoin's fame continued to grow. He traveled a wide circuit throughout Southwest Louisiana to the Texas border, playing in both houses and dance halls, riding in McGee's Model T or on his own horse, or hitching rides. "The black people that had no money, my daddy would go play a dance for them," Canray Fontenot remembers. "And sometimes they'd pay with some wood, and cut it and bring it at the house all ready to use. It was all right for him, because my daddy was a married man and he was a farmer. But Amédé didn't want that. He wanted some money."

Late at night, following the white dances, Ardoin would return to his community. It was then, Fontenot remembers, that he would unleash the blues and play old African "hollers" — perhaps even taking his accordion to the old *juré* songs. "He'd tell me he played at the church gathering, for the black people," recalls Vincent Lejeune, who knew Ardoin. "On Wednesday nights, there would be a religious meeting, maybe the whole neighborhood would get in one house, and Amédé would go play for them. All those country people. I used to say their bones rattle in them. But he'd play the music."

Vincent's father, Emar Lejeune, was a Cajun farmer who ran a dance hall in the town of Swords; for two years it was Ardoin's regular Saturday night stop. "Oh, people thought Amédé was the best," Vincent remembers. "The building was huge, it was eighty feet by eighty square. And they'd come from Church Point, Lewisburg, Eunice, Opelousas, Basile. People would come from miles. Wagon, buggies, old Model Ts, and horseback, every weekend. They'd charge the people twenty-five cents to come in to the dance, and Amédé got seventy-five, eighty dollars sometime. It was good money, because five or six dollars in those days for a musician, that was top money. They was supposed to shut everything down at twelve o'clock at night, but the people would throw a quarter, one would throw a dime, maybe one a nickel, and they'd keep him going. He'd never get tired, until two, three o'clock in the morning.

"Amédé would sing anything he wanted. His voice would go through you. He could play some music, every woman in the dancehall would cry. They'd stop dancing. Sat down and wiped the tears. Oh yes sir, he made the women cry, and the men would hang their heads down. Daddy said, 'He puts it to them.' Amédé used to say, 'Well, I'm singing about the facts of life.' And when he'd mix a little bit of the religious stuff with it, these women would cry like babies.

"I wasn't but eight or nine years old when he first started coming. Lots of kids would come with their parents to the dance, and Amédé'd get there early, about two o'clock, and he'd sit on the porch and sing to us. He'd ask you your name, who you was, and what you done, and where you went to school at, then he'd sing. And boy, he'd put in there, like if you had a girlfriend, then he'd sing about your girlfriend. I remember a song that Amédé played, that he was a hobo. He'd sing about him being on this train, and he had picked up this little dog, and you'd swear that dog would bark. He'd make that accordion bark like a dog. And he would laugh, he got a kick out of that. I believe he could make any sound he wanted on his accordion. He'd play that to us, the smaller kids, and he'd tell us, 'Get out of here! That's it!' and we'd all take off."

If Ardoin could put the devil in the dancers at Quincy Davis's club, Lejeune says he could take it right out again at his father's place. "He'd sing about the people at the place, and the people would get kind of rowdy. And when the people would get rowdy, he'd sing a religious song. That would calm them down, right there. And you'd never see anybody fight."

Lejeune recalls that Ardoin would play with Dennis McGee, as well as with a band that included a fiddle, guitar, triangle, and occasionally a washboard. Other times, he'd come and visit with the family, and make a different kind of music. "He'd sit there on the porch, and my brothers would be there, all farmers, and talk with him. And Amédé would sing to you, with no accordion. He'd pound on the porch and he'd make music with the back of his hand. He had a rhythm that he'd keep up with what he was singing, like somebody with drums. I don't think that nobody else could make up songs the way he done it, and sing it, and make good music out of it."

One day Ardoin played a wedding dance for Lejeune's sister Mamie. Everyone from the dance hall was invited, and more than a hundred cakes were given away as dance prizes. "He came there in the afternoon, and they had him sitting in a wagon," he remembers. "There were spring seats in the wagons in those days, and I can see him there, jumping up and down, and the people dancing in the yard, having a big time. It was about daylight the next morning before they quit.

"He played it all. He'd play a waltz, he'd play a two-step, he played a one-step. He played for people that used to do the Charleston. And he'd play the old New Orleans blues. I remember one man, they put a big red handkerchief on the floor, and that old guy would dance on all four corners on that handkerchief, and never move it. And he started Amédé to some kind of music special for him, and he'd hit on one corner of the handkerchief, hit the other, and keep the handkerchief straight all the time. And that would go for thirty minutes without stopping. He was old, a tall, skinny guy, and he'd drink lots of moonshine. Amédé would look at his violin player and he'd laugh, and he'd look at the people in the dance hall, and he'd smile.

"And there was Mr. Simon Guidry and his wife, Maurice Stanbar and his wife, and Jimmy Pitre and his wife. I was small, but I remembered those three colored couples, that came there in the dance hall. It was people we'd see every day, neighbors, and they asked Daddy if they could come there to listen. He'd say sure. Most of the people knew them anyway, because they were farmers, been there for years. The black people didn't dance, but I heard some of these white men tell them, 'Maurice, get up here and grab your old lady and dance, or I'm going to swing her around awhile.' But they had a corner, and they'd sit there, and they'd listen. After a while, one of them would walk out to that buggy, and my dad used to walk down the gravel road, as protection for them."

The dances kept going strong for two years, until Emar Lejeune decided he needed the building for a barn. "He put cotton in it, and corn," Vincent remembers. "He said he was tired of fooling with it. He said, 'Let somebody else go with it now.' When they closed that dance hall, I tell you, lots of people missed it. They told him he didn't need a barn. Because every Saturday night, that was the place. Well, about a couple years after that, Daddy had a heart attack, and he died. And then as the years went by, well, we lost track of Amédé."

Perhaps it was jealousy, perhaps he named the wrong people in his songs. Whatever the reason, it would seem that Amédé Ardoin was taking his life in his hands every time he played a dance. "I think what they hated the most is this habit that he wouldn't work, you know?" suggests Canray Fontenot. "They would call Amédé a bum, and in another word, that's what he was. Amédé would go someplace and play and take up a collection, but he always had some money in his pocket, when some of them were killing themselves working with no money.

"You see, Amédé was a little man and he had a lot of nerve," Fontenot continues. "He could come on the road there, and look both sides, and by the time he'd get here, he would compose something. So a lot of time, some of them fellows, them and their wife was in a feud or something, and Amédé would go sit down there and play, and the woman would go over there and he'd sing about a certain thing the man done to his wife. And the man knew who he was singing about, so he didn't like it. Said he had a bad mouth.

"One time they had a dance hall in Basile, and what saved him was some white guy who was learning how to play the guitar. Somebody threw a big ol' rock — whoever done it wanted to hurt him bad — and the guitar player put this guitar in front of Amédé, and the rock went through the guitar. But you know, he would take chances, and what he done, they kept on hiring him. They went and took some chicken wire and they made a pen there, and they would go get Amédé, and they had a bunch of men walking around him, and he would get in the pen there, and he would play anyway." Adam Fontenot warned Ardoin not to play in the Basile club anymore. Ardoin replied that it was good money. Adam, who farmed all his life and never made a record because it went against his religious beliefs, couldn't convince his friend otherwise.

The legends have it that Ardoin narrowly escaped death almost every weekend. An accordionist is said to have shot Ardoin one night through a church window, because of jealousy. Vincent Lejeune remembers that his father had to throw some men out of his sister's wedding; they had become enraged that Ardoin's music was making their women cry. "He'd leave the accordion and he'd run across the fields many a time," Wade Frugé once recalled.

"I remember he once played a dance somewhere, when he had a buggy," Milton Ardoin remembers. "And when he left that dance, he figured out he was going to have some trouble in the road, where them people were jealous of him. He'd take his handkerchief, and he tied that on the horse head, just like that horse had a white spot. When they saw that horse had a white spot, they thought it wasn't Amédé, and they let him pass."

Today not everyone agrees that Amédé Ardoin was beaten and left for dead on the side of the road. "Now, he didn't take no handkerchief from that white woman, that I know of," says Boozoo Chavis. "Somebody's putting that in there. In that time, them colored people wouldn't do things like that, they'd kill you. What they done, they poisoned him in his drink. Because them white women used to go there by the bandstand and ask him to play a number. They liked his music. And them people say, 'Well, we're going to fix the clock for him.' They wouldn't shoot him, because he had a white partner with him, so they poisoned him."

Other musicians believe that the poisoner was a black fiddler, enraged that Amédé chose to perform with whites. "There was a black man who played the fiddle and he wanted to play with Amédé," Dennis McGee told Ann Savoy. "And Amédé told him, 'I'm not going to play with you. If you and I play together, two blacks, the whites are going to kill us. There would be nothing to save us. I like to have Mr. McGee with me because Mr. McGee's going to help me.' The last time I saw Amédé he was in Eunice, planted between two railroad tracks. I said, 'What's wrong with you, Amédé?' He was right there, in front of the Blackstone, and he was lost, lost, lost. The black man had given him a dose of poison in whiskey."

Others think that if he was beaten for taking the handkerchief, it couldn't have been by locals. "There were some people, not from this area, at the dance who didn't like to see a black man use a white woman's handkerchief, so they followed him home and beat him badly," Cajun musician Joel Savoy told Ann Savoy. "There wasn't anyone in this area who would have thought twice about Amédé using a white woman's handkerchief. Everyone knew and liked him."

Milton Ardoin doesn't think it happened because of a handkerchief at all. He says he knows the names of the men who beat his uncle, and that they are no longer living. The problems started when Amédé took a ride in a car that belonged to one of Celestin Marcantel's friends. Marcantel sat in the front with his friend, and his friend's daughters rode in the back with Ardoin. "Them two daughters, they would sit down on each side while he was playing music, and they would kiss him, you know. He was playing music to go back home. And they were so happy." Without Marcantel's knowledge, says Milton, the friend paid two black men to ambush the musician.

Milton Ardoin isn't the only one who today considers the handkerchief to be just a polite metaphor for the obvious truth: that Amédé had relations with white women, and that's what killed him. "The story that we hear down here is that he had a secret affair with a white woman, they found out about it, and they beat him till he lost his mind," says zydeco bandleader Terrance Simien. Yet another theory holds that Amédé's condition was caused by a degenerative disease, such as pneumonia or syphilis. Whatever the cause, when his friends saw Amédé during the last years of his life, they knew that the man who made the people go "rolling in like balls" to see him, and whose music could make women weep and men stop fighting, was no longer the same man. "When he came to the house, he was not able to play his music like he used to," recalls Milton Ardoin sadly. "Something between his hand and his mind, it was off."

An official report of the attack has never been located. Milton estimates that it occurred in 1949. Others believe it was a decade earlier. All agree on the effect it had: Amédé tried to continue playing music, but his wanderings had lost their purpose.

"When I was about six years old, we were in the cotton field, right by Highway 190," remembers musician George Broussard. "I remember my father telling my mother, 'That's Amédé Ardoin walking down there.' So then I looked up, because I could remember them talking about his music. He crossed over the fence and walked in the field where we was picking cotton, and he asked my father, 'Which way is it to Eunice?' My father said, 'Well, just get back over the fence and go the same direction you were walking.' Then he walked away, and went that same direction. Then my father and my mother talked about it, and he said, 'I guess something just happened to Amédé.' "

Eventually, Ardoin was taken to an asylum in the central Louisiana town of Pineville. Mama Lena Pitre, a cousin of the Ardoins, used to go to hear Amédé play the dances, and she recognized him in Pineville one afternoon. "I went to visit my dad in the hospital, and I saw Amédé there," she recalls. "His hand was all crippled — he played so much accordion till his hand was just curled up. He was wearing blue pants, some old slippers, and a yellow T-shirt he had on. His hair was gray, he was all jammed up in the front. I went by the fence, and I was talking French. I said, 'How are you doing, Nonc Amédé?' 'Oh,' he said, *'bien, bien, bien.'*"

The only news that the Fontenots heard about their ailing friend came from one of Amédé's older brothers. Recalled Canray: "He told me, 'I went to Pineville to see him, and he never could remember who I was.' He said, 'That's what you call stone crazy.' He said, 'That man there, there's no need for nobody to go see him.' He says, 'They told me over there in Pineville, he ain't going to never ask for a drink, he ain't never going to never ask for something to eat.'"

One day Milton Ardoin visited his uncle in Pineville. "I said, 'Nonc, how you feel?' He said, 'I feel all right.' He said, 'I would be glad to go back home.' I said, 'You can't go back, because the doctor is still treating you.' He said, 'They're going to let me go?' But he was not good, you know, to take the road to come back home."


There are legends that Amédé Ardoin eventually left Pineville and took one last walk back home. However, it seems more likely that he died in the institution. The date is uncertain; jazz musician and writer Austin Sonnier obtained a death certificate from Pineville dated May 30, 1941 for "Amelie Ardoin," but the deceased was listed as being twenty years older than Amédé. Milton believes that Amédé died in Pineville in the early 1950s, that he had a girlfriend in Rayne who didn't want the body, and that he was buried in an unmarked common grave. He thinks about him every time he drives to Eunice. "There's a John Deere store at the place where Amédé was thrown in the ditch," he says. "Every time I pass, I look about it, I say, 'Well, that's the place they threw my uncle.'"

Both Canray Fontenot and Bois Sec Ardoin began their musical careers by playing triangle behind Amédé Ardoin. "When I was young I was watching how he was playing, and listening to his tune and learning the words," Bois Sec says. "We used to play in Basile together, at Quincy Davis's club." Canray Fontenot had been invited to join Amédé for his New York recording session, but his mother said he was too young. "Most of them old people, they didn't care for you to learn how to play music when you was young," he says. "Amédé was a good example and a bad example. Because they figure if you learn how to play music you was going to wind up like he was."

When Iry Lejeune reintroduced the accordion into Cajun music in the 1950s, he was inspired by many hours spent listening to his Uncle Angeles's old 78s of Amédé Ardoin — in fact, the celebrated return of the accordion into contemporary Cajun music was largely due to Lejeune's versions of Ardoin tunes. Boozoo Chavis also remembers those songs. "My uncle had that record, the 'Eunice Two-Step,'" he says. "Everyone had Amédé's record. Boy, that man had a fine voice. That's pure Frenchman from the heart." Clifton Chenier once said that he never heard Ardoin play, but that he had heard talk of him; he was the one who informed Arhoolie Records owner Chris Strachwitz that Ardoin was a black man.

Arhoolie has reissued most of Ardoin's recordings, and Columbia has reissued most of the others; his tunes frequently surface during zydeco nights, but usually with new titles and no mention of Ardoin. Despite the current trend toward a percussive, single-note accordion in zydeco, he is yet to be given his full due. Perhaps a restless orphan cuts too strange a figure as a king. Perhaps his life is too suffused with painful details of a not-too-distant past. So far, the only official records of his life to surface are a draft registration card, a census count, and a possible death certificate. Other documents were said to have been stored in a church in Eunice that burned in 1915. His most enduring legacy is thirty-four recorded songs and countless stories that recall the precarious road traveled by Amédé Ardoin.

*Canray Fontenot and Bois Sec Ardoin.*

*Canray Fontenot with the Ardoin family band at Carnegie Hall, 1990.*

# 5

# A WALTZ CAN TURN
# TO THE BLUES

---

SUNDAY AFTERNOON IN DURALDE, LOUISIANA; morning services have ended, and a priest changes from robes into black pants and a short-sleeved shirt. Dinners of pork chops and rice dressing are served in the community hall. Men gather in the shade of the church; there are words in French and a barrage of laughter, then Bois Sec Ardoin walks slowly from the group to a flatbed trailer. With a hand from his son Morris he climbs up.

Morris blinks sweat from his eyes and runs his bow across his fiddle. Bois Sec sits on a metal folding chair, then lightly rocks his shoulders and pushes notes from his accordion, launching into the tune "Eunice Two-Step." His cries fill the churchyard and the open fields beyond.

Watching the band is a man in torn jeans, a T-shirt, and a white cap. He identifies himself as a Marcantel. Yes, he's related to Celestin Marcantel, he nods, and everyone in his family knows the story. "But Celestin and Amédé, they were friends," he says. "That's what I heard."

A few couples are dancing in the sun. Some old men stand in front of the speakers, shouting out to Bois Sec as he plays. "It'll take three feet to dance that two-step!" yells one, and Bois Sec leans forward to drive out the last notes. Then a young boy in a wide-brimmed hat climbs on the flatbed, and he stares hard at the accordion. "Mr. Bois Sec," he demands, "play 'Bon-soir Moreau.'" Morris leans down. "Bois Sec doesn't play 'Bonsoir Moreau,'" he says quietly. "That was Mr. Canray."

For decades, the musical partnership of Bois Sec Ardoin and Canray Fontenot provided one of the last great chances to hear a passing Creole style: the accordion and fiddle trading the lead on playful blues like "Joe Pitre a deux femmes" ("Joe Pitre Has Two Wives") and the bluesy *baisse bas* "Bonsoir Moreau" ("Good Night, Moreau"), played in three-four time but sung in the emotional wailing vocal style first heard in Alan Lomax's record-ing of Cleveland Benoit and Darby Hicks's "Là-bas chez Moreau" ("Over at Moreau's"). Ardoin and Fontenot moved from house dances to clubs, and when the R&B-influenced zydeco bands crowded them from the local clubs, they began to appear on international festival stages.

But most of the great surviving pioneers of Creole music have not been as fortunate. Those who used to pack the floor have now retired to their porches and living rooms, where they teach young musicians and play for their families. There, the melodies, rhythms, voices, dances, and passions of another era can be heard in their songs and stories.

### Bois Sec Ardoin and Canray Fontenot

It is long past midnight in the fall of 1965, and a station wagon, filled with laughing men, barrels down the narrow Railroad Avenue in Welsh, Loui-siana. When Creole fiddler Canray Fontenot hears the commotion, he gets out of bed and pulls his clothes on. "There must be something serious some-where," he thinks, and watches as a car rolls to a stop in his driveway. Bois Sec Ardoin falls out, followed by a man Fontenot doesn't recognize: the folklorist Ralph Rinzler. Rinzler is looking for performers for the 1966 New-port Folk Festival in Rhode Island.

The party moves inside, and a late night audition becomes a party. Fontenot goes for the only fiddle he hasn't sold off. He tells them its story, that it was a "bad luck" fiddle that had been tossed out when its player fell ill and died. A trash-truck driver salvaged it and gave it to him.

While Rinzler waits, Fontenot tunes the fiddle to Ardoin's accordion. A few songs are played, there is more laughter; by sunrise, the pair is invited to Newport for the following July, when they would introduce Creole music to its widest audience yet. And returning home from Rhode Island, the two musicians would stop in Virginia to meet with producer Dick Spottswood and make their first album, *Les Blues Du Bayou*. Recalls Fontenot: "Boy, was

I embarrassed with this little fiddle here. But I said, 'Lord have mercy, what the hell' — I had never went to a festival before."

Never full-time musicians, Ardoin and Fontenot had put their instruments on blocks many times during their lives. "I had to put my accordion on the armoire because they all wanted rock and roll," recalls Ardoin of one dry spell. And both men always had other things on their minds besides music: Ardoin raised fourteen children by working as a farmer, Fontenot raised six by laboring in a Welsh seed store. But whenever they returned to their instruments, it was to give their rich Creole tradition new life, and to take one more turn around on "Bonsoir Moreau," the song they'd once used to sneak the blues into a house dance under the respectable mantle of a waltz. "You was out of business if you played blues," Fontenot explains. "That's where me and Bois Sec got the idea of 'Bonsoir Moreau.' It's kind of blues, but you could kind of slip it on them with something they could waltz, and you could play that all night if you wanted."

Canray Fontenot's musical family included his cousins Freeman and Bee Fontenot, as well as his father, Adam. During his childhood in the community of l'Anse aux Vaches, he remembers, life and music were entwined at the deepest levels: "At Christmas, my grandpa would get a bunch of men together and sing all night there. A little log was put in the chimney, and they'd let it burn all night long. Before sunup Christmas morning, everybody would make twelve coals out of the Christmas fire, and they'd use that to make a calendar in the barn. Then they would take some onion, some salt garlic, and believe me, they could tell you if this month was going to be a wet month, if there was going to be a lot of rain." Among Fontenot's later recordings would be some of the songs he heard around that Christmas fire.

His father, Adam Fontenot, was a popular accordionist, a peer of Amédé Ardoin. But it was his cousin Douglas Bellard who first put the fiddle in his hands, when Bellard separated from his wife and moved near the Fontenots. "I used to go fool with the fiddle, you know, I had learned how to tune it and everything from him," Fontenot remembers. In October 1929, Bellard went to New Orleans and made what would be the first commercial records ever released by a black Creole musician from Southwest Louisiana, including "La valse de la prison." His success was an annoyance to young Canray. "He started getting kind of popular and most of the time that doggone Douglas was gone," he says. "I didn't have nothing to practice. How in the hell was I going to learn? I was just getting in the groove to learn something, now he keeps taking the fiddle." The solution took the shape of a wooden cigar box, some screen taken out of his unsuspecting mother's new door, some sewing thread, pine tree rosin, and a knife swiped from a drunken meat cutter. With these materials Fontenot fashioned his first fiddle. "It didn't sound loud," he says, "but I could hear what I was doing."

During this time, Alphonse "Bois Sec" Ardoin was growing up in the nearby community of L'Anse de 'Prien Noir. Like his cousin Amédé, he lost his father when he was a child, and he and his brothers grew up helping his mother sharecrop. But, also like his cousin Amédé, he soon became known — or at least kidded — for avoiding hard work. That reputation is preserved in his nickname, which translates to "dry wood." The story — a family favorite — goes that when Bois Sec was young, he'd bring water to the field workers, and always make a dash to the barn when it started to rain.

As a boy, Bois Sec backed his cousin Amédé on triangle, watching his fingers dance along the accordion, learning the tunes. "It won't be long before I catch up with you," he told him. Then Bois Sec started stealing his brother's accordion, which he'd take to the top of the barn to avoid getting caught. "It was not a good hiding place, because you could hear me for miles," he admits with a laugh. But by the time his brother discovered him, Bois Sec had learned to play well, and his brother ended up giving him the instrument.

Fontenot also started out playing with Amédé Ardoin. He went on to form a string band in the 1930s, but by the late 1940s he had joined with Bois Sec to create the Duralde Ramblers, which began playing for community dances and for a live radio broadcast on Sundays on KEUN in Eunice. They played in towns throughout Southwest Louisiana, including Basile, where there was a club owned by Freeman Fontenot; their songs included numbers from Amédé Ardoin and Adam Fontenot, as well as a tune Canray reworked from Bellard's "La valse de la prison," which he titled "Barres de la prison":

Moi, j'ai roulé, je m'ai mis à malfaire.
J'avais la tête dure, j'ai rentré dans le tracas.
Asteur j'suis condamné pour la balance de ma vie
Dans les barres de la prison.

Me, I rolled around, I got into doing wrong.
I had a hard head, I got into trouble.
Now I'm condemned for the rest of my life
To the prison bars.

"If you were to hear the real 'Barres de la prison' that he made, you can't dance that, it's out of beat," Fontenot says. "I learned how to play it when it first came out, and I thought, if ever I make a record, I'm going to set it in my own way, and they're going to be able to dance it. My daddy always was talking about, 'Whenever you're going to play a tune, play a tune that the people can dance.' And that's what I did."

Both Ardoin and Fontenot are clear that their Creole repertoire should not be called zydeco, but their music has proved a trove for zydeco musicians. John Delafose's version of "Joe Pitre" launched both his band and the single-row accordion revival. More recently, both Geno Delafose and Beau Jocque put zydeco instrumentation and a contemporary dance beat behind their versions of other Ardoin and Fontenot tunes. Cajun bands such as Steve Riley and the Mamou Playboys and BeauSoleil have also adapted them to their styles, adding new arrangements, vocal harmonies, and usually faster tempos. Among the most popular Ardoin-Fontenot melodies are "Les Haricots," which was adapted in BeauSoleil's "Zydeco Gris-Gris," and "'Tit Monde" ("Little World"), which was retooled into the zydeco hit "Why Do You Want to Make Me Cry?" Contemporary interpreters of Fontenot's fiddle style include Doucet, D'Jalma Garnier, Mitch Reed, and Edward Poullard.

But to the older players, hearing new versions of old songs serves as a bittersweet reminder that times change. Once, Bois Sec recalls, his son Gustav was showing interest in the honey-smooth vocals of Cajun swamp pop musician Belton Richard. "That's the style he wanted to play and I stopped him," he says. "I said to take your time with that. You've been raised with that Creole music. We're not going to change it, we're going to stay there. And we stayed there, too." But he admits he can only listen now as the youngest in the family turn to contemporary zydeco. "All my grandchildren play zydeco now, but I can't change them," he says. Then he laughs. "Oh no, I got to let them go."

Following their appearance at Newport in 1966, Fontenot and Ardoin kept playing for festivals both around the world and in Louisiana, becoming the only Creoles to regularly play the old style long after it went out of fashion at the prairie dances. They tenaciously hung together through a series of health problems, and to the end they shared the kind of alliance in which information can be exchanged in a glance, and on a dime a waltz can turn to the blues. There would come a point in their songs when they would shoot each other glances, give each other slight smiles, and bear down on their instruments, tapping their feet harder, going to work, driving a deeper groove down the median of the tune. For their audiences around the world, their relationship defined Creole music.

"We can read each other's mind," Bois Sec Ardoin would explain. "It's not like that with anyone else."

## Bébé Carrière

Creole fiddler Joseph "Bébé" Carrière takes a sip of coffee, his eyes dancing over the rim of the cup. "The first time I came to Lake Charles, they threw me in the can," he begins. "I was going to play in Iowa, Louisiana, and at that time it was forbidden to have whiskey. They had none of that. The one had made that dance, he was living right along the highway, and before we got to the man's house, the law stopped us. And me, I had bought me a little apple punch to play the dance, you know."

He shrugs his shoulders. "They just had to stop the dance, they had no more musicians to play. And boy they hated that, yeah. We stayed in the can four, five days. The day of the trial, the judge said, 'Soon as you see two or three colored fellows in the car, you go and stop them.' And he let us go. I said, 'Well, well.'"

Today Carrière lives on the Texas side of Lake Charles, in the oil and sulphur city of Port Arthur. He's sitting with his grandson Greg in the kitchen of his daughter's house, tucked behind a manicured lawn, surrounded by a caring family, and a long way from his former home in Lawtell. Carrière had stayed in Lawtell his entire life, watching his friends and family, and even his wife and children, move on to Texas and California. He sharecropped cotton, corn, and sweet potatoes, raised hogs and cattle, and bootlegged white mule moonshine. When asked for details, he offers this recipe: "You'd take fifty pounds corn chop and fifty pounds of sugar in some wooden barrels, and you let that stay in there about five or six days. That stuff would start boiling, you'd swear they had some fish in there. And don't you know that when that stuff comes out of that still, it would be a hundred and forty degrees. And some of them fellows would drink it hot like that. I would reduce it to a hundred and five and put it in a wooden barrel, so it gets that poison out of it.

"When it would drip out, it was white — that's why they'd call it white mule. Then you could burn some sugar and make a syrup with that, and it would make it turn kind of red. And boy, I made that a whole lot. A white fellow from Welsh paid me so much a gallon to make it, and I'd take some of it with me to the dances. That stuff would make a person happy, you know."

Carrière may have left Lawtell, but he left behind a band name that forever memorialized his town in music: the Lawtell Playboys. Mention that

*Bébé Carrière.*

*Frank Andrus at home with his granddaughter Kara.*

band around Louisiana, and people shake their heads for the old days. With his brother, accordionist Eraste "Dolon" Carrière, Bébé started out playing house dances and went on to hold down Saturday nights at Slim's Y-Ki-Ki, playing the band's popular tunes "La robe à parasol" and "Blues à Bébé." When they stopped, they passed on the band title to Dolon's son, the fiddler Calvin Carrière, who joined with accordionist Delton Broussard to keep the name alive. "We used to work in the fields," remembers Calvin, "and every Sunday Delton would sit on that porch and take lessons from my daddy. He was kind of shy but he got it good." As the new Lawtell Playboys played on at Slim's, the Carrière brothers continued making music in Bébé's kitchen in Lawtell, where they recorded their songs for the 1976 Rounder album *Zodico: Louisiana Creole Music.*

But Dolon Carrière passed away in 1983, and Bébé admits that he doesn't even have a fiddle with him in Port Arthur. He thinks moving the bow might help his arthritis, but his music seems far away indeed. Yet there were some good years in there, he says with a smile.

There was even one time he had a chance to play a Lawtell house dance with Amédé Ardoin. "He came looking for me, heard there was a Carrière boy who could play the fiddle," he says. "The way he'd turn his number around, I followed him. I was right on his track."

The first music Carrière heard was from his father, Ernest Carrière, who played accordion at home. "I made me a violin with a cigar box," Bébé says. "I don't know how in the world I learned off that, because strings go by let- ters — E, A, B, G, you see — and those strings there didn't have no letters. But after I learned to play that thing, my daddy understood. He brought me to Church Point, where he bought a real violin from the music store. I must have been about fourteen years. And I took off."

Older players in the area taught young Carrière the secrets of playing, telling him that he needed to find rattlesnake tails to put inside the fiddle. Friends in the town of Washington killed some snakes and gave him the rat- tles. The sound was better. "But one day I was playing," he frowns, "and I kind of shake my violin. No more rattles. I don't know who done it, or how they got my rattle out. But I never had my rattle back."

Another local snake inspired one of his most popular compositions, the high-speed fiddle breakdown called "Blue Runner." Says Carrière: "That was a fast piece, because a blue runner is a fast snake. It runs with its head up, and when them things catch you, they hold on to your clothes and they whip you with that tail."

Bébé Carrière recalls that he kept the Lawtell Playboys up to date by learning new songs off 78s and introducing them in the dances. "I could tune up a violin three kind of ways," he explains. "I could tune my violin to play the blues, and that's why the people were attached to me so much. I'd play one they'd sing it there, 'Baby, please don't go back to New Orleans.' It's about how they knew that was a big city and everything that was going on there.

"I started that when I would hear that on records," Carrière continues. "If I wanted to learn the songs from the blues, I'd buy me a record and I'd play it on a graphaphone. And I liked some of them hillbillies. 'Kentucky Waltz,' Bill Monroe had made that, and I liked that very much. And poor Jimmie Rodgers's song, I could play, 'I'm going to California where they sleep out every night.' I'd sing all that, and people would find that funny that I could sing in English and French — you know, they thought I could just sing in French." Among the Carrière brothers' later songs was even a number they called "Deux Pas à Granny," or "Granny's Two-Step," a Creole version of the theme to *The Beverly Hillbillies*.

Early in his career — probably around 1929, when Amédé Ardoin was making his first records — a scout had offered Carrière a chance to record. But unlike Ardoin, Douglas Bellard, and others he played with, he never took advantage of the offer. Not, he says, because of any beliefs against recording. He was just young. The Carrière brothers would later record for Rounder, Maison de Soul, and Arhoolie, but Bébé admits that he still wonders what might have happened if he left Lawtell earlier. "My kin people, some of them are in California, but I acted like an old fool. If I had gone too, I'd have been way up yonder."

One of his sons, Andrew Carrier, leads the band Cajun Classics in San Francisco, and he's always trying to get his father to fly out to play for that city's eager zydeco dancers. "He tells me, 'If you want to play, I'll send a ticket,'" Bébé says, then laughs. "I say, 'That's too high up in the sky.' And my stepdaughter told me, 'Pop, you know what to do, get you a good swag before you get on that bird, and before you know you'll be landing in Oakland.'"

On this afternoon in Port Arthur, Bébé and Greg talk for another hour about how Greg and his brother would visit their grandfather in Lawtell, and how his brother would run to the outhouse because he was afraid of the bulls. Greg remembers that his uncle used to take him in his lap and play him his favorite song, "Blue Runner."

Then Bébé Carrière picks up a bright blue leather-wrapped cane with fringes up the sides — a gift from his nephew Mark Carrier, a safety for the Chicago Bears. He holds up the cane and admires it, then his slippers pad across plush carpet to the front door. "Yeah, I should have went out to California when I was about twenty-five or thirty years of age," he says. "Last August, I made eighty-eight years. But they're still trying to get me to go." He stops. "I'm thinking about it."

## Anderson Moss

"I'm going to get 'Eh 'tite fille,'" says Ernest Henry, looking to his teacher.

It's Saturday morning in Houston, and the heat rises from wide empty streets into Anderson Moss's screened porch. Moss is wearing a long-sleeved shirt, red suspenders, and a panama hat. This is his home; when a car passes in front of the house, he stands up to identify it. If he doesn't recognize the driver, he shakes his head in disgust. Then he brightens, and turns to his student. "You got to learn how to beat them bass," he instructs Henry in low tones, adding a rumbling laugh. "You learn that, you're going to go to Lafayette one day. Heh, heh, heh."

Moss keeps his own piano-key accordion in his lap. "The best they made, a Titano," he says. "I bought it about twenty-seven years ago." He runs his fingers along the keys while he talks, then he raises a hand and points to Henry. "That boy's going to learn, he pays attention. You see, I broke in about five or six men, in Houston. And that boy, he couldn't even hit a note. Now he hits notes." Henry nods.

"You see, I done hit my eighty," Moss says. "Try to live as long as you can. All my people are gone. The Moss family and Daddy, my sisters, all gone. Practically all the musicians is gone. Willie Green, Joe Jackson, they've faded away. Only one more is left, L. C. Donatto, and he ain't as old as me.

"One used to come pick me up all the time, he died about three months ago. They called him Mitchell. Lonnie Mitchell. Now, he was my best friend. He'd come pick me up, we'd go up to the zydeco. He always wanted to play. He was sick, but he kept on. Doctor had told him leave it alone. But he couldn't. He didn't drink, now, but boy, he played that accordion. That's what got him.

"I could still be playing," he continues. "But instead, I learn my friends. They come here, I learn them how to play. White or black. I'd rather do that, sit down in the house. Money's good, don't get me wrong. But what money do you have, when you're dead and gone. Heh, heh, heh."

Moss was one of the early Creole arrivals to Houston. He moved here with his family from their home in Maurice, Louisiana, in 1928, after the price of rice fell. "Louisiana people took over this town," he remembers. "All you had to do was say you was from Louisiana, and they would hire you right there."

"They know you sweat in the field with the cotton, sweet potato, cane," agrees Henry. "Myself, that's how I got hired. The man wouldn't hire nobody if he wasn't from Louisiana."

Moss laughs in appreciation.

"That's right," Henry says. "My foreman, he used to tell us on Friday, keep fingers, eyes, and a good back, and you was going to work. Don't get cut up on Saturday night, and you had a job waiting for you on Monday."

Moss nods slowly. It was a good town for an accordion player too, he says. When he was a boy back in Maurice, he'd sneak into the local dance hall to hear players like Sou-Pop, Bidon, and Amédé Ardoin, and when he hit Houston, he decided to learn to play. "I started with a big triple-note," he says. "They had a big tree in the yard. My daddy would say, 'Honey, he's learning.' Then I learned two pieces, 'Stormy Weather' and 'Driftin' Blues.' And then 'Black Gal.' After them three numbers, the people started knocking on the door. 'A musician lives here? I want you to play a party for me.'"

Moss played everywhere there were French people to hire him. He watched Clifton Chenier come out of Houston. "I have seen better players," he comments dryly. He played in the Catholic churches and in the country clubs where he couldn't afford to eat, and he remembered one night he filled a house with so many people the ceiling broke. "I played till four o'clock that morning," he says. "They danced on the other side. That zydeco was tough. Every night I had somewhere to play. Things were good and money was flowing."

Moss's Houston was a boom town, a city of quick riches and legendary characters. "Have you ever heard about Silver Dollar Wes?" he asks. "His mama lived about a block and a half from where he lived. He had a tunnel under the ground to her house, and that tunnel was full of silver dollars. He had a bunch of men working for him, just to shine the dollars. Sometimes he'd go to where you were working, he'd line you up, and he'd throw a bunch of silver dollars in the air. He'd say, 'Come on, fellows, I'm going to see how many y'all can catch.' It was just like feeding a bunch of chickens."

Henry laughs. "I know one white man, he said, 'If my mother and daddy were living to see how Mr. Wes is taking that money and giving it to them negroes, they'd jump out of their grave.'"

"Yes, when Silver Dollar Wes died," Moss agrees, "everybody missed him."

Moss left Houston once, for military service during World War II. He bought an accordion when he was in England, and he brought it with him to France, where he played on street corners. "You talk about some fine people who can dance all night long," he says. He says he was ordered to get rid of his accordion, because his music was making the other Louisiana men in his barracks too homesick. Instead, Moss stashed the accordion with his new French friends.

Moss continued his music when he returned to Houston, and he married a woman he met at a dance. "You get you a woman from Louisiana," he instructs, "you got you something, man." He made some records, but he still doesn't know exactly what happened to them, and he shied away from making any more. But onstage, he couldn't be beat. "I used to dance like I was Superman." He leans back and gives his accordion case a hard kick. "When I got happy on that box, I was something else. Then I used to play stage shows, on Friday and Saturday nights. I would play three songs, then someone would sing and dance, and some of them would do Amos and Andy, stuff like that. People would clap. I was a young man."

Moss hears a passing car and looks up. Early afternoon has come to his corner of Houston. His children shuttle through the porch with bags from Burger King, and his great-grandnephew is lugging around a shiny green toy accordion. "Come here, Tee-Tee, play something," Moss says. The boy stops in his tracks, mushes his fingers on his accordion buttons, and shouts, "What's his name, Keith Frank!" Moss lifts his eyebrows. "He's going to learn," he says. "Wait until he gets a little older, around seven or eight, and watch out. Heh, heh, heh." Tee-Tee runs off.

Moss takes out a cigarette. His doctor told him it was good for his nerves, he explains, so he smokes several packs a day.

"I'm going to tell you something, this will ease your brain." He pats the top of his accordion. "Just like I got old, now, I get to think about what I used to do. And the things I used to do, I can't do it no more, you understand. I think about it so hard, then I take that box and start pulling on it, and it just leaves me.

"That music is a pretty thing, man," he concludes. "It will ease your brains. You think about different things, you think about everything. You ain't got nobody to talk with, you see. So I get on that accordion and play about five or six pieces, I'm all right. I don't even have to drink. Yeah, you see, I'm blessed."

Henry puts his accordion in its case and gets ready to leave. I ask Moss to play one more song. He declines. "Maybe next time you come back, if I'm still living," he says. "Heh, heh, heh." Then, on my way to my car, the sound of his accordion fills the street. "Tell me what's the matter," Moss is singing. "What's the matter, now?"

### Hiram Sampy

Some Creole musicians made the switch from house dances to clubs. They plugged their accordions into amplifiers, and they added a drummer and a guitar player. "I had three clubs regularly," Hiram Sampy recalls. "The old Bon Ton, the one that burned down. And the Blue Angel, the one that they broke down. And I had two dances a month at Hamilton's, on Saturdays.

The clubs wanted the French music, because in our dances we had 'ageable' people, people that were responsible. Those that wanted to act right."

Today Sampy lives in the town of Carencro, where he works as a school crossing guard. Next to his house is another closed club that he used to play, the Rock and Roll. "I was there, playing Saturday nights, and my band was called Sampy and the Rock and Roll," he remembers. "So the man asked me, 'How about changing your name?' It was kind of funny, Sampy and the Rock and Roll, playing at the Rock and Roll. So he said, 'I'm going to call you Sampy and the Bad Habits.'"

The name stuck, and Sampy's career took off. He moved from single-row French songs to piano-key blues. He was one of the first to play the Southwest Louisiana Zydeco Festival, and he recalls that Rockin' Dopsie started out scratching rubboard for him. He made one record, with the late Lafayette zydeco entrepreneur J. J. Caillier; the cover showed Sampy's smiling face encased in a modern swirl of psychedelic colors. He played at the New Orleans Jazz Fest for two years, and believes he wasn't invited back because two members of his band ended up getting into a fight. Never hire a husband and a wife together, he advises. But he always played to packed clubs, because he followed his father's advice: "He said, 'Whatever you do, give the people a satisfaction.'"

The music Sampy grew up hearing included *bazar* marches and French-language ring games that couples would play during Lent. "We'd form a circle, and someone would go in the middle and say they fell in the well. You'd ask, 'How many feet did you fall in there?' She'd say, 'Five,' and you had to give her five kisses to get out. Then you'd go all around, clapping your hands and singing, *'Tombé dans le puits.'* That game had been there for a long, long time. No, Lent wasn't bad at all."

When he was older, Sampy tried out Houston for six months. He worked construction. But he gave up the city and moved back to Carencro, and he kept on following his father's advice. "I played what the people wanted, not what I wanted," he says. "Some people like the blues, some people like the two-step, and I'd play it all. Me, when I was on the bandstand, I was four or five musicians. I could play some Clifton Chenier numbers, I could play some Dopsie, and I play my own songs. Cliff wouldn't play nothing but his. He's like Boozoo. But me, it wouldn't make no difference."

Sampy reaches down and opens his accordion box, and he pulls out a piece of napkin. He unfolds it, revealing a request in blue ink: "Could you please play 'Just Because,' thank you." A souvenir from the Blue Angel Club. He folds it and puts it back in the case, then pulls out a single-row accordion and taps his fingers on the buttons and squeezes out a quick, buoyant tune. "They call that 'Mazurka,'" he says. "My daddy used to play it. That's a

*Hiram Sampy.*

one-step, not a two-step. You dance that almost with one foot, hopping around. It gets away from us, the old songs."

Then he pulls another accordion case over to him. "To tell you the fact, everything I own, this second-hand house I bought, and the lot, and all my cars, I bought with this accordion," he says, lifting up a triple-row. He laughs. "That's not heavy, yeah," he says, putting it in his lap and running the straps around his shoulders. "But you couldn't play the blues on that little one. I can play anything I want on that triple."

And for the rest of this waning afternoon in Carencro, he does.


### Walter Polite

Born on Christmas Day in 1910, Walter Polite was another musician who went from house dances to clubs. His band, Walter Polite and the Red Hot Swinging Dukes, had a club hit with the song "My Baby Is Coming Back Home to Me." Today, even though he keeps his accordion within reach, he admits he rarely takes it from its case.

But Polite has a clear memory of the sounds he heard during his childhood in St. Martinville: the French music on weekends, and the *bazar* marches during Lent. "That was on Saturdays, on weekends. They wouldn't make the fair at churches, they'd go to houses. They had a group sitting down, just like they were the band, but with no instruments — just singing and clapping hands. They'd sing:

*Quand m'a partie, t'allez manquer moi.*

When I'm gone, you're going to miss me.

and the couples would hold each other, and they'd just turn around, but they wouldn't dance. When you dance, your foot is going to jump. But they'd just march.

"Then on Easter Saturday, everybody would turn out," he continues. "That was when the dance would start. You'd see dances everywhere, because the people hadn't danced for seven weeks. And that marching was finished."

Polite first started playing music when his cousin gave him an accordion, and he performed at his first house dance two weeks later. He watched players like Bidon and Claude and Ernest Faulk, and soon he was playing for the priests in St. Martinville, who hired him for church dances. He also started performing for political rallies. "They'd give me a big glass of whiskey and a bowl of ice cream to cool me down," he remembers. "And I'd play in North Louisiana, I used to play for the soldiers in the camp. But Houston was the place. That priest there used to love me to play for him. Big church hall, and they used to lock my accordion in the church, so I couldn't go back home and had to play again the next day."

Polite was glad when he could add electricity to his accordion. "It could overtake the noise," he says. "Then I could play anything I wanted — hillbilly, rock and roll, church hymns." In their prime, the Red Hot Swinging Dukes were a zydeco big band, complete with trumpet, saxophone, organ, and a female vocalist.

"Cliff gave me a lot of learning," Polite remembers. "He said, 'When I die, they can call you Cliff the Second.' Now, there's a man that I'm learning how to play. John Wilson, he's in New York. I told him, 'I'm going to quit. What I want you to do, don't start playing music and bragging on yourself. Don't try to outplay somebody. Play your music.' And you ought to hear him now.

"My son could play a little bit, but he doesn't want to anymore, because he's a preacher," Polite concludes. "He used to be my drummer, and when he quit, that got me out of courage to play. Now, everywhere I go, people ask me, 'Why did you stop?' But I stopped."


### Frank Andrus

"'Pinetop Boogie Woogie,' y'all!" Frank Andrus shouts. "Now, when I say 'stop,' stop! And don't move a thing!"

His granddaughter, a preschooler named Kara, freezes.

"And when I say 'get it,' let's shake that thing!"

She starts up again, arms in the air, and Andrus goes back to his story.

Unlike Hiram Sampy and Walter Polite, Andrus had only a few nights in the clubs. He played a couple of times in Opelousas, he says, in a place owned by a man named Lastrapes. And he won't forget his show at the Silver Slipper in Pecaniere, a club famous for its "cool-down room," a small closet with a window where misbehaving patrons were sent. "I played there one night — me and another guy, his name was Thompson. I played accordion that night, and I beat him playing. I took him. I made a rag out of him." But that was one of his last public performances.

Andrus lives at the end of a quiet road in Port Barre, across the highway from Opelousas. Many of his stories speak of long-standing feuds and missed opportunities. But he delivers them as grand comic adventures, and he frequently stops talking to play the accordion for Kara, who dances around him the entire evening.

"My brother George, boy, could he sing," he starts. "And when he'd sing, the women would come to him. And his wife would be hiding in the yard, peeping through the window. And she'd come in there and beat the hell out of him, yeah."

He stops playing, and Kara reaches for the accordion. She sits on the floor and puts her hands through the straps, and starts playing notes. "Hey girl, keep going," he says, and she looks up.

"Now, we had children, so my wife couldn't follow me," Andrus continues. "So she wouldn't let me go to play dances anymore. And it didn't pay me to say no, because she was more strong than me!"

He takes the accordion from his granddaughter, and she gives a little shout. "She loves it," he says. "I have to hide it from her when I go out, up on the armoire." Then he puts it in his lap and launches into one of his old house dance tunes. *"Hey Zalee,"* he sings, *"where you left your drawers?"* He jerks the bellows open, and his fingers find the buttons. *"I left my drawers at Mr. Polen's cotton gin.*

"That man didn't know we made that song," he says. "That was a mean man. My boss at the lumberyard told me that if Mr. Polen found out about that song, he'd have killed somebody. Had a million dogs. I mean, you pass them dogs, they'd kill you. One of my buddies, he passed his place in Pecanierre one night, that dog broke the fence. And he cut that dog's head off. He was a knife man.

"My daddy was an accordion player too," Andrus continues. "He played the old-time fool songs, way back yonder." He comes up with an example. *"Open the door,"* he sings, *"and let the funky come out."*

Unlike many of his friends, Andrus stayed in Port Barre, and he seems glad that he did. He learned his destiny, he says, when a carnival came to town. "You talk about hoodoo, that's where they got it. The white people call it mojo, but we call it hoodoo. My buddy said, 'Come on, Frank, let's have our fortune read.' The woman said to him, 'If you leave Port Barre, you ain't going to live long.' But she told me, 'You got it made, you. You're going to live a long life.' Well, he left Port Barre, and he was sassy, and three weeks after he left here someone killed him in California with a shotgun.

"But I'm hoodooed, too," he continues. "In Lawtell, a girl put a white egg in a pound of coffee. If I'd have put an egg in a pound of coffee and brought it to her, there'd be nothing wrong with me. I thought she just wanted some egg and some coffee, and I didn't bring it." What was the outcome? Andrus shrugs. "I'm hoodooed, yeah."

Then he frowns, but not about eggs and coffee. He's thinking about a neighbor, a seventy-five-year-old man who rides around with his accordion in his truck and gets out to play when he sees a crowd of people. "He says he's the king, man," he scoffs. "I could knock him down. He says he's got five hundred acres of land, so many cows, so many chicken, and he says he can play accordion. But he lies."

Kara comes to her grandfather and puts her head on his knee. He picks up the accordion again, and shouts, "When I say 'go,' I want you to shake that thing!" She dances some more.

"One day, it was about twenty-five years ago, I was young," he remembers. "I could work all day and go out all night. And I stopped in Port Barre, I still had my accordion. I was at the store there, and the guy said, 'He can play accordion.' So I played 'Pinetop Boogie Woogie.' Man, the people that came there. They had gallons of wine, whiskey, gin coming out of that store like it was Christmas Day. That man said, 'Frank, I made some money off you today. Anytime you want to play accordion, you come here.'

"Before I met Clifton, I was the king. They said I was boss, I was about the best accordion player they'd hear. But when Clifton took over, he had me beat. Forget about me, man."

In the annals of zydeco, Port Barre is destined to go down as the boyhood home of Clifton and Cleveland Chenier, and nobody is more aware of this than Frank Andrus. "You know that song, 'Mailman, Mailman'?" he asks. "*Mailman, mailman, please bring my letter today.* I could blow that song, man. Clifton Chenier came to me one night and I played that song. He came and kneeled by me. Poor Clifton Chenier, he's dead and gone. But the man loved when I played that song.

"He would come to the house dance, you see, and ask me, please show him. And I would show him. I'd say, 'Go ahead, bro, kneel down there and look at me.' He looked at me and said, 'Do you think I would ever get to be like you?' I said, 'Here's what you do, bro.' I said, 'Put one song you like in your mind.' And I said, 'You go to bed with that song, the next morning, get up and play, and that way, you'll keep on like that.' And that man got to be the world king, the one to call it 'zydeco.'

"And after I showed him, he messed me up, you see. I was playing single-row. After I showed him, he bought a piano-note. He took the leg. He went to the heaven side of me there. He lost me.

"You see, it was just me and the washboard, that's all. I was too stupid to get me a guitar and a drum. Just the dry washboard. And when Clifton Chenier started playing, he had him a real circus. Drum, washboard, guitar, harp. He just went straight up in the sky, yeah, and left me way behind town. And that boy was the best accordion player I ever heard."

Andrus shakes his head. He puts a toothpick in his mouth and glares straight ahead. "You know that guy who lies so much, you know what he done? He goes and plays the accordion in the church house. One Christmas, he asked the priest if he could play the song 'Silent Night.' He must have had the accordion where the priests dress, because here he comes out playing. Boy, I can't stand him. He thinks he's king."

Andrus reaches for his accordion, and his granddaughter stands at attention. "I'll play one more 'Pinetop Boogie Woogie,'" he allows. "Then I'll put my accordion up."

## The Ardoin Brothers

It was time for his generation to play their piece, Morris Ardoin decided.

It was 1966, the same year that Bois Sec Ardoin and Canray Fontenot went to Newport. Morris, Bois Sec's oldest son, had been living in Mississippi, because the farming pay was better. But he returned home with an idea.

"I got together with my brothers, and I told them, 'It doesn't pay to have nothing going on,'" he remembers. "Daddy and Canray, they made their thing. We can't undo that. But if the brothers don't get together, nobody's going to know about us."

Morris was the guitar man, and with Lawrence on drums, Gustav "Bud" on accordion, Russell on bass, and Canray Fontenot playing fiddle, the Ardoin Brothers went to Lafayette's La Louisianne studio and recorded a 45. "Pine Tree Two-Step" was on one side and "La valse à Bud" on the other. Bud's delicate accordion runs and high-pitched vocal cries brought steady work for the Ardoin Brothers, who began playing every other week at Slim's Y-Ki-Ki, as well as at Morris's own Cowboy Club. They toured to festivals in New Orleans and Washington, D.C. The Ardoins were at it again. "We made a hit," says Morris. "And I mean a hit."

The Cowboy Club is now a closed building sitting in the tall grass next to Morris's home, which is just about a mile and a half of winding road away from his father's. One afternoon, with a few hours to spare before he is to drive his truck to Lake Charles, he recalls what it was like growing up as the oldest boy in a musical family of fourteen.

He was raised sharecropping with his father. "It was high land, and he was farming on thirds in those days," he explains. "He'd sell his crop at the end of the year, and there would be two for him, and every number three goes to the landowner. You have your own horses, your own plows. You could farm on half, but then you're not free, you have to do what the man says. When you're on a third, you're on your own. Yeah, I was raised farming.

"After I left the farm, I went into trucking," Ardoin continues. "They tried to send me to school, but you know how kids look at their daddy and mama and try to follow that step. You see, my daddy didn't have an education, but he had more skills than one. He could do a little carpentry, he could play a little music, and he'd farm. He'd do all kinds of things to help himself. So when I turned sixteen, they couldn't force me to go to school."

He was nine when he started playing the triangle behind his father. They played house dances, and they played Freeman Fontenot's club. He also remembers a grand event that took place every Fourth of July in the town of Elton: "For blacks, that used to be a big thing, as big as Mardi Gras. They had two clubs there, and they had dances at one o'clock. People that had left, gone to Lake Charles and Texas, they'd come back and you'd meet them at Elton."

The main attraction for children in Elton was a mule-drawn merry-go-round, called a swing. A center post was attached to a circle of benches, and as the mule turned the riders, in the center sat Bois Sec, acting as a Creole accordion calliope. "Daddy would play there all day," Morris says, "and I started young to play triangle with him."

Elton is fondly recalled by all who attended the festivities. "Daddy would always say, you all got to work if you want some money to go there," Mama Lena Pitre says. "The old mule was turning that swing — *zoom, zoom, zoom* — and Bois Sec was sitting in the middle, and the man with the washboard would play *backabackaback*, or the triangle would play *tingalingaling*." Bee Fontenot and Peter King are also remembered for playing the ride.

Another big day for the Ardoins was Mardi Gras; for years their family organized a traditional horseback run, and Bois Sec played accordion. And Morris remembers a Lenten game in which girls and boys would pass a ring back and forth, dropping it in the hand of the one they preferred. "All that good stuff faded out," he says.

As he grew older, Ardoin watched while his father's accordion started to fall out of fashion too. "The French music went down amongst us blacks," he remembers. "That's when the rock and roll started. But we'd play house dances for white people around here, and they would pay about four dollars a night." One time, Morris remembers, his father was accused by a Creole club owner of snubbing the blacks. He remembers that Bois Sec quietly replied that he played for whoever wanted to pay him. "They'd talk all kinds of things, and that never did bother him," Morris recalls. "But me, I was mad. I said, 'Why don't you tell him that they made you put your accordion on the armoire, that you never would have played if it had just been for them?' Boy, I was pissed off, how he let them off easy for that. 'No,' he said, 'you don't do that, son.' And after I got older, I started thinking that he put it in the right way."

In the early 1970s, Chris Strachwitz visited Bois Sec Ardoin's home to record the family for Arhoolie Records. In addition to the old-style two-steps and waltzes, including "Home Sweet Home," the tune traditionally played when it was time for the house dances to end, the sessions resulted in one of the more unusual songs in the Creole tradition: a kind of French talking blues played and sung by Morris. Titled "Le Boss (Rice Farmer)," it tells of the time when Morris decided not to bite his tongue, and it serves as an anthem for the many Creoles who gave up sharecropping for the opportunities of the cities.

It all started when Morris had a fight with his employer, he recalls. He wanted more money to feed his family. His boss told him that it wasn't his fault that Morris had so many mouths to feed, and he didn't say it that nicely. "I told him, 'It's because of your pocketbook and my mind that you're a rich man today,'" says Morris. "He said that he'd rather quit farming than pay me more money.

"I told him that when I work construction, after forty hours you get time and a half. Here, you put in all the hours you want, and you still get nothing. Boy, I was brokenhearted then. I had five kids, and I didn't know where to go. But I told him, 'When I came to work for you, you had a bunch of cattle and an old rotten fence. I built a whole new fence, and a big farm. And that's the thanks you give me. Oh boss, I can't take that. I got to go.' And those are the last words of the song."

The Ardoin Brothers kept their name going, with the extended family making a total of three appearances in Carnegie Hall, as well as several more recordings for various labels. Then one night the brothers were planning to tour to Canada, and Gustav went to visit accordionist Delton Broussard, to see if the Lawtell Playboys could cover their Saturday night at Slim's. His car collided with a truck, and he never made it back home. "For a while, we had the hottest band going," Morris says, and then he is quiet.

Morris goes outside to his truck. As he climbs to his seat for the ride to Lake Charles, he speaks of the future. One of his sons returned from the military a religious man, and won't have anything to do with music. But his sons Gus and Dexter are playing. "I have a hell of a time to get Dexter in the groove to learn the old French," Morris says. "I said, 'Learn this. It's a different stroke, but it doesn't stop you from zydeco.'"

Then he starts the engine and heads out of the woods for the highway, leaving behind a house noisy with grandchildren and beside it the overgrown Cowboy Club, a silent testament to the Ardoin family band.

\* \* \*

On a night not so long ago in New Orleans, Canray Fontenot was sitting on a wooden bench outside the Maple Leaf Bar, waiting to perform with the band Filé. He was talking about a tribute that was held for him in his hometown of Welsh. "It was good for them to do that," he said, then he laughed. "Most of the time, they don't care about music. They just care about who's got the biggest cow."

Fontenot died in the summer of 1995, after a bout with cancer. His funeral was held in St. Joseph's Church in Welsh, and his fiddle was displayed beside his coffin. During the eulogy, the priest spoke about reporters and photographers who were present for the ceremony. "Not too often is the media welcome in church," he said, "but Canray was in the press a lot, because that is how he made his music: through television and through records."

Three years earlier, Fontenot had told me about his father, Adam Fontenot, who never made a record. "'When I die,'" Canray recalled him saying, "'I want Adam to be dead. And that's it. Me and my music, we're going to both be dead.' He didn't like the idea of your music still going while he was dead, and that's why he never made a record. But I knew almost all his songs, and I put some of them on the record." Canray Fontenot made sure that his music would live on.

As the priest reaches the end of his sermon, he tells the congregation that Fontenot once said he wanted to play the fiddle in church. But it never happened. Then he walks to the altar, and the music of a fiddle and an accordion is heard. It is the blues waltz "Bonsoir Moreau," the song that Fontenot and Bois Sec Ardoin played so that the couples could dance close. Certainly, even Canray Fontenot never thought that this one would get played in a Catholic church.

*O bonsoir Moreau, O bonsoir Moreau*
*O je connais c'est l'heure je m'en va's*
*O bonsoir Moreau, O bonsoir Moreau.*

*O on a eu-z-un bon temps,*
*Un bon temps toute la nuit.*
*O je connais c'est l'heure je m'en va's.*
*O bonsoir Moreau.*

*O la lune après coucher,*
*Hé, soleil après se lever,*

*Hé, Caillette est pas tirée.*
*O bonsoir Moreau.*

Oh, good night Moreau, oh, good night Moreau,
Oh, I know it's the hour to go.
Oh, good night Moreau, oh, good night Moreau.

Oh, had a good time,
A good time all night.
Oh, I know it's the hour to go.
Oh, good night Moreau.

Oh, the moon is setting,
The sun is rising,
Caillette, the cow, is not milked.
Oh, good night Moreau.

The song ends, and the church is silent. As people step outside into the sun, there is a sense that a door has just closed to a great dance, that the world no longer sounds the same.

Yet with the songs and memories they made each Saturday night, the Creole players had also opened a door for the next generation. Beginning in the 1940s and 1950s, dancers left the houses for the bars and clubs in the prairie towns and Gulf Coast cities. But the dancing never stopped. The old French two-step is getting new hinges so she can swing, is how one accordion player would put it. He is the one who moved from Port Barre on to Houston, and he calls his music *zydeco*.

*Clifton Chenier.*

# 6

# THE KING OF ZYDECO

*You know, it ain't the man who grew*
*the sugarcane, it's the man who refined it.*

— *John Hart, saxophonist for Clifton Chenier's Red Hot*
*Louisiana Band*

## I

I T BEGAN ONE HOT DAY ON A PATCH OF LAND NEAR OPELOUSAS, he'd
tell them. With his older brother Cleveland, he was on his father's
field, working a hoe through heavy clumps of blackjack dirt. When he
came to the end of the row, he drove the hoe down into that blackjack
and left it standing. I am never going to put another plow or hoe or mule in
this hand, he said. I am tired of falling all over that dirt. His brother stood
there and watched him walk away.

Paul "Little Buck" Senegal is driving up Interstate 49 from Lafayette to
Opelousas, windows open, vents blowing warm air. "That cat could play so
hard," he yells into the wind, "that after the dance he'd take his shoes off
and pour the sweat out. All the while he'd play, it'd be just like you open up
a little faucet and let it run. I've seen it many times."

Senegal points east, behind a clump of trees, toward the towns of Port
Barre and Leonville. "That's where Clifton Chenier came out," he says, and
turns the van the other way, facing the sun and Opelousas. "It was a funny

thing how me and Cliff met. One day, I go to the Blue Angel, my uncle Claude Boudreaux's club. So when I walk in there, this big tall guy is standing by the bar with a three-piece suit. So he said, 'You Li'l Buck?' I said, 'Yeah.' He said, 'Look, my guitar player is stuck in Houston. You want to play with me tonight?' So I came down and played, and after we got off the stage, he said, 'Look, Friday, Saturday, and Sunday, I'm going to be in Houston,' and he told the drummer to pick me up. I didn't tell Cliff I was going to play with him regular or nothing. He just made me a band member."

Senegal put twelve years into playing guitar for Clifton Chenier's Red Hot Louisiana Band. These days, he's a blues guitarist with his own group, and he's en route to drive his friend and former Red Hots bandmate, the saxophonist John Hart, to a show in a Lafayette bar. Playing behind Chenier's accordion, Senegal and Hart and the rest of the Red Hots made records that introduced zydeco to the world, and created lasting memories of marathon dance sets in clubs up and down the Louisiana and Texas Gulf Coast. Chenier's band knew the King of Zydeco well. And they have plenty of stories.

How about the day, Senegal asks, when both the van and the instrument trailer caught flat tires at the exact same time, turning everyone upside down in the ditch, on top of two alligators? Or the cold day in Canada when Cleveland Chenier stole a blanket out of a hotel for the drive home, and the whole band got bedbug bites? When Clifton heard about that one, he laughed so hard that he fell to his knees in the dirt, even though he was wearing a suit.

Then there was that time they were playing at a club near the coast, and they caught the side of a hurricane coming out of Brownsville, Texas. The lights were blinking and the electric instruments were cutting on and off, but the people kept dancing. Another time, they played in Cameron on a Good Friday and everyone's amplifier blew up. They never played on a Good Friday again.

Senegal rolls through Opelousas until he reaches an outlying neighborhood of large, flat lawns. He chooses a driveway and cuts the engine. "Now, when he got sick, he wasn't into all the fun," he says, his voice dropping. "I remember one night he was parked in front of his house, going to Houston. His wife, Margaret, came and said, 'Clifton, I don't believe you're going to go try to play that dance tonight.' I was driving the truck. I'll never forget what he said. 'Die over here, or die on the bandstand,' he said, 'I got to go. Them people are waiting for me.' He jumped in the van and said, 'Let's go, let's go!' I didn't know what to do. He said, 'Come on, man! I said let's go!'"

Little Buck gets out of the van. "Here's John Hart's house," he says. "Now you're going to hear some talk."

Clifton Chenier was born on June 25, 1925, to Joseph and Olivia Chenier, in a sharecropping family of two boys and one girl. He followed his father into the vegetable and cotton fields, and when he was fifteen he followed him on the accordion.

He'd say that he had really been following that accordion since he was a child. One night Claude Faulk and the Reynolds brothers passed by the Cheniers' on their way to play a house dance. They stopped their Model A Ford long enough for Clifton to hide in the rumble seat. By the time he was discovered, he'd already made it to the music.

Another night he saw his father play a dance. He heard him sing a few words about another woman, and then he saw his mother walk up to his father, waving a razor in the air. She took the razor and sliced right through the center of the accordion. The bellows let out a little sigh and collapsed. That would become one of Clifton's favorite stories about growing up.

Joseph Chenier, like the other house dance players, played the single-row accordion. It's not clear whether his son ever played this accordion or if he started right out pumping the blues and R&B on the big piano model, which he went on to exclusively play for the rest of his life. There's a curious scene in Les Blank's 1973 documentary *Hot Pepper*, when Clifton visits his first cousin Carlton King. Everyone is sitting on the front porch, and when King starts playing a double-row, Clifton stands up and dances a little shuffle.

"That's where it's at," he shouts, shaking a finger in the air and pointing to King's old accordion. "That's where it's at, baby!"

Then he starts some more jokes, about how he doesn't really know his way around the country anymore. "Way out here in the country where you were born and raised, you don't know where you're at?" asks a friend, pouring a drink from an orange cooler. Then the friend points to the small accordion. "That's the thing there, right there, that's what Clifton Chenier was born and raised on," he announces. "That's what he started off on. That's how he got famous. Clifton Chenier from double-note to triple-note, triple-note to piano-note."

Chenier shakes his head. "No, I never played them kind."

"Yeah, you played them kind! You can play them kind!"

"No, I can't."

But his friend is insistent. "Yeah, that's how you learned 'Paper in My Shoe,' on them kind!"

Chenier picks up the small accordion and unsnaps the top, and puts it on his lap. He looks down at it, and tries a few notes, leaving the bottom strap snapped shut.

"This is where he started from, right here in the woods!" his friend encourages. "You know you can work that thing. You have to unsnap the bottom."

Chenier looks at him slyly. "If you know how to play," he says, "you don't have to unsnap the bottom."

Accordion player Frank Andrus lived near the Chenier family, and he remembers the young man taking his accordion when he went to work the sugarcane fields. He swears he saw Clifton starting on the little accordion, and Creole fiddler Calvin Carrière agrees. "I remember a long time ago in Grand Island, the church had a little hall over there, and he was playing single-note," he says. "That was before he moved to Texas, and his brother Cleveland was with him. He sounded good, he had a little different style. And they had so much people there they were looking through the window." However, other former neighbors from the Port Barre area remember seeing young Chenier sitting on his porch practicing a piano-key.

When he was asked, Chenier would always report that his first accordion was a piano-key that an Opelousas house dance player named Isaie Blasa gave him. In fact, suggests Chenier's old friend Herbert Sam, that particular accordion wasn't exactly a gift. "Clifton Chenier took Isaie Blasa's accordion, and came to Lake Charles," Sam remembers. "I was living there then. And somehow, Clifton Chenier didn't bring Isaie Blasa's accordion back. So his daddy came to Lake Charles to get Isaie's accordion." He adds that Chenier had to get by on borrowed instruments until he could afford his own.

But even if he never played his father's accordion, Clifton would often recount how Joseph Chenier gave him his first lessons about life and music. In an interview with Chris Strachwitz at the 1982 San Francisco Blues Festival, he provided the final word on his early days:

"My daddy used to play accordion, you see. And I used to follow him when I was a little boy. And where he'd move, I was right there with him. One thing he'd tell me all the time. He'd say, 'You want to play accordion?'

"I'd say, 'Yeah.'

"He'd say, 'I'm going to tell you something, son. If you're going to be something, be something. If you're going to be nothing, be nothing. But if you learn how to play that accordion, I want you to do one thing.'

"I said, 'What?'

"'Don't let nobody beat you. Don't let nobody get ahead of you, with your style.'

"I said, 'Well, I don't believe you have to worry about that.'"

*　*　*

By the late 1940s thousands of French-speaking Creoles were trading in their fathers' blackjack fields for hourly wages in the refineries and shipyards in the Texas "Golden Triangle" cities of Port Arthur, Beaumont, and Orange. On weekends they would crowd into clapboard shacks called icehouses, where the music sounded both familiar and new. The air buzzed with the electric sputter of Clifton Chenier's accordion being pushed through a rebuilt amplifier, while Clifton's older brother, Cleveland, scraped a piece of the same type of sheet metal they'd all been working construction with during the week.

Chenier moved to Lake Charles and then on to Port Arthur; by the early 1950s he had married his lifelong wife, Margaret, and was making a living pumping gas and driving trucks for the Gulf Oil Refinery. "He was very wild, he had ambition, he was actually unpredictable," remembers Wilbert Guillory. "We would drink, and he told me he was going to Texas, and he probably was going to spend some time there. I didn't see him for a few years until he came back and started playing at Richard's."

Herbert Sam's oldest son, Ronnie, recalls those days in Texas: "He was living off an alley behind a grocery store, in a sharpshooter house, just a couple little rooms in a row. At that time it was hard, he was just starting making money. Clifton and Margaret used to baby-sit me when I was a little baby. At first, he would sneak off and borrow my daddy's accordion, because his wife didn't want him to play."

But Chenier soon became a busy musician, playing in local clubs like the Spindle Top and Channel View. He and Cleveland performed for tips outside the local refinery gate at quitting time, and they made Saturday night runs back to country towns like Basile and Lawtell, returning to Beaumont, Texas, to play Mondays and Thursdays at Clarence Garlow's Bon Ton Drive-In. George Broussard, originally from the town of Tyrone, remembers those country dances. "I went to many dances where it was only Cliff and Cleveland and that was the band," he says. "When I was a teenager, he used to come from Port Arthur and play at Freeman Fontenot's little club in the country, by Basile. He would play there every other Saturday, and it was rubbing board and accordion, and that was the music that you called zydeco."

Soon Chenier's old friends noticed that the accordion player seemed to be a different person from the farmer's son who'd left the country just a few years earlier. "He came back from Texas, he was a changed man," Wilbert Guillory remembers. "He had all kinds of colored clothes, and he had his conked hair. Gold teeth, talked nice, talked proper. But one thing about Clifton that had never changed, Clifton was a man you could always reach."

*Cleveland and Clifton Chenier, circa 1949.*

Frank Malbrough, a zydeco deejay living in Church Point, also noticed the new figure that Chenier was cutting, and remembers the tremendous impact that it had on Creoles back home. "As a young man, he would play at Richard's," he says. "And hey, when they started putting that picture on that poster? Shit, it was just like when B. B. King, Chuck Berry, Gatemouth Brown, Wilson Pickett, or Fats Domino hit Opelousas. Now, we'd run to the corner post and look at that poster of Clifton Chenier. He brought in a new style, that's what I think it was. Texas always was ahead in fashion.

"I had three kids, and my friend next door had two or three kids, and we'd all get into the car and go to the back of the club. This was before drive-in movies. In back of Richard's, they had this certain spot with that little small window, and we could see him on the stage. One of us would describe him, and we'd all take a turn and see. 'Oh yeah, oh yeah, look at that processing!' Remember when he started wearing that conk. That was new to us, a black guy with straight hair, you know.

"So we'd sit there and watch him, and the window was pushing all that sound out. It wasn't an involved sound like we have today, just a regular amplifier. And we'd talk about everything. The color of the shirt, and the accordion, all that blue and that red and that white. Before that we had only seen the old French accordion, that these people had in the sack. They had no color to it, no chrome or nothing. But his accordion, it had glow into the color, man. And we'd go back home and tell people about what we had seen."

If a black Frenchman with a chromed accordion ever had a chance to make it onto the national charts, it was in the early 1950s. Independent record labels were flourishing, and guitar players were electrifying their blues and scoring hits like Muddy Waters's 1951 "Louisiana Blues." Musicians such as New Orleans pianist Professor Longhair proved that you didn't need to be smooth and polished. Many newly urbanized blacks preferred down-home music, and they didn't mind rough edges. To satisfy their demand, record men scoured the rural South for the next sound.

One afternoon in 1954, a former circus worker and drummer named J. R. Fulbright drove into Port Arthur, searching for a new blues harp player. A black entrepreneur and an independent spirit, Fulbright had become a record producer, pressing many of his own discs with handmade dies and a cooling system constructed from a Frigidaire, and then selling them out of his car trunk to local jukebox operators. As he drove through the commercial district of Port Arthur, he spotted a crowd of people. There in the center was Clifton Chenier. "One heck of a man," Chenier would say. "He told me, 'You play too much accordion to be in these woods.'"

Fulbright took the musician to the KAOK radio studio in Lake Charles for a recording session, but he later recalled for *Blues Unlimited* how his work was hampered by a racist sound engineer: "He got his cigar in his mouth and his newspaper and put his feet up on the desk. So I asked him, 'Ain't you doing no engineering work?' And he jumped up like I hit him and said, 'What the hell you talking about? You know where you at? You in Lake Charles.'" Despite these obstacles, Chenier's first session resulted in seven songs, two of which were pressed as a single on Fulbright's Elko label, under the name "Cliston Chanier." These records reveal how Chenier had been sounding in the East Texas icehouses. Backed by bass, drums, and his uncle Morris "Big" Chenier's guitar, his instrumental "Louisiana Stomp" is a flourish of accordion tremolos and blues harp-style train whistles. On the B-side, "Cliston Blues," Chenier showed off his great talent as a blues singer. "Whoa baby, what in the world will become of me?" he cried, not for the last time. "I'm just a little ol' country boy, and I don't know my way around."

Fulbright sold the Lake Charles masters to Imperial, and invited Chenier to stay in his home in Los Angeles. Chenier had long been covering popular tunes on his accordion — the first song he learned was Joe Liggins's "The Honeydripper" — and he traveled to California eager to make some hits of his own. Fulbright booked him into the prestigious 5/4 Ballroom, and under directions from Specialty Records head Art Rupe, Bumps Blackwell — fresh from recording Little Richard in New Orleans — auditioned the accordion man, and liked what he heard. Chenier signed to Specialty Records in April 1955, and immediately began the first of two sessions. From these came his biggest single, "Ay-Tete Fee," Chenier's French version of the tune "Hey, Little Girl," recorded by Professor Longhair six years earlier. The title suggests that Blackwell was bewildered by Chenier's native tongue, or perhaps he hoped to transpose the French "*Eh, 'tite fille,*" into a kind of jive talk, a la Little Richard's "A-wop-bop-a-loo-bop." Either way, the song became a national hit, and jukebox and radio listeners became acquainted with a rollicking accordion and some swampy French lines:

*Hé 'tite fille! O 'tite fille!*
*Où t'as été hier au soir?*

Hey little girl! Oh little girl!
Where did you go last night?

From the start, Chenier knew the sound he was looking for. "When we made a record, I had to stand right there and give him the rhythm that he wanted," remembers guitarist Phillip Walker, who played on those Specialty sessions. "We got in there and we just kept playing, and when we thought we really had something, we'd wave to Bumps Blackwell: 'I think we got it. Roll the tape.'" Blackwell added a piano and tenor saxophone, but he gave centerstage to Chenier's driving accordion solos on instrumentals like "Boppin' the Rock." One single, "Squeeze Box Boogie," went on to become a jukebox hit in Jamaica. Clifton Chenier had a sound, a band, and a key to the highway.

But he also had one last statement to make before he hit the road. "Clifton used to tell me this story about when he was working in Lake Charles," remembers former Red Hots guitarist Sonny Landreth. "He was working out in construction, and his boss used to give him a hard time. Then he got a record deal. And he bought him a Cadillac, and he said he drove back out to the construction site and hit the gas, and then the wheels started turning, and the gravel started flying. He said, 'I followed along them boys out there in the ditch and they're all waving back, and I drove off.'"

Back in Louisiana, Chenier had been performing in the time-honored fashion — seated against the wall, out of way of the dancers. Now he was appearing on bills with the likes of Little Richard and Chuck Berry, and he had to learn to put on a show. For instruction, he turned to one of his R&B heroes, Lowell Fulson.

From Tulsa, Oklahoma, Fulson was just four years older than Chenier, but he was already a seasoned veteran when his agent scheduled him to tour with the accordionist and his band, then called the Hot Sizzlers. "We worked together quite a bit, touring up and down the Midwest, and the East Coast, and up and down the South," Fulson recalls. "He could sit up there and take that accordion and make you think you've got a tenor horn with you. That man had shoulders like a football player from carrying that accordion. He'd stand up there for hours, like there wasn't nothing to it.

"But Cliff was a country boy, so you could always find something for him to tidy up a little bit," he continues, laughing. "He believed in that shirt and tie, but he didn't take time with the shoes. So one night I looked him up and down, and I said, 'Boy, you're dressed up.' And he smiled. And I said, 'But next time, shine your shoes.'"

Fulson tutored Chenier on fashion, saluting the audience, how to do an encore, and when to offer that final little bow before exiting the stage. He told him to draw the spotlight by letting the band precede him onstage. "And he'd get loose and he'd get to rattling that French, and he'd forget that all the towns weren't the French Quarters," he adds. "So I taught him not to talk so much French, and he had his head down low in the Midwest for a while. But if the audience didn't understand the language, they'd laugh about it anyway, because the sound was good."

A group of black men traveling through the South in nice cars ran the constant risk of being stopped by suspicious police, Fulson remembers. "If we ever got pulled over, I'd say, 'We didn't come down here to start a riot, we didn't come down here to join no march, we just came down here to play the blues and talk French.' And that tickled Cliff to death. He'd say, 'You hear that, fellows, we talk French and we play the blues!'

"We did New York, East Chicago, Indiana," Fulson remembers. "I wish I could hear what it sounded like, but we never did get a tape. They mixed their French and the two-step, and they'd dance, and then I'd slip in there on them blues. And boy, we'd tear down on it. So I showed him about all he needed, then after about a year I got hung up with another band. But I hated to leave them old boys. It seemed like a family."

In later years, Chenier would credit Fulson for his lessons in showmanship. "He really showed me the highway," he told interviewer Ann Savoy. "I'd ask him questions, and he'd talk to me and I'd listen. And I'd say, 'Yeah, I'll learn all that.'"

In 1956 and '57, Chenier had two sessions for the Chess Records group, the home of Muddy Waters and Howlin' Wolf. It was here that he made his great R&B original "My Soul," a song he'd developed on stage at the El Dorado Ballroom in Houston. With a thundering beat and an echoing accordion — and with a young, uncredited singer named Etta James wailing "M-m-m-m-my soul" — Chenier proclaimed his essence. "If I should sit and cry without a reason, it's my soul," he wailed. "And if I should jump up and holler, without a reason, snatchin' the collar, it's my soul."

Chenier's music braided these two moods — the low-down blues and jump-up zydeco — for the rest of his career. "I played my first dance with him in Houston, Texas, in the Third Ward, in a little pub called Irene's," guitarist Phillip Walker recalls. "It was a unique thing. I had played with him six months before we even left the state of Louisiana. And in Houston, he had a mixed crowd. There were Texas blues people, and zydeco people from Louisiana. And most of the blues people didn't like harmonica players and accordion players in the lower part of Texas. Well, that really put us against the wall. We had to really get in there and mix that stuff up. And I didn't know the guy had it in him, until he started off on some Jimmy Reed stuff.

After that, we started with a seven-piece band across the country. We had a couple agents behind us and a record company, and we were feeling pretty good.

"Back then, Cliff had a great opportunity to be known," Walker continues, "because they'd book us with people that had just done big hits, million sellers. It was big shows, and people like Clifton that didn't have a big name could take a coattail ride. So we would go on shows with Fats Domino or Chuck Berry, and Cliff had a great opportunity to get some exposure. He was a serious man about what he was doing, and he was a good man to work for. And he would fine you and fire you too, in a minute, because he was serious about the business."

Chenier traded in his station wagon for a bus, which he purchased from a country band in Wichita, Kansas, and he bought suits for the band. "We were fully uniformed," says Walker with a laugh. "Everything was matching: we had two sets, a pea green and a burnt orange. We was loud-colored, and man, we'd light the stage up. We was all young guys, cutting flips and doing all kind of things, we had a show. Most times, Cliff would come out in a different outfit, like a black against a green or a white against a burnt orange. It was something for the girls to look at, I'll tell you."

Along with Fulson and Walker, Chenier worked with blues musician Cornelius "Lonesome Sundown" Green. The Dallas-based booking agent Howard Lewis packaged the Hot Sizzlers with blues acts Johnny "Guitar" Watson, Jimmy Reed, and Rosco Gordon, as well as vocal groups like the Clovers and the Cadillacs. Many of the stories that survive about those years concern singer Etta James, who was just seventeen when she started touring with the band. She once recalled that Chenier used to give her supper and lock her in her hotel room to keep her away from one of the band members, adding that she circumvented his noble efforts by climbing through the bathroom window. "Clifton taught me a lot about the road, and he tried to really keep me off the guys," she told radio host Greg Drust.

Walker also remembers a time in Mississippi when a passing driver saw James in the bus and called the police. "We was in Mississippi, man. She was a girl, she used to have all that blond hair on her head. This man drove past us, he just knew we had a white woman, and he called the cops. And they pulled us over, and she said, 'No, I'm not a white woman, my hair is just bleached!' But we had some interesting times."

One of the Hot Sizzlers' most memorable gigs was a brief appearance at the famed Apollo Theatre in New York City. "We played the curtain," Walker says. "You'd come on there at twelve o'clock midday after they showed a couple movies, and you play the intermission. It was a rough one, because you came in just like trains, one band behind the other. If you weren't cutting it, they would just hook you right off the stage there. We got in there and did our song. I don't think the New Yorkers could really figure out what we were. By the time they figured out just what was going on, we were off the stage."

After only a few years on the road, things started to wind down for Clifton Chenier and the Hot Sizzlers. Walker thinks Chenier's early career was hurt by his reluctance to tour overseas. "Well, there was a lot of things going on," he explains. "Number one, we did have some opportunities. France was into the accordion at the time. But you couldn't mention an airplane to Clifton Chenier. Cliff wouldn't fly. So the band kind of shied down. I hung in there all the way, till he said, 'Well, I think I'm just going to stop here and reorganize.' That's when I came out West."

At the time, however, there probably wasn't much that Clifton Chenier could have done to stay on track. By the end of the decade, an accordion man's opportunities were waning. At Specialty, Chenier had crossed paths with rock and roll pioneers like Lloyd Price and Little Richard, and even though Chenier had recorded a tune called "Boppin' the Rock" back in '55, he couldn't make his swampy style flow into the emerging mainstream. He went back home and attempted a few more R&B singles for Jay Miller's tiny Zynn label in Crowley. The sides featured notable Louisiana musicians Katie Webster and Lazy Lester, but something wasn't clicking. By the end of the decade, Chenier was traversing old territory, and he wasn't sure where to go next.

"When I first met him, he ain't had nothing, man," former Red Hot Louisiana Band drummer Robert St. Judy remembers. "To tell you the truth, he was down in the dumps. He had an old 'fifty-six white Cadillac. And I think he had two suits, man. He had one brown one, he used to tie it up with a necktie. I'm serious, man."

At the time, St. Judy (also known through the years as Robert Peter and Robert Julien) was drumming with Rockin' Dopsie. But he knew about Chenier, and he knew "Ay-Tete Fee." In fact, he had first heard Chenier when he was nine years old and had snuck into a wedding dance. That was the night he started liking zydeco, he says. "So I was going back and forth between him and Dopsie, but I liked the way Cliff played, so I just stayed with him. But everyone would just come and go, because they weren't making money, you know? It was a scuffle."

For accordions, Chenier relied on second-hand instruments, which he'd bring to famed accordion builder John Gabbenelli, who had recently moved to Houston from Italy. "He'd always go pick junk accordions in a garage sale," Gabbenelli remembers. "And then he'd come to me, I have to fix them. He was looking for a peculiar sound, you know what I mean? These old-time accordions have different sounds than the new ones."

Then, one winter weekend night in 1964, the musician was playing a bar in Houston. It had been ten years since he was in a Lake Charles radio station with J. R. Fulbright. Four years since his last record in Crowley. Behind him was just a drummer, and before him a few dancers were staying warm on the floor. Then the door opened, and a new road rolled in and landed at his feet.

First to walk into the bar was Sam "Lightnin'" Hopkins, the blues guitarist who had just recorded an album for Folkways and was beginning to enjoy a prominent role in the nascent blues revival. Hopkins's wife was Chenier's first cousin, and the guitarist and the accordion man occasionally performed together around the city. One of those nights is remembered by Robert Burton "Mack" McCormick: "One time I ran into Lightnin' and he told me that he and Clifton were working together in some area around Houston. I thought, 'That would be interesting. What in the hell would Clifton and Lightnin' do onstage other than fight?' So I went to see them, and indeed they were fighting onstage. Literally. They were fighting over who was going to start the piece and who was going to stop it."

But Hopkins also seemed to use every opportunity to advertise his cousin. "I'd sure like to bring him over here," he told reporters during a tour in England. "He's just about the best there is in Houston. Plays like nothing, man. He has a mike on top of the accordion. He can play anything you like, any type of music."

And so, thanks to Hopkins's urging, the second person to walk into the Houston bar was a tall man with long arms and an eager, round face. He was a German immigrant, a former high school teacher, and a self-described "record-collecting freak." His name was Chris Strachwitz, and he had come along to the bar mainly because he went wherever Lightnin' Hopkins told him to go.

Clifton Chenier looked at the stranger. "You're a record man," he said immediately. "Let's make a record."

## II

From behind the gauze of a screen door thunders the voice of John Hart. "You ready?" he says, his hands reaching for the lock.

*Lightnin' Hopkins and Clifton Chenier, Houston, circa 1963.*

*Clifton Chenier and John Hart at New Orleans Jazz Fest.*

"If you want to get him mad, try that 'Blind John' stuff," says Senegal quietly. "He'll say, 'I was born like this. What's your excuse for being so damn stupid?'"

Hart comes to the door and lightly places his hand on his friend's shoulder, and walks beside him to the van. He stops to condemn the weather. "It's summertime," he thunders. *"Da-a-mn!"*

"Nice and cool out here. Better than in that truck."

"It ain't too damn cool out here!"

Hart's saxophone defined the zydeco horn in his days with the Red Hots, and his sonorous voice would proclaim Chenier's arrival on stage, with cheers of "The dyyy-namic!" and "Loueee-siana's own!" When the rest of the band wore suits, turtlenecks, or matching T-shirts, Hart always dressed in an old-school suit and tie. He maintains the self-possessed air of a bank manager taking his time deciding on a loan. We start the ride, and Senegal notes Hart's shoes.

"I put that old army shine on them sons of bitches," Hart replies, settling in. Then Senegal formally introduces me. Hart pitches his voice to the backseat.

"So, you're writing a book on zydeco? *Goddamn,* that makes twenty-five or thirty of them I know writing books on zydeco. I'm wondering, what is the scenario of the book going to be?"

Senegal smiles.

"I've been around this world sixty-four years, and that's a hell of a long goddamn time," Hart continues. "The word 'book,' it means that you got to roam around, you got to seek, you got to turn over things. People like Claude Faulk and Isaie Blasa, the Johnny-go-luckies don't even know about these people. Clifton Chenier, he's the author and creator of zydeco. You know, it ain't the man who grew the sugarcane, it's the man who refined it."

Senegal steers back to the open road and the wind picks up. "You see, the word 'zydeco' ain't shit," Hart roars. "That word don't mean nothing. But I can tell you one goddamn thing it allowed. It allowed simplified persons to grab an instrument and have it for a few days, and the next thing you see, a damn placard says zydeco this and zydeco that. And they're not playing zydeco!"

When we stop at a gas station, Senegal passes a Coke through the window and offers Hart his change. "Man, you're always bringing me something, so don't worry about that little fucking change!" Hart booms. Senegal slides back in the van and starts the engine.

"Today, the word 'zydeco' ain't nothing but a fast name for a fast dollar," Hart continues. "You can buy some of the material that Clifton did back in the game, or buy what they call zydeco today. You compare it."

"It's no comparison," Senegal nods.

"It ain't no comparison. So it ain't zydeco. You see, you're sitting down with two cats who've been through zydeco music. We played with the man with the plan, brother."

"What we tell you, it's authentic."

"When they closed the lid on Clifton's coffin, they closed zydeco out."

"That's right."

Clifton Chenier didn't ever say he wanted to hire a sax player, but Hart remembers that he was traveling with soul singer O. V. Wright and was getting tired of the road. "So I went down to the Blue Angel," he says. "And I said, 'Man, I'll tell you what, just allow me to sit in, we'll see how it goes, and you gather from there.' In other words, I was putting words in his mouth. And I guess I played an hour and a half, an hour forty-five. So I reached for my horn case — I keep it by me all the time — and I said, 'Well, man, I think I'm going to sit down and listen to you, I enjoy this stuff.' 'Oh no, man, don't put your horn up now.' So I played, and when the dance was over, he come to me before he put his accordion down. He said, 'Hey man, would you like to join?' I said, 'That was my purpose here.'"

"When I heard you playing," says Senegal, "I said, 'I know we're going to get it on now.'"

"Oh ye-e-ah."

"Not bragging, but Jumpin' Joe, Robert St. Judy, John Hart, myself, Cleveland, and Cliff, you couldn't pass through that band, brother. You couldn't get through that band. I don't care where we go. Albert King told his agent, as long as I work for you, don't ever put me behind that Frenchman. You remember that, John?"

"I remember it."

"Man, don't ever put me behind that Frenchman."

"He'd make your road rock."

"Then, if they had two or three other bands there, he'd tell me and the bass player, y'all go sit down. He wanted just the washboard, the drums, and the accordion."

"He'd play his own creation."

"His own. There you go. That's all it was, his own creation. The song I liked the most with John and Cliff, when they would do 'Pinetop Boogie Woogie.' The horn and the accordion."

"See, it took a whole orchestra to play that tune with Woody Herman," Hart says. "This cat did it all on one accordion."

"Sometimes, we'd sit down for an hour and a half, bro. Two hours. One time, it was just him and his brother and the drummer that were playing the song. Jumpin' Joe and me and John Hart got off the stage to go to the rest room. Then on our way back, he got on the mike and said, 'Hey y'all, don't get off my bandstand like that.' He told us next time to get a bucket. A bucket!

"And the night he played, you wouldn't go by his table at all, he wouldn't even talk to nobody," Senegal continues. "The band would sit at one end of the club and he'd sit on the other end. Nobody would fool around with Cliff. In the day, he'd sit down with us, have a drink or so and laugh. Come that night we're having a gig, he's an altogether different person, man. You wouldn't even go by him."

Not surprisingly, accordion players rarely tried to challenge Clifton Chenier on the bandstand. Few even asked to sit in. "Nobody had that kind of nerve," Hart explains. "It's just like you trying to race with a helicopter. He's up there and you're down here."

"He'd spellbound people, man," Little Buck says.

"Oh ye-e-ah."

"Clifton had three or four guitar players before me, but some of the guys they had, after they played two nights, they couldn't find them for the third night."

"They were wayward kind of people, you know. They didn't recognize their opportunity."

"Hey, John! You were there when Elvin Bishop dropped that little pipe and I kicked it under the piano, man!"

Hart rumbles with laughter.

"I played on the album *Out West,* with Elvin Bishop and Steve Miller. Elvin played with that pipe, that little wrench. But boy, I was so mad at Chris Strachwitz. The cat brings me all the way to California and doesn't let me play one solo on his album. Last song we're going to do, Elvin lost that little pipe. It fell on the floor. They're looking for it, but I kicked it under the piano. So Chris said, 'Well, you play that solo.' That's the only solo I played, but I was playing it." Little Buck starts humming the line.

"Cliff was a good man to work for," says Hart.

"I'll tell you what, man, he helped me in my life, just by playing with him."

"We were very knowledgeable when we left."

"And in the studio, he never would do it twice, either. You ain't doing it no two times or say to do it again. That's it."

"But you know that's the way it should be," Hart says. "That's your creation. How in the hell you're going to tell me about my creation? You're going to tell God how to make you? Or how to make the next man?"

The wind whips through the back of the van.

"No-o-o," Hart answers.

\* \* \*

Above a cluttered labyrinth that includes a warehouse, distribution center, retail store, archives, and a kitchen currently stocked with leftover gumbo sits the office of Chris Strachwitz. This is the home of Arhoolie Records in El Cerrito, California. Strachwitz launched the label in 1960, and it has become one of the world's great sources of traditional music, ranging from blues to Tex-Mex to zydeco; it's where Chenier made his best records.

When Chenier met Strachwitz, he must have realized he was a kindred soul. Accordion players are a one-man band, and at Arhoolie, Strachwitz runs his own show as much as any record producer ever has. It started when Strachwitz took a bus to Houston in 1959 to find Lightnin' Hopkins. He returned to Texas the following year to make his first blues recordings, and he heard his first zydeco the next year in Houston's Frenchtown neighborhood, where he taped accordionists Albert Chevalier and Herbert "Good Rockin'" Sam during a jam session at DowMcGowan Lounge, and Willie Green at Irene's Cafe. That same year he went to a house dance in Lafayette and recorded musicians Paul McZiel and Wallace Gernger, and in 1962 he drove to Lake Charles and recorded Peter King at the Goldband studios, then visited Rayne to make the only recording of Boozoo Chavis's great-uncle Sidney Babineaux.

"I'd just ask people, do you ever know any zydeco," Strachwitz recalls. "Somebody told me the oldest man around is Sidney Babineaux, so I went to Rayne. Mack McCormick had told me the sheriff will know every damn musician in town. And sure enough, the parish sheriff knew him and drove me over there. I followed his goddamn sheriff car, and I'm sure poor old Sidney Babineaux and his family were probably having a heart attack, 'Here comes the high sheriff, God, what do they want with me?'

"But my whole ambition was to hang around Lightnin', because I thought he was the key to the whole mountain," he continues. "And one night he just said, 'Hey Chris, you want to go see my cousin?' I said, 'Who's your cousin?' He said, 'Cliff.' I said, 'Cliff who?' 'Clifton Chenier.' That rang a little bell in my head, because I had that Specialty record, but I really didn't connect it with anything great. At the time, I just loved what Lightnin' was doing, and all I wanted was nasty low-down blues. But what the hell. If he's going to hang out with somebody, let's go.

"So we went over to Frenchtown, that area along the ship channels. I remember that a rat ran across the street, and I'd never seen a rat as huge as that. And we went into this teeny beer joint. I already knew about zydeco, but I really didn't think that Clifton was going to be in the same league as the guys I'd seen already. But here was Clifton. He had that big piano accordion, and he was such a singer. He was amazing."

Strachwitz immediately called Houston producer Bill Quinn and arranged to go in to his Gold Star studio. But his heart sank when the accordionist showed up the next day with a full band in tow. "He said, 'Oh man, I got to have an orchestra,'" Strachwitz remembers. "I said, 'Shit.' Because I loved what I heard the night before, when he played his ass off." But the fates seemed to be on the side of Strachwitz. "He said, 'Oh yeah, we got to have the band.' And then the bass player plugged in, and the goddamn cone wasn't connected to the paper, so there was just nothing there. And then the guitar amp started literally smoking. I mean, actual smoke came out of it. I said, 'I believe we better pull the plug on that thing.' And that was the end of that."

That day resulted in an enduring Chenier blues classic, "I'm on the Wonder," ("I'm on the wonder, baby / Do you ever think of me?") but that great recording wouldn't be issued until decades later. In fact, the singles released from the session were largely noisy barrelhouse shout-alongs, with Chenier's singing and accordion almost lost in the ruckus of the drums and piano on the calypso-tinged "Ay Ai Ai" (with a melody possibly derived from the song "Polly Wolly Doodle") and the beery "Why Did You Go Last Night." But Strachwitz had some connections on Houston radio, and the songs received play. A partnership was launched.

The two tall men had yet to see eye to eye on the future of zydeco, however. In 1965 Chenier showed up for his next Arhoolie session at the Gold Star studio with another R&B outfit in tow. This time the amps didn't explode, and the musician and the producer were at a standoff. Strachwitz knew the tastes of white college-educated blues fans like himself, and he knew there was a market for the sounds that he had heard in that Frenchtown bar. But Chenier had his crowd, too. And he knew that if he wanted to attract black dancers in Louisiana and Texas, he had to take on the hits of the day and put them over on his accordion.

"He was very insecure about his ability to sell with his French music," Strachwitz remembers. "He'd say, 'All these kids want Ray Charles, and I'm going to beat Ray Charles.' Later, every time we went to the New Orleans Jazz and Heritage Festival, he would say, 'I'm going to take New Orleans this time. I'm going to whip that goddamn Fats Domino,' or Ray Charles, or whoever was on the opposing bill. It was always a contest for him.

"That very first Specialty thing, that 'Ay-Tete Fee,' had a little French in it, but it had the R&B sound, and that's the combination that made it," Strachwitz continues. "If he had put out a down-home record at the time, it probably would have never sold. I think it needed to be in that modern suit.

But you see, I never cared about that. I just thought he sounded so much better singing in Creole."

Negotiations became heated. Strachwitz may not have spoken French himself, but he knew he wanted to hear its cadences in zydeco, and he told Chenier he didn't come all the way to Texas to record warmed-over radio hits. Chenier answered that he wasn't going to do any more of that god-damn old French. Finally, a bargain was struck. "He finally said, 'All right, we'll make a deal,'" Strachwitz recalls. "'I'll make half the numbers in French, if you let me do half the numbers in rock and roll.'"

So on one side of his first Arhoolie album, *Louisiana Blues and Zydeco*, Chenier played accordion and harmonica, and his five-piece band included guitar, bass, piano, and Robert St. Judy on drums. They turned in a new version of "Eh 'Tite Fille" (now spelled in more or less proper French) and three confident English blues numbers, and Chenier even tossed in an accordion riff on Henry Mancini's theme to *Peter Gunn* that he called "Hot Rod." For the second side, Cleveland Chenier, who had been playing with Lightnin' Hopkins for the past few years, rejoined his brother on rubboard. Backed by drummer Madison Guidry, they played a couple of waltzes that infused "Jolie blonde" with blues-style vocals. Then, for the first time on record, Chenier started singing a blues in French.

"I'll never forget it," Strachwitz says. "Old Quinn was standing behind me, and we had a real good engineer, Doyle E. Jones, and he got this kick drum recorded with a real heavy sound. And Clifton started in on this '*Tous les jours la même chose*' and all this shit, and while he was playing that, Quinn said, 'Chris, that thing will sell down here. That's got the feeling.' And sure enough, as soon as he finished, Clifton comes running out of the control room. 'I got to call my old lady, she's got to hear this one.' So he called Margaret, and we played it back, and he thought that was one of the best things he'd ever done."

The phrase, which translates to "every day is the same thing," is a common Creole axiom (as is its inverse, "every day is not the same thing"). But when Strachwitz asked about the spelling, Chenier replied that he could spell it any way he liked. Strachwitz titled the song "Louisiana Blues," and he recalls that it became Chenier's first Arhoolie hit. "That's the one that sold," he says. "It had this blues feeling that people loved to dance to, and there wasn't a lick of English in there. That gave him confidence that there are enough people down there who can speak Creole and who are willing to buy his music."

But not everybody remembers it that way. Robert St. Judy says that it was Chenier's most contemporary song of that session that really recharged his career. "After we recorded 'Hot Rod,' the hits started coming out, and we started out on the road," he says. "And then Cliff was really happy, man. There were some good days."

There is no way to prove whose memory is the more accurate, because "Louisiana Blues" and "Hot Rod" were released on the same 45 single. At any rate, the lines between Chenier's two sides quickly blurred. He always sang the traditional material with soulful blues and R&B inflections, and he played the modern songs with swampy, down-home feeling. And when he combined these two approaches on one song, "Zydeco Sont Pas Salé," he created his most influential recording.

Although Strachwitz had already recorded tunes with this title — and Babineaux had dated his version as originating before his birth in 1895 — Chenier's rhythm sets his "Zydeco Sont Pas Salé" apart from the rest. St. Judy remembers that Chenier gave him specific instructions on how to play it. "He told me, try this or try that," he says. "Especially on them zydeco songs, he gave me the idea to just play on my snare drum." The result was a song that recalled the *juré* style more than anything recorded before or since, and it set the pace for zydeco to come.

Chenier and Strachwitz worked together steadily over the next decade. In short time Chenier himself became a crusader for the Creole French language and the old accordion-rubboard combo, and started looking for ways to bring these traditional elements into his music. In 1966 he surprised his producer by suggesting his uncle Morris "Big" Chenier, who had played guitar back on the Fulbright recordings and was now running the Horse Shoe Club in Lake Charles. Clifton wanted him in Houston to play fiddle, and the unlikely result was the biggest Arhoolie hit of his career.

"Clifton knew I loved that old shit, you see, so he introduced me to his uncle Morris," Strachwitz says. "I never had any money, but I paid his bus fare from Lake Charles, and the poor man came. He had a beat-up old fiddle, and he had a tendency to sound out of tune most of the time. I didn't want to bother him, because I figured, well, this is down-home music, and I'm not going to mess with him, if they're happy with it. But after the record was over, he came and said, 'Chris, I got to apologize. You know what happened to my fiddle? That bridge inside, plum fell down.' I don't see how the hell he even kept anything halfway in tune. I wish I'd recorded him again, but he died shortly thereafter."

That session resulted in Chenier's second Arhoolie release, *Bon Ton Roulet*. The selection of songs ranged from the title track's French spin on the Louis Jordan classic "Let the Good Times Roll" to Amédé Ardoin's "Eunice Two-Step" (released as "Sweet Little Doll") and an instrumental version of Don Gibson's "I Can't Stop Loving You," a recent hit for Ray Charles. But the biggest success was a tune recorded with Morris Chenier, an astonishingly dissonant accordion and fiddle blues called "Black Gal." The demand for this tune was too great for recordman Floyd Soileau, who was then distributing Chenier's singles, so the song was licensed to the national Bell Records. "This 'Black Gal' is so funky, but that's the one that really sold — it was a monster," remembers Strachwitz. "Floyd has so much calls on that, and he says, 'This Bell company thinks they can make a national hit out of it,' and they damn near did. Maybe twenty or thirty thousand. Clifton never sold that much of anything else."

Although Chenier recorded for a number of independent labels throughout his career — including Maison de Soul, Alligator, and Huey Meaux's Crazy Cajun — he also kept working with Strachwitz, eventually becoming Arhoolie's biggest-selling artist. But Chenier was frustrated that greater success eluded him, and there were few studio sessions with Strachwitz after the 1960s. In 1975 he would refuse to go into the studio to make the acclaimed *Bogalusa Boogie* album until Strachwitz paid him five thousand dollars up front, more than five times his usual advance.

"I always felt bad, because I thought he was doing OK, but he wanted to be a big star with lots of money, you know, and lots of Cadillacs like Ray Charles," Strachwitz recalls.

"So one time he called me from Los Angeles, he says, 'Listen, this man at the Ash Grove saw me last night, and he wants me to record. It's Atlantic Records.' Ray Charles's label, oh man. Strachwitz had always asked Chenier to tell him if he received an offer, and he went to Los Angeles to negotiate with producer Jerry Wexler. Chenier needed a new trailer, Strachwitz recalls, so he asked for four thousand dollars. The producers also discussed advertising and the length of the contract. No deal was struck.

"It sort of hurt us all," Strachwitz admits. "Clifton really wanted to be on a major label, but that's the way it went."

Clifton Chenier may never have had a major record deal, but he was fast becoming a star of Creole dances from Louisiana to California. He had played the bars in Louisiana and Texas, and he'd played the 5/4 Ballroom. He filled the country dance halls, and he'd taken a shot at the Apollo. But it was in the churches that the king came into his glory.

In 1958 St. Francis of Assisi Catholic Church in Houston was operating in the red, and a parishioner named Clarence Gallien had an idea. He'd recently moved to Houston from Opelousas, where he had once built a dance club in his front yard, and he'd seen the way zydeco could fill a room. He suggested putting on a dance right at the church school. The event was packed with Louisiana people of all ages, and the church made money. The next month he hired Clifton Chenier, and the church made even more money. Soon a dozen other churches in the city started holding dances, and Gallien began training recruits for a new ecclesiastical position: dance chairman.

Within a couple years, Gallien's idea had moved westward. In Los Angeles, Father Fisher Robinson held a dance to benefit Verbum Dei Boys' School, and Clifton Chenier played. Then in San Francisco, George Broussard approached All Hallows Church about having a dance in the gym. "I suggested to the membership that this man Clifton Chenier could make us a profit," Broussard remembers. "And everybody was wide-eyed and scared to death, because at that time, six hundred dollars to pay the band was a lot of money. They wondered if they would make enough money to pay this guy. I said, 'Oh yeah, you take my word for it. He's going to draw the people.'"

The church dances drew together the people from Louisiana who'd moved west for better jobs in the shipping industry. Thanks to these zydeco nights, the Creoles of California reconnected in a community to find new expression for the values and aesthetics they'd left behind. "It would bring people together that probably wouldn't have been together otherwise," Broussard explains. "You run into somebody at one of these events you hadn't seen in a long time: 'Oh, I'm glad to see you,' and so forth and so on. And if it wouldn't have been for the zydeco event, you probably would have never laid eyes on that person again for a long time or never. Because you kind of lose track of people when they move here, when they're scattered all over the Bay Area.

"You love to see people out there enjoying themselves," Broussard continues. "Because after all, you got to have a little fun sometimes. Father Faringo was the priest at All Hallows. He used to stick around and listen, he liked the sound. But then he would go home because, you know, being a priest, he'd say, 'I'm not supposed to be dancing all night here.' But we had another priest in the area, he would even get up and dance."

Strachwitz became Chenier's unofficial booking agent in California, bringing him into folk clubs in Santa Cruz and Davis for the nights he wasn't booked at the churches. "They're real quiet in these hippie joints," Chenier complained to *Rolling Stone* in 1971. "They don't dance — don't do nothing but sit there. And if they don't dance, how are you supposed to know if they dig what you're doing?" Chenier played a solo show at the Berkeley Folk Festival in 1966, and the accordionist was even teamed for a night at the Avalon Ballroom with the heavy metal band Blue Cheer. It was that performance, he later remarked, that convinced him to travel with his own group. "They told me, 'That boy sure can play some drums,'" he said of Blue Cheer. "And I said, 'Oh man, you're sick!'"

One of Chenier's regular church stops was St. Mark's in Richmond, where he stayed in the home of Mama Lena and Houston Pitre. "He was playing for us to St. Mark's Church, my church," remembers Mama Lena Pitre. "He started here around 1965. My husband and I wanted something you can dance to that'll fund-raise for the church.

"Clifton would never touch an accordion before he was ready to go play," she adds. "Never. He'd make one song in the back room, he was sitting in there, and he'd make it with his hands like this, clapping. It was 'O ma negresse,' something like that. He'd say, 'Oh, that does it, I make me a song, girl.' And that night we went with him to the dance in Berkeley, where he used to play in that club, and he played that song. He said on the speakers, 'That was a new song I make today. I made that in Houston Pitre's bedroom.'"

The Pitres' church was the site of Chenier's only live recording at a zydeco dance, taped in November 1971 and released on Arhoolie as *Live at St. Mark's*. The recording provides a rare glimpse of just what type of nights Chenier was providing for his Louisiana-born audience. Standing on a bandstand only slightly elevated above the dancers, he extended his height an extra foot by wearing an elaborate gilded crown. "You know, it's good to be here with all my home people," he pronounced. "Lawtell, Opelousas, St. Martinville, Lake Charles, Baton Rouge, anybody from New Orleans? Basile, have mercy. Anybody from Frilot Cove?" The crowd shouted and hollered. "Y'all are looking good," Chenier went on. "When you come home, I want you to be looking just like that." Then a voice rose from the din. "You know you're lying," it countered. "'Cause you know there is one person who don't look good. He just wants to make everybody feel good." But Chenier stood his ground. "Everybody's looking good," he answered. "Aw, you know better than that," replied the skeptic.

Chenier remained in charge for the rest of the night. He ran through nearly forty songs, interjecting cries of *"eh, toi"* and "I feel good, baby! I feel like a champ!" He joked about the title of his new song, "I'm a Hog for You," laughing that "it sounds bad but it ain't bad." He pointed out Chris Strachwitz in the crowd, teasing him about the time they went to Paris and he had to order his food for him in French. And he informed his crowd that they were all making their own record that night. "You don't know it, but you're on record right now," he said. "Every now and then, come up and holler your name. Say, 'I'm so-and-so.' You're going to be on there."

Nights like these secured Chenier's reputation as the King of Zydeco.

In songs like "Tu Le Ton Son Ton,"(also known as "Tous les temps en temps," or "Every Now and Then"), "I'm a Hog for You," and "Black Snake Blues," he celebrated the rural life that California Creoles had left behind, and his dances were as hot as anything back in Louisiana. With Clifton Chenier at the accordion and dancers on the floor, everyone felt at home. "I think he really made it because when he started playing a dance, that was four hours, straight," Robert St. Judy says. "No break. And I think that's why people started liking him so much. When he got up there from nine to one, that was nine to one. And when he was done, it was a finished thing."

By the end of the decade, Chenier overcame his reluctance to travel overseas. In 1969 Strachwitz organized the American Folk and Blues Tour. In London, critic Simon Napier reviewed the Royal Albert Hall performance, declaring Chenier "a fine artist and a showman," with a repertoire that ranged from "Jolie blonde" to "Release Me." Backstage, Chenier entertained Earl Hooker, John Jackson, and the other musicians on the tour by playing piano in the dressing room. "I never thought I'd ever hit Europe, but I know one thing: the way I was playing that accordion it was going to go somewhere," he would tell writer Ben Sandmel. "I mean I ain't bragging about it, but I knew what I had going was going to go somewhere, and that's what it did."

On tour in California, Chenier also had the opportunity to hook up with friends from the old R&B days. "We went in 1967 to Los Angeles, but we were staying at a motel, and that wasn't a place that Cliff wanted to stay," remembers Red Hots bass player Jumpin' Joe Morris. "So he went to find a man he knew from way back, his name was J. R. Fulbright. He said, 'You all leave this motel, you all are going to stay at my house.' So we left the motel and we went to J. R.'s place. We stayed there a whole month.

"The nights we had off, J. R. would make arrangements for us to play at a club. Then one night Cliff asked J. R., 'Man, where can I find T-Bone Walker?' He said, 'Cliff, we can run by T-Bone's house.' So we get in the station wagon, and we got to T-Bone Walker's house. He was just having dinner, but he hadn't seen Cliff in so long, you talk about something. So he got on the phone, he said, 'Man, they got somebody that want to talk to you, you know him?' It was Lowell Fulson, and he said, 'I'll be damned, if that's not the Frenchman!' So we all went over to Lowell Fulson's house. T-Bone Walker, he was drinking gin, and Lowell Fulson, he was drinking gin. But T-Bone, him, a fifth of gin wasn't nothing for him, come to find out he had an all-plastic stomach inside.

"So Lowell said, 'Cliff, you got your accordion with you?' He said, 'Man, I stay with my accordion, you know.' He had put it in J. R.'s station wagon, and he said, 'Joe, go get my accordion,' and I went and got his accordion.

The three of those guys hook up together, boy. They played so many songs, and it all sounded so sweet and level. And man, each one of them guys would take a solo. Lowell would take a solo off of his record, and T-Bone would take a solo off of his record, and Cliff would take a solo off of his record. And then what they did, they combined them together, and I didn't think it could work like that. Man, that worked out so beautiful together. T-Bone was so drunk, he couldn't hardly walk. Cliff had been hitting the bottle too, and me and Big Robert had to help him take his accordion off. You talk about something."

The end of the 1950s had left Clifton Chenier nearly destitute and searching for a way to rekindle his career. A decade later his star was polished and gleaming. Then, back in a Houston recording studio with Strachwitz, he announced his next move when he recorded his most personal song: "I'm Coming Home," planned as a gift to his widowed mother, now living in Opelousas. "You know, when he wrote that song, we was coming back from California," Morris remembers. "We left for Houston Texas, he said, 'You know, fellows, I'm thinking of a song, we're going to record that. We're going to record that song for our mothers.'"

Running his fingers across his accordion in a melody that evoked Sam Cooke's recent hit "Bring It on Home to Me," Chenier sang in a plaintive voice:

I'm coming home
'Cause I feel
You know I feel so all alone.
I'm coming back home
And meet my dear old mother
'Cause that's where I belong.

He couldn't wait for his mother to hear it, but the album was delayed until more songs could be added the following year. Finally, on a tour in California, he was able to pick up a copy of the record. Sadly, he was too late. "Clifton called and said he was coming in," recalls his mother's sister, Oreile Thibeaux. "But before he got there, she never heard the record. She died before he got back home on his tour. And he was bringing that record with him. I don't like to hear that song, it brings back memories."

For the rest of his life, this sadness would revisit Chenier and his family whenever he sang "I'm Coming Home." Yet he would play it nearly every time he performed.

## III

"Man, you remember what Cliff used to do?" Little Buck Senegal asks, shaking his head. "He'd play all night Saturday night, and start a dance on Sunday at ten o'clock in the morning. I remember one Sunday morning, Cleveland was sick. And he had an upset stomach, you know, and he did a number on the stage. He made the band get off the stage, made Cleveland go get a bucket and a mop, and mop that whole bandstand. I'm telling you I was there. You see, Cleveland used to stay up and drink that whiskey straight. And eat just pork chops, man. Those pork chops would mess him up, man."

"That all happened before Lent." John Hart nods. "On Lent, the people that Cliff would play for, no dancing, no liquor, no smoking."

"And one time, Cliff was hot then, the place was packed. He got on there on his accordion, boy, he took his necktie, put it back, and he started playing. First song, he said, 'I hope you all had a good time. Good night, everybody.' I said, 'Cliff, we just started, it was the first song.' He said, 'What?' He said, 'Go get me a pitcher of ice water.' After you bring him a pitcher of ice water, they had to stop that man from playing. We'd be coming in there from St. Martinville or New Iberia, play there, then go do another one Sunday afternoon and another one that night."

"You see, Catholic people, they were not oriented like Protestant people, so that didn't make them a difference."

"Yeah, Sunday morning, man, people wouldn't go to church, they'd be in that club. I mean wall to wall, man, ten o'clock. Suit and necktie."

By the start of the 1970s, a surge in oil prices flooded Southwest Louisiana with new jobs, and no longer was it necessary to go to Texas to find work. By Friday night, pockets were full and zydeco clubs were packed. Lording over the new prosperity was Clifton Chenier, who was now frequently wearing his tall crown that glimmered against the chrome on his accordion and the gold caps on his teeth.

Everywhere he went, people hailed him as king. When zydeco accordionist Nathan Williams was growing up, he would watch in awe as Chenier rode in an annual parade through his hometown. "They always had a salute to Clifton Chenier in St. Martinville," he remembers. "They put him on a float, then the next thing you know, *'Eh, 'tite fille.'* Man, you could hear people all down the street, they'd boogaloo, 'Go Clifton, go Cliff!' Before they put him up to the Casino Club, the club's packed. Now he's sitting down in the chair — this is Cliff on the chair, drunk. He's got a big fifth of VO and a gallon of water. They take his chair and they pick it up with him like that, into the club. Here comes the dance. And they put him on the bandstand like that, and he'd say, 'Bring the accordion over here, boy.' And he'd say, 'Well, we're going to play all night now.' And the next thing you know, that floor caved in and everything, and he's still jamming. I'm not lying, I'm talking about seven, five, six hundred people in the club, and the club boogaloo'd."

Touring the countryside in his Cadillac sedan, Chenier moved from crowd to crowd, from city to country, from black to white. From the Casino Club in St. Martinville to the Dipsy Doodle in Breaux Bridge, from the Bon Ton Rouley in Lafayette to Richard's Club in Lawtell, he stretched the weekend to its limits, and he made friends at each stop. "Clifton and the old man were very close," remembers Kermon Richard about his father, Eddie, who started Richard's Club in Lawtell. "He'd play every first Saturday of the month when he wasn't on tour. And on Sunday morning, boy, he'd leave from Lafayette, come over here and he and the old man would sit down and reminisce about the dance and joke and talk in French. They'd gossip about who left with somebody else other than their wives, and they would laugh about that, and drink their coffee."

A club on the seven-hundred block of South Orange Street, just a couple of blocks from his and Margaret's home on Magnolia, was where Chenier made his base of operations. "This was his home, at the Blue Angel," former owner Claude Boudreaux remembers. "That's why he made that record, 'Party at the Blue Angel.' My brother had to come open at eight in the morning for Cliff, and shit, he used to get on that telephone like that was his place. That telephone was his telephone. You'd swear that Blue Angel was for him. And everybody was calling for Cliff. They call at the Blue Angel, 234-9289. I ain't going to forget that number."

Boudreaux is sitting quietly in his living room in a Lafayette retirement community, with shades pulled against the bright afternoon sun. He's a month shy of his eightieth birthday, and after a lifetime of speaking over blaring accordions and jukeboxes, his voice is reduced to a whisper. He once smoked sixteen cigars a day. Now he just keeps one in his mouth, unlit.

When he bought the building in 1965, Boudreaux was working as a plumber. "Another guy had built that with some old lumber from the railroad," he says. "He called it the Tango Club. They had the Four Aces on Twelfth Street. They had the Peppermint Lounge on Twelfth. Oh, they had a bunch. When I took it, I put 'The Blue Angel' on it, and it put me over the top.

*Claude Boudreaux at the Blue Angel, circa 1970.*

"Wood, everything was wood," he describes. "There was some steps. Two jukeboxes. No cement. Now if I would have remodeled, the people would have stopped coming. Fix it too nice, and they think they have to dress up to go in it, so you don't have no business. When they get off work, and their shoes were kind of messed up, they'd come. That's who spends money. Now on the weekends, everyone would dress clean."

Boudreaux says there are many qualities important to a club owner, not the least of which was discretion. "Those ladies used to come there, talk to those other men, you know," he says. "When I go somewhere I see them with their husbands, I don't know you. But my oldest brother, one time we went to St. Martinville, and he saw those ladies. He said, 'Hey, you all were at the Blue Angel!' Oh! They had to quit coming. I told him, he put his nose in it. As long as there's no fight or no argument, I do like I don't see nothing. If I see your wife doing something, that's none of my business, you got to see for yourself.

"And poor Cliff, he was playing one night in Arnaudville. And a woman was dancing with her husband, and he's looking at her while he was playing. He was singing to her, 'Call me at the Blue Angel at nine o'clock.' I was there. And her husband, he was busy dancing the whole time. He never even heard him."

Boudreaux first met Chenier in Port Arthur during the war, when he was working construction. They stayed in contact through the years, and Boudreaux remembers that his friend was still having hard times when the Blue Angel first opened its doors. "When he came here, he was doing bad," he recalls. "I had to give him an undershirt, no undershirt. His shoes were bust. I had this old place, my mama and them's house, and I let him stay there, no rent.

"Then he started playing those dances, all right. He'd play for the door, a dollar and a quarter. He used to pick up six hundred, seven hundred. But he was messing up all that money. And his wife, Margaret, started coming. I asked, 'How's Cliff doing with that money?' And she says, 'Sometimes he comes home with one hundred, sometimes two.' I said, 'If you want to save some money, come follow him more often.' We were like brother and sister. And when she came and started holding the door herself, it went up just like that. She used to collect at the Blue Angel, and at one dance, he'd make six hundred on Saturday, and six hundred on Sunday. And he worked hard."

Soon it seemed that everyone in Southwest Louisiana was making it to Clifton Chenier's legendary "Blue Monday" dances. For advertising, Boudreaux hired a man to drive to Breaux Bridge and St. Martinville with a loudspeaker, and play Clifton Chenier records in the street. Chenier helped out whenever he would play out of town, by passing out pencils embossed with Boudreaux's name and the Blue Angel's phone number. But as Boudreaux sees it, Chenier's personality was the main reason for his success. "He was a good player, and he was so good with the people, it made his music better, you see," he says. "Sometimes he was drinking hard, and he missed some words there. But they wouldn't see that, because they liked him so much.

"I don't care how ugly you were, or how old, he'd sit down and drink all day long with you," he continues. "He knew how to mix. If you was ugly, you was his friend. They had another guy that lived by the Blue Angel, he's dead too, he used to make a show at the Blue called the Ugliest One Wins. It was five or ten dollars sometimes. So a guy there with Cliff, he was ugly-ugly, and he used to win all the time. That was Percy. That was Cliff's boy. Cliff was tight with Percy. All them broke people, you know, trying to make themselves ugly, but Percy was the king. And every morning he was right there waiting for Cliff."

Boudreaux always knew his friend was blessed with talent, especially when he witnessed how he'd come up with a new song. "He'd talk to anybody, sit down there and talk. When he'd get in that car, he'd start to mix those words together, and make a record. He'd make a record about how he wants you like you came into the world, with no clothes on. *'Mo lé toi comme to vini dans le pays.'* Like you came into this world, *pas de linge,* no clothes. *'Otez tout que'que chose. Otez ton bas. Otez to' robe.'* Take off everything. Take off your stockings. Take off your dress. When he say, *'Otez tes caleçons,'* that's the last thing he said, to take off your drawers." Then he said, *'Tout que'que chose est correcte.'* Everything's all right."

Today Boudreaux spends his days at the horse track, or at home, listening to zydeco on the radio. He often thinks about the years when he was the Blue Angel man. He had a new car, and he lived like he wanted. It was a good business place. And he made it all happen with his friend Clifton Chenier. "They got a lot of players, they ain't ever going to be like him," he explains. "He's dead and he's still the king."

The trick to finding Joe Morris — born Joseph Brouchet — is to know who to ask for. "Around here, if you don't ask for Jumpin' Joe, they ain't going to know who you're talking about," says Clifton Chenier's longtime bass player, in a conversation over dinner in his home in Lafayette. "The name started because when I get up and start playing music, I start jumping up high. The audience, they liked that, and everybody would shout, 'We want Jumpin' Joe!'"

Morris collects old 45s, which he stores on broom handles that tower in his dining room like black vinyl trees. He lives with his wife, Theresa, who is having her dinner in the kitchen tonight. She frequently calls out to prompt his memories. "Tell him about Africa," she says, and her husband doesn't miss a beat. "Oh man, it was wonderful," he says. "I was playing bass and I was dancing and jumping. I tore up a lot of clothes, man, playing on my back. In Africa, the people would be dancing but they don't know what you're saying."

Her voice returns. "And all of a sudden, he passed out like he had died, God forgive me."

"People thought I had died, and when they were crowding around me, they were sending for a doctor," Morris continues. He laughs. "Then Cliff kicked off the song again, I start playing right along, and I jumped up. Man! You talk about a trip!"

"What Cliff is to your mama, honey?"

"Huh?"

"What is Cliff to your mama? Cliff is your cuz."

"Yeah, that's my mama's nephew," says Morris. Jumpin' Joe's brother Jerry was one of Chenier's first drummers, and his other brother, Gene, is a singer who recorded with Rockin' Dopsie and Fernest Arceneaux. But as Clifton Chenier's bass player for fifteen years, Jumpin' Joe is the member of the family who took his music the farthest.

Born in Crowley, Morris began playing music as a child after meeting Clarence "Gatemouth" Brown, who showed him how to tune a guitar. He built his first guitar from a cigar box, which he eventually traded in for the real thing, and then he started backing local accordionists, including Claude Faulk, Sou-Pop, and Bidon. He switched to bass in the late 1960s, when Chenier invited him into the Red Hots. "My big break came when Clifton Chenier asked me to be in his band," he remembers. "I used to do plumbing work. So one Friday night, my boss came there to Jay's Lounge to see me play. He stood right by the bandstand, and he told the waiter to bring me a drink. Then that Monday, I told him, 'Clifton asked me to go and play with him, and I believe I would like to go try music.'"

Playing in the Red Hots, Morris witnessed how Chenier would rework an old house dance song in his own style. "You heard that record 'Oh, Lucille'?" he asks. "We were playing a dance in Scott, and Claude Faulk was sitting in. A lady asked him to play 'Lucille,' because that was his record. So he kicked it off and it sounded good, and he went all the way through with his own accordion, a button accordion. So Cliff got back on the bandstand, then he played that song over. But he played it on a piano accordion. Then we went to Houston that next week, and that Monday the first record we recorded was 'Hey, Lucille.' And on that record, Cliff bought himself a brand new Lincoln Continental, man."

Morris becomes most excited when he recalls meeting his musical heroes. Being in Chenier's band gave him the chance to know most of them. There was the day that Cleveland Chenier took him by the arm to go see Lightnin' Hopkins. And the time when Lowell Fulson got short-changed at a hotel in Switzerland, and showed up on the plane with a suitcase full of tiny liquor bottles. "Man, when we got off that airplane, we got off of cloud nine, and we were still on cloud nine," Morris says, laughing. They played with Albert Collins and even backed Big Joe Turner, but best of all, Morris remembers, they played with Big Mama Thornton at Carnegie Hall. "Man, I didn't mess around and do my show in Carnegie Hall," he says. "Those people were standing up, applauding, and I thought that whole thing was going to fall down. We had us a time, boy."

But Morris also wants to talk about other times, and how playing in the Red Hot Louisiana Band was not without its struggles. His eyes still hurt from all the smoke and dust, and he says his bladder is wrecked from those four-hour sets. And the leader and the band didn't always come to terms on the proper pay. "Lots of times, we'd get to the motel, you see, and the rooms would be already paid for. But he'd put the whole band in one room. The contract said two men to a room, but he had us all in one, sleeping on the floor. Then the drummer, he said, 'Man, we're tired of sleeping on the floor like that.' And that's what made him straighten up and fly right. Because he didn't want to lose that drummer.

"But let me tell you one thing. I wasn't ashamed to say it then, I ain't ashamed to say it now. Cliff done humbugged us out of a lot of money, man. I tell you, if I had every dollar that Cliff done beat me out of — "

"Not just you, the whole band, man," adds Theresa.

" — the whole band, I'd be living in a brick home, man. I'd be fixed for life."

"But he was a good musician."

"Man, he was the king."

"Where did he win that accordion at, honey?"

"He won it overseas, in Italy, they give it to him."

"That's right."

"I'm going to tell you what, they got nightclubs, if they had a dance, if Clifton Chenier was playing in their town, they'd cancel their dance. They wouldn't give their dance at all."

"They had to respect him."

"And Cliff built a lot of clubs. They got a place in Texas, and Cliff started playing there. Man, in three years' time, the man rebuilt his club. They could count on that crowd. Sometimes they'd fight over who had a table."

"They should have called in for their table."

"Some of them, they'd call two weeks ahead of time. They'd put a bottle on the table, and reserve."

"That's right."

It was hard to keep your money in the Red Hot Louisiana Band, Morris adds. "The guys, they was all hard gamblers, and I mean for money, man," says Morris. "But they'd never catch me in that, no. One Friday, Freddie King pulled up there with his boys, and they wanted to take each a turn playing cards, and each one of them got cleaned out. Because they had professional gamblers in Chenier's band. Especially the drummer and the driver, Big Charles White. Man, he'd get up there and drive that van, sometimes he'd drive a day and a half, two days, without even taking a break. That's just how hard he was. And a nice guy, but he could play cards."

Morris's favorite Chenier songs were his blues, such as "I'm on the Wonder" and "Ton Na Na." He says he will never forget a time in San Francisco when he witnessed just what Clifton Chenier's blues could do. "I tell you what, they called him to go play at a prison in San Francisco," he says. "We got out there, and there were benches and everything for the prisoners, and the ladies were in one section and the men were in another. Then he kicked off. It's a lot of them, they hadn't heard accordion or seen anybody play accordion in prison. And man, he was jamming. He was making that accordion smoke. And then when he broke it down, he said, 'Well, now we get down with the blues.' Now when he started playing that song, them ladies started fighting in there. And they had guards up there with them guns, so they all went down and stopped them ladies. I tell you, Robert got under the chair! He hit the deck. Oh man, I said, 'Cliff, I got a good idea. Let's get the hell out of here.' But we finished. After that one, the guy told him, 'Don't play no more blues,' and he started playing zydeco."

After staying with Chenier for fifteen years, Morris began playing with Hiram Sampy. But for all the good and bad times, he acknowledges that nothing will compare to his time in the Red Hot Louisiana Band. "You see, we were like family," he concludes. "And the way we played music, the way we had it going, it was like telepathy. All Clifton would do is just hit his accordion, and that's it, we knew where he was going. And when he put his head down like that there, we knew he was going to stop. Right on the money."

\*     \*     \*

Like Amédé Ardoin before him, Chenier took his music across the invisible color lines that cordoned the Louisiana prairie. Early in his career, he played segregated clubs like the Silver Slipper, a two-room dance club that stood in the community of Pecaniere, near his boyhood home. Chenier would perform on the white side of the club one week, and for the blacks the next. "You could hear the music on both sides," recalls Wilbert Levier, a frequent patron of the club. "But coming up in our time, the blacks couldn't go in there. They might be good friends with a white family, and they might dance with one another on their porch. Or you could be army buddies, both in the same platoon. You'd come home and come to Leonville and go to the dance, and you'd be on that side, and you on this side. You understand that, because that's the way it was."

Each side had its own music preference and way of dancing. Claude Boudreaux remembers seeing how Chenier would oblige a crowd in a white club by playing mostly up-tempo tunes. "It was a big place, and you'd see the dancers in one place, and they'd be way over yonder in no time," he says. "At the black dances he'd play more slow. The black people used to like to dance tight."

By the beginning of the seventies, Chenier's records were receiving play on Louisiana radio stations, and he gained greater fame as the subject of Les Blank's 1973 music documentary *Hot Pepper*. Young whites flocked to hear him at Willie Purple's in Lafayette, and in the nearby town of Cankton he played regular shows at a combination dance hall and rooster arena named Jay's Lounge and Cockpit. Some whites also began venturing into zydeco clubs, where they usually met warm receptions. "The place over here was big enough for Cliff to play, you know," remembers William Hamilton, owner of Hamilton's Place in Lafayette. "Before my daddy died, them whites started coming. They'd ask us, 'We ain't going to have no trouble? Sure we ain't going to have no trouble?' I said, 'No, y'all can come, y'all ain't never going to have no trouble.'"

Another Lafayette club, the Bon Ton Rouley, established the institution of the weekly "white night," which featured a local band called the Red Beans and Rice Revue. Guitarist Sonny Landreth frequently sat in with the band. "Cliff would come by with some of the guys from his band," Landreth remembers. "So he came out one night, and he invited me to play at the Casino Club in St. Martinville. I was thrilled. I thought, this is it."

Ten years earlier Landreth, then a high school student, had gone to hear Chenier play the Blue Angel Club. "I had never done that before, a white teenaged kid, but as soon as we got to the door, the vibe was so cool. Cliff was sitting at a table not far from the door, and he saw us and said, 'Hey soul, come on in.' He just took you in and made you feel right at home. And he got ready to play, and he was already hitting the stuff. So we started drinking a little beer, the band was so great, and it was quite a religious experience, really. I was never the same after that.

"A few years after that, things started really peaking out at Jay's," Landreth continues. "By 'seventy-two, everybody was packing the joint to hear Clifton. It was a lounge and cockpit — you could walk right in and there's the cockfights. But it was rocking, and that's when people started learning to dance, picking up on this jitterbug two-stepping style. Cliff tapped into the younger, white, post-'sixties generation that was kind of out of school, just really coming into its own, kind of feeling its oats."

Landreth learned the difference between black and white audiences when he began traveling with the Red Hots. "When we played the black joints, he might take five minutes in between a song to open another bottle of gin, but basically we partied the whole night," he remembers. "But he told me that when we play them 'hippie joints' — that's what he always called them — you got to take a break, let everybody go outside. He said that when you're playing these black joints, you can't take no breaks, they'll all go home."

After the show at the Casino Club, Chenier asked Landreth to come to New Orleans for the weekend. "At that point, everything was an initiation," he recalls. "Going down there, that was my first ride on the van. I think it was an old Dodge, and he called it SWAT, because they always had these red suits they all wore, and one time when they were all climbing out of it, Cliff said they looked like a SWAT team. And the van had rolled over, and the top still leaked from where it had been bent. Jumpin' Joe always sat in the back, and when it started raining, he'd put his umbrella up. I sat with him.

"Oh man, there's a ton of stories, most of them X-rated. And Cliff told me, when I first came into the band, he said, 'Look, you don't let them boys get your money. No matter what you do, don't you gamble with them.' But mainly, I could never get over how loose everything was. He told me to be over at his house at something like eight-thirty in the morning. I thought, 'Wow, they're getting an early start.' So I got over there, and it's me and Jumpin' Joe, and then they'd go by to pick everybody up. And this would take the course of the day, literally. You go to somebody's house, and then you're there for an hour, and he'd go back to the house for something else. So I go back in the van with Joe, and he's got his little bottle of Crown back there, and he says, 'Come on, cuz, have some of this.' So I was drunk by around five-thirty in the afternoon, and we hadn't got out of Lafayette yet.

"Cliff's wife, Margaret, would put sandwiches or something together and sell them to the band. It was something like six bucks, and I thought that was outrageous, so I decided to wait, you know. I guess the Crown does have its merit — you start nipping on that, and it kind of kills the appetite. But Margaret was getting on Robert St. Judy about a Moon Pie, because she thought he had gotten one and he didn't pay for it. 'Robert! You pay me for that pie!' 'Oh yeah, Margaret, I paid for that pie!' And when she walked away, he'd turn to me: 'I ain't paid her shit.'

"We didn't even start playing till like ten o'clock that night, and it seemed like the Exodus, just getting down to New Orleans. When we arrived in New Orleans, we checked into London Lodge on Airline Highway, and everyone went to the gas station next door to load up on microwave sandwiches. That's when Cliff summoned me to go to his room, and they came and got me. And he put his arm around me and said, 'I'm going to take you all around the world.' I was so honored."

Landreth recalls a night at Tipitina's, when Chenier pushed him into the spotlight, as being one of the most pivotal moments in his career. "I'd been with the band a while, and we were playing 'Mojo Working,' and he reached over and grabbed me — literally grabbed me and pulled me out — and said, 'Come on.' And this roar comes out from the crowd, the whole bit. It was just really happening, the magic kicked in. And he was loving it, he was just grinning from ear to ear, you know. It was a moment I've carried with me ever since."

But in South Louisiana, not all white clubs were hippie joints, and Landreth also saw how Chenier carefully navigated his band through the lingering racist attitudes of the day. "I never saw a gun, but I've heard there was one there," Landreth says. "Maybe he had a compartment in the accordion I didn't know about. But if there was ever a time to pull one out, I guess a club in Bridge City, Texas, would have been the place.

"Right as you're coming off the bridge, there it is, the Sparkle Paradise. It was a really classy joint, a long affair with two shotgun rooms. Clifton would play there on Sundays, and they would just revere him — it was another perfect example of how he crossed these barriers. They loved him. This old guy was telling me in the bathroom about how he'd been hearing Clifton Chenier for years. I always thought that was really amazing, they really treated him with respect. Go figure, right?"

The crowd at Sparkle Paradise also revered Cleveland Chenier, and even built a wooden box and placed it next to the rubboard player. "That was for Cleveland's donations," remembers Mabel Chenier, Cleveland's widow. "Sometimes they would give him maybe two or three hundred dollars." But she adds that the love for the Chenier brothers' music didn't extend to their families, and the band was once told that their wives and girlfriends weren't welcome at the club. "But Clifton said, 'If you want to hear me play, our women come in there.'"

The club owner would stand at the bandstand to try to deflect trouble-makers, but sometimes that wasn't enough. Landreth recalls the night he saw what steps Chenier would take to make sure his friends were safe: "Blacks weren't allowed in the place, to my knowledge, except when we played there. Well, there was this guy who used to hang out with the band, his nickname was Black. And we were playing, and all of a sudden, Clifton stopped the band. The reason was that Black was dancing with a white girl. And man, Clifton stopped the band in the middle of the song, and he got all over him. He was over the microphone, and he just shame-faced him all the way back to his table. I thought, 'Man, I can't believe this.' I mean, he stopped the band and said, 'Nigger, I told you to don't never do that,' and he started screaming and hollering and cussing him out, and shaking his fist at him. The girl just freaked out and ran outside, and Black went over and cowered off and sat down at the table. I thought that was pretty brutal. I mean, Cliff loved this old guy. He was always around, one of the cronies, part of the court.

"But as soon as we took a break, man, Cliff went out of his way to pull me over and explain it to me. He gave me the law about this place. He said, 'They don't want any of that in here. They could have taken him out and that could have been the last you'd ever see of him.' Cliff had this thing worked out. Wherever he played, he really knew the people. He knew what he needed to do, and it was all part of him keeping it together."

Despite the obstacles, Chenier continued to work in both black and white clubs, and he became a major musical inspiration for both Cajuns and Creoles. In 1976 he teamed up with Rod Bernard, a popular singer and guitarist who helped pioneer the musical hybrid of Cajun, Creole, and rock and roll known as swamp pop. The two men recorded an album of their favorite R&B tunes for Floyd Soileau's Jin Records. The title of their project made it clear that the musicians had succeeded in crossing the color barrier: *Boogie in Black & White.*


*"Bonjour, comment ça va, monsieur?"* Clifton Chenier greeted his cheering crowd at the 1975 Montreux Jazz Festival. "They call me the black Cajun Frenchman."

By now Chenier had become a veteran of the world's largest festival stages. "You never get tired of the road," he would tell interviewer Ben Sandmel. "The more you go, the more you want to go, because you got a lot of friends out there." He kept an eye on music trends, and he added a popular young R&B bandleader named Stanley "Buckwheat" Dural Jr. to the Red Hots roster, putting him on Hammond B-3 organ. He appeared on television on *Austin City Limits*, and was a regular fixture on Lafayette's *Passe Partout* and other local TV shows. He played for the first five Festivals Acadiens in Lafayette, and performed regularly at the New Orleans Jazz and Heritage Festival.

During this time he also captured the interest of a local composer and saxophonist named Dicky Landry, who was splitting his time between Southwest Louisiana and New York, where he was a member of the Philip Glass Ensemble. In 1972, Landry remembers, he was back home, and he took his saxophone and went to hear Chenier play the Dipsy Doodle. "Clifton gets on the mike: 'We have a white boy from Cecilia's going to try to play some zydeco.' So I played a couple of songs. I told him, 'Thank you,' but he told me to stay. So two hours later, I'm playing away and my lips are about to fall off. And ever since then I'd go sit in as many times as I could."

Like so many other blues musicians before him, Chenier was also beginning to attract the interest of players in the rock world. Lake Charles record producer Eddie Shuler recalls that members of Led Zeppelin once called his studio, looking for the accordionist to perform on their tour plane. Then one night in Los Angeles, Mick Jagger heard from Landry that Chenier was playing a dance at Verbum Dei. "So I call Cliff the next morning," Landry remembers. "I said, 'Cliff, I got this guy, Mick Jagger, he wants to come and hear you tomorrow night.' He says, 'Who's that?' I say, 'He's with the Rolling Stones.' 'Oh yeah,' he says, 'that magazine. They did a good article on me.' I said, 'No no, this guy's sold millions of records, he's a singer.' 'Oh, bring him. I don't care, bring him.'

"So we get to the high school in the limo. Jagger says, 'Go check it out. I don't want to go in if it'll be a scene.' So I walk in, and there's about eight hundred people in there, and they were speaking French. So I walk out to the limo and I say, 'I think it's cool.' And sure enough, we walk in, nobody recognized him, and we all danced all night, and finally in intermission I introduce him to Clifton and they're talking, and a couple of photographers take some pictures, and all of a sudden this group of people come with autograph papers. Jagger starts backing up, and they walk right by him to get to Clifton."

In 1978 Landry was asked to be an advisor for a "Boogie 'n' Blues" program at Carnegie Hall. He agreed, but only if Chenier was on the bill. The accordionist hadn't performed in New York since his brief appearance at the Apollo Theatre twenty years earlier, and the organizers were skeptical. Landry prevailed, but Chenier was scheduled for the end of the long night. "By the time Clifton came on, it was after midnight, and people were snoring," Landry recalls. "Then Clifton walks out on stage, he's got his accordion strapped to his chest, he's got this crown on his head, and he has his arms outstretched, and he looked like a god. He looked huge. And he steps up to the microphone and he says, 'I know I'm supposed to be playing some zydeco, but if it wouldn't be for this music, I wouldn't be here today, so my first song's going to be 'Jolie blonde.' And the minute he started playing, the house erupted. Everybody just jumped up from their seat and were dancing in the aisles, and he went out and did an incredible concert."

Reviewing the April 10, 1979, show, *New York Times* critic John Rockwell raved about the accordion player, who had shared the bill with such players as John Lee Hooker and his cousin Lightnin' Hopkins. "As the only band on the bill with a lively vital relationship to its home audience," Rockwell wrote, "it could be argued that Mr. Chenier's Red Hot Louisiana Band played the best blues of the night." Clifton Chenier had conquered New York.

Just as Clifton Chenier had launched a new sound when he traded in the single-row accordion for the modern piano-key model, his older brother Cleveland transformed a relic of the house dances into the second lead instrument in a zydeco band. Today, Cleveland Chenier is universally acknowledged as the rubboard's innovator as well as its most accomplished musician.

When he first began playing the oil town bars with his brother, Cleveland held a corrugated metal tray in his lap, and rubbed its surface with the back of a spoon. By all accounts, it was Clifton who invented the modern design — with collars over the shoulder, allowing greater movement of hands — when he drew a picture in the sand for a Port Arthur metalworker. But it is likely that the two brothers at least discussed the idea. "Clifton would say that the Cheniers were the only people smart enough to put such a washboard together," remembers Wilbert Guillory.

The new rubboard allowed Cleveland the freedom to experiment with new techniques as well. He varied the tone by leaning forward or by elevating the board with one shoulder, and he decided to use twelve church-key bottle openers — six on each hand — as scrapers. "I wanted it to be different from the others," he told Jean-Pierre Bruneau in the 1983 documentary *Dedans le Sud de la Louisiane.* "Some of them would play one-handed, some of them would play double with two spoons. I started with three keys, six keys altogether, and I jumped up to twelve and I quit at that." When Bruneau asked why he stopped at twelve, Chenier laughed. "I had enough," he said. "I was loaded there."

Cleveland Chenier was also Clifton's most constant band member. They had started out playing with no other musicians behind them, and they were together for the trip to Los Angeles to record for Specialty. Lowell Fulson recalls that Cleveland also went on the tours in the late 1950s. "We liked

*Cleveland Chenier and Sonny Landreth.*

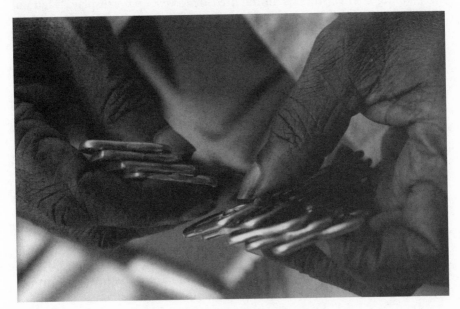

*Cleveland Chenier's church-key bottle openers.*

Cleveland because he stood between the bass and the drums," he says. "His brother fit right in there, him and that rubboard. I liked that funky beat." But by the early 1960s, Cleveland was mainly performing in clubs around Houston with his cousin Lightnin' Hopkins. "Cleveland used to play with Lightnin', I think Lightnin' would insist on the washboard, the actual washboard," remembers Robert McCormick.

Chris Strachwitz recalls that, by the mid-1960s, Cleveland was exclusively playing the new rubboard. Strachwitz considered the instrument to be as integral to zydeco as the twelve-string bass guitar called the *bajo sexto* was to Tex-Mex and conjunto music, and he featured it prominently in his recordings. The accordion and the rubboard might have been inseparable, Strachwitz adds, but that didn't mean their players always got along. "There was sort of a jealousy," he explains. "On that green record, that *Black Snake Blues*, man, they threw them whiskey bottles across the studio. The engineer said, 'Listen, if Clifton throws one more bottle at his brother, I'm going to throw you all out of here.'"

Yet the two brothers stayed at each other's side through four decades. One afternoon in her home in the town of Duson, his widow, Mabel Chenier, takes her late husband's last rubboard from its permanent place in the closet. She describes how devoted he was to his music. "Cleveland, he loved his rubbing board," she says, lifting the ridged vest up for display. "That was his life, that."

In 1966 Cleveland Chenier moved into this house with Mabel and her nine children from a previous marriage. One of Mabel's daughters, Rita Mouton, has joined the afternoon conversation. Rita's twelve-year-old daughter, Laqashia, has her grandfather's board around her shoulders. "He enjoyed playing, but he was so tired when he would come back," Mabel remembers. "We'd meet him at the corner there on Highway 90. Clifton would drop him there at three, four o'clock in the morning. When he'd get home, he takes a shower, and he would break that bread in the bowl, and put a little milk and sugar in that, that was his favorite."

Laqashia looks up. "He used to bring me and my brother some Reese's Pieces back."

"Yes indeed, it was fun in them days," Mabel continues. "I remember one time in eighty-one, he was in New York, and he said, 'Mabel, your son graduated this week.' I said, 'Yeah, he graduated.' I was ironing. He said, 'Go up there to Dallas and get you the beautiful and expensive dress, we're going to get married.' And that's what we did."

She takes the wedding photograph from the mantel and dusts it. "I met him in Carencro to a dance in 'sixty-four," she says. "I was thirty years old. My husband died when I was twenty-nine. I was sitting to a table, me and a girlfriend, and they had another guy sitting with my girlfriend. About eleven o'clock, he signed me with his hand. So I got up, and I went to the bandstand. He said, 'Where's your friend?' I said, 'I don't have any friend. I'm a widow.' He said, 'Oh, can I be in your company?' I said, 'I don't know.' He gave me some money for me to go buy what I wanted, and after the dance was over I said, 'Here's your money back, thank you.' I didn't know him, you see.

"So he said, 'Give me your phone number,' and he called me that Sunday afternoon. They were in St. Martinville at the Casino Club, and when I walked in there he started whistling, and he said, 'Look at that fine lady coming in.' I said, 'Oh Lord.' He said, 'Mabel, can I be still in your company?' I said, 'I don't know,' and they left three days after that to Los Angeles. They stayed there about three weeks and they came back, and that's when we started dating. He raised all nine of my kids."

Laqashia stops scratching the rubboard and listens to her grandmother.

"I never could understand how his playing was so beautiful," Mabel Chenier continues. "My kids would say, 'Mama, we could stand up all night and just look at Mr. Cleveland play the washboard.' They called him Mr. Cleveland. I thought Cleveland was going to be a hit-and-run, just come and pass, and go about his business. But he decided to stay right there. After he moved in, and the kids met him, my son said, 'Mama, nobody else is going to pass in between him. This is going to be our stepdaddy.' And he was only about nine years old.

"Cleveland played all weekend, and then on Monday morning, first thing he'd get up, he'd eat his breakfast, and all he'd do was polish. I mean, you'd swear it was a mirror. I had a carport, and he'd sit out there and clean. First he'd use SOS, and after that, he'd rub it with a dry towel until it was a shine. After that was clean, it was in the closet. Make sure nothing touches it so it don't scratch. He was particular."

Mabel Chenier and her daughter recall the times when they joined the band for trips to New Orleans and Houston. They were there for Lafayette dances that started at two in the morning and lasted through the next day, and for early Christmas mornings when the family would leave straight from midnight mass and head to the Blue Angel. "The next day, we couldn't cook our Christmas dinner, we were so drunk!" Rita Mouton laughs.

"Sometimes Cliff couldn't hold the accordion," her mother says, nodding. "In St. Martinville, he was so drunk one night, he said, 'Sister-in-law, go get me Alka Seltzer,' and I go get him that, and he said, 'Baby, you done it for me.' He drunk that and he started playing and he never stopped."

"They'd go four days without hardly no sleep."

"It was a killing! My little shoes, when I was ready to go dance, I didn't have to go get them, they jump out of the box and come meet me! That was how we used to do it."

"That was some good times."

"Monday I had to go to cook at the store, sometime I catch myself falling asleep standing around that crawfish etouffee."

"You couldn't sleep for sure," Mouton says. "Oh no, there's no way. It was just too live."

"Dress up to kill. Party dresses. They come there with that big old fifth, half a gallon of Crown Royal, VO. Sometime we had long dresses. I know, me, many time I went to Houston. I would go over there and borrow from my daughter-in-law and pretend it was mine, and nobody knew. I'm telling you."

"But not too long, because I didn't want nothing in my way!"

"She didn't want nothing to twist in her legs," laughs Chenier, "because she stays on that floor."

"I used to be there all the time. Oh Lord, you name it. Anywhere around here or Houston, Port Arthur, I was there. I used to drive them everywhere to them dances. With Big Charles. It was Cleveland, Little Buck, Robert, Joe Morris, they had John Hart, and C. J. And C. J. couldn't find another uncle like he had in Cleveland. Cleveland would take time with him, explain how to deal with the family, with his dad."

"Sometimes they had to look and see that they had no ladies for them to talk, because they had some strong jokes. Yes, indeed, it would make your hair rise sometimes."

"You just had to cry," Mouton says. "Laugh and cry at the same time, with those jokes they would come out with. From way back."

"And when he'd come back after being gone for a few days, he'd open that door and throw his hat first, to see if he was welcome."

"When Cleveland moved here I was ten. And I really enjoyed that man. I mean, he did a whole lot for us. I can just see him now, sitting here, joking with us."

Laqashia has returned to playing the rubboard, and Mabel Chenier positions her wedding picture back on the mantel. "Many times I'm sitting down in here by myself," she says. "I play the music and I say, 'Lord, remind me of the good old days.'"

## IV

By the 1980s, Clifton Chenier was beginning to receive the honors that crown a distinguished career. He was given a National Heritage Fellowship from the National Endowment for the Arts, and played in the White House for President Reagan. But the greatest satisfaction came in 1984, when he won a "Best Traditional or Ethnic Recording" Grammy for his Alligator record *I'm Here*. Whenever he played a dance, he'd remind the audience that it takes a lifetime of music to win an award like that. In an interview with Barry Ancelet shortly after the Grammies, he acknowledged the stubborn traditionalism of his former producer Chris Strachwitz. "What fits you, stick with it, you know," he said. "That's what I did. I figured French music fit me and I stayed with it. Rock and roll didn't get me that Grammy. Zydeco got me that Grammy. Maybe that's going to show some of the young ones that's where it's at, right here."

He continued to live in Lafayette, sharing his home with his wife, Margaret, and a frantic Chihuahua named for his father, Joseph. The Cheniers opened a zydeco club in Loreauville, near the sugarcane fields where Clifton once worked. He had new hits with songs like "Oh, My Lucille" and "Hot Tamale Baby," and after years of plying his trade in bars and churches, he could name his price. "People ask me how can I get up on the bandstand and play four hours without stopping," he told Ben Sandmel. "It's because I've always been a hard worker, you see. And when I tell you good night, you can hand me a thousand dollars and I ain't going to play no more."

Chenier remained particular about how his music should sound, traveling with a separate sound system just for his accordion. His battles with record producers also continued. In San Francisco he abruptly canceled an Arhoolie session after a dispute over his choice of bandmembers. When he went into the studios with Bruce Iglauer to record a follow-up record to *I'm Here!*, the results were disastrous. Alligator had licensed the first Chenier album from producer Sam Charters, and Iglauer remembers that he was looking forward to the chance to make one himself. But things started badly and slid quickly downhill.

"We went into the studio in Chicago after he had done four or five days at Fitzgerald's," Iglauer recalls. "We made a deal and shook hands on it, and we agreed on some of the songs. He had to have his check cashed before he started, and then he was determined to do the whole album in three hours. He was doing one take on everything. The first songs sounded terrible, and the engineer realized there were dead speakers in his amp. So he remiked it, and we continued, and it became clear that he was not doing the songs that had been discussed. So we got about ten songs in the can, including the first ones where the amp was working improperly, and he said, 'OK, I'm done.' I said, 'What?' and he said, 'I'm done.' He was adamant that he wasn't going to record anymore."

Throughout his career, Chenier was always suspicious that any alternate takes might be used for another record. It was a lesson, Strachwitz recalls, that Chenier picked up on from his cousin, Lightnin' Hopkins. Iglauer says he promised to give him the tapes for those songs, but Chenier wasn't satisfied. As it had during his first session with Strachwitz twenty years earlier, the discussion grew heated. But this time no compromise was reached. Iglauer told Chenier that he'd spent a lot on the session and didn't have an album to show for it. Chenier asked how much money had been spent. Remembers Iglauer: "I turned to the engineer and we figured it out, and it was eleven or twelve hundred dollars. So I told him that, and figured that would stop him. But he reached in his pocket and pulled out a wad of money, and counted off the amount. Then he took the master tape and walked out. Somebody in the band said, 'Oh God, now I'll never get paid.' It was one of the most horrifying experiences I ever had in a recording studio." Chenier took the tapes back to Louisiana. After several frustrated attempts to release the record himself, he leased it to Floyd Soileau, who titled it *Country Boy Now Grammy Winner 1984!*

"He was pretty hard-headed," recalls Landreth. "He didn't like nobody telling him what to do, that's a fact. One time in Minneapolis, he became convinced that he was being recorded without his permission. He stopped right in the middle, he just started cussing out the sound guy, 'I know what you're going to do with this tape, you're going to take it and you're just going to steal it and make an album.' And it was hilarious watching this little Woody Allen type of university guy try to explain: 'No, Mr. Chenier, sorry, Mr. Chenier.' If he wasn't happy with something, he'd just stop right then and there. And everybody in the band was just like, 'No big deal. King has spoken.'"

But there was one thing even the King couldn't control. By the early eighties, Chenier's health had begun to deteriorate. He was diagnosed with diabetes, and his body had clearly suffered from decades of hard drinking and hanging a thirty-seven-pound accordion from his shoulders for four straight hours. Mabel Chenier remembers that Cleveland took it hard when Clifton's health began to fail and he had to start canceling gigs. "Because, you see, they never spent a weekend at home. Never did. All Saints week, that was the only week they wouldn't play. And Good Friday. When Clifton took sick, he missed that music, and missed to be on the road with his brother, and he would cry many times."

Chenier received dialysis treatments three times a week, and part of his foot was amputated. The dialysis made his fingers numb. He spent his days squeezing a rubber ball to try to rebuild his strength. When his doctors told him not to tour, he routinely defied their warnings. Soon, Louisiana musicians began to hear of how Clifton would get an overnight pass from the hospital, jump in his car, and drive to a dance. And when he was too weak to squeeze the accordion, he played harmonica and sang, hiring a cousin from Galveston to fill in for him on the lead instrument. "Every now and then Cliff would reach over and he would push the stops on the accordion to get the right sound that he wanted for a particular song," Landreth remembers.

Occasionally, when Chenier was too weak to leave his bed, he'd send his band on without him. This prompted a series of rumors in the zydeco world. Some said that he had died, others that he could no longer play accordion. Then, one memorable night at Antone's in Austin, Texas, he proved them all wrong. He had started the night by coming out onstage with his band, playing harmonica and singing. Then he stopped in the middle of a song and shouted, "Give me that thing!" He took the accordion from his cousin and strapped it on, and played it for the rest of the night. "He cut loose, and people went nuts," Landreth recalls. "After that, he started playing the gigs again."

Chenier bought a custom-built accordion that didn't require him to squeeze the bellows. "They said I was down, but I'm back," he told the dancers at Grant Street Dance Hall in Lafayette, as recounted in Barry Ancelet's book *The Makers of Cajun Music*. "Everything's just fine and it's going to get better after while. I've got this new accordion, special-made for me in Italy, and I'm going to sit down to play. But I'm going to make sure that you don't sit down tonight."

And on the title track of *I'm Here!* he responded directly to stories that he was on his deathbed:

> Everybody talks about me,
> Say, well I'm dead and gone.
> The good Lord left me here for a purpose
> And I'm back again. . . .
>
> Well, I'm the zydeco man —
> Everybody knows I'm here.

Chenier's tours had always been unpredictable; now they seemed to become life-threatening on an almost regular basis. Little Buck Senegal remembers a trip from California to Austin, where the band was scheduled to play a week before returning to Lafayette: "I was doing the driving for the band, and we got to our first stop in Arizona. We had an ice chest, where we kept our baloney and bread, soda water, beer. But we didn't know Cliff kept his insulin in there. He said, 'Hey man, next time y'all stop at that rest area, you clean that ice chest, take all of that old ice, and all that baloney and bread, and we'll get some fresh stuff.' So Cleveland grabbed the ice chest and just threw everything away in a big barrel. Man, about fifty miles from Austin, Clifton goes in that ice chest for his insulin to take the shot, and he can't find it. We cleaned the thing out. All he said was, 'Buckaroo, get me to Austin. Don't worry about no ticket, man.' I must have drove that little truck with a trailer eighty-five or ninety miles an hour."

They finally reached Austin, and took Chenier directly to a hospital. The musician was furious when he heard that the club was considering canceling his show. "Clifton said, 'We ain't canceling nothing,'" Senegal remembers. "That was about maybe around seven o'clock. That cat's feet was so big that he couldn't put slippers on. And at ten o'clock, Clifton walked on the bandstand and played till two o'clock without stopping. I said, 'That's an iron man.'"

Despite these efforts, Chenier finally had to slow down. Many of his original Red Hot Louisiana Band members were forced to move to other bands for steady work, and he surrounded himself with new players, including guitarists Sherman Robertson, Danny Caron, and Harry Hypolite, and bassist Wayne Burns. Perhaps recognizing that he could no longer play all the parts on his accordion, he created an expanded horn section with his son, C. J. Chenier, on saxophone and Warren Ceasar on trumpet. But if he was moving more slowly, he was still conquering new territory for zydeco, including the blues capital of Chicago.

"I was at Jazz Fest in New Orleans, and Marcia Ball told me to check Cliff out," remembers Bill Fitzgerald, owner of Fitzgerald's club. "I talked to him and told him I was from Chicago, and he came and played four nights. By the end of that weekend, he had a line down the block. I think it was exciting for him to come into the home of the blues and kick ass, and he did. He played here a couple times a year, and all the time he was getting dialysis treatments, which I set up for him. All the nurses got to know him, and then they'd all come to his shows."

Fitzgerald took the band to Cubs games, and he also helped Chenier get a spot playing the Chicago Blues Festival. Most gratifying to Chenier were visits from Chicago bluesmen such as Lonnie Brooks, who had come up playing in his first bands. But other nights in Chicago were rough going. Fitzgerald remembers that he could chart Chenier's performance by his dialysis treatments. "Sometimes he could hardly even talk. He'd get a sore throat from the dialysis, and he just kind of kept to himself. He'd like to have salted peanuts sometimes, and a little something to drink. And he'd be back there sometimes with a five-gallon bucket because he would keep getting sick.

"One Friday night, he couldn't play. C. J. had to lead the band. People were running up to me and asking if Cliff needed a doctor. I'd have to tell them, 'Listen, he wouldn't be doing this if he didn't want to do it.' Then next night, he showed up, he had his blue King of Zydeco jacket on and felt great. He had this chair with a blue crushed-velvet cushion that he'd bring with him. Big Charles would wheel him out, and he would lift himself up and put himself in the chair. Then he would get up there and just kick ass.

"Some of my best memories are due to knowing him and being involved with these guys," Fitzgerald concludes. "Even after his amputation he was supposed to play up here, and he had to call me and cancel. It was the day after Father's Day, and he called me and said, 'We're ready to come up when you want us.' That was very moving to me, that after all the things that he had going wrong with him, he just wanted to be back out there."

Chenier was telling his musicians, his crowds, and the club owners that he was doing fine, but he knew the tours were becoming more taxing. He had already lost part of his foot to his diabetes; now he had to have part of his other leg amputated. "One time, I really didn't think he was going to make it," Sonny Landreth recalls. "I went to the hospital, and there was nobody there but Margaret. And I went in and, man, he looked bad. He had constant hiccups, he was in really bad shape. And he said, 'I'm going to be all right, I'm going to come out of this and I'm going to get up, and I'm going to take you with me, and we're going to hit the road again. I'm going to bring you with me.' He was laying in the bed, he had tubes in him and all this stuff. I just started crying. I said, 'Man, when you're ready to go, you just call me, I'll be there.'"

During one particularly strenuous trip, the band was detained at the Canadian border. The promoter had failed to get all their papers in order. Chenier was forced to leave a five-hundred-dollar deposit, and his accordion was sealed inside the trailer. On the same tour, Chenier became upset with his trumpet player, Warren Ceasar, and a fight broke out in the van. Chenier's endurance reached its limits. Ceasar recalls that the bandleader went into the glove compartment and pulled out "Hawaiian," his pistol. While Charles White sped down the highway, the band jumped in and tried to retrieve the gun from their leader. "I never will forget that day until I die," Ceasar says. "It was like it all stopped there. He had just had enough of it."

In the summer of 1987, Wilbert Guillory and Ruth Foote visited Clifton and Margaret Chenier to bring the musician his contract for the fifth annual Zydeco Festival. "Clifton was so weak he couldn't raise his hand hardly, and his

*Clifton Chenier and Rockin' Dopsie at the Southwest Louisiana Zydeco Festival, 1987.*

*Clifton Chenier on stage at the Zydeco Festival.*

wife had to sign the contract," remembers Guillory. "When I left from there, I said, 'I just booked this man, but I don't know if he's going to make it to the festival.'"

But that September, Chenier was at the festival in Plaisance, Louisiana. As he waited for his turn, he escaped the hot sun in the shade beneath the stage. He sat there through the day, dressed in his blue King of Zydeco tuxedo jacket, talking with friends. Then the Red Hot Louisiana Band started the set, and the crowd danced as C. J. Chenier led the musicians through a couple of R&B standards. When Chenier began to make his way up to the stage, the dancers stopped and pressed forward. "Hold the king, we're going to bring on the bishop," said the announcer, introducing a local church official who was to give his benediction. When the bishop was through, Chenier approached the center of the stage, supported by Rockin' Dopsie — who was then being billed as the Prince of Zydeco — and a local sheriff. Dopsie removed Chenier's tuxedo jacket and draped it around his plush chair, and helped lower the accordion to his lap.

"How many times in your life have you had the opportunity to see a prince present a king!" the announcer called out. "Look at them! What a beautiful sight in Plaisance, Louisiana."

Chenier seemed pinned to his chair by his accordion, but he leaned his head forward to the microphone. "Yeah, yeah!" he whispered. He ran his fingers lightly down the keys, deciding on the position. He looked down the line at his band — all younger men, for Cleveland was sick that day. He started with a blues, barely moving his hands, focusing all his strength on his voice. Then he looked out at the crowd, said in a near whisper, "Hello, world," then went into "I'm a Hog for You." The crowd cheered.

That title isn't really bad, he had once promised a church hall full of dancers in California, it only sounds like it's bad. "I'm a hog for you, rooting around your door."

Behind him, the scene on the stage was close to a circus. Musicians and public officials wandered about, and local sheriffs took advantage of the campaign season to throw trinkets into the crowd. He finished the song, left his fingers on the keys, and launched into another blues. A small child wandered into the commotion of the stage. The sheriffs took her backstage. For the first time that day, the man, the accordion, and his band were alone. Chenier leaned into the microphone again, and, in a voice that began to build in strength, he sang the words he once wrote for his mother:

> Remember
> When I get home,

I'm going to start,
Lord, start
All over again.
I'm coming home.
I'm coming back home.
'Cause that's where I belong.

He swayed in time to the song. A tear clouded his left eye and traced down his cheek. He looked up, and saw that his young niece was standing next to him on the stage. She moved over to his chair to put her arm across his shoulders. He finished playing, and she quickly bent down and kissed him. Then the song was over.

Chenier next launched into a fast zydeco, repeating *"Bye-bye, maman"* over and over. He looked up again at his crowd. "Hello, world," he repeated, a little more loudly than before. He ran through Ray Charles's "What'd I Say," and his niece moved to center stage and danced. Then he stopped, and held his accordion shut. He looked out at the audience with a stern expression.

"You know, they had a rumor around here that Clifton Chenier done died," he scolded. "So now you can see if I'm dead, right? All right." The crowd cheered, and he laughed softly. "I'm in the 'B' class," he promised. "I'm going to *be* here."

At the end of his set, he pushed his microphone away and waited for Big Charles White to remove his accordion and help him offstage. He left the King of Zydeco jacket behind. One of the sheriffs picked it up and folded it, then looked around, uncertain what to do.

Following the festival, Chenier took his Red Hot Louisiana Band on another tour to the Northeast. He seemed to know that it was his last time on the road. "We were in Boston, and I'll never forget that day," Ceasar remembers. "He had his own room and was real pale, and he didn't want any reporters to come talk to him. So I went and checked on him, and C. J. came. And he said, 'You all sit down. I want to tell you something. I want you all to go ahead on with the band, I'm going to let you young boys go on with it. I'm going to stay home with my club.' I could see it in his eyes, he knew he was dying."

When he returned home, he immediately checked into Lafayette General Medical Center. "When he fell sick, real bad, they rushed him to General, and I was at Cleveland's house," remembers Senegal. "We all took off. Cleveland and his wife and one of Cleveland's stepsons was there, so I brought them. His wife was in there, two or three other ladies. When I

*C. J. Chenier ( front left) and the Red Hot Louisiana Band in Clifton Chenier's funeral.*

*Clifton Chenier's grave, Loreauville, Louisiana.*

walked in, his face just lit up. He had them big old long fingers, and he grabbed my hand like that, and he said, 'It's rough, Buckaroo.'"

The next day, December 12, 1987, Senegal left to play a date in Houston with Rockin' Dopsie. As soon as he checked into the hotel, his phone rang. Clifton Chenier had died. He remembers that night at the Catholic church hall. "Dopsie made the announcement. He said, 'Ladies and gentlemen, I got something sad to tell y'all. Clifton Chenier passed away.' A lot of them picked up their stuff and left. And the rest couldn't believe it, you know. But I had gotten word from Cleveland's house, so I knew it was true.

"That night, I couldn't even play myself, man, everything just dropped out of me. It looked like the music went bad. Nothing was sounding right, it's like we couldn't even start the songs or end them. A lot of people started crying in that place, man."

The funeral was in the Immaculate Heart of Mary Church in Lafayette. While Clifton Chenier's body lay in the coffin, a crown next to his head, C. J. Chenier played "I'm Coming Home." An estimated four thousand people turned out in furs and hats, driving a fleet of Cadillacs. Jumpin' Joe Morris admits that he stayed home that day. "That would have been too emotional of a thing for me," he says. "You see, I'd been with the man so long. One of the boys, Robert St. Judy, he told me he got sick, because he couldn't stand it. He went to the church, and he had to go to the doctor, he got so upset behind it."

Chenier's passing was marked throughout Louisiana. Accordionist Walter Polite was playing a dance in Eunice the day of the funeral. "And the bossman told me, he said: 'I want you to play just Clifton's records. Don't play nothing else. His funeral is on now.' So that's what I did, played Clifton's records. The people didn't dance, they just sat down and listened."

Clifton Chenier was buried in Loreauville, near the sugarcane and his zydeco club, which remains open to this day. His grave, like Amédé Ardoin's, is unmarked.

Cleveland Chenier continued to play rubboard with Sonny Landreth and his nephew C. J. One Sunday afternoon in 1991, he took his wife, Mabel, to a community dinner. He ate two plates of barbecue, and turned to her. She remembers what happened next: "He said, 'Come on baby, some gin!' I said, 'What are you doing drinking?' He said, 'Mabel, I feel so good.'" Then Cleveland suffered a stroke, falling into a ditch and breaking his collar bone. Mabel rode with him to the hospital. "I said, 'Let's go say the prayers, we're going to forgive one another.' I said, 'We never did a bad thing in our lives till now, but we're going to forgive one another.' I recited the Our Father, the Hail Mary, the Act of Contrition. While I was saying that, he had tears, and then he passed away."

Cleveland Chenier died on May 7, 1991, nine days short of his seventieth birthday. Mabel buried her husband in a cemetery in Scott, and ordered a tombstone decorated with a carved rubboard and a wreath of bottle openers.

The music of Clifton Chenier still plays loudly on zydeco radio stations throughout Southwest Louisiana, as well as on a few remaining jukeboxes along the Gulf Coast to Houston. His son continues to lead the Red Hot Louisiana Band, and many of the musicians who passed through Clifton's ranks are bandleaders today, including Buckwheat Zydeco, Warren Ceasar, Sherman Robertson, Sonny Landreth, Little Buck Senegal, Lonnie Brooks, and Etta James. Robert St. Judy lives in Dallas and drums with Li'l Willie Davis. Jumpin' Joe Morris has recently started playing bass again; he had stopped for a while after the death of a family member.

Chenier's contributions to zydeco extend beyond his own music and band. Mama Lena Pitre recalls one night when the musician was staying with her family in Richmond, California. "My grandson Andre was about seven years old, and he'd catch Andre and laugh and hold him right on the arm," she says. "And then Clifton'd say, 'See how his arm bends? See that arm make a curl right here? That's going to be my man. That's going to be an accordion man.' Today, Andre Thierry leads his own band in the Bay Area.

Clifton Chenier's influence is acknowledged by a long list of musicians. "When I'm playing my accordion in a blues club, my mind's on him all the time," says Roy Carrier. Young accordionist Corey Arceneaux served as an altar boy for the funeral at Immaculate Heart of Mary. He can recite from memory the lines that Clifton once heard from his father: "If you're going to be something, be something. If you're going to be nothing, be nothing."

Chenier also inspired players of an earlier generation. Creole fiddler Canray Fontenot remembered one day in the early 1960s when he ran into the accordionist at a bar. "Where are you working tonight?" Chenier had asked.

"I ain't working nowhere," replied Fontenot. "Man, it's eight years now I don't play. I done sold my stuff."

"Aw man, you quit at the wrong time!" Chenier insisted. "Things are just beginning to get good. That music is going to move up North. Go get you a fiddle and start playing, and the first thing you know they're going to want you all over the world." Not long after, Fontenot was visited by Ralph Rinzler, seeking artists for the Newport Folk Festival.

"It was nineteen seventy-four or seventy-five when Clifton Chenier came to visit at the record shop," remembers producer Floyd Soileau. "We were about ready to do this *Boogie in Black & White* album with Rod Bernard. And he said to me, 'Soileau, you better get with that zydeco, because it's coming on strong.' It reminded me of when Dewey Balfa had tried to tell me that I should be recording traditional Cajun music. That was when I decided I was going to establish a label, and we called it Maison de Soul, and we were going to do zydeco recordings."

Explains Sonny Landreth: "He's like any of the great bluesmen that people are writing all this history about. I mean, that's Cliff on the accordion. He had this rare combination of gifts. Sometimes I remember back to those days to remind myself why I'm doing this in the first place. It's influenced me in the songs that I write today. That's where I really learned about rhythms. And there was an amazing energy that would come off that bandstand with him. It's something I can still tap into."

Other musicians also speak of his impact as a spiritual experience. Ambrose Sam once had a dream that Chenier came to him at night and knelt by his bed, and asked him to pray. Nathan Williams had a similar experience. "When Clifton Chenier died, and after I went to the wake, I came home," he remembers. "He came to me like natural, like in my sleep. He said, 'Keep on going, you're going to make it.'"

His name has been memorialized in song by many zydeco and Cajun bands, including Rosie Ledet, BeauSoleil, and Zachary Richard. In 1985 Paul Simon came to Louisiana hoping to record with Chenier. He was disappointed to learn that he was too sick to play, and penned his devotion in the song "That Was Your Mother," where he sings of "standing in the shadow of Clifton Chenier, dancing the night away."

In fact, the scope of Chenier's influence may be the only thing that nearly every zydeco musician can agree on. Clifton Chenier may not have been the first to call the music "zydeco," and other players of his day may have also been mixing blues, R&B, and old Creole songs on the piano accordion. But the zydeco accordionist from Port Barre commanded respect like no one before him. He embodied the qualities necessary for a postwar black Frenchman from the state of Louisiana to be a success. He was as sophisticated and urban as he was down-home and rural. He and his hot rod piano accordion — some models came complete with a shiny grille and taillights — were versatile. When Clifton Chenier stood on the bandstand, his tie flung across his shoulder or turned completely backwards, and sent his fingers up and down his keyboard, he showed the world just how far his music — his culture — could go.

* * *

"Three-piece all the time," Little Buck Senegal says, pulling his van onto a gravel parking lot in Lafayette. "Big tie all the time. You never saw him just with a shirt and pants. Not from the time I knew him."

John Hart packs tobacco in his pipe. "Oh, he was a mighty man, you know."

"I'll tell you what. That was a man. Nobody can compare with him. He had that feeling, that touch, and them big old hands. His hands were two times like mine. But that's from years of playing, you know."

"There will never be another man like him," agrees Hart.

"We played one night in St. Martinville, and we're on the stage, waiting on Clifton," Senegal remembers. "The place is packed. And Cleveland's tall, and he busted a lightbulb that was hanging from the ceiling. So Cleveland turned it off. Clifton said, 'Hey, we've been in the dark all our life.' He said, 'It's time to hit the light, put that light on, and don't touch it no more!'"

Senegal steers across a bumpy dirt parking lot, and Hart reaches for his saxophone case. They will play a lot of Clifton Chenier songs tonight, and next week Senegal will be back on the route to Opelousas to do the same. "We had the feeling," he says. "And that cat used to praise us. He'd say, 'Man, y'all played tonight. Y'all pushed, man.' And he would laugh. He laughed on all his albums. Listen to them. After almost every song. He'd laugh, and he'd say, 'That was good.'"

*C. J. Chenier.*

# 7

# CARRYING ON

T HE DUET WASN'T PLANNED. One afternoon in the early 1980s, in a basement apartment in Chicago, Clifton Chenier pulled out a chair from the kitchen table, and he sat down with his favorite accordion — the one he called Black Gal — and started playing. His son, C. J., sat across from him with his accordion. For the first and last time in their lives, the two men played together.

There had been other times when Clifton would watch C. J. play, and give him advice. "Don't pull so hard, you'll tear that accordion," he'd shout over the notes. "You're running them together," he'd say about his son's left hand. "You have to separate them."

C. J. Chenier knew that his father had good reasons for teaching him about the bass hand. He'd watch when other musicians would come up to the bandstand to try to steal an accordion lick. Clifton would just drop his right hand from the keys and keep on playing his bass. He could play the whole song like that. The other players would shake their heads and go back to their tables.

If they remained up there, Clifton had one more secret weapon: he would lay the "monkey" on them. That's what he called pressing the accordion up against his stomach and shaking the bellows, and sending the vibrato out into the crowd. That always put them back down to their chairs, he'd say.

Those were some of the lessons that C. J. Chenier had been receiving from his father. But that day in the 1980s, they both had their accordions out and just played. It wasn't even a song. They made it up as they went along. When they were through, they put their accordions down and got ready for that night's show.

"That was a long time ago," C. J. Chenier is saying. He's back in Chicago, in his Holiday Inn room, on the six-thousandth mile of a three-week tour, leading the Red Hot Louisiana Band. Chenier has a couple hours before he goes onstage at Fitzgerald's, the club where he and his father used to play. He's wearing dress pants and a white T-shirt. Two suits — decorated by his wife with spangles, bandleader-style fringed shoulders, and a tiny stitched guardian angel — are spread across his bed. Chenier chooses the blue and black double-breasted, and hangs the royal blue behind the door. Then he sits down, ready to talk about how he became a zydeco man.

"I guess it was meant to be, you know?" he starts. "Who would have thought I would end up in this position, from the refinery town of Port Arthur, Texas. And I think if my dad wouldn't have been in the business, I probably would still be there, weighing three hundred pounds and working at the Gulf or Texaco, if I didn't get blown up. I was doing all that when I was twenty years old, chipping sulphur, busting concrete, digging holes looking for gas leaks. But then I got a call, and it all started from there."

Clayton Joseph Thompson was born in Port Arthur in 1957. His mother, Mildred Bell, worked as a housecleaner. His father did not have any children with his wife, Margaret, and was then dividing his time between Lafayette and Houston and the road. C. J. was given his mother's maiden name. "All my life he's been there, but it's just like he wasn't there all the time," he says of his father. "I knew he was a musician, and I knew he did records, but I sure didn't know he was as popular as he was."

When C. J. was growing up, he explains, zydeco music was for the old people. The kids in school told him that his dad was playing "chanky-chank." But if the accordion was the furthest thing from his mind, he also discovered he could play just about anything else he put his hands on. In third grade he picked up the saxophone, because his mother told him it was a good blues instrument. Then he went on to play piano and organ, and even flute and tuba. "I always had this knack for picking up an instrument, as long as I can remember," he says. "My mother used to get mad because they'd tell her, 'Your son was at church playing the blues.' I'd be in church, and I'd just sit down and I'd start to boogie. You know, it's just been there with me all of my life."

A teenager in the disco era, C. J. was a sax and keyboard player in a local cover band called Carl Wayne and the Magnificent Seven. But after he graduated from high school, he recalls, he couldn't get anything started. He got a music scholarship to Texas Southern University, but stayed only six months. He started a funk group called Hot Ice, but it was only part-time. By the time he was twenty, he was living at his mother's house and figuring on joining his friends in the refineries. Then came the call.

It was on a Sunday, she remembers. Hot Ice was playing a church bazaar, and C. J. looked up to see the mother of one of the band members standing in front of him. "She said, 'Your mama wants you to call,'" Chenier says. "So I went to her house and I called, and she was like, 'You need to come home, because your daddy wants you to go on the road with him.' I said, 'Huh?' You know, out of the clear blue.

"I said, 'Mama, I don't know.' But she got me. She said, 'Well, if you don't want to go, that's up to you. But y'all ain't got no job, and you better get over here.' I said, 'Oh man, what am I going to do?' Because here I was, one week before my twenty-first birthday, getting ready to hit the road with all these old dudes."

There was no time to practice; the first show with his father was scheduled that night. "I didn't even have a chance to prepare myself or nothing, man," Chenier says. "So I went on home, and I threw my little stuff in a bag or whatever I had. I didn't even have too much to wear. And I went to Bridge City, to the Sparkle Paradise. I was expecting to see John Hart there. But when I got there, John Hart wasn't there, he was sick. So I was like, 'Man, what's going on?' Because I hadn't really played my saxophone for six months, and I'm going to stand right in the center of the stage with my daddy, not knowing a single song they're playing. I didn't know what to do."

His father wasn't offering a lot of advice, so C. J. turned to the Red Hot Louisiana Band. "The guys in the band — Little Buck, Big Robert, Jumpin' Joe, and my uncle Cleveland — they were all so much fun-loving guys, man, that they started making me feel comfortable right away. They weren't pushy, they weren't demanding, and they knew I didn't know nothing. I always liked his song 'Hot Rod,' because that was just *Peter Gunn*. I knew that. The rest of the songs were boogies and waltzes, and they all sounded like Japanese to me. But the guys allowed me time to learn the song without giving me a big hassle. And that first tour, that turned out to be the best time I ever had in my life."

The band drove from Bridge City, Texas, to Austin, where they stayed for a week. From there they went on to California to play church dances in

Los Angeles and San Francisco. They continued up the west coast to Canada, and then returned along the same route. "For somebody that had never been out of Port Arthur, Texas, I couldn't believe it," Chenier remembers. "I was used to playing a disco, where they do a little cool dance and all that. But man, I started playing those zydeco gigs and seeing those people having such a good time, that's what really drew me into that music. I thought, 'Man, if those people are having this much fun, there's got to be something good about this stuff.'"

Over time, the saxophonist began to distinguish one song from another, and he learned the secret to being in the Red Hot Louisiana Band: following the private cues that his father used to communicate with his players. "When he was talking to Warren Ceasar, he'd say, 'Blow your horn man,'" C. J. explains. "When he was talking to me, he'd just say, 'Aannhhh!' That was my signal. And when he wanted to play just accordion and drums together, and he wanted the band to lay out, he'd just make a little head motion. He'd throw his head back and close his eyes, and that was our signal: OK, it's time for him to play by himself."

Along the way, his father also told him stories about where his music started. He talked about the house dances, where you'd pay a nickel to come in and get a plate of snap beans and fish. He told him about playing all night with just an accordion and a washboard, and about the days when a man might be told to wear white gloves and play his accordion through a window. C. J. also got to know his uncle Cleveland, and learned to stay out of the way when the two brothers argued. "But you could tell they loved each other, too," he says, and then he shakes his head. "I miss them cats so much, it's a shame."

When Clifton Chenier invited his son to join the Red Hot Louisiana Band, did he plan on grooming him to be its leader? C. J. isn't sure of the answer, but he knows that his father was pleased when he started to show an interest in the accordion. "When we used to get ready to play, I would plug it up for him," he remembers. "And as I was doing that, I'd play a few notes. And I think he was proud of that, because every time somebody would come in the room, he'd say, 'C. J., run him a scale, run him a scale.'" Chenier laughs. "And it just went from there."

Clifton Chenier bragged about his son's progress when he was interviewed by Ben Sandmel in 1983 for *Louisiana Life* magazine. "All them youngsters, I want them to know to follow in their daddy's footsteps sometimes," he said. "See, I got my boy C. J., he's moving on pretty good now."

When Clifton Chenier's health had begun to fail, he first hired Jumpin'

Joe Morris's brother Gene to open his shows. Eventually he turned that task over to his son, and began to let him know that his time to lead would come: "His exact words were, 'C. J., the ol' hog ain't going to always be here. One day, you got to take over for me, and you got to learn that accordion.'"

The two became closer than ever before. Some Sundays, Clifton would pick up C. J. and bring him along on his regular route to see friends, to drink and gossip. But there was still another important step, C. J. recalls. "I was Clayton Thompson when I first started playing with him, because I had my mother's maiden name. As time went on, I'd have chicks start calling me 'Chenier,' and when they'd talk about me a little bit in the papers, it was 'Chenier.' So he and I sat down and talked about it. I said, 'Hey man, I don't know what to do, everybody calls me Clifton Junior.' So one thing led to another, and it was decided between us that it was time for me to have his last name. We went to the court and did the thing, and then I was Chenier. And there it went."

"I never caught myself going to imitate him, or try to play like he played, because that ain't going to happen," C. J. Chenier continues. "I could only do like I do, because the man was incredible. So if I play one of his songs, instead of trying to play his stuff note for note, I play it the way I play it. All he really told me was to do the best I could do with my own style. That's the way he said to do it, and that's what it is."

Like his father, C. J. Chenier plays only piano-key accordion, and he mixes slow blues into his dance sets. "I might add a few things, but basically everything I know now, I learned from him," he says. "Way back there, man, when we used to play the Blue Angel, by one o'clock in the morning it'd be smoking in there. He'd be hitting those blues, and everybody would be just feeling good. But today, there's a lot of times I go to zydeco, you don't even hear the blues, man.

"You know, my daddy was the King of Zydeco, but sometimes you'd see him walking around just humming the blues to himself," he remembers. "He just had the blues in him. And through my years of playing saxophone with him, I automatically thought all these different things he's playing belonged here, because that's what made up his dance all night. He's the one that showed me the boogie belongs here, he's the one showed me that waltzes and blues belong. He's the one that showed me you can play what you want on the accordion."

Among Chenier's duties were arranging charts and helping out with payroll — "Math was one of my better subjects," he says — and he also began to exert some control over the band. When his father fired one of the musicians, C. J. went around him and hired him back, telling him to just show up and get onstage. "There wasn't nobody too special for him to do without, including me," he says. "He just figured he could play by himself if he had to. He was very set in his ways. He was stubborn. And my mom always tells me I'm just like him. One time she got so mad at me, man, she punched me. 'Yes,' she said, 'you're just like your daddy.' Pow. I didn't know how my daddy was, I was growing up like *I* was. But if I turned out like him, it just happened that way, you know."

Over the years, Clifton loaned and gave his son several accordions to practice on and play. One day he told C. J. to bring in a Hohner he had recently given him, because the Hard Rock Cafe had called and wanted to buy it. C. J. was disappointed, but he brought it back. Then, on his way out, he saw his father reach down and grab another accordion. He couldn't believe what was happening.

"He said, 'Take that one.' I said, 'Huh?' He said, 'Take that one.'" The accordion was his father's favorite, a black Soprano model with his name emblazoned in white block letters running down the center. He'd used it for his best Arhoolie recordings, and as much as he'd tried, he'd never been able to find another accordion quite like it. It was the Black Gal.

"He said, 'I'm letting you use it now, I'm not giving it to you. I'm letting you use it.' I said, 'All right.' I took off, man, it's been mine ever since. He just told me to keep it, and then he passed away. His wife tried to get it back, but there wasn't no way I was giving that thing back. That accordion has got a sound that just won't quit."

At first, C. J. played Black Gal regularly. But his father was right, he says. He pulls too hard, and he's tough on accordions. He has since retired the instrument.

From the time he started in the band, C. J. Chenier knew his father was having health problems. But Clifton would get sick, then he'd make another seemingly miraculous recovery. "Out of the hospital, he'd hit the bandstand that night, man," he says. "When he'd get sick sometimes, he'd fumble the blues, sometimes he'd fumble the boogie, but he played the zydeco like there wasn't nothing wrong with him."

When he went to his father's hospital room one night in 1987, C. J. never imagined it would be the last time he'd see him alive. "He called me. He told me he was in the hospital, so I went to see him. He looked at me, and kind of shook his head like that. You know, sick again. I stayed there for a couple hours, and we were supposed to play El Sid O's that night. I said,

'Well, I'm going to go home for a while and get ready for the gig tonight.' I hadn't been home thirty minutes when a lady called and said, 'You better come back to the hospital. Clifton Chenier just died.' Man, my whole world dropped, right there."

His relationship with Margaret Chenier had always been strained, so he was both surprised and grateful that she included him in preparations for his father's funeral. Then she asked him if he would sing for the service. "As much as I wanted to be close to his wife, she never really did open the door for me too much," he says. "But when that happened to him, she didn't exclude me. I felt like I was really part of the family then. She asked me to sing, which meant a lot to me. So I sang a couple songs, and then I did 'I'm Coming Home.' That's still a rough song for me. I jive you not, sometimes I just can't sing it."

The night after his father's funeral, C. J. Chenier took the Red Hot Louisiana Band to play a dance in Houston. It was a difficult gig, but he got through it by imagining what his father would have said if he canceled. The following week, he was called for new bookings, and the next year he went back to Arhoolie and made his first record as leader of the Red Hots, *Let Me In Your Heart*.

"I had to come up on my own merit," Chenier says. "I couldn't ride on my daddy's name, because it wasn't happening like that. Everybody always asks me, is this like Hank Williams Jr. and Julian Lennon and all of this. I just play, you know. I can't be him, I can only be me. So I do the best I can do, and hope that people accept that."

C. J. Chenier is the premier interpreter of Clifton Chenier songs, but he has also gone on to distinguish himself in his own right. He released two albums on an alternative rock label called Slash, which attempted to market him to college radio markets. He played on *Rhythm of the Saints*, Paul Simon's follow-up to *Graceland*. Then in 1995 C. J. hit his stride with the first of a series of acclaimed records for Alligator Records. Working closely with Bruce Iglauer — the man Clifton Chenier once walked out on, carrying the master tapes with him — C. J. expanded into a wide range of material. For his 1996 disc *The Big Squeeze*, the multi-instrumentalist even plays flute on a swamp pop tune. Today, his Red Hot Louisiana Band now has only one band member remaining from the old days: the blues guitarist Harry Hypolite. Yet if Chenier is traveling his own road, he also sees that he's keeping his father's name and music alive. He's even trying to learn French. "It's hard to learn that stuff," he says with a laugh. "This town is talking one way, that town talks the other."

Like most piano-key accordion players, he also crusades against many of the current trends in zydeco. "Today, zydeco has got to be played a certain way at a certain tempo, so they can do a certain dance," he says. "There's nothing wrong with it whatsoever, because it's a funky beat. But when I started playing with my daddy and these guys, you started rocking the house, man, everybody just went to boogie. So he got in, and the faster he went, the faster they went, and they didn't care what kind of dance they was doing, they just got in there and had fun.

"They still do the two-step down in Lafayette, that's been a dance forever," he continues, building steam. "But to me, they're refining it a little too much these days. I liked the days when the shoes came flying off, shirts came flying off, sweat was flying, people was sliding across the floor, hopping, skipping, jumping, doing whatever they felt like doing, you know? And they all fit when you're playing zydeco. That's the way I remember with my daddy.

"Even people my age, who used to tell me when I was in school, 'Your daddy plays the chank-a-chank.' Now all of a sudden they think they're zydeco experts. I tell them, 'You learn how to do this dance, all of a sudden you think you can give me advice? What's wrong with you?' But they just know what they're hearing. The radio stations down South, you might hear just one or two songs a day by piano accordion — maybe one by Nathan, one by Buckwheat, maybe one by me. The rest of the time, you got these buttons, playing the same beat thing.

"I play different. I like the freedom. Whatever I play, you can still get that hop-skip-and-jump if you want to. I just can't refine myself to playing the style everybody wants to hear. I got more things inside than that. I have ballads. I have waltzes. I have blues. I have boogie. And I can't keep that bottled up on the inside."

C. J. Chenier was born into this argument, and he's clearly just getting warmed up. But a knock comes on the hotel room door. The Red Hot Louisiana Band has left for Fitzgerald's, and the accordionist has promised to call his wife before he leaves. He's returning to Houston after this gig, he says, and he's ready to be home. "My daughter has started to play flute," he explains, seeing me out. "I sit down and she tries to fool me sometime, acting like she doesn't know how to play something. I used to grab a flute and show her how it goes, but now I got hip to that little scene."

C. J. Chenier folds his large hands together. "She just likes me to play for her," he concludes, with a father's smile. Then he returns to his room to suit up for the night.

# 8

# A ZYDECO SUCCESS STORY

CCORDING TO NBC'S ESTIMATES, three and a half billion people around the world tuned in to the closing ceremonies of the twenty-sixth Olympiad in Atlanta, Georgia. They saw the event begin solemnly with speeches from President Clinton and Juan Antonio Samaranch, the president of the International Olympic Committee. Then, as jazz trumpeter Wynton Marsalis started to perform, the network's sportscasters offered a play-by-play of the musical proceedings.

"There's a feeling of looseness, a festive feeling here," Eric Engberg announced.

"This is the night that sends the athletes home with the good feelings of fun and camaraderie and romance," added Bob Costas.

"The final Olympic jamboree, a celebration of all the rich music from the South," Engberg explained. "Jazz, country, rhythm and blues, Latin, Southern rock and roll, zydeco — Creole dance music."

A voice echoed over the stadium loudspeaker, describing a "musical quilt" about to be draped across the viewers. Country musicians Mark O'Conner and Faith Hill sang "Will the Circle Be Unbroken," followed by B. B. King, Al Green, Tito Puente, and Gloria Estefan.

"A conga line has formed amongst the athletes," Costas noted.

*Stanley Dural, Senior, and Stanley "Buckwheat" Dural, Junior, at the elder Dural's house.*

*Eric Clapton and Buckwheat Zydeco at S.O.B.'s in New York.*

When Little Richard began singing "Long Tall Sally," the event started to look like a crazy quilt. The international competitors abandoned their reserved seating and thronged over the stadium field to dance. The stage was set for the final entrance: the electric signboard announced ZYDECO, and Stanley "Buckwheat Zydeco" Dural Jr. entered, standing tall in a starched white shirt and black vest, hoisting a glittering white accordion. He played "Jambalaya," the Hank Williams tune based on a traditional Cajun melody. Zydeco artists had been covering the song since Clifton Chenier played it at the 1975 Montreux Jazz Festival. But nobody had ever played it like this. As the accordionist towered over the athletes, everyone from Little Richard to Tito Puente joined in the song.

"This is strange," intoned Eric Engberg, "but delightful."

Two days after he introduced billions of new ears to zydeco, Stanley Dural is elbow deep in a less glamorous pursuit. He is behind the gates of his sprawling ranch home in Carencro, his hands buried in the mechanical guts of his tour bus, installing a new radiator.

As he finishes the job, his manager, Ted Fox, waits in his home office. The room holds a large desk, a collection of photos and music awards, and two closed accordions. Fox is describing the past weekend, and how the featured musicians were waiting in the dressing room as speeches were being made in the stadium. Everyone started singing "When the Saints Go Marching In," joined by a large gospel choir. They kept that up until one of the Olympics organizers had to ask them to please keep it down, the crowd was trying to hear Samaranch's speech.

Did the other musicians know zydeco? Fox considers the question. "They know Buckwheat Zydeco," he replies.

Fox is slumped a bit in his chair, wearing a T-shirt and shorts, exhausted from the trip and slightly wilted from the summer heat. He may not immediately appear to be one of the most important figures in modern zydeco, but as the manager of Buckwheat Zydeco, he is. Fox had authored books on record producers and the Apollo Theatre before he put a hold on his writing career to manage Dural, and like any good manager, he quickly passes the spotlight to the musician. "It's him," he says. "I give all credit to Buck. I don't want this to come across in any other way. Musically, I couldn't hum do-re-mi."

But he also acknowledges that their relationship goes beyond artist and manager. He has produced, coproduced, executive produced, or co–executive produced all of Buckwheat Zydeco's records since 1987. That same year, he helped make Buckwheat Zydeco the first zydeco artist to sign to a major label. The team of Buckwheat Zydeco and Ted Fox is largely responsible for the appearance in the mid-1980s of hundreds of zydeco movie soundtracks and zydeco television commercials.

"I think my main contribution is that I know him really well," Fox says. "He's the godfather of my boy. He gets sick with something, I get sick with the same thing. It's bizarre. This white Jewish kid from New York and this French-speaking Creole black guy from southwestern Louisiana. But it's like we're twins sometimes."

Dural walks into the room. He's wearing jeans and a work shirt and is wiping engine grease from his hands, but he carries himself as regally as he did at the Olympics. The most successful player in his field, he began his zydeco career when Clifton Chenier asked him to join the Red Hot Louisiana Band as an organ player. After he left the Red Hots, he went on to stretch the music's inherent elasticity — some critics have said to the breaking point — by recording with Dwight Yoakam and Eric Clapton, and covering songs by the Rolling Stones and Bob Dylan.

Buckwheat Zydeco keeps to his roots by performing several times a year at El Sid O's in Lafayette. He also repairs his own bus. Nonetheless, the musician's upscaled life sets him apart from most zydeco players. His estate near the Evangeline Downs racetrack is a large, ranch-style home, home to chickens, ducks, rabbits, goats, sheep, peacocks, and emu. It is the most visible sign that this accordionist is on a different path.

Dural is reminded of this today, just two days after Atlanta. He returned home to find no mention in the media that a local musician just closed the Olympics. "Let me tell you something," he says, closing the door behind him and settling on the couch. "When I come back and I see what's going on here, it sort of makes me sad. I think our people here should put full force behind the artists and the culture, because that's what we live by. If it's bad, try to help it. If it's good, continue to push it. That's what I'm about."

This is the other side of Buckwheat Zydeco. A virtuoso musician, he is also the most influential advocate of black Creole cultural identity currently strapped to an accordion. Success has allowed him to be more stubborn than most. There is a story about Buckwheat Zydeco frequently told by Louisiana musicians: Did you hear about the time, they ask, that Buckwheat Zydeco was playing a festival, and there was a banner that said CAJUN MUSIC, and Buckwheat refused to play until they took the banner down?

The story is true, and it's a side to his personality that springs directly from his music. Just as Clifton Chenier put the blues into his father's music, Dural fuses his zydeco with the sound and attitude of 1960s and 1970s funk and soul. In Buckwheat Zydeco, "Zydeco sont pas salés" and James

Brown's "Say It Loud (I'm Black and I'm Proud)" have found common ground.

Dural was born November 14, 1947, one of thirteen children of bilingual parents who worked as farmers near the present-day location of El Sid O's. "It was nothing but woods," he recalls. "When I was seven or eight, I used to come here to Carencro and pick cotton. I'm the fourth kid, and I always used to scream and holler to go where my brothers and sisters would go: 'I'm going to go pick cotton!'" He laughs. "Man, what a mistake."

At nine, Dural worked as delivery boy, and he used his earnings to buy chicks to raise in his yard. His family homestead was less than an acre, and nearly every available spot was filled with pigs, chickens, and ducks.

He also remembers fishing for crawfish with sewing thread, and spending afternoons hunting for the family's food. (As a traveling musician, he has been known to fish from his hotel room window, then cook his catch on hot plates.) "I recorded this song, 'Madame Coco Bo,' and that was this old man that lived in the pastures, right in the back where I was raised," he says. "I used to go on his property, hunting rabbits with a stick — man, I'm serious. And that was a meal for me, my brothers and sisters, and my mom and dad. You hear what I'm telling you? I used to hunt armadillos, possum, and nutria. I'm a woodsman. If nature is there, I will survive."

Although Stanley Dural Sr. would never take his music into a club, he played accordion at home. In fact, Stanley Dural Sr. played so much at home, his son thought he'd never want to hear the accordion again. "Coming up, I heard him play every day. You better believe, every day, that's how come I was sick of the accordion, man. Morning, before he'd leave to go to work. Come to lunch, the accordion. At night, accordion. Next night, accordion. I said, 'Oh man, it's a trip.'"

When Stanley Jr. proved himself to be a musical prodigy, his father desperately wanted him to also play accordion. But his son was moved by other sounds. An older brother taught him to play piano when he was five, and his professional career in R&B began when he was only nine, when he made the rounds of local nightclubs, accompanied by present-day zydeco bandleader Lynn August, who was then playing drums. Before he hit his teens in the early 1960s, Dural was playing keyboards for Sammy and the Untouchables, opening for Fats Domino, Ray Charles, and Little Richard.

His career in R&B and soul continued when he joined Paul "Little Buck" Senegal's band, Little Buck and the Topcats; among their regular gigs was backing an Ethiopian snake dancer named Prince Savannah, who performed with giant boas and pythons. Dural left the Topcats in 1971 to launch his own funk outfit, Buckwheat and the Hitchhikers. "My best friend, Eddie Taylor, gave me that name," he explains. "We were five brothers and we all went to school with long, braided hair. This guy says, 'We got a name for you — Buckwheat.' It came from that TV show. I hated it, but once something like that sticks, you can't get it off. Now, not too many people know my real name."

At age twenty-four, Buckwheat was covering the latest funk hits in tailor-made spangled suits and towering platform shoes. "I had a fifteen-piece band and five singers, two male and three female," he recalls. "I was doing Bobby Womack, Sly and the Family Stone, Ohio Players, all R&B funk. And I played everything James Brown did." By now he had even changed his hair from his childhood braids to a style that accented his resemblance to the Godfather of Soul. "James, when he first met me many years ago, he was shocked himself," Dural laughs. "He thought he was looking at himself in invisible glass.

"See, James was an inspiration, man," he explains. "He was telling us, 'This is who you are, don't be ashamed of it.' When he made the song 'Say It Loud (I'm Black and I'm Proud),' that meant a lot to me. Some of the kids felt like they had to be ashamed of their nationality. Today, you're not going to see that as much anymore."

But not everybody was a fan of Buckwheat's new band. From the moment he started playing R&B, Dural found himself in an argument with his father that would last for two decades. "Me and my dad, we had a big problem," he says. "He'd never been out to see me perform from the age of nine until 1979, because he didn't want me to play R&B. I don't think he even drove around the club while I was performing."

What were those discussions like with his father? "Discussions?" Dural exclaims. "You didn't have no discussion! He wouldn't sit and talk to you. He'd just tell you: 'It's no good music, what you're playing.' I'm serious as a heart attack. And he and Clifton were very good friends, and he'd say, 'You need to play music like Clifton Chenier.' He was a true Frenchman, you know. And I was one of the biggest critics about accordion music, but I wouldn't tell that to him. In my generation, you don't tell that to your dad, man. You'd be waking up a couple days later, after he bust you out. But I couldn't stand it.

"As a matter of fact, you know what happened to me? We always had one or two pianos, and he used to tune the piano by ear, with his mechanic tools. And he would lock it up for me not to play it. Because I was playing rock and roll, that's me. Some Fats Domino, Little Richard, at an early age. I had my first organ for a year, and my organ was taken away from me. I couldn't play it, so I had to quit the band." He turns to his manager. "Did I tell you that?"

"You did, yeah," Fox replies.

Dural shakes his head. "I didn't like him for it, either."

Buckwheat and the Hitchhikers enjoyed a regional success. They backed Solomon Burke and Barbara Lynn, and their circuit ran from Texas to Mississippi. Then in 1975 — with eight months of scheduled bookings and a new tour van — the bandleader decided the show was over. There were "too many personalities" in the fifteen Hitchhikers, he explains. He went home, intending to take a year off. Then he received a call from an old friend.

"Little Buck called me from Austin, Texas, and I said, 'News travels so fast.' And he spoke to me and said, 'Man, why don't you come and play with us for a little while?' Now me, I was really against it. I mean, bad against it. Because I heard that every day at my house. But I said, 'OK, I'll talk to Clifton.'

"And Clifton came back and, please believe me, he drove off I-10 up to my house before he even went to his house, him and Little Buck. They came and talked to me, and Clifton told me, 'Buck, if you like it, I'd like you to play with my band. If you don't like it, I'll understand.' And I had my big Hammond organ in the house, and he said that he was going to play Antlers in Lafayette."

Dural was still skeptical, but he agreed to play the show. Chenier wanted to send the van to pick up the organ, but Dural said he'd get a truck and bring it himself. "If I don't like it, I would take my organ off that stage, I was gone," he remembers. "I'm serious, I was getting out of there, man. I was bad against this man. I knew Little Buck can play, but I didn't like him playing with Clifton Chenier either, because he was unique. Paul Senegal, he's bad. Clifton had John Hart playing saxophone, he had Jumpin' Joe, he had Big Robert playing drums, his brother Cleveland. So that night, I got onstage and I set my organ up.

"And there comes Clifton. Man, knocked my socks off. I couldn't believe that. He got onstage and kicked off, man this guy's got it going — the energy, the people jumping and hollering. He got onstage and he got to playing and he got to rocking and, please believe me, man, as I played — and I'm playing the way I played with the Hitchhikers, just feeling the music and just chomping, man — the time just went away. The next thing, I hear this man telling people good night. Four hours, nonstop, it's like we just started. I couldn't believe that I was doing this, and I couldn't believe that the music was sounding that way."

Dural didn't tell his father he was going out to play with the Red Hot Louisiana Band that night. "No, he didn't know that," he starts, then he reconsiders. "But he might have known something, because he and Clifton used to be together almost every day. That's one reason why my dad would tell me I have to play accordion like Clifton Chenier. Because he and Clifton had been talking." Dural nods. "He never told me that, but I know that's what it is. Like a setup. That's what I think it was. They were plotting."

Just as he credits James Brown with teaching him about black pride, Dural says Clifton Chenier taught him not to undersell his Creole tradition. "What I learned from him was that this is your culture, this is your roots, and don't be ashamed of it," he says. "You see, my dad played good, but he played all the time. It was nerve-racking. Give me a break. And when I got on Clifton Chenier's stage, that's what I thought I'd be hearing, too. I got a good education from that. Clifton Chenier was the man who put this music on the map."

Chenier must have also known that hiring Dural would help the Red Hots stay on the map for a new generation of Louisianans. Remembers Red Hots bass player Jumpin' Joe Morris: "You see, Buckwheat and the Hitchhikers had a lot of fans. And a lot of youngsters started coming in to hear Buckwheat play the organ. Come to find out, they start loving that zydeco, and man, they had more youngsters than they had some older people."

Dural played with the Red Hot Louisiana Band for two and a half years. He joined them for several live and studio albums, and he learned that zydeco could take him farther than he'd ever been with the Hitchhikers, including tours to Europe and Africa. In 1979 Dural decided to teach himself accordion, and Buckwheat Zydeco was born.

He determined to give himself two and a half years — the time he'd spent with the Red Hots — to find out if he could lead a zydeco band. "When I got out of Clifton Chenier's band it was October, and I rehearsed for eight months," he says. "Just me, no band, playing, playing, playing. I had my father come over and listen to me, and he would bring his button accordion, and I'd listen to him."

His fans from the Hitchhiker days may have followed him to the Red Hots, but when he picked up the accordion, it was more than many of them could take. "They said I was going crazy," he laughs. "They said Buckwheat was going crazy. I'm serious as a heart attack. They'd say, 'What's the matter with him?'"

He also faced a tougher challenge: he had never sung in public, and a stutter kept him away from the microphone. He'd hired five vocalists for the Hitchhikers, but now he decided to force himself to learn to sing, and he did.

Many of Dural's early songs were in French, a language he'd learned from relatives while working in the cotton fields. He also chose a band name from the French expression that local racetrack announcers use when the horses leave the starting gates: *"Ils sont partis"* ("They're off"). "The first night I performed was this place in Arnaudville, the Gypsy Club," he says. "Buckwheat Zydeco and Ils Sont Partis. And I can remember twenty, twenty-five people. And I was willing to pay people's way in to come and listen to me. But something happened. In October of 'seventy-nine I built the band, and between 'eighty and 'eighty-one I was touring Europe."

Buckwheat Zydeco and Ils Sont Partis preserved many of the show-band elements of the Hitchhikers, yet their early repertoire was surprisingly traditional. Their first record, *One for the Road*, recorded for J. D. Miller's Blues Unlimited label, was emblazoned with a kaleidoscopic photomontage of the accordionist in a disco shirt and silver vest, but the songs were a mix of two-steps, waltzes, and blues, such as Chenier's "Oh, My Lucille." Dural wrote "Madame Coco Bo," a French-language waltz about the lands he used to hunt. He also penned a Creole French-English blues about his favorite pet, a raccoon named Jack:

> *Tu connais a chien c'est un bon ami pour un homme,*
> *Mais chaoui vas trapper to*

> You see, a dog is a man's best friend, honey,
> But the raccoon won't put you out.

The song was autobiographical. In his early career, Buckwheat was known to travel with his raccoon, which would drape itself across his shoulders while he played. Jack, the first, was with him during the Hitchhiker days. The second, Tina, often joined him on the zydeco road. As he tells her story, he reaches above the couch and takes a photo from the wall. "She used to go with me everywhere," he says. "As a matter of fact, Tina got me in a lot of trouble. She'd always come onstage with me. But one night I decided to leave her in a La Quinta motel in Houston, Texas. And she got under the covers, she had her chips, she'd take them out one at a time, watching television. I'm serious. Come ready to leave, she hurried and jumped for the door. I said, 'Tina, get back in the bed.' She'd get back in the bed. Very smart coon. But it was the biggest mistake I ever made, because she got angry. Come back, total destruction. Fellas, that coon did everything she was big enough to do. She didn't miss nothing. She tore up the bed, she tore up every sofa in that damn thing, she tore up everything in that motel. She didn't like being left."

The song "I Bought a Raccoon" became Dural's first local zydeco hit, convincing him that he was on the right track. He made three more albums for Blues Unlimited, and then recorded one album for Black Top and two for Rounder. It was on these labels that he began to stretch out and define himself musically, and he scored his biggest hits with soul and R&B covers such as "Take Me to the Mountain Top," "Turning Point," and especially the Lee Dorsey tune "Ya Ya," which received play on regional pop radio. "I was doing the zydeco, but putting a touch of myself, too," Dural says. "I wanted to play the funk on the accordion, so I started mixing it, to see if I could put them both together, and that's how I came up with that sound I got now."

His roots in Lafayette Creole life grew deeper. When his friend Sid Williams told him he wanted to open a zydeco club, he played a dance that raised enough money to make it possible, and he became El Sid O's Saturday night house band. When Rounder approached him to record a live album, he suggested they record Sid's brother, Nathan Williams. That album gave the young player his first break.

It was also during this time that Ted Fox came down to hear Buckwheat Zydeco play a rural dance. "I had written about zydeco for *Audio* magazine, and I met you in some club, north of Breaux Bridge," Fox says. "Some valley. Hidden Valley? Happy Valley?"

Dural laughs. "But I met you before in New York, in the old Tramps," he reminds him. "That's when you refused to be my manager. He says, 'I'm a book writer.' I was talking to him for a while and I say, 'This guy has got his head well screwed on, you know. Intelligent guy.' And here I am, I've been managing myself for the longest time. I had a manager before and I got rid of him. So we talked some more, and I said, 'Think about it.'"

At the time, Fox had been conducting a series of interviews with music producers to be collected in his book *In the Groove*. Island Records founder Chris Blackwell had agreed to do an interview during a plane ride, and following the interview Fox had seven hours left in the air. Seven hours to tell him about Buckwheat Zydeco.

Dural smiles. "He probably said, 'What's a Buckwheat?'"

"He did. And I said that zydeco could be the next reggae music. Because Chris is the guy who discovered Bob Marley and launched the whole reggae sound. So when I got home I made him a tape from the old Blues Unlimited stuff. I started hearing stories from people that the tape was getting played at Compass Point Studios in Nassau at two o'clock in the morning, so I knew he must have been hooked. I sent him another letter, and I said, 'What's the big deal? You make records with all kinds of people. Make a record with Buckwheat.' Two days later he called me, and he said, 'Not only do I want to make a record with Buckwheat, I think you ought to manage him, and you ought to produce him, and I want to sign him to a five-record deal.' Boom, out of the sky."

Remembers Dural: "Ted gave a call and says, 'Tell me something, buddy. How would you like to record for a major label?' I said, 'OK, now talk English to me.' It was a big surprise to me. You never had an accordion band to record for a major label."

The recording sessions were scheduled for New Orleans in spring 1987. The plan was to throw a listening party for music journalists in town for Jazz Fest. Songs included Bob Dylan's "On a Night Like This," the Blasters' "Marie Marie," Booker T and the MGs' "Time Is Tight," and Chenier's "Hot Tamale Baby." But as the journalists started filling their plates with catered soul food, the first song they heard was Dural's seven-minute "Ma 'Tit Fille," a dizzying reading of Cajun musician Nathan Abshire's "Pine Grove Blues" that presciently adapted the title of Chenier's 1955 breakthrough hit. Dural had first recorded the song for Blues Unlimited five years earlier, but now his accordion was showcased by crisp production and an arrangement burnished with a full horn section, including members of the Dirty Dozen Brass Band. Remembers Fox: "I remember we put up 'Ma 'Tit Fille,' and it was like some movie or something, because everyone just burst into applause."

Before the record was released, Dural was invited to England to play Island Records' twenty-fifth anniversary concert. When Fox and Dural arrived at the venue, they received word that they had been bumped to make room for a jam by Eric Clapton and Ringo Starr. But the manager had intended this night to be Buckwheat Zydeco's coming-out party, and he acted quickly. Dural's Hammond B-3 organ was still set up, and as the rockers launched into the set, Fox grabbed the stage manager and insisted that Buckwheat join them on stage. Recalls Fox: "So the guy's got a flashlight, we're going through the backstage and tripping over cables and stuff, and the organ was up on the back. Buck said, 'No, you got to come out and sit on the bench with me.'

"Ringo is like six feet away on the right, and he's looking over like, 'What the fuck is this?' And Clapton was maybe five feet in front of us, and Buck gets up there, and Clapton does this solo, and Buck played it on the organ and he bumps it up a notch. And Clapton plays what Buck has just played, and he bumps it up a notch. And they're getting into this furious cutting contest, and Clapton hasn't even turned around at this point. And all of a sudden four thousand people are screaming, and Eric just stops playing, and he turns around and he puts his hand out to Buck and he says, 'I'm Eric Clapton. Who are you?' It was just one of those kind of moments."

From that point on, the barriers that most zydeco bands are still trying to break through began to tumble like dominoes before Buckwheat Zydeco. *On a Night Like This* received an enthusiastic review in *Rolling Stone*, and the *New York Times* ranked it one of the year's top ten albums. As the night was closing for the New York release party at S.O.B.'s, Clapton walked in with his guitar, and the band kept playing. "The next thing I knew, I was touring with Eric Clapton in the United States," says Dural. "Next thing I knew again, I had an invitation to tour with him in England. Twelve nights at the Albert Hall." Reviewing a show in East Rutherford, New Jersey, *Billboard* magazine's Bruce Haring wrote that Buckwheat Zydeco "made an easy transition from the bars to the arena."

Buckwheat Zydeco was a success. He recorded with Clapton, Willie Nelson, Dwight Yoakam, Mavis Staples, and Keith Richards. Los Lobos' David Hidalgo produced his third Island release. The combined sales of his five Island records (including a "greatest hits" collection called *Menagerie*) topped the half-million mark. Says Fox: "We did the *Today* show, the *CBS Morning News,* we did David Letterman four times, and they always asked Buck to stay and play through the show. You gotta do the interviews, you gotta do the TV, you gotta play in front of the right people, and do the conventions and the glad-handing, you gotta do the in-stores, and it's a lot of work."

The work paid off. By the end of the 1980s, it was safe to say that more people had heard of Buckwheat Zydeco than knew about zydeco itself.

But Dural was taking care of that, too.


When the conversation returns to the Olympics, I say that I thought it was remarkable when sportscaster Eric Engberg described zydeco as "Creole dance music."

Dural snaps his head up. "He said that?" he exclaims. "Cool!"

"We got to them," Fox smiles.

"We get to them, because that's what it is," Dural says. "Why call it something that it's not? It's just that simple."

The stories that Buckwheat Zydeco will refuse to play if the show is billed as "Cajun" are all true. Following the explosion of Cajun cooking and music in the early 1980s, zydeco musicians started to see their tradition labeled as "Cajun's younger cousin" in the national press. Often, they complain, people outside Louisiana miss the distinctions between Cajun and zydeco, or can't distinguish between New Orleans and Lafayette. But Dural won't stand for it happening at one of his shows. "If you're calling it a Cajun band, or you're calling it a jazz band, then you have the wrong people performing for you," he says. "You see, I didn't come this far saying that I'm somebody that I'm not. And if you don't have that identity, man, you're just lost.

"Why do you say that this area is Cajun country?" he continues. "You have black, you have white, you have some Indians, Vietnamese, and we're all here in Louisiana. We all make Louisiana work. And please believe me, I know I pay more taxes than the average person here in Louisiana. I'm not passing through here, I live here. And I won't accept it."

Dural grew up hearing about the Creole musician who was told to play his accordion through the window. He saw something similar happen one night in a white club in Lafayette. He had been asked to play with a black R&B band, and he arrived to see the musicians set up behind a sheet. "I wouldn't play," he says. "They didn't want to see the band but they wanted to hear the music.

"When I think about it, it makes me angry, because I've been through some of the changes like that," he continues. "Blacks, people like me, couldn't even come to the door of these clubs. That's my experience with this. I've been in a club, if light-skinned people are dancing, dark-skinned people can't get on that same dance floor. Now, what it has been with me in my generation, think what it has been to my father in his generation."

When Fox heard of the problems the accordionist was having with promoters, he sat down with Dural and the two drafted a form-letter addendum to the contracts that states, in big red letters, that zydeco is Creole dance music — the letter Engberg read from in the Olympic broadcast — and that the contract will be considered void if Buckwheat is billed as a Cajun. "The letter happened because I got a couple calls from Buck in the early days," Fox recalls. "He pulls up to the front and a sign says the 'Wild Cajun Sounds of Buckwheat Zydeco.' And he says, 'Man, they got the wrong band!'"

"If it's being advertised like this, I can have my equipment onstage set up ready to play, and I'll take them offstage," Dural promises. "I put them back on my vehicle and I get out."

"I tell you what," Fox recalls, "we had a couple times where Buck called and I called the club owner and said, 'Look — '"

"I was leaving."

"' — he's gone unless you change all the signs now.'"

"I've never seen a black Cajun in my life," says Dural. "It doesn't make sense, huh? It don't even ring a bell. So why call me something I'm not?"

"I don't want to make it sound like Buck's out there to pick a fight with these guys," Fox adds. "Most people, they want to know, and they're glad.

He's really been an ambassador for this, and he's really been enlightening people. I've read a zillion interviews, and I've never seen anybody but Buck talking about the Cajun-Creole thing."

As far as Dural is concerned, it's something every touring zydeco musician should consider. "He should demand it," he says. "If it's not right, leave. If they don't want to take it off, leave. A dollar bill ain't going to bother me."

About two hours into our conversation, a knock comes on the office door. A mechanic wants Dural to check on the bus. Also, his daughter is looking for her book of autographs from the Olympics. Fox checks his watch for the third time. Dural hasn't unpacked from his tour yet, he explains.

So I decide to close by asking Dural about the regular shows he still performs at El Sid O's on Mother's Day and other holidays. And about how he's become a role model for young accordionists like Li'l Brian Terry and Corey Arceneaux. He feels good about that, he says. He once rejected his musical culture, but now he's helping it continue for another generation.

As we're about to end, Fox leans forward. He doesn't seem pleased. "You know, we basically stopped in 1987," he says, frowning. "You're doing the book on zydeco, and we really got to talk about the records that we made, because that is the big story that is really underreported. It's like ethnomusicologists who want to put Buckwheat in this little box that they can understand."

Dural turns to me. "You're not going to do that, huh?"

"I hope you're not going to do that," Fox says, building volume. "It's not just a thing that's played in little clubs around Lafayette. This is the guy who's played the closing ceremonies of the freaking Olympics! How did that happen? You do not jump from being a session player with Clifton Chenier to playing the closing ceremonies of the Olympics!"

Dural leans back in the couch. He can see his manager is on a roll.

"After all, even the great Clifton never had a major label deal. This is an important part of the history of zydeco music!" Fox waves his hands at Dural. "This is why! Buck onstage is a world class entertainer. En-ter-tain-er!" He chews the syllables and spits them out. "That's what the eth-no-mus-i-col-o-gists don't get!"

Fox keeps on. "In front of seventy thousand young U2 fans is no different from the Buckwheat Zydeco show that I have seen at El Sid O's. Well, maybe a little bit different from El Sid O's. But certainly no different from any of the one hundred and fifty road dates that we do in clubs all around the country. Because he's the real deal. That is the bottom line.

"But no one's gotten the story." Fox sighs. "*On a Night Like This* is the most important zydeco record ever made, as far as I'm concerned, period. I'm not going to claim it's the best, but by any count, it's the most important, except maybe the first zydeco record. But why is nobody talking about it? Why is nobody writing about it? I guess they don't consider it zydeco anymore. But that's total bullshit.

"Look, the machinations of what happened from *On a Night Like This* — that's what led up to that scene at the Olympics. All the TV commercials. Watch TV any day, you're going to hear half a dozen spots that are basically zydeco spots. You never heard that ten years ago. We started that. We did the first one. We sat down with the editor in chief of *Advertising Age* magazine, hipped him to this new thing that was coming out, just before *On a Night Like This.*

"You know, that's really in some ways even more important than all the zydeco records," Fox continues. "When you turn on your freaking TV now, in America and in a lot of places in the world you're hearing zydeco music every single day. Everyone may not be able to say, 'Oh, that UPS spot that I heard ninety-eight times on the Olympics is a zydeco spot. 'They may not know that, but we know it. Even *Ad Age* named zydeco as one of the up-and-coming trends in advertising.

"That doesn't fit into the discography-ethnomusicology-blah-blah-blah," he continues. "But it is a social phenomenon that every damn day you turn on the TV you're hearing this sound. And maybe it's one song away, maybe it's one film away with the right zydeco soundtrack to really crack this thing open. But to me, that's the real story of zydeco over the last ten years."

It's another half hour into the night. Dural seems really ready to unpack, but he also admits he is enjoying himself. "This was rolling. I don't get in conversations like this too often. But if you're going to hold a straight, good conversation, that's what it's going to be like. Ted and I sit and talk sometimes, and he knows I don't like hogwash. I like a real conversation."

He opens the office door. "How about if you and Ted get together later?" he asks. Everyone nods, and Buckwheat Zydeco walks out.


And so, a couple months later at a bar in Lafayette, I meet Fox to finish the discussion. He's back in town to coproduce Buckwheat Zydeco's first CD in three years, *Trouble,* for Atlantic's Mesa Blue Moon label. It's an unusual project for Buckwheat Zydeco: the only cover tune is Robert Johnson's blues classic "Crossroads Blues," and many of the originals wouldn't sound out of place in a rural dance club. "I think we're going to get the Plaisance crowd," Fox says. "The key phrase is 'getting back to the roots.'"

Tonight nobody brings up ethnomusicology. Instead, Fox is here to explain the marketing of Buckwheat Zydeco — and zydeco in general.

"I think a lot of guys have been hurt because they didn't have management, or they had bad management that was giving them bad advice," he believes. "You know, Chris Strachwitz made a lot of cool records with Clifton Chenier. But Chris is completely anticommercial in any way, shape, or form. And I've had a problem with these people, because these musicians got to make a living. Clifton Chenier should have been sitting like B. B. King is now."

Live performance has been the key to Buckwheat Zydeco's success, he says. Fox recalls a night when the accordionist played WEA, a record industry convention; a crowd of jaded record executives started a conga line. Following the show, Atlantic Records founder Ahmet Ertegun came backstage and said, "I think you guys are the best band in America." Explains Fox: "So it was always, who can we get Buck to play for? Whatever influential group, let's do it. And it really helped, or otherwise they wouldn't have had a clue about zydeco.

"Another thing I really worked hard with Island was the concept of filing the records in the rock and roll bins. Because the big problem with anything that's perceived as ethnic music is that it gets stuck in some ridiculous place in the back corner of the record store, and is usually mislabeled under 'Cajun' or 'blues' or 'country.' You can't even find it. It's hopeless. But if you look for Bob Marley in most stores, you're going to find him under 'rock and roll.' I said, 'Look, if the Gipsy Kings can be positioned that way, we can be positioned that way. Let's be crass about it. Let's put a big goddamn sticker on everything saying to file this in the "rock" bin.' And they did put some stickers on some of the early records saying, 'Buckwheat Zydeco will rock your socks off.'"

Fox admits that they have had only partial success with other attempts to make zydeco cross over into commercial markets. A video for "Ma 'Tit Fille" received some play. They scored higher when a duet with Dwight Yoakam on Hank Williams's "Hey, Good Lookin'" was placed in heavy rotation on VH1. But an attempt to push the song to country stations flopped. "They sort of embraced Cajun music with Doug Kershaw, and Michael Doucet did that duet with Mary Chapin Carpenter," Fox explains, "but country has that black-white thing, and the only zydeco that ever made it to the Nashville networks was Rockin' Sidney's 'My Toot-Toot.'"

Fox also suggested the zydeco versions of rock songs to attract new listeners. He remembers when he first brought a cassette of Bob Dylan's "On a Night Like This" into the band rehearsal in Paul's Playhouse in Sunset. Ashe played the original version, and he sat on the pool table with his feet dangling, waving a pool cue around like a baton. The band just looked at him. "It sounded to them so rinky-dink and kind of corny." Fox laughs. "But the guy is game, he'll try anything. Both of those became real crowd-pleasers." Another cover, the Rolling Stones' "Beast of Burden," was suggested by bassist Lee Allen Zeno. "I will say right now that Lee Allen is the Rock of Gibraltar, an amazing bass player and a really key guy," Fox says. "At first I thought 'Beast of Burden' was a terrible idea. Now it's usually the finale at the encore."

Buckwheat Zydeco's first television commercial was a zydeco rendering of Lincoln Mercury's theme song. His music has been used in movies from *The Big Easy* to *Fletch Lives*, on television programs ranging from Super Bowl broadcasts to *Northern Exposure*, and on commercials for Isuzu, Budweiser, Coca-Cola, and Apple Cinnamon Cheerios — in the latter, the zydeco rubboard is used for the sound of an apple being grated over the cereal. But success has created its own problems: the music is becoming so common that ad agencies have begun to hire New York studio musicians to play accordion for scale.

"I'm telling you, this is a sound now that is pervasive in American culture that was not there ten years ago," Fox says. "And it's an endless thing. I'm amazed at how much interest there is in Buckwheat Zydeco around the country. It is an interesting story, and he can talk about more than his latest record. He can talk about growing up and learning on his father's knee, and playing from the time he was five, and picking cotton with his brothers and sisters and living with twelve people in this tiny house. When we first started working together, it was just him and the guys in Old Gray, his famous favorite old Chevy van, which he still has, with I don't know how many hundreds of thousands of miles. And this is it. This is going on right now. It's a real American success story."

*Sid Williams.*

# 9

# THE ONE-STOP

SID WILLIAMS LOOKED UP FROM THE CASH REGISTER. He nodded at a local real estate agent entering Sid's One Stop convenience store. "Come with me," he said quickly. "I want to show you something." He told his brother that he would just be gone a few minutes; bells jingled against glass as he pushed open the door and went out to the parking lot.

His blue truck reversed around his gas pumps and sped away past his club, El Sid O's. It left behind the housing projects and Catholic churches of the neighborhood and turned onto University Avenue, then right to Interstate 10, which cuts across this section of Lafayette on its way from New Orleans to Houston. It took the on-ramp, entered the freeway, and sped up until it reached the top of an overpass. There, on the bridge, Sid Williams braked and swerved to the right.

Parking his truck on the three-foot shoulder, he went around to open the passenger door. Standing by the short guardrail, oblivious to the cars and trucks that whipped past him blasting their horns, he surveyed the landscape from the highest point in the area. He pointed out his store, Sid's One Stop. He dragged his finger to El Sid O's. Then he turned around and faced his house, which opened to the interstate with a large metal accordion affixed by the front gate. He leaned over to the real estate agent. "I like to come here," he shouted over the traffic, "to think."

Here, he can remember when he left his mother's home in St. Martinville. He recalls his hands in cold soapy water, washing dishes, and his weeks on end in the oil fields, and the sweet smell of blood in the meat markets he cleaned. Then he thinks about the dollars he made, and the dollars he spent to build his store and his club. How he started it with Buckwheat Zydeco, and then watched his brother Nathan Williams become one of the most popular young musicians in the zydeco field.

Sid Williams looked at the rooftops, roads, and trees. Then he opened the door for the agent and merged back into traffic.

By Sunday afternoon at Sid's One Stop, Sid Williams has been working almost nonstop for three days. Last night, he stayed at the store until eleven o'clock, and then he moved down the street to El Sid O's. He closed those doors at four in the morning. He woke up at seven for church, and he's been back at the store since. He inherited this schedule from his father. "He worked himself to the ground, the poor man," he says, shaking his head.

He is currently sitting on some grocery crates in the store's back room — a vantage point from which he can see his interviewer, the cash register, and most of the store. He works out of what he calls this "ragtag" office, and keeps most of his business on index cards. "They want me to get a computer," he says. "Now what the hell am I going to do with a computer?"

Then he looks up. "Just a second." A customer has found him in the back room. She wants to come back later with the money for her cold drink. "Let her go on with that!" he yells up to the front.

After his father died, Williams quit school to work with his grandmother, grinding sugarcane. His grandmother — whose son Harry Hypolite has played guitar for both Clifton and C. J. Chenier — would come by in the morning and bring the family biscuits, rice dishes, and bread. But others in the family were less supportive, he says. "They'd tell my mama, 'All your boys are going to be in prison.' They'd say, 'Sid ain't going to be nothing.' I was the oldest brother, I didn't have nobody to take care of me, and they'd want to mess with me."

At home, he'd watch his mother cope with the family's poverty. "I'd see her take the same slip at night and wash it and hang it over the fire for the next day," he remembers sadly. He decided to go to work at his father's old job with J. B. Talley's construction company. "I worked there about seven months, and I think I took about five dollars out of my check to buy me a little bottle of Thunderbird and two packs of cigarettes, and I'd give Mama the rest.

"Then I got an offshore job in Venice, Louisiana, but I had no ride to get there," he continues. "So I hitchhiked all the way to Venice. I slept in the heliport. I had fifty cents in my pocket. I bought me two bags of chips and drank water for two days. And then I went on the boat. I stayed there for fifteen days, and the man wanted me to come back in. But I said no, I ain't got no money to get a bus back, and I don't have no cigarettes. So I just stayed out there. When Mama called me, she said, 'I got a big check over here for two thousand dollars — are you sure you haven't stolen nothing over there?'

"Just a second." A man is asking Williams to cash a check for twenty-five dollars. He bounced a check here last week, but this is his wife's account. "All right my man, handle up on him good!" Williams calls out, making a note on an index card.

The oldest brother had three thousand dollars in his pocket when he returned from Venice, enough to buy the family a car and put school coats on his brothers and his sister. "Oh, we were in high cotton," he says. "So I worked offshore: help my mama, help my mama, help my mama." This lasted for three years, until he had an injury in the oil fields. "That was when the pipes fell on me," he recalls. "The pipe broke on me and messed up my hip and spine and everything." He underwent back surgery and received a settlement from the company.

As soon as the money came, he knew he wanted to build a nightclub. But his wife, Susanna, wouldn't allow it. Instead, there was some land available in Lafayette on what is now Martin Luther King Drive. Three years later Sid's One Stop opened for business, and Williams put his family, including his teenage brother Nathan, to work.

Music was always part of the life that revolved around the Williams' home in St. Martinville, and it followed them to the store. Behind the One Stop stood a little house where Sid would fry hog fat into cracklin'. Musician Clayton Sampy was a frequent visitor. "He used to come back here all the time and play his accordion for us," Sid remembers. "Nathan would come back there and we would just humbug, you know? And one day he went and touched the man's accordion, and Clayton said, 'Don't put your hands on my accordion.' He really made a stink about this thing. That's when we broke friendship. I felt Nathan was insulted, and when my Daddy died, Nathan was seven years old and I raised them. If somebody was insulted, they'd come to me."

Sid told Nathan that he was going to the apartment building across the street, where Buckwheat Zydeco was then living. He said he was going to buy him an accordion. Nathan said that he didn't want anything to do with an accordion. "So I went across the street to Buckwheat," says Sid, "and I reached down and I got that accordion."

Soon Nathan was practicing around the store. Recalls Sid, "Clayton would stop back — we made friends again — and he'd show Nathan a little piece, and Buckwheat would show Nathan a little piece." Nathan began to follow Buckwheat Zydeco from club to club, and the already famous musician would frequently call his protégé onstage for a few numbers. Then Nathan was hospitalized for eight months by a thyroid condition. While recuperating, Nathan decided that he was going to play zydeco and form a band called the Zydeco Cha Chas.

Meanwhile Sid Williams was also making plans to deepen his connection to the zydeco scene. To block plans for a competing store, he had purchased some nearby property. Every time he looked at that corner lot, he remembers, he saw a zydeco club. This time, his wife agreed. Buckwheat Zydeco gave a dance at the nearby King Center to help raise funds, and the club began to build up, piece by piece, whenever Sid had enough money to take it a little higher. Finally, after three years, El Sid O's was complete. Opening night, Mother's Day 1985, featured Buckwheat Zydeco.

"It's the first zydeco club that has ever been built from the ground up in Lafayette," says Williams, adding that its name, El Sid O's, came from an old nickname. "Mr. Brown, the welder, he said, 'You ought to open that club and call it El Sid O.' I wore my big cat hat, and I must have about eighty pair of cowboy boots, and maybe about a hundred hats. I got one hat I bought, it cost me five hundred dollars, with this lizard on there. When we got some big shows, I got some tuxedos with rhinestones. So Mr. Brown says, 'Hey, El Sid O.' I told him, 'That's what I'm going to call it: El Sid O's Zydeco and Blues Club.'"

Nathan Williams calls his brother "the Don King of zydeco," and the eldest Williams does have such a flair for publicity that it is sometimes hard to know just where Sid ends and El Sid O begins. "I never was able to go to school," he explains. "I've just been promoting myself all my life." He sports gold rings and bracelets trimmed with accordions, and the accordion on his gate is also designed to attract attention. "So when a tour bus is coming," he says, "they say, 'Ladies and gentlemen, we are now entering into the city of Lafayette, and we are now headed for the fabulous El Sid O's Zydeco and Blues Club. To your right, ladies and gentlemen, is Mr. El Sid O's Zydeco and Blues Little Villa.'"

Local officials have led visiting dignitaries to El Sid O's, he adds, and Rounder has made live recordings in the club. David Hidalgo and Buckwheat Zydeco have rehearsed here. Every year, Sid passes out thousands of

T-shirts and key chains and cup holders, and he rides in a parade every Mardi Gras in St. Martinville. His Thanksgiving food drive is also a local tradition, and his club has become an important stop for politicians stumping for votes.

"Just a second, look who's here!" Williams exclaims. "A visiting celebrity to Sid's One Stop!"

C. J. Chenier walks into the store.

"You ain't played around here — what?" asks Williams. "Eight, nine months?"

"Well, here is the only place I play when I'm here, man."

"We go way back, actually way back with his daddy."

"And he spanked me a few times, everything." Chenier laughs. "That's my big brother."

Williams laughs. "I straightened him up a little bit."

Chenier sees my tape recorder and waves his hand. "I'll stop by later," he tells Sid. "Let's have a bottle of something."

Williams turns to me when he leaves. "You always see some celebrities that come around here," he says.


Nathan Williams lives one block behind the One Stop — a short walk when he is called into the store to help out. On this Sunday in July, he's just home from Europe, and he only has a few days until he hits the road again. His son, Nathan Jr. — nicknamed Pum, short for "Rum-pum-pum-pum" — is occupying most of his day. Pum has a drum set in the back of the house, and he has also started to play accordion. He listens closely as his father recounts how he became a zydeco man, and how he used to get in trouble. Pum likes that part.

"I used to go listen to Clifton Chenier play at the Casino Club in St. Martinville," remembers Nathan Williams, his quiet voice reflecting the strain of the seven-week tour. "I had to be out back, standing on this washing machine and watching through the window. This old lady would always run us out of her yard. One time, she came out with her purse and beat the hell out of us. We used to peek in and see if she was on the dance floor to see if we were safe."

As a child, Nathan was most famous for being the best boxer in St. Martinville. Older boys would meet at the barber and place bets on their kid brothers. They'd set up matches, and the boys would start throwing punches until somebody fell. He wanted to go on and play football, but his mother didn't approve. "So in ninth grade I left St. Martinville and hitchhiked to Lafayette to work with my brother," he remembers. "I never went back."

*Nathan Williams and the Zydeco Cha Chas in Mardi Gras parade, St. Martinville, Louisiana. On guitar is Dennis Paul Williams.*

*Nathan Williams with a masked Chuck Williams on rubboard.*

While at the One Stop, he also met Clayton Sampy and Buckwheat Zydeco, and he talked to older musicians such as Claude Faulk. He had been hearing music since he was a child, he remembers, including several older men in his family who would meet on the front steps and make what they'd call *bazar*. "Four or five guys would get together," he recalls. "They'd be drinking some wine, one would be clapping his hands, the other's got a spoon, the other's singing:

> Going to the war, eighteen, nineteen,
> Very good man going to the war,
> Motherless child, going to the war.
> *Juré, juré, juré* going to marry me.

I'd be watching all that, and some of those old guys would sing till you'd cry, man. One of these days I'm going to record that. I have a lot of stuff stored in me that I haven't shared with nobody yet."

Williams remembers that he first received the idea to play professionally when he was hospitalized with his thyroid condition. Lying in the hospital, he dreamed that he was playing accordion in front of thousands of people. He decided then to form a band called the Zydeco Cha Chas, taking the name from a Clifton Chenier instrumental.

At the time, Buckwheat Zydeco had been El Sid O's house band, playing at the club twice a month. But his star was quickly ascending, and he was starting to spend more time on the road. Remembers Sid: "I asked Buck what I was going to do, with him on the road. He said, 'Don't worry, bro, I'm recruiting Nathan.'"

Nathan Williams's first gigs at El Sid O's drew few people. Sid let customers in free and passed out beer, and a few more started showing up. Attendance steadily increased. With Sid's backing, Nathan cut two 45s on the El Sid O label, including his version of an old Clifton Chenier song, which he titled "Everybody Calls Me Crazy (But My Name Is Nathan Williams)." Sung in French and English, the lyrics provided an introduction to the brothers from St. Martinville:

> Everybody call me crazy,
> But my name is Nathan Williams. . . .
> They say I come from the country, y'all,
> And don't know what I'm doing.
>
> Everybody call him crazy,
> But his name is El Sid O. . . .

> They say he come from the country, y'all,
> And don't know what he's doing.

"They were calling him crazy, because of his thyroid," explains Sid, who had begun to manage Nathan's career. "And they were calling me crazy because of my gun." (Sid is a registered sheriff's deputy, and explains that his "peacemaker" helped to clean up his neighborhood.) The song received extensive airplay on zydeco radio shows, especially on Lester Thibeaux's program on KJCB. Then Rounder approached Buckwheat Zydeco to cut a live record with Boozoo Chavis. Buckwheat had just signed with Island, but he recommended Nathan for the project. The result was *Zydeco Live,* and the album introduced Williams to a new audience.

By now the accordionist had also acquired a new look: wraparound sunglasses and a gleaming cowboy hat. The outfit was his brother's idea. "At first he didn't want to wear them," Sid says. "Now he can't go onstage without it."

Following the live album, Nathan Williams continued to work with Rounder; his first studio record was *Steady Rock,* and he scored a regional hit with his reggae-zydeco treatment of the Paul Kelly–penned title track. Soon the song could be heard everywhere; it was even played by marching bands during football games. "When I went over to St. Martinville for Mardi Gras, I saw a parade band on the street, and they were playing 'Steady Rock,'" says Williams. "I'm proud, man. My music reaches a lot of younger people."

It was also on *Steady Rock* that Nathan Williams first revealed himself to be zydeco's best young songwriter. He traces his family roots back to Haiti, and St. Martinville is known for a distinctive Creole French language that reflects that area's Caribbean roots. Williams's songs are steeped in his home culture, and he draws inspiration for many of his original songs from the daily life he recalls from St. Martinville, as well as the street-corner bustle of his brother's store. From his first studio album came the modern classic "Everything on the Hog," a grocery list sung in both French and English of the products behind the glass of Sid's butcher counter:

> Everything on the hog, everything on the hog is good.
> Everything on the hog, everything on the hog is good.
> Except the eyes, baby, the eyes ain't no good.
>
> I like that good ol' time hoghead cheese.
> I like that good ol' time hog cracklin'.
> I like that good ol' time boudin.

> I like that good ol' time backbone.
> Everything on the hog is good,
> Except his eyes ain't no good.

Williams traces the source of another of his regional hits to a line he heard from Clayton Sampy. One day, he recalls, Sampy walked into the store and announced, "Follow me, chicken, I'm full of corn." The line gave Williams the title for his fourth Rounder release; it also dates back to a century-old Creole song first listed in the 1945 WPA Louisiana Writers' Project book *Gumbo Ya-Ya: Folk Tales of Louisiana.*

For another song, "Alligator," Williams again drew from the trove of Creole folklore. At first listen, the lyrics would seem to be a fairly simple celebration of Louisiana food, not unlike what can be heard every day in local tourism jingles:

> Alligator, sauce piquant,
> Tomato gravy will drive you crazy.
> Hmm, all right.

But Williams explains that the song refers to a traditional Creole belief: that a woman can cast a spell on a man if she places a drop of her menstrual blood in tomato sauce. "A long time ago they had a saying where if a woman wanted a guy she'd mess him up in tomato gravy," Williams explains. "He'd fall in love with her because of that gravy. That's an old remedy.

"My music is from everyday life," he continues. "People talk slang and I pick it up, and I do something with it. You know, I'm never going to be better at doing what Clifton did, because Clifton created that, or better than Buck, because Buck created himself. But nobody is ever going to be better than me at doing my music, because I created that."

Sid Williams may have built a zydeco empire on Martin Luther King Drive, but the success of the Zydeco Cha Chas has also helped a third brother establish his domain in St. Martinville. Guitarist Dennis Paul Williams has performed with Nathan from the beginning, and he is also a painter who stores his works in six buildings along Port Street, not far from the family's first home.

Dennis Williams' work is exhibited in galleries around the world, and he recently contributed the official poster to Lafayette's Festival International. He also has a portrait of fiddler Canray Fontenot currently hanging in El Sid O's. A deeply religious man, he draws a clear connection between his work and his childhood experiences in St. Martinville. Most of his paintings depict females, he explains, because he believes that when he was a child the Virgin Mary healed him of congenital heart disease.

"I can remember when I was eight or nine, I asked Mama why she used to dress me in blue and white," he says one afternoon in his St. Martinville home. "She told me that those were the colors of the Virgin Mary, and that one day the doctor had told her that I wasn't going to make it. On that day she sold me to the saints." He pulls out a purple rosary and places it on a table. "That day was the beginning of wisdom for me."

Dennis was schooled in the lore of traditional remedies. As a child, he used to crawl under houses to gather dirt-daubers — mud wasp nests — for a local treater to use as medicine. He also began collecting pencil lead off the streets, and he first painted with twigs and thorns. He even invented his own method for keeping his watercolors free of roaches: mix them with Joy detergent. But he received little encouragement for his innovations. "We were all considered lower class — the troublemakers," he explains. A teacher told him that art was no good for him, and kicked Dennis out of the program. He adds that support finally came, from professors at the University of Southwestern Louisiana.

Dennis plays both guitar and triangle for the Zydeco Cha Chas. "After our father died," he says, "Sid made workaholics out of all of us." Family relations are close, he says, and he remembers the months when his brother Nathan was hospitalized with his thyroid condition. "They tried to make me leave the hospital," he says. "But I slept on the window ledge. I read in the Bible that you should anoint the sick with oil, so I went down to the gift store and got a bottle of baby oil, and I greased his head like a pig, and I prayed. And when the nurse came to see him, he was a different man."

When he paints, Williams says, he listens to both zydeco and Handel's *Messiah*. He admits that some people at his church criticize him for playing at clubs. "But when I've got my guitar, it's a revival for me," he says. "If I got to catch the Holy Ghost, then that's what I do."

As the afternoon light fades from his corner of Lafayette, Nathan "Pum" Williams Jr. can stand it no longer. He has gone into some back room and is now carting out an electric organ, an accordion, and a mouth organ.

"I don't want to brag or nothing," says his father, "but Pum has the best rhythm of any young rubboard player around."

His son grins and picks up a duct-taped fork. "Hey, Dad," he says. "I have a good idea. Let's play two songs!" In the lengthening shadow of Sid's One

Stop, a young boy puts on his metal vest, and his weary father picks up his accordion.

When the Zydeco Cha Chas are in town, El Sid O's becomes the site of an extended family reunion. Sid is behind the bar, Nathan and Dennis are onstage, and other brothers and cousins are either helping out or are on the dance floor. The next day, the family can be found back at the store, minding the till, swapping stories, selling boudin, inspiring new songs, and entertaining the celebrities of the neighborhood.

"There's one thing people may not understand about my family," Sid Williams says. "All we've ever had is each other."

*Rockin' Sidney Simien at his radio station, KAOK, Lake Charles, Louisiana.*

# 10

# THE HOUSE THAT "TOOT-TOOT" BUILT

*Well, she was born in her birth suit,*
*The doctor slap her behind,*
*Said you're gonna be special,*
*You sweet little Toot-Toot.*

— *Rockin' Sidney, "My Toot-Toot"*

"WHEN I WENT OUT INTO ZYDECO, it was tough," admits Rockin' Sidney Simien. "I'll still say it: Cliff was a monster, man. And Buckwheat was no slouch himself. My thing was show biz."

He leans back, rolling an orange office chair to the wall. There's a hum of fluorescent bulbs and the faint murmur of his grandson announcing a Keith Frank song in an adjacent room. Old sound equipment is stacked in the corner, along with cardboard boxes labeled "Rush Limbaugh" and "G. Gordon Liddy." We're in the studios of KAOK, one of two radio stations owned by Simien that boast an unusual format: zydeco, blues, and right-wing talk shows. The business cards read "Toot Toot Communications, Inc."

This station is a jewel in the crown of an unusual career. Born in 1938 to a French-speaking family of farmers in Lebeau, Simien went on to blaze a trail through Louisiana music like no one else's. "When I started, I never dreamed of doing a French song," he says. Instead, as a young swamp pop and R&B performer, he was inspired by his flashy hero Guitar Slim. "He had a red suit and red drawers, and a way of making his pants drop," he remembers. "I had a cream suit, and the next day I was downtown looking for red dye."

In his early twenties, Simien made a series of successful swamp pop recordings on Floyd Soileau's Jin label. Eventually, the success of Clifton Chenier inspired him to switch to zydeco, and he set out to become a court jester on a stage of accordion kings. He starred in his own vaudeville-style zydeco shows complete with multiple costume changes, a live goose, a Clifton Chenier suit, and a ventriloquist's dummy made up to look like Buckwheat Zydeco. And when he started making zydeco records, he did them his way: writing, producing, publishing, singing, and playing all the instruments himself.

This is what he was doing one summer night in 1982, when he cut off the air conditioner and went alone into his garage studio. He emerged twelve hours later, after recording the biggest single in the history of zydeco. The song, "My Toot-Toot," became a worldwide phenomenon, the "Macarena" of the mid-eighties. Among other things, it bought the radio station that Simien is currently sitting in.

"I was really influenced by my daddy, which he doesn't even know today," Rockin' Sidney Simien says. "He's a hard worker, and he'd buy one thing at a time and pay for it. I remember when he brought his first cow home, and he bought his first mule, his first tractor. But farming wasn't for me. I wanted to be in the movies."

More specifically, Simien adds, he wanted to be a singing cowboy. He was bitterly disappointed when his brothers told him that no black man could be hired for that job. Then, one day at his Catholic school, a priest came to his class to discuss careers. Simien watched the other kids stand up to declare they wanted to be doctors, lawyers, or farmers. On his turn, he recalls, he announced, "Well, it's not what I want to be, it's what I'm going to have to be. And I don't believe the Lord can do much about it, either." The priest asked why, and Simien said it was because he was black. "That's when the teacher told me to wait in the hall," he remembers.

Simien figured the priest was going to hit him. "But he said, 'You want a soda water?' I guess when I said 'black,' he had to approach it right. I guess it's in the teaching. He said, 'What is it you want to be?' I said I wanted to be in the movies. He said, 'Well, lots of people are in the movies.' I said, 'Well,

I want to be a cowboy.' He said, 'Hmm.' I told him about Roy Rogers playing guitar and cleaning the town and getting the girl, and everybody respected him. He said, 'That's it! You want to be an entertainer.'"

Simien knew about musicians. Both his grandfathers played accordion for house dances, and his uncle played saxophone. His corner of Louisiana picked up both Duke Ellington and hillbilly programs on the radio stations of Ville Platte and Marksville, and he remembers one of his grandfathers playing "Tuxedo Junction" on the piano accordion.

Three days later, he went back to talk with the priest. "That's when he turned my life around, man," he remembers. "He told me to study piano, and he paid for it. I was maybe ten, eleven years old. I started playing at school, and he started calling churches and booking me. That was Father Mulkeen. He heard some of my records, but he never saw me get famous." His eyes start to mist, and he apologizes. "I get emotional when I talk about it, man."

Simien continues the story. "By the time I turned twelve, I started playing professionally. I took over my uncle's band when I was fifteen. I was making five, six hundred, and I bought my first station wagon. In Lebeau, just me and the priest had a station wagon, man."

With his uncle, Simien began traveling to New Orleans, where he met his next teacher: an old piano player who taught him the secret hustles of the performing life. "I'd go around to these clubs around Bourbon and Toulouse, and I'd show the band my guitar pick, just to make them nervous," he remembers. "I looked older than I was. I had a moustache and sideburns already. You see, when I was a kid, I'd entertain my family. I'd mock my daddy and act like I was shaving. First thing you know, I had sideburns.

"Anyway, I met this old man, he said that he played with Duke Ellington and Count Basie. I still wonder about that. But he played the piano, and his wife was the drummer. I showed him my pick, and he said, 'Man, I see you're a musician.' But he said 'moo-sician.' He could tell I was from the country, and he was kind of making fun of me. He said, 'Are y'all making money?' I said, 'Man, we're making money all the time.' He said, 'If you're making money, I'll bet you'll buy us a drink.' So I bought a drink, and he kept talking to me, and he said, 'Son, what you're doing, you're spending all your money proving to me you're making money. I know y'all ain't making no money.'"

The piano player — Simien says he has been trying to remember his name for years — promised the young musician he'd show him the game. "He'd tell me, 'You don't want to be a *moo*-sician, you want to be a star. Go out and make you a damn record. Then go and make you some damn placards. Put on there that you're a recording star, jack! And if you say that, one day somebody will repeat it.'"

Simien returned to New Orleans six times. He learned about booking a gig by telling a club owner he'd just run out of gas, and then talking him out of ten dollars in advance of his first booking. Or how to give a waitress a box of candy and money to play his song on the jukebox, and then return a month later and ask the owner for a gig. "He'd say, 'You got records?' I'd say, 'Oh yeah, that's my record playing now.' He'd say, 'They sure play this son of a bitch in here, man. Let's talk.' It was hard work, but once I laid the foundation, I was in."

When Simien graduated from high school, he went to Opelousas and ordered a pink and green Plymouth, and began playing clubs in Alexandria, Morganza, and New Roads. He was having trouble breaking into the prime markets of Opelousas and Lafayette until he signed to Floyd Soileau's Jin label. Here he first became Rockin' Sidney, scoring regional hits with a series of lively R&B and swamp pop tunes, including "She's My Morning Coffee," "You Ain't Nothin' But Fine," and "No Good Woman," which hit number one on local radio. In 1965 he moved to Lake Charles and started recording pop and soul for Goldband as Count Rockin' Sidney and the Dukes. Hits were now eluding him, but songs from this era would later be rediscovered by groups such as the Fabulous Thunderbirds, who included Simien's "Tell Me" on their album *Tuff Enuff.*

"We made a lot of money on that," Simien says. "All it cost me was a loaf of bread, a pile of baloneys, a couple soda waters, and a trip to Lake Charles." But a scheduled tour to Europe fell apart because Simien couldn't keep his band together. He began looking enviously at Clifton Chenier's crowds.

His father was a Chenier fan, and Simien had been aware of the accordion player since the 1950s. "The thing that amazed me was that he was on Specialty with that kind of music," he remembers. "I used to go watch him in the Yambilee parade in Opelousas. And this guy has got his own float in the parade, and the rock-and-roll people ain't got nobody in the parade. And when people ran for the sheriff of Opelousas, you didn't hear Fats Domino on the speakers, you didn't hear Guitar Slim or Chuck Berry, you heard Clifton Chenier. That was the politicians' way of getting the people to vote.

"But that accordion was something I never had the mind to play. What really turned me around was this guy Eddie Shuler at Goldband. I had bought a television from him, and he used to come by my house to collect the money. And after my contract ended with Floyd, Eddie told me he had a song that could be bigger than 'No Good Woman.' He said I was the only guy who could play it. In other words, he was putting butter on it. And he said that after I signed a contract, he'd show me the song."

Simien signed the contract, but his heart sank when he saw the song in Eddie Shuler's hands: a French tune called "Lâche pas la patate." Shuler believed Rockin' Sidney could be the next Clifton Chenier, playing harmonica instead of accordion. "I went in and cut the song, but it didn't do nothing," Simien says. "People just didn't buy that harmonica, and they didn't buy that French. They knew what I was trying to say, but they also knew I wasn't a true Frenchman.

"But after that, I kept looking into Clifton Chenier, and I decided I was going to buy an accordion. I used to go to his dances, and I went up to him one night and whispered to him, 'Cliff, I want to buy me an accordion, you mind if I — ' And he turned around and said, 'Man, don't bother me.' Now, he had five hundred people at the Sacred Heart Church over here, and I keep bothering him about his accordion. And I was drinking a little bit, and then I asked him if I could play harmonica. So he made an announcement on the microphone, about how Rockin' Sidney wants to play the accordion and the harmonica. He kind of embarrassed me a little bit."

After the Count Rockin' Sidney experience, Simien had decided to take time off from leading a band, and he spent the next twelve years doing one-man shows on organ and drum machine in local hotel lounges. He wrote and produced for a number of local soul and disco bands, and he started several of his own record labels. Then he decided to try a new door into zydeco.

"I said, the only way I can do this thing, I got to be the Muhammad Ali of zydeco. So first of all, I went around and watched Cliff. He dressed nice, he wore a suit to the place and came home with the same suit. But he didn't excite me, because all he did was sing his song, talk to the people, and stayed right there. He didn't perform. I said, well, I can outdo this. I figured I can't be Clifton Chenier, but I can be Rockin' Sidney. So what I did, I bought me a motor home, forty thousand dollars. I would dress before I go to the gig, change twice on the gig, and wear another suit to leave."

His first zydeco release was an eight-track called *Zydeco Fever*, followed by the album *King of the South*, which featured his first local zydeco hit, "If It's Good for the Gander." This song became the showstopper at places like Richard's Club. "I used to dress this goose up with earrings and lipstick, and the goose messed the floor up a lot, so I decided to put a diaper on it. And I'd come out with this goose on a leash, and we'd go in the audience. I knew the first thing a goose does when it gets to a door is it wants to go in, so I'd go by the women's bathroom, and the house would go wild."

Then in 1982, as he was playing the first Texas-Louisiana Blues and Zy-deco Festival in Houston's Summit Auditorium, he debuted his latest inno-vation. "I had a deal, it looked like my accordion would blow up. I had this magic powder that the rock bands used to use. So I'd be playing, and I'd hit this note and I'd fall to the floor, and as I go down, I press this little button and this flame goes up, and the people thought I'd exploded."

Simien had spent a month planning his entrance, packing the front rows with family members to cheer his every move. Then he dropped to his knees. It burned his pants leg, he remembers, but it was worth it. "From that date on, everybody wanted to book me in Houston, and Clifton was mad about that," he says.

But it was the main event of that evening that really drew his attention: the first joint appearance of Clifton Chenier and Buckwheat Zydeco since the two men had played together in Chenier's Red Hot Louisiana Band. The meeting was publicized as a battle for the crown of zydeco. The show made an impression on Simien, who went home and sewed a homemade Clifton Chenier wig. He filed down some plastic vampire teeth and painted them gold. Then he fashioned a crown from a plastic mixing bowl and stitched together a cape. When that was finished, he bought a book on ventrilo-quism and taught himself how to sing without moving his lips. Then he bought a dummy, painted it, and added glasses.

Remembers Simien: "After that, when I came on stage, I dressed like Cliff. I had a portable dressing room I'd set up, and the emcee would say, 'Ladies and gentlemen, we just found out the King of Zydeco has just walked into the house, let's give him a big hand.' And then he'd sweep his hand and my spotlight would fall on me. The first thing they'd see is the gold teeth, the crown, and the cape, and I'd do a song like him. Then I'd take out Buckwheat, and it looked just like him, with a suit, accordion, glasses. And I'd put the microphone up to the little dummy, and I'd start singing, 'It's all right, it's all right tonight.' Just like Buckwheat. The trick was for words like 'body,' you say 'dody': 'Everydody dancing, everydody having a time.' People used to stand right up front to see that thing. Then I'd stick that little neck way up and I'd say, *'Ils sont partis!'* Buckwheat stayed mad a long time.

"But that's what made me real popular. And actually Clifton Chenier and Buckwheat both would catch my show to see if I was going to do them. So when Cliff would come, I'd do Buckwheat, and when Buckwheat would come, I'd do Cliff. I wasn't really making fun of them. I was telling them they were actually the king, and I'd interview him, just like you're doing me. A few people came to me and said I shouldn't do it. In fact, even my daddy didn't like it. He said, 'I don't see why you have to do that.'"

His last big show was at a club in Lafayette, Simien remembers. "All of this was before 'Toot-Toot,'" he says. "After 'Toot-Toot,' I just went in and did two or three songs, and I did 'Toot-Toot,' and the show was over."

Following his grandson's zydeco broadcast, Simien closes the station for the night. He leads the way to a large building behind his house, down a narrow hall, and through the door to his office. The room is a shrine to a two-and-a-half-minute song: "My Toot-Toot." Behind his desk, a gray safe houses song masters, stacks of self-shot publicity photos, and tapes and records of over seventy-five versions of the song, in various languages. A glass cabinet displays an array of prestigious awards: the 1985 Best Ethnic or Traditional Folk Grammy, the W. C. Handy Single of the Year, the Handy Best Blues Song of the Year, and a trophy from a St. Francis of Assisi Church that names him "Most Fabulous Band" of 1985.

Simien rifles through some papers and pulls out a mailing from the Jim Halsey Company; after "My Toot-Toot" hit it big on country radio, the talent agency put him on the roster alongside Roy Clark, Conway Twitty, and the Judds. Then he goes to the wall and pulls down one of his most cherished souvenirs: a framed letter from Little Rascals star George "Spanky" McFarland. "We were playing a celebrity gold tournament in Chattanooga, Tennessee," Simien remembers, dusting the frame and putting it back on the wall. "I never played golf in my life. That night, I went down to the bar, and Spanky and Leslie Nielsen and I started drinking. We found out that we all kind of thought alike."

Simien takes a seat behind the cluttered desk to recount the story of his song, drawing back the curtain for the opening scene: his garage, on a warm night in 1982. "My wife was trying to sleep that night," he starts. "My studio was the garage, right next to the kitchen, and I'd back the cars out. I had a little old Tek four-track, and I finished that whole album at seven o'clock the next morning. I have my best time at three o'clock in the morning, and I don't come out till I finish.

"At the time, you didn't hear much zydeco on the radio," he continues. "So I wanted to come up with something that the black people and the Cajun people could both relate to. I kept looking for words and I used to go to all the Cajun dances, and then I started going to some Clifton Chenier dances. And Clifton Chenier would say, *'Eh, toi, fais attention.'* Like, 'Hey, you, pay attention.' The Cajun people would say *'Fais pas ça'* — 'Don't do that' — and 'aieee.' Clifton Chenier would holler 'aaaahh' or 'waow.' It's all different, you know. Then the Cajun people, when they would stop a number, they would say something in Cajun, and then they would say, *'ma chère*

*Rockin' Sidney as Clifton Chenier, circa 1983.*

*tout-toute,*' the people would just react to whatever the guy would say. It meant, 'my sweet little everything.' Well, I don't speak French, so what I'm hearing is, 'Blah-blah-blah-blah-toot-toot.'

"I had already written a song called 'Toot-Toot' around 1972, for this disco band I was producing. When I got ready to do my zydeco album, I was one song short. When I get ready to record, I just go in the studio, and I do all the parts. If I need a line, I go in a big brown book that dates way back, where I put my ideas. And I'm looking through that, just trying to find words. I found that song, but the disco arrangement didn't work. So I said, I'm going to do this thing simple, simple, simple.

"I had a little electric drum from way back, it didn't play but one beat, and no bass pattern would fit. Then I thought about a bass player I knew that was playing with John Delafose, a guy named Slim Prudhomme. And Slim played one pattern all the time and it was choppy, but he had that little groove. And I used to listen to that and say, man, it's the same thing and look at the people dance; I'll put that damn thing on there and I'll bet the people will dance like hell. So I put that in.

"So then I sang it one time, and I made a bunch of mistakes on that thing. One place I said, *'C'est pas ça,'* but it's supposed to be *'Fais pas ça.'* But I was playing my accordion and singing, and I had to pull the slide down on the four-track, and I looked to see and I was a little late, so I just said, *'C'est pas ca.'* And all this made the record. Now, it turns out the Spanish people would think I was trying to sing, *'¿Qué pasa?'*

"Then I added some new lines to the song, like 'the other woman' and 'break your face.' At first I had it 'You can look but don't touch.' And I thought I'd be clever with my words and change them around, because I used to like the way Chuck Berry would write. Chuck Berry wouldn't say 'under the tree,' he'd say 'beneath the tree.' He doesn't say 'grass,' he says 'evergreen,' and 'gunny sack' and stuff like that. So I said, 'You can look as much, but if you much as touch.'

"Then I said, 'You're going to have a case, I'm going to break your face.' Now, I'd heard some kids talking one day, and one kid took a kid's popsicle and the little kid said, 'Give me back my popsicle, or I'm going to break your face.' So I wrote that down. Lord, that was twenty or thirty years ago, but I always try to remember things like that when you need something to put down on songs.

"But in 'Toot-Toot,' when I changed the song around, I got the idea that I was going to let people try to figure out what I was trying to say. I said, 'She was born in her birth suit, the doctor slap her behind.' So when the baby was crying he slapped her, and when he turned her over to see if she was all right, even then he noticed how she was going to be built. I thought that was a clever thing, but nobody ever questioned me about that.

"But the main thing I can remember about that night is that my wife wanted me to come to bed or cut that noise out. She used to make me so angry, and she'd kind of take my soul away from me, because I'd be in that groove. And that particular night, I happened to look at the side, and I saw her standing with her hand on her hip, watching me. But I just pretended I didn't. That went on, and she woke up around six o'clock to make her coffee, and I was playing this song back, and I said, either that son of a bitch is going to make them knock chairs down to go dance, or they're going to say, 'Man, what the hell was he doing?' But the more I heard it, the more it would hit you. So my wife is standing by the door drinking her coffee, and I could see she's kind of angry. I said, 'What do you think?' She said, 'I think it's silly.' And she turned around and drank her coffee. But my wife put up with me. I kept her up many nights."

He took the tape to Ville Platte; Floyd Soileau wasn't immediately impressed with the home studio sound, but in 1984 his Maison de Soul label released *My Zydeco Shoes Got the Zydeco Blues.* The song "My Toot-Toot" was buried on the second side.

Then things began to move quickly. Within a month, Simien recalls, dancers were knocking down chairs. A Baton Rouge disc jockey named E. Rodney Jones went to a dance, saw the reaction to "My Toot-Toot," and began playing the song on his show. Soon Soileau noticed something strange on his sales sheets: a zydeco record was selling east of the Atchafalaya Basin. He called his stores and heard the story, and he called Simien to Ville Platte. The two men listened to the song again. "I said, my God, it's empty," Soileau recalls. "I mean, there's no middle, there's no bottom, and it's hardly hanging on by a thread. This guy in Baton Rouge is picking this to be the heavy song of the album, and it'll never carry the weight." Simien took the tape back to his garage and applied a newly purchased drum machine to the project, adding drumrolls, hand claps, and the sound of a slap after the line "The doctor slap her behind." Continues Soileau: "He said, 'What are we going to do now?' I said, 'We're not going to say nothing. I'm going to change the mastering of that side of the album, and we're going to send some new LPs out to the disc jockeys.' And we didn't say anything until long after the fact."

Also in Baton Rouge, a Cajun programmer named Mick Abed began playing the song on his Saturday morning show on the country station WYNK. Listeners began requesting the song during the rest of the week, and country radio in Houston also put it in regular rotation. "We pressed over a hundred thousand singles," Soileau remembers. "Any spare time we had, we were putting product on the floor."

As Soileau pushed "My Toot-Toot" to country stations, female R&B vocalists Jean Knight and Denise La Salle recorded disco versions of the song. And by that year's New Orleans Jazz Fest every performer seemed to have a version of the song, including Cajun fiddler Dewey Balfa and the Olympia Brass Band. When Rockin' Sidney played it on a main stage, thousands sang along. Jimmy C. Newman and Ralph Emory recorded it, Fats Domino and Doug Kershaw filmed a video, and former Creedence Clearwater Revival frontman John Fogerty flew to Louisiana to make a record and video for a Showtime special, which featured Rockin' Sidney on accordion.

Simien was both an overnight sensation and a hometown hero. "I remember the first time I heard 'Toot-Toot' on the radio, I must have been twelve," remembers Lafayette rock and roll musician C. C. Adcock. "My dad and I were coming back from fishing, out from Intracoastal City, and that song came on the radio, and we thought it was so funny and we liked it so much, and we spent the whole drive just trying to find every radio station that would play it. And then it was on Casey Kasem, and it was on the TV, and the very next morning I rode my bike down Camellia Boulevard and that very same guy was playing at Wal-Mart on a flatbed and throwing out all the 'Toot-Toot' T-shirts you could catch."

After selling forty thousand albums and cassettes, Soileau realized he couldn't press enough copies to keep up with demand. Huey Meaux, working as Rockin' Sidney's manager, brokered a leasing deal with Epic for a four-song EP. Bootlegs of Fogerty's Showtime performance began airing on Atlanta radio, but Warner Brothers went along with the singer's promise to Soileau and Simien that he wouldn't compete with their version.

Rockin' Sidney climbed the country charts until he stalled in the top twenty, but the life of the song was just beginning. Around the country, the phrase "toot-toot" began to transform from a Cajun term of endearment into a bayou-born sexual innuendo. Simien, it turns out, had coined a catchphrase for the mid-eighties. "I was having so much fun, it was like I was in dreamworld for a long time," he remembers. "I had people calling me for interviews, from seven to seven, every day when I wasn't on the road. They were playing games on the radio, saying, 'We got the man on the line to tell us what a toot-toot is.' People were having so much fun with this thing. Hell, everybody was just 'toot-toot-toot-toot-toot.'

"They had all those versions with Jean Knight and Denise La Salle, so people were familiar with those records," Simien continues. "I had the accordion, and they had the keyboard, and they wanted to take it to another part of town, and that's not what the people wanted. I think what really opened up a lot of people's minds was *People* magazine. When they heard about it, they sent a guy down here to interview me. They wrote, 'If you think you heard "Toot-Toot," you need to hear the original.'"

In short order the song crossed national borders and became a global phenomenon. La Salle's version topped the charts in England. One day Simien wandered into a disco in Frankfurt, Germany, and heard his own version blasting from the speakers. "That was the biggest thrill of my life," he says. "They're playing Michael Jackson and Madonna, then all of a sudden 'Toot-Toot' came up, and everybody starts dancing. I started walking around and I had me a pretty good time."

But "Toot-Toot" made the most noise in Spanish-speaking communities and countries. In the United States, Tex-Mex accordion star Steve Jordan used "My Toot-Toot" for the title track of his 1985 RCA album. Then the *New Orleans Times-Picayune* ran a story about two movies, *One Tough Cop* and *Pure Luck*, which were including Spanish-language versions in their soundtracks. Soileau read the article, called his lawyer, and eventually discovered that the Cumbia superstar group La Sonora Dinamita had scored millionsellers with two versions of the song: "Tu Cucú" in 1988 and "No provoques mi pichichí" in 1989. But "Toot-Toot" was just starting to turn a profit.

The elusive meaning of "toot-toot" fueled much of the song's appeal. In English, the phrase seemed to slyly refer to the woman's anatomy. In Spanish, the *pichichi* belongs to the man. Simien and Soileau stoked the fire by adding a line of T-shirts, including a model that illustrated "Don't Mess with My Toot-Toot" with an arrow pointing south. Other zydeco musicians joined the conversation. John Delafose scored a regional hit with an answer song, "Ka-Wann," which plays off a local Creole and Cajun French double entendre:

> Well now, you got Buckwheat talk about a Ya Ya
> Then you got Boozoo talk about a Deacon Jones
> Rockin' Sidney talk about a Toot Toot
> But now myself, John Delafose, I want the best
>
> Come on *'la ka-wann,'* come on *'la ka-wann'*
> *'Ka-wann' est meilleure,* come on *'la ka-wann'*

"It all depends on what part of the state you're in," Soileau explains. "See, over here, around Ville Platte, *ka-wann* is a good turtle meat, but around Morgan City, that's not what it is. There, you're talking about a woman, about sex. And John knew that when he recorded it, and it was the last big song that he got.

"Some people said that 'Toot-Toot' was not exactly zydeco music as we dance to it today," Soileau continues. "But I always use 'Toot-Toot' as an example when I talk to these young performers who are just starting out. That's why I say, 'You need to write a hit song. You might be old and gray some day and you can sit back in that rocking chair and let the mailman bring you your profits.' That's what it's all about."

Rockin' Sidney Simien's solo recording technique paid off. He maintained full author credit of "My Toot-Toot," and publishing proceeds were split between his Sid Sim company and Soileau's Flat Town. When his share of the profits started to arrive, Soileau bought a motor home with the license MY2TOOT. Simien bought a bus and two radio stations, and opened up a Lake Charles zydeco club called Festival City. Recent royalty checks include one from a 1995 German beer commercial that paid $140,000 to record a new version with a German vocalist. "I've got about sixty-seven songs that are still making me some money right now," Simien says, "but 'Toot-Toot' is the only thing really keeping me going. I'm blessed. Everybody made some money on 'Toot-Toot.'"

Simien winds up the night with a tour to the second floor of the house that "Toot-Toot" built. He hopes to move his family here someday, but for now these unairconditioned rooms serve as a giant attic for his souvenirs, and for raw materials for new projects. Near the door, next to a stuffed deer head, are vinyl seats from his old tour bus. Propped against a wall are three plaster mannequins. "This is supposed to be Queen Ida and Ann Goodly, and this other one is Rosie Ledet." Simien wipes sweat from his face; the heat is stifling. "Wal-Mart moved and they had all this stuff. They told me if I want them, take them. I want to paint them and fix a little motor in the arm to make it wave: 'Come on in to Festival City.'"

He leads the way to a room with racks of vinyl records and eight-track tapes. "This is 'Joy to the South,'" he says, wiping a dirty cellophane wrapper. "When I brought this one out, I got some bumper stickers that said 'Joy to the South, Rockin' Sidney.' I went to the Greyhound station in Lake Charles, and I put all them damn stickers on the buses. Do you know how many people saw those before they pulled that off? Those buses were going to California, man."

In the corner is a small multicolored mountain of "Toot-Toot" shirts, all small sizes. "This woman came up to me and said, 'Tell my husband that a

"Toot-Toot" is your little girl.' I'll never forget, I was wearing that nasty shirt with the arrow pointing straight down. And I folded my arms over myself and I said, 'Yeah, well, "Toot-Toot" is whatever you think it is.'"

He kneels on the dusty carpet and goes through the shirts. "Man, everybody was selling these shirts. They had one with a pistol." Then he looks up. "Where's Buckwheat? Anybody know?"

Simien's grandson has followed him upstairs. "What, that doll thing?" he calls out from another room.

Simien goes to some brown paper bags and pulls out some leather shoes, painted purple, and finds a black wig. "Now, when I put this thing on with the teeth, shit, that's Cliff all the way," he says, overturning bags of fabric. He finds a cardboard crown and a robe with blue fur trim. "This is my cheap little thing. But I put a lot of work into it, man. Took me a whole week. When I stepped into that spotlight, that shit would glit."

Then he finds one of the items he's searching for: a cardboard placard from the 1982 Texas-Louisiana Blues and Zydeco Festival in Houston, back when he played with Chenier and Buckwheat Zydeco, and fell to his knees and made his accordion go up in flames. "That's where it all started," he says. "I've done some things. I've done what nobody has done. But I still admire Cliff."

He lifts up a spray-painted 45. "I made me a gold record, before I got a real one," he says. Stacks of sheet music are left over from a music store he owned and closed, and there's a box of stationery with DANCE AND SHOW BANDS ATTRACTIONS on the letterhead. "That was me." He laughs. "I'd tell them, 'My agency demands so much money up front and I got to pay them fifteen percent.' I learned all that shit from that old guy that I met when I was a kid in New Orleans. I still don't remember his name, but he was the man that started me making records." He pulls out stacks of 45s and reads the labels. "Sid Sim Corporation. Disco Weather. Nifty Records. Bally-Hoo. These are all my record companies.

"You see, Quincy Jones was doing a lot of stuff, and that's what I admired. I am the writer. I am the publisher. I am the producer. I did the whole thing. Just like I played all the parts in all my records. I built my own studio. I had my own radio show in Sulphur in 1982. I went on *Hee-Haw*. They didn't believe I could be a country star, but I went on the road in my cowboy hat and I played my song."

Simien straightens up and wipes his hands. "I never finished telling you that story. After I made my first record, I drove all the way to New Orleans to show that old guy. He said, 'How many records you got?' I told him that I got a box. He said, 'When are you going to learn? You mean you drove all the way from Lebeau and you ain't made no money? You know how many jukeboxes you passed from there to here? You could have made a hundred dollars.' He said, 'Damn a dance hall. If they got a jukebox in a church, put it in there.'

"The first time I went in a place I was nervous. Then I started acting like the old guy. I'd say, 'You mean you ain't got *this* record?' Finally this big man come up to me, 'Who are you, you got a band?' I'd say, 'I'm in Monroe. Working with Fats Domino.' And I had an uncle in the band who looked just like Fats Domino. And one time Fats Domino was playing the White Eagle in Opelousas, and I went by the bus and acted like I was getting out of the bus, with my coat like this, carrying my guitar, and my uncle would be turned sideways — he's real short and dark, and he cut his hair like Fats — and I would lean in like I'm telling him something. And I took a roll of pictures like this, and I'd show the man this. And he'd say, 'Yeah, man, that's you and Fats!' Back then, my little record was sad, but I got my price.

"That old man hipped me to a lot of things. I used to stop at all the Denny's and I'd park my bus up front and tip the waitress ten, fifteen, twenty dollars. I'd have my drummer go up there and say, 'We have Rockin' Sidney out there, we want to bring him in if you can make room for him.' So they'd fix them tables up and all my guys looked like football players, they had uniforms to travel in. The drummer would walk me in and sit me down, and he'd call the manager and say, 'Rockin' Sidney wants to meet you.' All this to make me look important, and all those people eating in there would see that. So they get the manager to come meet me, and get the cook, and all that. I had to tip the waitress, tip the cook, tell how good the food is, and they put a picture up. And coming back, we'd stop at the one at the other side.

"But it's a new day and it's a new way," Simien says. "They don't even have jukeboxes. I've been following this new zydeco for the past five years, and I've tried to help some of the young bands out. I try to put them on the right road, give them a lot of advice, try to tell them how to approach a bandstand. If they say, 'We got So-and-so in the house,' and if you stand and keep waving, they might keep that light on you. But I don't know, the younger people don't seem to think that's any good today. Maybe it is the old days. But I still think it's powerful.

"Another thing, I look at the young guys, they ain't got no women screaming at them. They come and sit down. They hide from the public. They all got their wives with them. They don't sign autographs. They don't dress nice. They don't even have lights on them. That might be the day of the past, but I don't know. I still think, the president still wears suits, he's still running this town. So I just think that young guy has just got to put that in his mind.

"And it's still sex that keeps fans and makes artists. If you're popular with all the women and girls, you're going to get a crowd. But you know who's the stars in zydeco today? The dancers are the stars. These little black guys with them cowboy hats and them boots, and they're standing there like that. And them little gals are waiting, and as soon as the music hits, man, they run and grab them. They don't even look at the band. They are the stars amongst themselves. And the guys on the bandstand can't see that."

Simien picks up the Texas placard to carry down to his office. Then he turns back. "But there's something about that 'Toot-Toot' that's weird," he says. "I'll play that record, and I don't care what key it is in, if I have a kid, they're going to move. To me, it seemed to be in the bass. I have this crazy notion that when I was putting that bass pattern together, the Lord put something in my playing that went on that tape. Because if I put it on and pay attention to that bass, I can still feel that little thing I was doing."

He shuts off the light and walks down the dark hall, past his office, out into the Lake Charles night. He's talked long past dinner, and his grandson is shooting baskets, waiting to go eat. Simien holds out a "Toot-Toot" shirt as a gift. "I'm fifty-eight, but a young guy could do it, and do it with the zydeco," he says, getting in his car. "Someday there's going to be that one little guy who can get popular and just say, 'Hey, I'm up here.'"

# 11

# GULF COAST WEST

DANNY POULLARD WAS TWENTY-ONE YEARS OLD, just out of the military, and new to California. A cousin had helped him find a job at a local slaughterhouse; another cousin was renting a place in San Francisco's Fillmore district, where Poullard also took a room.

One day Poullard was returning from work when he met his neighbors in the upstairs apartment and learned that they were also from Louisiana. "The man said, 'I'm going to the dance tonight, you want to come over?'" Poullard remembers. "I said, 'What dance?' He said, 'French dance.' I said, 'Yeah, I'll come over.'"

When he arrived at the dance at All Hallows Church in the Bayview district, Poullard couldn't believe his eyes. On accordion was "Li'l John" Simien, whom Poullard had heard years earlier at a dance back in Mallet, Louisiana. In fact, every time Poullard turned around, he recognized another face from Louisiana or Texas. Around him, people ran up to each other, checking last names, looking for relatives. "It felt like home," he remembers.

*Queen Ida.*

Nobody can say how many Louisiana black Creoles now live along the West Coast. The 1990 census was the first to allow people to check themselves off as "Cajun," which nearly twenty thousand Californians — five percent of the nation's total number of Cajuns — did. The census gives no option for "Creole." But starting in the 1940s thousands of farmers and sharecroppers made the trek west, going first to Texas and then, in search of jobs on military bases and in shipyards, to California. When they arrived, they faced new choices about who they were and who they wanted to become. "People here in Lake Charles were moving to California and people from Opelousas were moving to Lake Charles," Rockin' Sidney Simien says. "The ones that get there first can get their nose up a little bit. Sometimes they're the ones that don't want to associate."

In California some Creoles had the opportunity to abandon their previous identities altogether. "You got people come here, want to pass for something else," says Mama Lena Pitre, a native of Basile who moved to California in 1961. "I'm going to tell you just like it is. They have a lot like that. They get in their minds that if they pass for something else, they get a better job. White, Mexican, everything they could pass for but black. I know where they come from, that's why I don't say anything."

George Broussard moved to San Francisco from Lake Charles in the late 1950s. He wasn't sure if he wanted to stay, but by the mid-sixties he had settled into his new home, where he worked in a steel shop, played drums in a zydeco band, and organized dances. He also recalls that some Creoles weren't interested in keeping old ties. "You got some from Louisiana here in California, they don't really want to identify with the rest," he says. "These same people wouldn't even dance. They don't want to turn loose. What goes into their mind, I really don't know. Because if you look long enough and you listen to the way they talk, eventually you're going to catch on that they are one of you."

By this time, however, greater numbers of people were becoming eager to see familiar faces and dance the old songs. Even before Clifton Chenier began playing the churches in Los Angeles and the Bay Area, families gathered in their basements (a new room for those just relocated from the Louisiana wetlands) to dance, either to French records from home or to live music played by relatives. Soon professional musicians started to find work. Accordionist Ambrose Sam began to perform in Los Angeles at private parties, accompanied by fellow Louisiana transplants Jack, Albert, and Wilson Perkins. Sam soon moved on to clubs and church halls.

George Broussard remembers the first house parties in San Francisco. When he lived in Lake Charles, Broussard had played drums with an R&B band called the House Rockers, which featured Leo "the Bull" Thomas playing guitar and occasional appearances by another young guitarist named John Delafose, then known as "Snook." Recalls Broussard: "I grew up in Tyrone, right between Eunice and Basile. Every time my father picked up his accordion, he wanted to play 'Eunice Two-Step.' But at the time, I wasn't interested in Cajun music. To me, this was sort of outdated."

Broussard left his drums with Thomas when he moved to California. When he arrived at his new home, he realized that what he really longed to hear was his father's French music. "You don't miss it until you don't hear it anymore," he says. "So we formed a little group, and we decided to see if we could give a regular dance. Home people from Louisiana would show up. So we had it at our house, and that was the beginning of it."

By this time, accordionist Li'l John Simien had already played a few dances at local longshoreman halls, and he and Broussard formed the Opelousas Playboys, with Ben Guillory on fiddle and Junior Felton on guitar. A stubborn traditionalist, Simien had moved to California but continued to farm, as well as to play and to speak French. "Some people thought John was crazy," recalled his brother, Joe Simien, in an interview with Freida Fusilier for her book *Hé, Là Bas! A History of Louisiana Cajun and Zydeco Music in California.* Joe Simien recounted how his brother once visited him with his accordion and played a song. When John left the room, Joe picked up his accordion and played the same song. John told Joe to leave his accordion alone. A week later, he sent him a new one in the mail.

By the late 1960s the Opelousas Playboys began to play for larger crowds in the Bay Area, expanding their audience beyond the transplanted Creoles. "When we did our first event, we contacted mostly the people we knew that had moved here from Louisiana," Broussard says. "But it didn't take long for others to find out about these events, and that's what made it possible for us to continue." But in the heyday of such San Francisco bands as Sly and the Family Stone, not all locals knew what to make of a group of black men playing accordion and fiddles and singing in French. Writing in his "On the Town" column in the *San Francisco Chronicle,* even esteemed music critic Ralph J. Gleason seemed as perplexed as he was entertained by the Opelousas Playboys' performance at the 1969 Berkeley Folk Festival. "A black Cajun band from Louisiana (turning out to be not quite that black) did its set with charm," he wrote.

Danny Poullard remembers when his music started to spread throughout the area. "The Catholic church scene was always big," he remembers. "Then I met Les Blank, and he got together with Chris Strachwitz and put us on KPFA one Thanksgiving Day, and then we started playing more on the East Side. We'd play these Polish halls and Slovakian halls, for these hippy dances, we'd call them. These people just ran up and down the hall, jumping up and down. You couldn't watch anybody and play at the same time, it would throw you off."

Poullard was born to a musical family in Ritchie, Louisiana. He recalls that his father, John Poullard, was a farmer and accordion player who had played with Amédé Ardoin but had moved the family to Beaumont, Texas, when Danny was thirteen. "When we started school in Beaumont, we were speaking broken English, and the kids would call us Frenchies," Poullard remembers. "A lot of them were from Louisiana too, but they learned to speak English at a younger age."

Following a stint in the military, Poullard decided to leave the Louisiana-Texas area for good. "They were hiring for refinery jobs, but they were bypassing me," he says. "With all the racism down there, I decided I wasn't going to stay in Beaumont for the rest of my life." Things seemed better in California, he adds. "They have so many kinds of ethnic backgrounds here in the Bay Area, they just didn't give a shit who or what I was."

Poullard didn't begin playing accordion until he was well into his thirties and living in California. He had joined the Opelousas Playboys as a bass player, and began taking a series of unusual accordion lessons from John Simien. Recalls Poullard: "I was going to his house every week on Wednesdays and he'd give me lessons. But I didn't show him I was learning anything, because I knew his ways. But I'd take what he'd give me, and go home and practice. Then one day we were all in John's house, and he said, 'Danny, how come you don't ever play the accordion here?' So we had a few beers and I finally cut loose, and I played one of the tunes he had been teaching me. And when I kicked off that tune, he was pissed. After that, he wouldn't show me anything anymore."

Poullard remembers that his father had never wanted him to play accordion. Like Amédé Ardoin, John Poullard had once been ambushed on the way back from a house dance. He had been shot in the back and left for dead. But after Danny started playing, his father would visit him in California and teach him both his style and his old songs. In time, Danny Poullard began to play accordion with a splinter group from the Opelousas Playboys called the Louisiana Playboys.

Both the Opelousas Playboys and the Louisiana Playboys continued to build devoted followings around the Bay Area. In 1975 George Broussard was excited to hear that the *San Francisco Examiner & Chronicle* was going to send a reporter and photographer to cover a Mardi Gras dance at All Hallows. "We were up there trying to look good, because this guy's going to write a big story about us," he recalls. During the dance, Broussard introduced a friend of the band who had started playing accordion during informal jam sessions. They had thought it might be fun if she sat in with the band during the Mardi Gras dance. She was reluctant, but that night, when she picked up the accordion, the effect on the crowd was immediate. "Believe me, all the focus became on her," Broussard remembers. "I knew right then, boy, we're not going to get too much in that paper."

When Broussard had introduced this friend, Ida Guillory, as "the queen of the Mardi Gras," the writer, Peter Levine, picked up on it. A month later, the title was displayed on the cover of the newspaper's Sunday magazine. The minute she picked up her accordion that night at All Hallows, Guillory was beginning her lifelong reign as Queen Ida.


Queen Ida Guillory lifts thirty pounds of accordion and hands it out the front door. "Good luck, kid," she calls out. "Just don't leave that on the plane. You know, Myrick did that once." She starts to close the door and then turns back. "Tell Al 'good luck,'" she adds.

She locks the door, pulls back a curtain, and watches the teenager struggle with the box up the steep San Francisco street. "Don't drop it, kid," she mutters.

Guillory goes into the kitchen to make coffee. Except for the 1983 Grammy displayed in a glass cabinet, her living room seems typical for many homes in this pleasant suburb just south of San Francisco: a comfortable sofa on thick carpet, an old low-tech stereo against the wall. And Guillory herself, a tiny woman dressed in a pink pants suit, doesn't immediately strike one as a performer who makes national television appearances or who is on first-name terms with Francis Ford Coppola. Then, after returning with two cups and saucers, she launches into the tale of Queen Ida.

She was born Ida Lewis in Lake Charles on January 15, 1929, the fourth in a family of seven. When she was nine, her parents, Ben and Elvina Lewis, moved the family to Beaumont, Texas. On her eighteenth birthday they moved again, to San Francisco.

"My sister Hazel got married and her husband was stationed here," she remembers. "In July 1945 my dad went to visit her. He left this hot weather in Texas, and when he came back, he told my mother she might like it in California. He was getting tired of this sunup to sundown, no clocks. The farming life. He said, 'You got to pray all year, and it's just a pressure on the mind.' And they made that decision, and we moved in 1947."

Guillory's youngest brother is musician Al Rapone, born Al Lewis, who currently lives in New Orleans. Rapone was ten years old when the family made the move to California. "My brother and I went up with one of my cousins on a train," he recalls. "My dad sold everything he had but two trucks, an International and a GMC. That International was a big thing that he used to use to haul the rice. So it was like the Beverly Hillbillies going out there, man, only this was the San Francisco Creoles. I swear, we had tubs and pots hanging on the side of that thing."

Ben Lewis had written ahead and been granted permission to bring sacks of his own rice into California, but the family still had problems at the border. "Mom had peaches, pears, watermelons, and she was going to start her big patch in California," Rapone remembers. "But when we got to that border, they made us leave all that stuff. She pulled out her rosary, said a prayer, and was crying. First time she'd been out of Louisiana. My dad, he just sat there and ate all the food. They ate everything, and got sick. But that's how they got here."

The Lewis family settled in the Bernal Heights district. "It was a conglomeration of Italians and Latinos, and that was about it," Rapone says. "One of my first friends was an Italian, and I had dinner at their house. They had spaghetti, and I was scared to tell them I ate rice. Finally, I had dinner at a Mexican house, and they had that rice, and I said, 'All right!' So I started hanging out with the Latino guys, and we were like brothers. They loved gumbo, and I loved menudo."

Ben Lewis found a job as a meat packer, and his family settled into their new lives. "John Simien used to come around, and he'd bring his accordion, and my brother Willie would play rubboard," remembers Queen Ida Guillory. "We had met some guys that were playing in a jazz band, so we left the old folks at home with the little accordion. They'd have a little party, have a few friends over for drinks and gumbo, and they'd sit down in the basement or garage and dance."

Elvina Lewis began to make annual trips back to Louisiana, and would return with suitcases filled with food and records. "That was a four-day journey in those little cars," Rapone recalls. "She would bring back homemade smoked sausages, and by the time she'd get here, there's be a little bacteria forming on those sausages. She'd go and get her rag with vinegar and clean it up, man, and resmoke it. I mean, where were you going to find this stuff in San Francisco? Safeway? Hey!"

Elvina Lewis also returned with music. Each trip, she bought stacks of Cajun and zydeco 45s and albums, usually warped from the journey. One day she came back with an accordion. Remembers Guillory: "Everybody wanted to see that accordion. She sat the boys down, three boys: Willie, Al, and Paul. She said, 'I brought this accordion back for you boys to keep the music alive, because it's dying in Louisiana and Texas.' And she opened the box, and there was the accordion. But she had said 'boys,' and that was a message to us. When Mom would leave, us girls would grab it too, just to see. And then we'd hurry up and put it back in the box! At the time, I didn't think an accordion was very ladylike, anyway."

Al showed the most interest in the music. He'd first heard the accordion back in Lake Charles, when his uncles Louis and Marius Broussard played house dances on Sunday afternoons. "When they were playing waltzes and dancing close, they'd get rid of me," he says. "But the house was built on stilts, so I'd go underneath, where I could find the accordion. Then

*Mary and Egan Perkin, Al Rapone, Hazel Bellow, and Edna Bordelon,*
*Hoffman Hall, San Francisco, circa 1950.*

I'd serve coffee and tea, whatever I could do to get in there. I'd grab the accordion, and they'd smack me on the hand and say, 'That's not a toy, son.' But they'd take their time playing the melody, so I could look at their hands. It wasn't really lessons, but those were the guys that were really responsible for me and Ida's band. If they had been rice farmers, maybe today I'd be designing farm equipment."

When he was thirteen and living in San Francisco, Rapone formed a band with two brothers originally from Lafayette. A friend from Mexico played maracas, and they began performing at a local Latin bar called La Bamba. "I was playing my Cajun-Creole music, and the Louisiana people would come and get down," he says. "We'd be doing 'Hip et Taïaut,' and we'd do 'Les flammes d'enfer' — 'The Flames of Hell' — five different ways. The Mexicans were looking at us, trying to figure out what's going on here. They played the same style accordion, so it sounded familiar. So I went down to the record shop and picked up a couple 45s by Flaco Jiminez, just to get by. They served free menudo every Sunday, and it got to be a weekly thing. This is when my music started to get a little Latin flavored."

*Dancers, Hoffman Hall.*

Like Danny Poullard, Rapone soon found a reluctant teacher in John Simien. "He wasn't really a tutor, because that wasn't his bag," he says. "But he'd at least indulge me for an hour, and play his licks. I was clever enough to keep them in my head, and when I got home, I played them one note at a time."

Rapone's uncle Marius was George Broussard's father, and Rapone remembers his cousin organizing the early San Francisco dances. "George had one of the 'forty-eight Chevys with the torpedo back, and he was one of the ones that came and went between Louisiana and California," he recalls. "He's an idealist, and he got the idea. He said, 'Wait a minute — music, money, hey!' And he started bringing musicians up from Louisiana."

Rapone went into the military for four years, where he played cymbal for the drum and bugle corps, and began to receive formal music training. He came home to enroll in college with a major in music, and performed in a trio at local cocktail lounges. He also played with Jimmy Reed and Lowell Fulson, and had a two-year stint playing guitar for Big Mama Thornton. "She beat the shit out of a guitar player and came to the club where I was working and said, 'Hey, pretty boy, I want you to play some guitar for me,'" he remembers. "That's where I learned about the blues."

On Sundays the family would gather, and Al would play accordion. By this time his sister Ida had also settled down in San Francisco, married to Raymond Guillory, a man she'd met years earlier at a church dance in Lake Charles. Soon Al began teaching her the accordion. "We'd go downstairs to my little bedroom, and we'd practice like hell," he remembers. "Then we'd go back upstairs, and we'd bring Mom and Dad in. My brother Willie would play rubboard, and my sister Hazel would get them up to dance. Ida and I would be playing our hearts out. It was just partying, our style, for our elderly parents, and our own faith."

At the time, nobody could have predicted that Ida would go on to a career in music. Her uncles Louis and Marius Broussard had performed for dances, but her mother, Elvina Lewis, had always confined her accordion playing to the house. "If she had an accordion when you came into the house, by the time the door slammed, it'd be put away," Rapone remembers. There were few examples of women who played dance hall music in Louisiana and Texas. "You didn't participate in a man's world, like playing guitar and drums and accordion," Ida Guillory explains. "The only person that I knew of was Joe Falcon's wife, Cleoma, who played drums with him. But he was there, and they were always together. It's not like, 'Hey, I'm going to play drums with this band.' This was a husband-and-wife situation."

"Someone once asked me, 'Are you liberated?'" she continues, laughing. "I said, 'Well, not necessarily liberated, but I did manage to push forward into doing something different, like the accordion. And when I finally did pick up the accordion, I looked at Mom and wondered what she would say. I said, 'Mom, where's Al's accordion?' She said, 'Well, I guess it's in his room downstairs, where he does his rehearsal.' And I said, 'It sounds so good, I have to try my hand at it.' And I watched her. She just smiled. The only thing she said one day was, 'You keep at it.' Well, that was the encouragement."

Her lessons with her brother continued. "He would pick it up and I'd watch him," she remembers. "He was very technical when he wanted me to play a song, and he would go button to button and give it back to me. I'd say, 'But, Al, this sounds — .' 'No, I want it just like this.' By this time Al had been studying music in college, and he taught me how to work with a band. In fact, I got most of my music training from Al. You can't learn that accordion in school."

During this time Ida and Raymond Guillory started going to the Opelousas Playboys' Saturday afternoon jam sessions. "The wives of these

men were there, and finally one day they said, 'Why don't you grab the accordion?'" Ida remembers. "I checked with my husband, and he said,
'That's OK.' And I would jam a little bit with the guys, and all the wives
would say, 'Go ahead, Ida, get in there with those guys.' That was a big help,
because I still kind of felt like I shouldn't do it."

After Ida's three children started school, she began to drive a school
bus. She soon discovered that the job provided many opportunities to practice the accordion. "I was around forty years old at the time, playing a little
bit at these parties," she says. "I used to take the accordion with me on the
bus, and while they were playing their football and basketball, I would park
the bus a long distance from the field, and I would be sure nobody else was
around, and I'd get the accordion and practice. They never even knew that
I had it."

Then came the night at All Hallows, and soon everyone in town knew.


It began innocently enough: George Broussard was helping organize a benefit for the parochial school athletic program. Al asked his sister to sit in
with his band. "And I said, 'Oh God, not for the public,'" Ida remembers.
"And my husband said, 'Why don't you do it? It's for a good cause.' And of
course Al repeated that too. That night, I remember people taking pictures,
but had I known that this guy was going to write about me or take my picture, I would never have gone on that stage."

When the article came out, club owners contacted All Hallows trying to
find the accordion player on the cover of the Sunday magazine. The church
passed them to George Broussard, who passed them to Ida. "I kept getting
these phone calls, and I kept saying, 'I'm sorry, but I was only sitting in for
the good cause of the benefit,' and I gave them my brother's number.

"And finally Al calls me, and he says, 'Well, Sis, you're going to have to
come sit in with us.' I said, 'Are you kidding?' He says, 'They want to see the
lady.' I said, 'Al, you know I only have five songs.' He says, 'Well, you'll have
to play the five songs.'"

Al Rapone was confident that his sister had what it takes to play zydeco
accordion. "When we got together to do this thing, I knew she had the guts,"
he explains. "When we were growing up in Texas, she was always out there
beating the boys, solid. Ida was outrunning the boys in the footrace. Out-
riding them in a horse race. Outswimming them across the canal. And when
we'd be visiting Mom, the accordions would break out. Every time I played
a new lick, she started daring me that she could do this and do that. So I
knew she had the competitive nature."

The calls kept coming. With Al Rapone arranging and playing lead guitar, Queen Ida and the Bon Temps Band started on the festival circuit by
playing the San Francisco Blues Festival. "When we played that, it was the
headlines again," Rapone recalls. "Clifton Chenier was the man all the time,
but we were getting all the publicity, because we were on the West Coast.

"After that we played the Haight Ashbury," he continues, laughing. "Oh
man, what a place. They were selling gingerbread, you know, space cookies.
You know what I mean. And then we played at parties, where it was all sit-
down. But I was happy they all liked the music."

One year at the New Orleans Jazz Fest, Rapone talked to Clifton Chenier, who was following Queen Ida on the same stage. He asked Chenier if
he'd like to perform together on his next trip to California. He recalls that
Chenier was hesitant, but finally agreed.

Queen Ida also remembers that show: "I didn't know how Clifton would
take that. I didn't know how the men, period, would accept a middle-aged
woman on the stage with an accordion. That was my concern for a long
time. So Clifton and I played together that night at the Mainliner Club in
San Mateo. And he sat right down at the front, in the first table, and he just
watched me the whole time. And I kept thinking, 'Oh God, is he just going
to think that this little lady should be home with her kids?'

"And then he said to me, 'Lady, you're tough.' When he told me this,
I felt really good. I knew if he accepted me, the other male performers
will, too."

Less than a year after the Mardi Gras show at All Hallows, Queen
Ida and the Bon Temps Band signed with the Los Angeles–based label
GNP/Crescendo. Although Al and Ida sang in French, the songs on their
first album, *Play the Zydeco*, revealed that the San Francisco experience and
the La Bamba days had an influence. The rhythms, accordion work, and
vocal harmonies introduced a Tex-Mex flavor that would become Queen
Ida's signature sound, coming to full flavor on a later song, "Zydeco Taco."

Among the selections on *Play the Zydeco* were a number of traditional
tunes Rapone recalled hearing his uncles play, as well as originals such as
"Rosa Majeure," which he based on an old folk tale that all of Elvina Lewis's
children heard growing up. "My mother did most of the storytelling," Ida
recalls. "She told us all about Barbe Bleue, which means Bluebeard. He
would kill the women and put them in a room, to scare us from going into
empty buildings. And 'Rosa majeure' means Rosa of legal age. The story is
about a girl who asked her parents if she could go to a dance on this big
bridge called La Pont du Nord. They said no, but she went anyway. The
bridge collapsed, so Rosa fell in the water and drowned.

"So Al wrote a song about that," she continues. "And I said to Al, 'Do you think we should translate that, because the music is very lively, and the words are sad.' And he said, 'No, we'll just leave it in French.' And when I play that song, the music is so lively and people are just dancing, and here comes *'Rosa Majeur était au bal, samedi à soir,'* which means Rosa went to the ball on Saturday night. And that's when the bridge collapses. But that's the nature of the music and the culture: the lyrics are sad and the music is lively.

"My mother was still living, but she was blind at that time, and she was bedridden. But she knew all about our music. Al would tape whenever we played together, and he'd bring it to her and have her listen to it. She was very pleased, very proud, and she'd say, 'Hmm, you guys are sounding good.' In other words, 'Well, they're doing what I asked.'"

From her base in California, Queen Ida continued to blaze new trails for zydeco. In 1979 she began working with agent John Ullman, whose Seattle-based Traditional Arts Services — launched with funding from the NEA — brought her into museums and other fine-arts venues throughout the country and overseas; she was the first zydeco accordionist to tour Japan. In 1983 *Queen Ida on Tour* became the first zydeco album to receive a Grammy. By the mid-eighties, she was on the road two hundred nights a year; she opened for the South African group Ladysmith Black Mambazo at Carnegie Hall, and performed on-camera in a street dance scene in Francis Ford Coppola's *Rumble Fish.* Perhaps no artist but Buckwheat Zydeco would make more television appearances: her trademark headband and peacock feathers were displayed on both *Saturday Night Live* and *Mr. Rogers' Neighborhood.* "They had to keep reshooting my scene," she says about the latter. "I got so excited watching King Friday I forgot my line." Her presence in mid-eighties pop culture reached a curious zenith in the Clint Eastwood movie *Sudden Impact;* before Dirty Harry utters the phrase "Go ahead, make my day," he calls in a license plate number by reading "Queen Ida" for the letters Q and I.

Al Rapone produced *Queen Ida on Tour,* and brother and sister went on stage together to accept their Grammy. Today they lead separate bands, but in the Spring of 1998 they started work on new material for a family album. They also reunited for their older sister Hazel's fiftieth wedding anniversary. "Hazel is the duchess — you put that down," says Rapone. "It was the biggest family reunion since the move to California." Rapone currently works with the Minneapolis-based band The Butanes; in 1997 he released *Al Rapone Plays Tribute,* a collection of songs associated with Clifton Chenier. Queen Ida continues to record for GNP/ Crescendo. In 1990 she published a cookbook, *Cookin' With Queen Ida,* which she dedicated to her mother. Included in the book are stories of growing up in Lake Charles, as well as instructions for making gumbo, etouffee, and tamale pie. Her son Myrick "Freeze"

Guillory has followed her into zydeco, first playing with her band, and now leading his own group, Nouveau Zydeco.

Ida admits that now she is being more selective about her touring schedule. "I'm tired of being away from home and living out of a suitcase," she says. "Now I say, 'Get Myrick.' I'm still booked into next year, but not as much. My husband used to be with me, and my brothers, so my family was there. But my oldest brother retired from the rubboard, and now my husband doesn't take long trips anymore. I remember going on tour once this year, and my son couldn't be there, and I felt very lonely."

But Queen Ida had one last recourse. "I called my daughter," she says, "and she flew out and joined the band."


Not everybody who moved to California stayed. "A lot of them, after they've been out there, and they made the money, they're coming back home," says Al Rapone. "Way back when we left, there's no air conditioning. And they'll take a chance on a hurricane as opposed to an earthquake. I've talked to several people there who are thinking along those lines."

George Broussard is one of them. "My intention is to return to Louisiana and see if I can do a little bit of fishing and sit back and relax after all this hard work," he says. "It will be over thirty years since I left." Broussard doesn't expect to retire completely: he is already planning to stage zydeco and Cajun dances at a new Broussard Community Center, a building next to his boyhood home off Highway 190 in the town of Tyrone. "When you retire from music, you got something to look back on," he says. "You can say, 'Well, that was my accomplishment.'"

Many of the founders of the West Coast scene have passed away. The music of John Simien, accordionist Wilfred Latour, fiddler Edgar Leday, and accordionist Ambrose Sam can no longer be heard in houses and church halls on Saturday nights. Some of the finest dancers are gone, too. "Ullus Gobart was a left-handed fiddler, and he was probably the best dancer we had," Broussard remembers. "He could go to one of them dances and never quit, until his shirt was wringing wet."

In San Francisco, Danny Poullard has seen a number of musicians pass through his carport accordion university, including Kevin Wimmer and Suzy Thompson, who plays fiddle with Poullard in the California Cajun Orchestra, which also features Lake Charles native Charlie St. Mary on rubboard. Covering songs by everyone from Boozoo Chavis to Iry LeJeune, the California Cajun Orchestra typifies the West Coast's unique contributions to the music: women musicians, racially integrated bands, and the joining of styles that are usually maintained as separate entities back home. "In

Louisiana, they want to label the music behind who's playing it," Poullard explains. "I sat in some festivals years ago and they had a bunch of accordion players from Louisiana, and we all played the same tune. But when I got to play the tune, they said it was Creole music. I don't see how it could be called Creole style or Cajun style. It's a personal style.

"In Louisiana, the Creoles and the blacks think the Cajun is for white music," he continues. "Hell, the Cajun playing is what Amédé really paved the road for. And how the hell are they going to be prejudiced against that music? All the years we fought like hell to get it together, and you got some people in Louisiana trying to tear it apart.

"Oh yeah, I've heard a lot of people criticize it. I don't sit too well with that. You hear, 'Oh man, Danny Poullard's just playing the Cajun music, he can't play no zydeco music.' And those guys, they don't know what I can play. I can play Clifton music, I can play Boozoo music, Beau Jocque, I can play Amédé's music, I can play any damn thing I want to.

"Once, I bet some guys that I would play all the way to Los Angeles in a mobile home and play the dance and then play all the way back to San Francisco, and not play the same tune. They said, 'Oh, I doubt that very seriously.' I put out two hundred dollars, I said, 'This is the money I'm making tonight. Put it up.' They didn't take it, but I showed them anyway."

Danny Poullard counts himself as one Louisiana expatriate who has no plans to return. "I like to visit, but things are not right down there for me," he says. "You can see it all and it reminds you of the reason why you left. I can't see anybody going back over there that's been gone a long time like I have."

As in Louisiana and Texas, the California zydeco scene is thriving. It is a bit more centrally organized than its Southern counterpart: monthly calendars are posted on the Internet, and there are zydeco telephone hotlines available in every major city. Busy promoters such as "Louisiana Sue" Ramon regularly bring Louisiana bands to scores of clubs and festivals along the West Coast, joining homegrown bands such as T-Lou, Zydeco Flames, Bonne Musique, Motor Dude Zydeco, and Benny and the Swamp Gators. Los Angeles–based fiddler Lisa Haley used to play with Queen Ida; today she leads her own popular band, the Zydekats, and works frequently with accordionist Joe Simien, who still lives in south-central Los Angeles. Widely considered a patron saint of the Southern California zydeco scene, Simien admitted in an interview with Jim Washburn for the *Los Angeles Times* that he still misses much about his old home. "Onstage sometimes it makes me think of things when I was young," he said. "Some of these pieces remind me of going out riding on a horse, when you'd go way out there on the country road, just sing and test your voice out. There's nothing bad to the memory, but you can get so deep into it you feel kind of blue."

The church dances that began in the early 1960s can still be found in both Los Angeles and the Bay Area. This is the scene on a recent Saturday night at St. John's Church, located on the outskirts of San Francisco. The dance, sponsored by an association of Bell System employees called the Telephone Pioneers, is in the gym; the basketball hoops are latched to the ceiling, and the electric bingo boards are dark for the night. Paul Ardoin — "Yes, one of those Ardoins," he says, nodding — is checking on the gumbo. A local cable access program called *Soul Beat* is interviewing an elderly Creole man, who wears a three-piece suit and blinks in the light, talking about how zydeco is a snap bean. Behind him, rows of dancers are learning the "zydeco shuffle," a line dance that Californians seem to enjoy more than their kin back home.

On the bandstand in the corner is Andre Thierry, a high-school-age accordionist and one of the most popular young players in the Bay Area. Thierry is grandson to Mama Lena Pitre, the friend of Clifton Chenier who, with her husband, used to bring the Zydeco King to her St. Mark's parish in Richmond. The St. Mark's events continue to this day; piled on Thierry's bandstand is a stack of pink leaflets advertising Pitre's next dance.

Although Thierry has been playing accordion for several years, he originally limited himself to instrumentals. But recently he's been building up the confidence to sing in both English and French, and he's now in the middle of a tune he learned from the band Zydeco Force:

> I'm on my way,
> I'm on my way,
> And I ain't coming back no more.

Walking through the crowd is R. C. Carrier, a local rubboard player with a band called Zydeco Slim. He's carrying plastic cups of beer for his table, but he's stopped by a thin man in a black suit and yellow-tinted glasses who puts a hand on his arm.

"You a Carrier?" the man asks.

"Yeah."

"My mama and daddy, they're from Opelousas, Lawtell. He's a Carrier, she's a Simien."

"Yeah!"

"Where are your people from?"

"Church Point."

"That's the same one, the same one!"

"If you keep to the zydeco, you're going to meet a lot of people here," promises Carrier.

Continuing back to his table, he passes two men talking.

"I know all your people," says one. "You're the Lake Charles Thibodeaux."

"That's right," says the other.

"Your auntie ran the Cotton Club."

"That's right."

Andre Thierry goes to the microphone. He looks at the lines of dancers taking steady, short steps, moving in waves up to the stage, and he keeps the song going:

> I'm goin' to stay,
> I'm goin' to stay,
> And I ain't going back no more.

*Clifton Chenier at 1975 Tribute to Cajun Music, Lafayette, Louisiana.*

# 12

# CORONATION BLUES

O NE NIGHT AT THE BLUE ANGEL CLUB, Clifton Chenier took the bandstand with a giant red crown rising above his head. "I want you all to take this," he taunted the crowd. "Take it from me, take it. I said, if you all beat me playing accordion, I want you to take it. But now remember, you got to beat me now. And I ain't lying, either."

The scene, filmed by Les Blank for *Hot Pepper*, was repeated at the Blue Angel and at other dance clubs and church halls where Chenier played throughout the 1970s. To Clifton Chenier, the zydeco crown — he also wore a jeweled leather diadem, which functioned to keep the sweat from his face — was very real. "I heard somebody make a statement one time, where it's all a gimmick," says C. J. Chenier. "It wasn't no gimmick to my daddy."

But there is little agreement about where Chenier got his crown or under what circumstances. Theories variously advanced by zydeco musicians are that it came from Lafayette, St. Martinville, California, Spain, the Queen of England, or the Pope. The possibility that Chenier crowned himself is widely considered heresy. That is, however, the view of his former producer Chris Strachwitz.

"I think he was a self-crowned king," Strachwitz suggests. "I don't think there was any ceremony, he just started putting it on. It was just there in the

221

box one day. At the same time, I heard there was this guy that was selling cars on that Channel 10 in Lafayette, where Clifton was appearing on *Passe Partout,* and this guy was calling himself the king of cars.

"But I think the main thing was that he took it after James Brown. James Brown would do this cape business, and Cliff would say, 'You know, James Brown got this thing, man.' Then he came out with the crown, and he had these pictures made of him wearing it. I don't remember what year that was, nineteen seventy-something. But he was really crazy about that crown."

In a rare interview on the subject, Chenier offered a different origin. "That goes back to 'seventy-one," he told writer Ben Sandmel. "In Europe they had an accordion contest and they had about five hundred accordion players, but I was the only one — in other words, they had a lot of accordion players, but they couldn't capture my style. But I could play their style, so that's how I walk out with that crown. I've been having it ever since. I tell you what, to get that crown, you have to roll me."

A writer faces certain obstacles when he tries to dig too deeply into the story. I learned this the hard way during a brief telephone interview with Clifton Chenier's widow, Margaret Chenier:

Q: Do you have Mr. Clifton's crown?

A: Well, I have it put up.

Q: Is it displayed in the club?

A: No, no, not in my club. Not in my house either.

Q: So you have it in storage?

A: Uh-huh. Clifton's crown is Clifton's crown. Their crown is theirs. He has his own crown. He won that crown from judges.

Q: Where did that crown come from?

A: Overseas. They judged that crown there. They had judges sitting there. I don't know about the others.

Q: Do you know what country that was?

A: No.

Q: He used to wear that —

A: Sometimes.

Q: Was the crown important to him?

A: Oh yes. It meant a lot.

Q: What would he say about it?

A: If I tell you that over the phone, that's going to mean a lot of money.

Q: In your opinion is Clifton the King of Zydeco?

A: I can't give you that answer, baby, I can't. All right? All right.

The origins of the crown may be forever buried in self-generated mythology. Yet no matter who glued the rows of blue, orange, and silver paste jewels to the headpiece, or stuffed the red velvet cap, it was commonly agreed that the crown was Chenier's birthright. It looked good on him. It accented the gold in his teeth and rings, and the glitter of his accordion. Most important, Chenier's music established a proper measure for zydeco — much as a king's foot established the measure of a foot.

Most of Chenier's moves were imitated by other players, and the crown was no exception. By the mid-1970s placards tacked to the peeling paint of country dance clubs billed Hiram Sampy as the Zordico King, or Wilfred Latour as the King of French Music. From Houston came Jabo, the Texas Prince of Zydeco. From Carencro came Fernest Arceneaux, a talented triple-row accordion player who scored a hit when his instrumental "Zydeco Boogaloo" became a club standard, and who was thenceforth pronounced on placards the New Prince of Zydeco.

But these were mostly jovial riffs on the theme of royalty, not serious challenges. As in the world of boxing, there was a shared understanding that rivalries built interest and fattened the purse for all players. In his lifetime, Chenier faced only one challenge for his crown that he — and his fans — took seriously. It came from within the ranks of his Red Hot Louisiana Band, from Stanley "Buckwheat Zydeco" Dural Jr.

Dural had decided to form his own band in 1978, and guitarist "Little Buck" Senegal went with him. While Buckwheat Zydeco was making his name, Chenier's illness was slowing him down, forcing him to cancel some performances. Then came this article from the Houston *Forward Times* of August 2, 1980: "Stanley 'Buckwheat' Dural was recently crowned King of Zydeco. The crowning event highlighted Buckwheat's colorful career and brought to a close the reign of Clifton Chenier."

His official title was Texas King of Zydeco, but Dural now remembers that he went to the coronation reluctantly. He offers his final words on the subject: "They gave it to me at a church hall in Houston. I didn't like it then, but I didn't tell them that. And I don't like it now. Because if it hadn't been for Clifton Chenier to pave this way, there wouldn't be no way of doing it. Clifton Chenier's the King of Zydeco today and tomorrow, and always will be. You see what I'm saying? All the other stuff is just kind of silly. It's obsolete. I don't have no time for it, to be honest with you."

But in the early 1980s, Senegal was calling Dural to the stage as the "crowned king of zydeco." The title of Dural's Blues Unlimited album *People's Choice* was interpreted as a claim to the throne, and Dural posed in his sequined cape and purple crown for the cover of his first Rounder album, *Turning Point*. Then came a showdown: On Halloween weekend 1982, at the first Texas-Louisiana Blues and Zydeco Festival in Houston's Summit Auditorium, the two accordionists faced a highly anticipated shared billing.

Rockin' Sidney Simien opened the show, and he remembers that he watched the proceedings in amazement. "Back then, Buckwheat was calling himself king, and they crowned him up in Houston," Simien recounts. "Clifton and them was mad about that. So first, Buckwheat came on. He had his little short cape with this little crown, and when they brought him up there, he came on running. Then Cliff came on, and he was mad at Buckwheat. Cliff had just had his foot operated on, so he walked slow. And Cliff looked like more the real king. He had that big old long blue cape, it looked like it had diamonds on it. And he had this big old crown, with rubies and stuff. Fake, but it looked like the real thing. And Cliff had that little smile where he'd show the gold.

"So when he walked up there, he sat down, and he took his time. Then he started talking. '*Eh toi*, I've been up here, all of them talking about playing zydeco. I ain't heard no zydeco yet. I'll show you how zydeco would go.' Man, people just jumped out and they hollered and started dancing. Then he said, 'I've been all over the world' — and he's talking about Buckwheat here — 'and I'm not just a king in Houston. I'm king all over the world.' And he took that little crown off and he threw it. He said, 'I don't need this. Everybody knows that I'm King of Zydeco.' And he threw that damn thing." That was the performance that made such an impact on Simien that he would devote the next couple years of his career to restaging it as a puppet show.

The Houston festival would also prove to be one of Chenier's last performances with his crown. "He didn't want to wear that no more," remembers Warren Ceasar. "He didn't care about being no king. He just wanted to live the rest of his years out." Instead, when Chenier talked to his crowds, he repeatedly referred to his Grammy as his crowning achievement. Buckwheat Zydeco also began to look at his costume as so much velvet and rhinestones. "I don't really know where it now is," he says. "The Hard Rock Café called and said, 'Do you have anything to donate?' I said, 'Yes, you can have that.'"

When Chenier died, his crown was placed in his casket near his head. Many believed it was buried with him, both literally and symbolically. But after his death and burial, while his fans were still in a state of shock, the problem of the crown quickly resurfaced. For among those many players billing themselves as the Prince of Zydeco at the time of Chenier's death, one had plans to elevate his status: Rockin' Dopsie.

Born in 1932 in Carencro, Louisiana, Alton "Rockin' Dopsie" Rubin began playing accordion when he was eight. He became famous as the left-handed musician who could play his accordion upside down. Among his many accomplishments was an educational tour of Southwest Louisiana schools with Cajun fiddler Dewey Balfa. He also toured extensively, becoming perhaps best known for his regular Friday night shows at the Maple Leaf Bar in New Orleans. In 1986, he joined Paul Simon on his *Graceland* album in a song that paid tribute to "Clifton Chenier, King of the Bayou."

Rockin' Dopsie was a friend of the Cheniers; his son David "Rockin' Dopsie Jr." Rubin received lessons on rubboard while sitting on Cleveland Chenier's front stoop. Rockin' Dopsie Sr. even escorted Clifton Chenier to the stage for his final performance at the Zydeco Festival. Shortly after Chenier's death, however, Rockin' Dopsie stumbled into a public relations nightmare. On January 3, 1988, just three weeks after Chenier's death, he and his family staged an event that suggested to many observers that he was attempting a zydeco coup d'état.

That winter's night, about three hundred people responded to the promise of a coronation in a banquet hall in Lafayette's Hotel Acadiana. A handful of zydeco musicians were present, including Major Handy, Fernest Arceneaux, and Rockin' Sidney Simien. But any questions about who was sponsoring the event were answered when patrons paid their six-dollar cover charge and their hands were stamped "Rockin' Dopsie King of Zydeco." Then, to the delight of some present — but to the shock of many others — Lafayette mayor Dud Lastrapes went before the crowd and ceremoniously placed a crown on Rockin' Dopsie's head.

Years later, Lastrapes couldn't recall much about the night. "There was a request from Rockin' Dopsie and his people," he said. "I mean, this is not something we normally do in the city, but I like to take part in a lot of events. This guy was recognized as one of the outstanding musicians in zydeco, and I was happy to respond."

Writing in the Lafayette weekly *Times of Acadiana*, Katrinna Huggs reported that Dopsie's acceptance speech paid tribute to Chenier: "'He told me on his deathbed, "I'm going, but keep the thing going." We started in 1955 and they didn't have nobody but me and Clifton. Well, ladies and gentlemen, I'm going to break myself in two if I don't keep it going.'"

But the nod to Chenier didn't smooth ruffled feathers. Louisiana is a state known for clownish behavior by its elected representatives, but musicians are somehow held to a higher standard. Huggs echoed the sentiments of many when she editorialized: "Is an elected city official knowledgeable enough about the merits of a musician to declare him 'king of zydeco' in the first place, implying endorsement by the city? And secondly, how legitimate is a crowning of any sort when the 'king' calls for his own crowning?" The issue was the subject of a brutal volley of letters to the editor. "I have not been lately as embarrassed or outraged by any public figure as I am by Rockin' Dopsie," started one of the milder responses.

Among those unhappy about the event was Clifton Chenier's son, C. J. Chenier. "It was just a couple weeks after my daddy died, and I was riding to Lafayette one day, and I was listening on the radio about the crowning of the new king," he recalls. "It kind of upset me, because it seemed like they didn't give us a chance to put my daddy in the ground and here's somebody trying to jump on him. I don't know, I was just upset, so I wrote that song." His song "You're Still the King To Me" was released on his *Hot Rod* album.

> There was a lot of folks
> Always hanging around
> Telling a bunch of jokes
> Like, "Hey, I got the crown."

> But like he used to say,
> "You can have this crown, you see,
> But if you want to wear this crown,
> You got to take it away from me."

David "Rockin' Dopsie Jr." Rubin remembers that the criticism caught his father by surprise. "He'd sit at home a lot," he says. "A lot of times he said, 'If I had known that's how it would have been done toward me, I never would have done it.' That's why we hardly ever played in Lafayette. We didn't have a lot of support from the people. And to be honest with you, I still don't care to play the band here."

Rubin acknowledges that his father paid for the crown himself — he believes the bill was around $3,800 — and that it was custom-built by a Lafayette jeweler. But the controversy was misguided, he says. "See, after Clifton passed, when my daddy was crowned the king of zydeco by the mayor of Lafayette, it was a big turmoil. The *Times of Acadiana* just shot my dad down every week. But my dad was in the hospital the day Clifton Chenier died, and Clifton Chenier told my daddy, 'You know it took a long time to get where we are today.' And he said that back in the nineteen fifties, it was hard for them to do it, especially trying to win over a white audience. Clifton said, 'If anything happens to me, I want you to just keep the legacy going.' I was in the room. So I just let them write that criticism."

Rockin' Dopsie decided not to sport his $3,800 crown in most dance clubs or church halls in Southwest Louisiana or Texas. Instead he settled on a metal diadem and a brass plate for his accordion. Then, in 1993, he apparently started to consider the transfer of the zydeco crown. He approached musician Boozoo Chavis. Recalls David Rubin: "During the Jazz Fest, he and I and Boozoo were talking in the lobby of the Bayou Plaza Hotel. My dad still had the prince crown, and he said he wanted to crown Boozoo the prince of zydeco."

Rockin' Dopsie also contacted a private nonprofit organization, the Louisiana Hall of Fame, and announced his decision. The organization's founder and president, Lou Gabus, set out to make the coronation official. To her, this meant procuring documents signed by the mayor of Lafayette and Melinda Schwegman, the lieutenant governor of Louisiana. Another crowning was on the horizon.

Rockin' Dopsie's actions suggest that, all along, he had been sincerely concerned with the issue of succession. A prince, he must have figured, should become a king. And a king should anoint a prince. But when news of this impending coronation hit the zydeco community, old furies were instantly reignited, and the focus of criticism was again Rockin' Dopsie. Typical was this response from Herman Fuselier, writing in his "Bayou Boogie" column for the *Opelousas Daily World:* "When Chenier wore it, the crown was a symbol of achievement, kindness, and charisma. Musicians trampling over one another to anoint themselves king makes the culture look simple and tasteless."

Then, while the storm was still building, Rockin' Dopsie died. He suffered a heart attack on August 26, 1993. During the funeral, his family placed his city proclamation beside him in the coffin. Lou Gabus, head of the Louisiana Hall of Fame, found herself caught between lingering public outrage and a strong desire to honor a dead man's wishes. She decided that the best thing to do would be to crown as king the man Rockin' Dopsie wanted as prince. Carrying out such a task would have required an enormous amount of diplomacy. Unfortunately, Lou Gabus would prove herself no diplomat.

I first heard about the controversy in 1993, when I was told of a dispute backstage at the Zydeco Festival, which I was covering for *OffBeat* magazine. At first I thought I'd be writing a lighthearted tale of accordions and kings, perhaps a cross between a lively zydeco cutting contest and a Monty Python sketch. Then I began to hear that there were racial overtones in the struggles between Gabus, who is white, and the musicians and promoters involved with the festival, who are mostly black Creole. I called Gabus for an interview, and she picked up the phone on the first ring.

It became quickly apparent that having to defend her recent actions had put Gabus in a combative mood. Most of all, she said, she resented people who challenged the legitimacy of Dopsie's reign. "Mayor Lastrapes is the one who crowned Rockin' Dopsie and — honey, I don't give a damn — it's time to lay it to rest," she started. "The man was legally crowned king." As the conversation continued Gabus herself brought up the incident at the Zydeco Festival:

A: You know what the zydeco association did to me? They sent me two backstage passes, OK.

Q: These are the people who put on the Zydeco Festival?

A: Wait. So my friend and I, we get dressed, and Wilbert Guillory said they were going to read the proclamations in French and English. That Dopsie — see, Dopsie, he trusted me. As you know, Dopsie wasn't well educated. You know that. But yet, he put his trust in me. And he said, "If anything can be done right, Lou can do it." Getting the proclamations correct, and making sure that he's crowned. So he put his trust in me. The day after Dopsie died, I called Wilbert Guillory with the zydeco association. And before they jumped the gun, I told them, "Now, you better be careful. Dopsie did appoint a prince. So we got to be awfully careful before anybody jumps the gun." I said, "I have a proclamation from the mayor here of Lafayette, a hundred and five thousand people. And I have a proclamation from the lieutenant governor." And I said, "Since Dopsie is not here, we will not crown Boozoo prince." I said, "He will automatically become king."

Q: So this was —

A: So now, Wilbert Guillory says, "Well, come for the Zydeco Festival. We got to read it in French and in English, that poor Dopsie had appointed a prince." We were reading it around two-thirty, three. So around two I went up to the emcee. And I told him all about it. He said, "Well, it did not go through the zydeco association." I said, "Look, Mr. Wilbert Guillory told me to come here, and you all would read it in French and in English." And he said, "That has to be voted on." I said, "Voted on what!" And then he started on and on and on and on, and he said, "Well, we can't do this, because the zydeco association didn't vote for it." I said, "Hold on just a minute." I pulled the proclamation out. I said, "You see this is marked July the twenty-eighth," and I said, "You see Melinda Schwegmann's signature here?" I said, "That is just as legal as legal can be." You know what that smart son of a bitch answered me? "Well, maybe she better crown him." I said, "Well, maybe she will." I packed up my shit and I left.

Gabus talked about the various performers she's included in the Hall of Fame, then her voice began to rise as we went back to the subject of the Zydeco Festival.

A: I mean, you're well respected when you can bring in these people. And I'm not going to have a penny-ante outfit like the zydeco association telling me what to do. When they are just an association. They're not even registered with the state, did you know that? They don't have no state proclamations!

I was confused about who signed what proclamations, so I started an exchange that would end our conversation:

Q: So Dopsie had a certificate from Melinda Schwegmann?
A: No, Dopsie did not have that. Not Dopsie, no. Dopsie had the one from Mayor Lastrapes here in Lafayette when he was crowned king, but that's all he has. Now, Boozoo would have had one from Melinda Schwegmann, and one from the current mayor here, Kenny Bowen. But we did not do anything because of respect for Dopsie's family. That's in the future, babe.
Q: I think I have it straight.
A: Now, don't be like — do you really have to mention people's names? Just put a state proclamation and a city proclamation, without naming any names, because I don't want to have to kill a bunch of niggers.
Q: I'm sorry?
A: I don't have to kill a bunch of black ones.

Gabus then apologized, explaining that she was tired, and that it's not like her to be ugly. Of course, I knew she was not intending to make a serious threat. But I had identified myself as a journalist. From where did her comment — or joke — arise? I doubt I'll ever know. The conversation ended and I hung up the phone.

The story of the crown had changed, to say the least. It was no longer about Chenier's talent and how it had once shaped and shaken the zydeco scene. Nor was it simply about one man's ill-advised attempt at innocent self-promotion. Instead, I have come to believe that it has become bound up in the issue that has stayed on people's minds since they first heard from their grandparents about the dark-skinned accordionist who had to play his music outside the window. Or about Amédé Ardoin, the best musician of them all, beaten for accepting a white woman's handkerchief. The matter of crowning is subsumed in the larger question of whether black Creoles can feel at home within their own culture, and whether or not the rest of the world recognizes their prerogative to interpret — and argue over — who is the best exemplar of the spirit of zydeco.

"Zydeco musicians, man, they're basically not selfish people," Terrance Simien once told me. "They're just trying to maintain their position in the world of music. A lot of them know certain ways and can be mistaken by other people. So we have fucked-up silent little wars about this and that, and who's better, who's worse. You know, I think a lot of the competition comes from racism, thinking that one is better than the other.

"You see, when I was growing up, the bright-skinned Creoles discriminated against the dark-skinned Creoles — what sense did that make? And I've been discriminated, growing up with blacks, just because I wasn't all black, and that hurt just as much as the other. Nobody's better or worse than the next man. We all want to be able to rest when it's time for us to rest. Be able to do our job when it's time for us to do our job. And I believe that if

*Rockin' Dopsie coronation, 1987.*

*Boozoo Chavis coronation, 1994, with Lou Gabus on left.*

you go to any zydeco musician and ask them for help, they're going to try to help you, and that's the main thing."

The spirit of competition can take many forms. As Simien points out, it coexists with an equally powerful spirit of cooperation, dating back to rural traditions of *boucheries* and *coups de main* and afternoons when the community gathered to snap *les haricots*. Zydeco dancers are participants in the common experience of making music, much as *juré* singers were two generations earlier. A kingdom of zydeco, then, is a delicate balance. A monarch is ultimately decided by dancers voting with their feet.

Indeed, when Creoles go to the dance, they are making judgments on much more than how to spend a weekend. They decide how to dance, how to dress, and what type of food to eat. What language to speak and sing. How to live musically. They are determining just what it means to be Creole. It takes a king or queen, speaking through the accordion, to lead a crowd to agree on these matters. Doing so requires both talent and a deep under-standing of one's culture and one's times. That's the one-two combination of Clifton Chenier.

Today's zydeco players often use gestures to explain the effect of a suc-cessful song: they join their hands together and then make them crest like a wave. The motion symbolizes the way it looks and feels in a club when people abandon their tables and meet on the dance floor. There is no surer way to the zydeco throne than to play a song that creates that surge of bodies. And because zydeco emerges from this relationship between musicians and dancers, matters of royalty are taken seriously. When they dance out their culture and honor a zydeco king, Creoles are exercising that most funda-mental of human rights: self-definition.

"I don't really think Miss Lou represents the Afro-American Creole zy-deco artists," Wilbert Guillory explained after the incident at the Zydeco Festival. "I don't think it's fair for someone to come and dictate to us who should be the King of Zydeco. What if I went to the Cajun music association and said who would be the Cajun King of Music? They would kick my be-hind, or they would try. Excuse the expression.

"I look at zydeco music as a music that creates unity," he continued. "When you get twenty thousand people here for the festival, all day you don't even get so much as one person calling another a liar. I don't see any-thing here but zydeco that could do that."

But objections were futile: the machinery was in place for the crowning of the new king. The proclamations were signed. On April 10, 1994, Boozoo Chavis — an incorruptible musician if ever there was one, whose participa-tion in this event escaped criticism from nearly all quarters — boarded a white limousine. With his wife, Leona, he was driven into the center of Aca-dian Village, a collection of restored and replicated wooden buildings de-signed to be a simulacrum of a nineteenth-century Louisiana village — the kind of place Amédé Ardoin once hitchhiked to.

As their car approached, Lou Gabus, dressed in a pinstripe blazer and hoop earrings, was giving a final interview to filmmaker Bob Mugge, who had come to Louisiana to make the music documentary *The Kingdom of Zydeco*. "It's been pretty tough in the zydeco industry, about going back and forth with so many problems," she admitted. "So finally we're going to put it to rest, and Rockin' Dopsie will be able to rest in his grave. Thank you. I got to go."

She hurried to the ceremony. Shouts of "Long live the King!" were ris-ing from the small crowd. Chavis, dressed in a blue double-breasted suit and a white Stetson, followed the red carpet to the podium. The crown was placed on his head. Then he went to the microphone and politely thanked each and every one, and said he was honored. He thanked his children and talked about how they put up with him when he gets crabby.

"And, ladies and gentlemen, I appreciate this to the highest position," he concluded. "I want to say a little thing, no offense to nobody. But you know what, all these years back, I like to say that nobody didn't see me. I was the king all the time."

The crowd cheered. Then Chavis thanked the Dopsie family, and he nodded to producer Scott Billington from Rounder records. He pointed to Floyd Soileau and said he looked like a dude in his straw hat, and he waved to an old friend named Shine. Then he looked around. "Look here, I ain't going to talk no more, but this thing here is going to fall," he said about his crown. "You all are going to have to take that off."

"You're looking for that cowboy hat!" boomed his son Charles.

"Boozoo's looking for that cowboy hat!" repeated the announcer. "That one's going to stay on."

Then Charles took the microphone, and he told his father that he'd always been the king to his family. Later, he would admit that he had been crying behind his sun shades.

Following the event, Boozoo Chavis stood with his wife and son for a filmed interview with Bob Mugge. By now he had returned to wearing his cowboy hat, and Charles was beside him, holding the crown. "I was there all the time," Chavis repeated, a smile playing beneath his frosted moustache. "They just overlooked me, I was kind of short."

He went on about how he used to play at Club 15 in Lake Charles, while Clifton Chenier played Club 16. He talked about the house dances, and how long he'd been married, and how old he was, and how he got cheated out of money when he made his first record, "Paper in My Shoe," in 1955. He started to talk more about that topic, but he stopped himself.

"What I was doing, Clifton used to come and listen to me play," he said. "And when he had the Red Hot Louisiana Band, he was going to California and play, and Boozoo Chavis was going to run horses in Evangeline Downs. I met him. We crisscrossed."

He took the crown in one hand and began to wave it wildly in the air as he spoke. In his other hand he held an open can of Budweiser with considerably greater care. He was asked if he planned to wear the crown in the future.

"I don't want to be rude," he answered. "I wear it if I have to. But sometimes I'd be ashamed to put this on. I can't wear that to church. I ain't going to bring it with me there. And when I die, I ain't going to be able to take it there. So I'll bring it to the Jazz Festival, and maybe I'll bring it to Slim's

Y-Ki-Ki when I play down there. But I'm not going to wear it steady. Ever since the people know me, I've been wearing cowboy boots and a cowboy hat. And this becomes me more. I'm natural. I'm Boozoo, natural.

"I don't try to act and perform and get out there and rent a tux," he continued. "Try to be this and that, try to be a dude. I'm sixty-three, I've got chickens, dogs, and ducks and stuff. You know, I'm not trying to brag of what I got. I'm saying I've been raised on a farm, and I'm natural. And I say, 'Yes sir,' 'No ma'am,' and 'No sir,' and I was raised that way. You know what I mean? All I need is my ten fingers."

Boozoo Chavis never refused the crown when it was offered to him. But the bejeweled hat soon became lost in the general ruckus of his life and music. A few months after the coronation, he affixed a silver tiara to the front of the cowboy hat, which he continues to wear to this day. This seems to have decided the matter, at least for now.

By early 1998 the argument over who was the proper king of zydeco had subsided. Today, a struggle for dominance over the weekend dance floor has taken its place. Meanwhile, a general consensus seems to be emerging that there have been three kings: Amédé Ardoin, Clifton Chenier, and Boozoo Chavis. The king is dead. Long live the king.

# 13

# DOG HILL DAYS

---

*Don't you worry about Boozoo,*
*Because you know he ain't no fool.*
*Don't you worry about Boozoo,*
*Baby, just keep cool.*

*Some flying high, and some flying low,*
*But you know, and I know, he better take it slow. . . .*

— *Boozoo Chavis, "Don't Worry about Boozoo"*

L EONA CHAVIS LOOKS THROUGH THE KITCHEN WINDOW as a line of
trucks pulls up to her house, and watches as chaos erupts in her
front yard. Her sons climb out of the trucks, hollering instructions
at each other as they unlatch horse trailers; hooves land on hard
ground; dogs bark; a rooster and a turkey noisily battle each other for the
roof of a chicken coop.

She sighs. "Boozoo, he's just like his mom," she says, turning from the
window to the stove. "If she wanted something done, y'all was going to get
it done." The phone rings. "He's always into something, I don't care what it
is," she adds, waving the receiver in the air as she talks. "'I'm going over
here, Leona, but I'm getting ready to come back over here.' 'Hey Leona,
I'm going over there, I'll be back.' Just like that — boom, boom."

*Boozoo Chavis.*

Welcome to Dog Hill, a slightly elevated one-acre farm of horses, dogs, guinea fowl, chickens, ducks, turkeys, and calves, located just outside the city limits of Lake Charles in a dusty network of winding roads and small farms. It got its name when city dwellers began coming here to dump their pets, but it gained fame as the subject of a Boozoo Chavis song. Thanks to Chavis's music, this farmland has become his own Noah's Ark: from here have emerged the dogs of "Dog Hill," the goats of "Johnnie Billie Goat," the donkeys of "Zydeco Hee Haw," and the horses of "Camel" and "Boozoo's Baby." Because of Chavis's great influence on the modern zydeco scene, his menagerie has multiplied: nearly all young bands today can be heard barking and braying in musical imitation of a Dog Hill morning.

But on this summer morning, Dog Hill is in an uproar. The nearby Delta Downs racetrack has closed for the season, and the new barn isn't ready for the nine incoming racehorses. Clearly, interviews with visiting writers — scheduled or not — will have to wait. Leona Chavis sends me through the kitchen door to find her husband, and I follow the sound of shouting coming from the half-finished barn. Inside is Boozoo Chavis, dressed in brown work pants and a plaid Western shirt, stamping through sawdust into a barn stall.

"Look," Chavis bellows, waving a Stetson at a carpenter. "I'm the racehorse!"

He aims his mouth at a mess of exposed wires and lunges his head over the gate. "I'm the racehorse!" he repeats.

The carpenter, with an uneasy smile, says he doesn't think the horses can reach the wires.

Chavis glares at him. "I'm sixty-five. I know what I'm doing."

"I guess your trip to Washington," the carpenter drawls, "didn't help your disposition none."

Chavis stops in his tracks. Yes, he has just returned from Washington D.C., where he stood before a hundred thousand people as part of a Fourth of July show. But when he's standing on a shag carpet of hay and sawdust and staring at a string of loose wires, he doesn't want to hear a line like that. He slams the gate, puts his hat back on, and hurries through the barn. "He's a good carpenter," he mutters as he passes. "He don't know horses."

Chavis's problems are just beginning. Outside, his sons have hitched the horses to the arms of a metal walker that is supposed to keep them pacing in a circle. The walker isn't turning, and the horses are starting to jump around nervously. The sight of nine expensive horses tied to a metal tree, kicking their hind legs in every direction, is especially alarming. "One of those kicks lands and it's a thousand dollars or more," says Leona Chavis, who has rushed from the kitchen and is balancing on a wood plank in a field of mud, trying to calm the animal.

What makes matters worse for Boozoo is that he has the use of only his right hand, and he's left-handed. A couple months before, he was hooking a heavy barbecue pit to a trailer hitch, and it crashed down, tearing the flesh from two fingers. His wife drove him to the hospital. Recalls Leona: "All the way he was saying, 'All the other musicians, they've been gunning after me.

They done got one damn hand, so now they'll be shooting at the other one.'" The fingertips were amputated at the top joint, and he played a dance that weekend in great pain. Working with horses is even harder.

The morning passes, and the barn slowly gets finished. As the noontime heat settles over Dog Hill, Boozoo Chavis is storming — boom, boom — from one end of his farm to the other. He checks on his wife and the harnessed horses. Under control. He checks on the visiting writer, who has found himself cutting wires and hanging box fans in the barn. He goes back to the carpenter. He's covering the wires.

Leona Chavis returns to the kitchen, where she starts making preparations for the upcoming Dog Hill Labor Day Festival that she and her husband throw every year. She's also watching a soap opera, and cooking an incredible multicourse lunch of beef and squirrel stew, gumbo, and greens.

Then — boom, boom — Chavis strides in, followed by his sons Rellis and Charles, and the kitchen suddenly comes alive with activity. The phone rings, the screen door opens and slams, and family members file through the house, dipping spoons into pots, standing around the table with bowls of food.

Chavis isn't eating; he skipped breakfast and doesn't take time for lunch. He tentatively sits down at the table, his eyes darting across the room. "Sometimes a lot of people come to interview me, and I get so furious," he begins. "I'm not talking about you, I'm talking about these other guys." He shoots me a look, and family members bring their food over to listen. Then he lights up a cigarette and begins his story.

The first hit was the 1955 anthem "Paper in My Shoe," and the most recent was a reworking of the 1930s Western swing standard "You're Gonna Look Like a Monkey." In the years between those songs, Boozoo Chavis launched many zydeco standards being played today. It is no exaggeration to say that he has redirected the course of the music. He is regarded as the living legend of zydeco, and his style is imitated by dozens of younger bands.

But imitating the idiosyncratic Boozoo Chavis isn't easy. When he speaks, the words speed from his mouth like horses bred to sprint a quarter mile at a time — the sort that he's trained all his life. And when he plays a zydeco dance, he can clip through his songs just as quickly. "I can play fifteen to twenty songs in fifteen minutes," he boasts. "Shit. Sometime I'll be playing them so fast, one after another, I got to stop. I'll just turn around and get me a cigarette and light it, to kill time. Get me a beer."

Wilson Anthony Chavis was born on October 23, 1930, near Church Point, Louisiana. Soon after that — for reasons nobody remembers — he started to be called Boozoo. His family moved to Lake Charles to become tenant farmers and settled near Dog Hill. "You had to scuffle for what you wanted," he remembers of those days. "Your mama and daddy would work in the field and try to make ends meet. You'd farm on half — you'd farm for a share — and any crop you'd give the boss man. That boss man would take five hundred, you had three hundred."

His parents separated when he was three, but Chavis maintained ties with his father, who played accordion. Other musicians in the family included his great-uncle Sidney Babineaux, the well-known triple-note player from Rayne who recorded his version of "Zydeco sont pas salé" for Chris Strachwitz in 1962. Chavis also remembers going to hear singing cowboys Gene Autry and Roy Rogers at the Lake Charles rodeo. But the primary influence on Boozoo Chavis was his mother. From her, he says, he learned about scuffling, and that the surest way to make money is to move quickly in many directions.

"She would drive a team, work behind a plow, she just had that energy," he says proudly. "She'd know how to make that money, and she never stopped. She was a midwife, yeah, deliver that baby. And man, you'd bring her half a calf, she'd cut all that meat by herself. I'd hold the leg." She also ran informal horse races called bushtracks, making money by selling homemade barbecue, pies, and gumbo, and later operated a dance club. Her efforts yielded three acres of land; Chavis remembers that the family moved across the highway when he was fifteen. That was the age, he says, that he started smoking in front of his mother.

By this time Chavis's personality had taken its shape. "Boozoo was bad," says Leona Chavis. "He used to ride his horse to school, and when he passed the girls, he lassoed us with that rope. And start dragging them girls down that gravel road. And if it wasn't that, he always rode a bike. And if y'all was in that group, he was coming through there. We'd catch him and we'd whip him and let him go."

Boozoo and Leona were also the best dancers in the area, so a teacher asked them to perform a popular step called the "truck" for a high school program. "He'd always say he didn't like to dance with me because my hands would sweat," Leona continues. "The teacher said, 'Wilson, that's going to be your wife.' And he just said, 'Whoo! My baby's going to have long, coal black, curly hair!' I said, 'I'm going to fix you.' That ol' little bitty thing running around there saying, 'My baby got long, coal black, curly hair.' He caught a whipping for that."

It was during a Christmas house dance that Leona first heard about Boozoo's intentions of marriage. "Oh Lord, he didn't tell me anything. Daddy brought us to the dance, and Boozoo said, 'You know what? You're going to be my wife. I'm asking your daddy tonight.' I said, 'You got to be kidding!'" They married in 1952.

As a young man, Chavis kept his personal scuffle to farming, horse training, and jockeying. His music career started with a horse race. "I rode a race and I won, and I bought me a calf," he recalls. "A heifer. So after a while I sold that heifer and I took the money and bought me an accordion. And I started then. I was bad then."

Among his teachers was an accordionist named Elridge Davis, a rice farmer who met Chavis at lunchtime and showed him how to play. The two began to perform at house dances on the weekends. And when the house dances began dying out, members of Leona's family were among the first in the area to start their own clubs.

Here, as in the rest of Texas and Louisiana, there was much demand for the young Clifton Chenier, and a rivalry between the two very different men was perhaps inevitable. Remembers Leona: "Clifton used to play for Boozoo's mama every fifteen days, with that white piano accordion, and his brother Cleve was on the washboard. He had the gold teeth, but he didn't comb his hair that slick way, yet.

"And they had two clubs out here, Club 15 and Club 16. My daddy owned Club 15, and my aunt owned Club 16. Mama had hired Cliff to play one night, and Aunty offered Cliff more money to go play at the Club 16. So my mama called over here and she said, 'Boozoo, Clifton was supposed to play for me, and the rest of them paid Cliff more money to go play at Club 16. Can you come and play my dance tonight?' He just had the washboard and the accordion, and Boozoo closed Clifton's dance. He closed him down. Oh yeah, they had some people there."

Chenier and Chavis were born within five years and thirty miles of each other, and they both started their careers in the house dances, where the accordion alone could keep people on the floor all night. Like Chenier, Chavis continued to lead his band as if the accordion were the only really necessary instrument. "Follow me," goes Boozoo's famous instruction to his musicians. "If I'm wrong, you're wrong, too."

But it's the differences between these two men that delineate the two sides of zydeco today. For if Chenier always reminded his audiences that he came from the country, Chavis makes it plain that he never left. Instead of Chenier's crisp suit and tie, Chavis makes his statement in a Stetson hat and a plastic apron (to prevent sweat from drenching the accordion bellows). And while Chenier played the big piano accordion, Chavis stays with the old French single- and triple-row boxes. These small diatonic accordions may not play the blues as fluidly as the piano-key, but they have a punchier, more percussive sound; after Chavis, many of the major innovations in modern zydeco have been in rhythm.

The difference also expresses itself in geography. Chenier's R&B influences suggested that the action was to be found in cities like Houston, but Chavis's danceable mix of rural humor, rough blues, early Creole tunes, one-chord instrumental vamps, and autobiographical originals has shifted the scene back "down east" to country towns like Opelousas and Lawtell.

Finally, the two musicians would have different experiences with the record industry of the mid-1950s. Around the same time Chenier met J. R. Fulbright in Sulphur, Chavis landed just a few miles from his home, in the tiny Goldband studio owned by a Lake Charles electrical appliance salesman named Eddie Shuler. It was here that Chavis made his first record, "Paper in My Shoe." It was 1955, the same year that Chenier hit with "Ay-Tete Fee."

But Chavis became suspicious of the record scuffle. He soon grew to believe that the boss man was getting more than his share. So he took off his accordion and spent the next twenty years training racehorses. He speaks bluntly of that time. "That dude stole my money. That's why I quit playing," he told a reporter in 1990, and when asked about it today, he doesn't add many details. For the longer version, it's necessary to take a twenty-minute drive from Dog Hill into downtown Lake Charles, to a siding-covered music landmark that sits behind a sign that reads Eddie's Music House.


Eddie Shuler once made a picture that he passes out as a free souvenir to music fans who visit Goldband studios to see where Dolly Parton and Freddy Fender made records before they were famous, where the swamp pop hit "Sea of Love" was recorded, and where Boozoo Chavis started out. Over a photo of his storefront he's pasted a cutout photo of himself, standing with his hands halfway inside his pockets, giving a kindly but no-nonsense look to the camera. The first thing you notice is the scale: Shuler seems to stand about twenty feet tall.

Inside Goldband, Shuler looms just as large. In the front of the store, creaky wooden floors are covered with racks of records and tapes, a few Cajun trinkets, appliances in disrepair, and a jukebox, vintage 1933. Holding forth in his back office, Shuler — who still makes TV repair calls — is an immediately charming man who speaks in a musical Texas drawl and has a penchant for saying things like "It took off like a ruptured duck."

Born in 1913 in Wrightsboro, Texas, he moved to Lake Charles to work as a dragline and heavy crane operator during World War II. He also worked for a time as a vocalist for the Cajun string band the Hackberry Ramblers,

*Boozoo Chavis, circa 1954.*

but when he tried to take guitar lessons, he realized the discipline of music wasn't for him. "Just sitting here for two hours at a time — plink, plink, plink, plink — didn't suit me at all," he says. "Because I'd rather be out there making money, you know?" So, like Boozoo Chavis, Shuler diversified. He hosted a radio show, he fixed appliances, and he sold insurance. But also like Chavis, he continued to make music his life's work.

Shuler's new Goldband label took off in 1949, when he met the legendary blind Cajun accordionist Iry LeJeune. When Shuler recorded LeJeune's version of the Amédé Ardoin tune "Tante Aline" under the new name "Lacassine Special," he had his first successful artist. Even more important, Shuler says, he had a hit song. "People die and songs live forever. That's the lesson of the music business. It's not the musician — they're just a necessary element. You got to have that song."

In the postwar record business, that philosophy often translated to producers making overstated claims for songwriting credit. Shuler is listed as co-composer on all of LeJeune's songs, although he freely admits he doesn't understand the Cajun French lyrics. And among the 741 songs that are registered with Broadcast Music, Incorporated (BMI) as full or partial Shuler compositions are a number of tunes in Boozoo Chavis's repertoire, including "Paper in My Shoe," "Forty-One Days," and "Oh Yae Yae." This is what Chavis is referring to when he charges that Shuler stole his music.

Shuler and Chavis first met in 1954, when a Cajun accordionist named Sidney Brown dropped by the studios. "He said there's a little black boy out there that's got a real good song," Shuler recalls. "So I said, 'Well, bring him in.'" Chavis brought his accordion into the studio, sat down, and played "Paper in My Shoe." Shuler agreed that the song was good, but Brown begged off from recording with Chavis, saying that the black and white styles were too different. Shuler called up a local R&B player named Classie Ballou, who fronted a local band called the Tempo Kings.

"So I told him I got a boy down there that plays this black Cajun music," Shuler continues. "I said, 'Can you play this stuff?' 'Oh yeah.' Well, he was lying, because he couldn't." In the studio, the styles of the accordion player — who had previously only played with a rubboard or by hitting his foot on a Coke box — and the R&B band collided head-on. "It kept going downhill, and on the third day it was worse off than it was when we started," says Shuler. "So I said, 'Boozoo, do you drink any at all?' He said, 'Yes sir.' So I went out and got a pint of Seagram's Seven, and after about halfway into that jug of whiskey, it started to sound better."

What next happened in the studio is a matter of long-standing disagreement. According to Shuler, the band was almost through their best take of "Paper in My Shoe" when he heard a terrific crash. "But the music never stopped," he says. "So when they finally got down to the end of the song, I opened the door. Well, there lay Boozoo on the floor, still playing the accordion. That's why the music didn't stop. The stool fell over and he didn't stop playing." By that time Shuler was ready to give up. He says he paid the band $250 and figured it for a loss.

Boozoo Chavis's tumble has become a well-known anecdote in Louisiana music lore, appearing in liner notes, music histories, and even in the E. Annie Proulx novel *Accordion Crimes.* But Boozoo Chavis insists he never fell half-drunk in Eddie Shuler's studio. "How the hell are you going to keep playing like that?" he once snapped to interviewer Ben Sandmel, a quote that appears in the liner notes to Chavis's Elektra album.

Yet Shuler not only sticks by his story — he is dumbfounded that Chavis doesn't appreciate it. "He's always denied falling off that stool, but that's the best commercial he could ever have," he says. "You couldn't even dream up something that valuable. But he doesn't look at it like that, you know. He looks at it as something else. But I told it just like it was, and it got in print, and that got him the attention that he needed, you know?"

There is another person who was in the studio that day: guitarist Classie Ballou. Now living in Waco, Texas, where he leads Classie Ballou and the Family Band, he was eighteen years old when Shuler called him to come into Goldband. "I was a little ol' teenager back then, I was just starting out," he remembers. "Eddie Shuler called me, because I had the hottest little old thing going on in Lake Charles back at that time."

Ballou didn't know the accordionist at the time of the recording, although his wife is a distant relative. He had, however, grown up in the Creole house dance tradition. "Before I was a kid, I started playing rubbing board with a great-uncle of mine, his name is Letell Thomas, now he's been dead," he says. "And we used to play in the houses, they used to have them big pitty-pat games back then, and people used to gather around on a Saturday night and have a big gumbo. But back then I was about ten years old, and he looked at me one day and said, 'Man, you got good rhythm. Why don't you tell your dad to buy you a guitar?' And that's how I got started."

If Shuler was hoping to find a black artist familiar with Chavis's music, however, he found the wrong man. By this time Ballou was playing in area clubs, covering Fats Domino and Little Richard for mostly white audiences, and hadn't been around accordion music since he was a child. "It was kind of a long session," he says of his experience at Goldband. "At the time, that music wasn't really appealing to me, to be truthful about it. I can't recall exactly how long it took, but I knew it took a little time, because we had to keep running the tracks over and over until Eddie finally got what he wanted.

"Oh, it was kind of wild." He laughs. "Back then, they used to like that

Old Crow. I don't know if they brought it in, or Eddie had it, but it was just a wild session. Boozoo was stomping so loud, the sound was bleeding into the mike, so they had to put pillows and all kinds of quilts under his foot. But he had a hit, and I guess none of us knew it at the time, even Eddie. But 'Paper in My Shoe,' one of the greatest hits out there in zydeco."

Ballou remembers that Chavis was one of the ones who was drinking, and that he did fall off a stool. But he can't say whether he kept playing accordion. "I heard that he kind of got insulted when he heard about that, he said it wasn't true," he says. "But he fell off a stool."

The recording done that day — or days — makes two things clear: the band was not used to backing an accordion player, and Chavis was not used to working with a band. "Listening to the record, one is awestruck by the fact that no two instruments — in fact, no two strings — appear to be in tune with each other!" wrote critic Billy Vera for a Capitol reissue of the sides. On Chenier's first recordings, also made in Lake Charles, there is clearly a musical visionary mixing the blend of Creole music and R&B. At Goldband, Chavis's accordion and Ballou's guitar — as well as a band that included a Lafayette saxophonist named Danny George — fitted together uncomfortably at best. But Ballou is satisfied with the results. "It was very different from what I was doing back in that time, but I guess we did a good job with the music, because the record made a hit."

At first Shuler just stored the tapes of the session and put the whole thing out of his mind. Then, two months later, he was out on the road on an insurance run and thinking about his $250. He went back and listened to the tapes, and says he got the idea to fade out the ending before the crash. And that, he says, is how "Paper in My Shoe" saw the light of day.

For all the disagreements about its origins, the song has proved an enduring classic in both zydeco and Cajun music. Like Chenier's "Zydeco Sont Pas Salé," the lyrics of "Paper in My Shoe" are built around a metaphor for poverty. In this case, instead of referring to the lack of salt meat in the beans, they tell of padding your shoe with paper for warmth:

> *Pour ça to' mami connaist pas et to' papa fait pas*
> *Mo gain papier dans mon soulier*

> Oh, what your mama don't know
> And what your papa don't allow
> I got a paper in my shoe.

"If you got some socks, well, you'd rather keep it for on the weekends, for going to church," Chavis explains. "Or when you dress up to go somewhere.

When you go to school, you're ashamed to go without socks. Some of them children would laugh at you. But in them days, it was just rough for everybody."

Although Chavis was the first person to record the song, he acknowledges that he first heard it from Ambrose "Potato" Sam in the 1940s. Shuler didn't really know what the song was about — "I thought it meant he had a letter from the girl or something like that," he says — but he released the record, and he remembers how he watched it take off like a ruptured duck. Impressed by its success, he sent a copy of the song to Lew Chudd at Imperial records, who agreed to lease the track and distribute it alongside the latest tunes by Fats Domino and other Imperial artists. Shuler believes the song sold between 100,000 and 140,000 copies, although he has no sales records to validate these high estimates.

Yet despite this success — or perhaps because of it — the relationship between the musician and the producer quickly broke down. "At first he was a very humble and compatible type of person," Shuler says of Chavis. "Now in later years, he's got real talkative, like the rest of them do. When in reality, there wasn't any money to be made back in those days off of records anyway."

When "Paper in My Shoe" became a hit, Shuler continues, Chudd called to ask for a follow-up song. Shuler called Chavis. Chavis asked for his money. Shuler said that Imperial only paid twice a year, and there wasn't any money yet. Chavis refused to come in. Eventually, Shuler says, Chavis was told by a club owner that he had to put out a new record to keep his gig, and he returned to Goldband. Shuler was still smarting about missing out on the follow-up song and he charged Chavis $375 for the session. This experience resulted in another memorable song, "Forty-One Days." Chavis says he first heard it from Herbert "Red" Sam. Eddie Shuler is listed as the sole composer.

Although Chavis would return to Goldband over the next ten years to make a few more records, he never had another "Paper in My Shoe," and the chance of a lasting business relationship between the two Lake Charles music men was clearly over, if it ever existed at all. Chavis collected his unbroken pride and went back to breaking racehorses, playing accordion only for parties and, he says, "under a tree." For years, little was heard from him. In 1967 British writer Mike Leadbitter, writing a series of articles on Louisiana music for *Blues Unlimited,* drove out to Dog Hill with Shuler and Cajun accordionist Jo-El Sonnier. He later reported:

> It is a great pity that this fantastically good musician should be
> so poorly represented on record and forgotten by most. He is
> far better than Clifton Chenier, who has used many of his orig-

*Boozoo Chavis at home, 1967: (top) with his daughter, Louanna;
(bottom) with his wife, Leona.*

inal songs and ideas, and he should be getting as much publicity as his rival. When he and Jo-El started a two-accordion
session the stomping feet shook the shack — in fact the TV set
couldn't stand the vibration and finally flickered out. . . . I
begged Eddie, who was nearly as shook up as myself, to get
him back to the studio and convinced Boozoo that we in Europe were interested in him and would try to help.

But if any encouragement came to Chavis from across the sea, it was too
little, too late. The session was never released, and the musician continued
to break horses.

Chavis remembers one recent night at the Liberty Theatre in Eunice,
when he and Leona ran into his old producer. They made small talk: "Oh,
Boozoo, you never knew you would be up in the world now." "No, I sure
didn't."

Concludes Shuler: "We're friendly enough, one businessman to another one. But I wouldn't want to record him, and I'm sure he wouldn't
want to record for me."

But Boozoo Chavis's experiences in the music scuffle weren't over yet.


One day in 1984, Boozoo and Leona Chavis were pulling horses to run at
Evangeline Downs, and they turned on a zydeco radio show. Leona remembers it well: "And the man said on the radio, 'Boozoo Chavis going to
be at Slim's Y-Ki-Ki.' He looked at me and he said, 'Leona, where is Slim's
Y-Ki-Ki?' I said, 'Don't ask me. I don't know.' He said, 'I sure would like to
know where Slim's Y-Ki-Ki is. And who done this.'"

She recalls that the two drove up the highway to visit Slim's, where they
were shocked to learn that another player was using what was left of Chavis's
thirty-year-old reputation to get gigs. "So I told Boozoo, I said, 'Well, man, you
can play accordion. If I was you, I'd cut me a record, and I'd keep trucking.'"

Boozoo Chavis knew he didn't want to go back to Goldband, so he
packed up his accordion and his sons and went down the road to Rockin'
Sidney Simien's house. "He had the music but no song," remembers
Simien. "And I just told him, 'Man, why don't we make something like
where you live at, Dog Hill?' Because they used to have them parties and
rodeos over there. He said, 'Yeah, we had them pretty women over there,
you remember.' I said, 'Yeah, make something about Dog Hill.'

"So that particular night we was just rehearsing, and Boozoo's son Poncho was singing it for him. It was sounding pretty good, so I said, 'I'm going
to put it on tape so y'all can rehearse it.' So his son started singing and we

put it together. Then I thought of that Clifton Chenier song 'Josephine c'est pas ma femme,' where he hollers 'Weeow!' and he started playing, so I told Boozoo, 'How you say Dog Hill in French?' And he said something and it floored me. That magic was right there."

The first six hundred copies of "Dog Hill" sold out quickly, thanks to Lafayette record store owner and disc jockey J. J. Caillier, who played the song repeatedly on his popular radio program. The single "Dog Hill" became just the first of many new songs to celebrate the world that had sustained Chavis for the past two decades. It all began with the opening lines shouted by Boozoo Chavis:

*Hé! on est parti dessus où habitent les chiens!*
*Ay où tous les jolies femmes est!*
*Ça c'est pour ici où habitent les chats!*

Hey! We're off to where the dogs live!
Where all the pretty women are!
This is where the cats are!

Released as a single, "Dog Hill," backed by the exquisite *baisse-bas* "Goin' to la maison," began getting play on local radio. J. J. Caillier produced Chavis's first album, *Louisiana Zydeco Music,* for Maison de Soul.

Chavis's next stop on the comeback trail was the dance clubs. "In 1984, Boozoo wasn't doing nothing," says Kermon Richard, owner of Richard's Club. "But he had a record out, 'Dog Hill' and 'Goin' to La Maison,' and I liked it. When I told people I was getting Boozoo, they said, 'That old man? What do you have, a special ramp for him to roll his wheelchair up in the club? You got some crutches for him?' They threw all kinds of stuff at me. Boozoo was charging four hundred dollars at that time and I made four hundred thirty-two, but boy, I loved his music. I kept on booking him and the crowd kept getting bigger, then his head got so big it wouldn't fit in my double door. But the best zydeco musician I've heard that ever walked was Boozoo."

Chavis soon proved himself to be a zydeco Midas, turning everything and everybody he touched into song. He honored his wife by reworking "Bad Bad Whiskey" into "Leona Had a Party." He named one song for his daughter, Do-Right, and teased a daughter-in-law with "Lula Lula Don't You Go to Bingo." Among his animal songs were several tributes to his racehorses, including "Boozoo's Baby," "Camel," and "Motor Dude Special." He is now regarded as the personal chronicler of family and friends. "People come up to me now and say, 'Write a song about me, Boozoo!'" he says.

Chavis also confidently brought back much of his old Goldband material, including "Paper in My Shoe," "Forty-One Days," and "Tee Black." For his new songs, he drew from the same well of Creole melodies and language as Clifton Chenier, but with different results. In his hit "Zydeco Hee Haw" Chavis sings the axiom *"Tous les jours sont pas la même chose"* ("Every day is not the same thing"), but it's not the blues lament Chenier recorded; it's a rodeo of a song complete with mule snorts and a tag line that turns the whole thing into a joke: *"Tous les soirs sont pas la même femme!"* ("Every night is not the same woman!").

Suddenly, Boozoo Chavis was taking on all comers. Appearing at the Zydeco Festival with Clifton Chenier, he used the opportunity to face off with his rival, telling the audience that he could outplay the king, just as he had thirty years earlier. Festival director Wilbert Guillory recalls that he had to hold C. J. Chenier back that day. "You know Clifton is the best," he kept telling him.

Chavis achieved local notoriety with four raunchy singles, "Deacon Jones," "Uncle Bud," "The Monkey and the Baboon," and "Boozoo's Blue Balls Rap." Like many of his songs, these had lyrics drawn from oral tradition, but this particular tradition had to be sold under record store counters with XXX labels and warnings about radio play; onstage, Chavis usually stays with sanitized versions. "One time a woman came up to me in Houston," he explains. "She said, 'You're a nasty little man.' But she already knew all those words. It wasn't nothing new." Chavis also became identified with his most popular souvenir: underwear featuring his picture and some more lines from an old song: "Take 'em off! Throw 'em in the corner!"

Boozoo Chavis's comeback has been aided by his new manager, Jack Reich, and his producer Terry Adams, a founding member of the rock band NRBQ. Although Chavis has largely confined his playing to the Texas-Louisiana circuit, hooking up with Reich did increase his out-of-state work: in 1990 he took his first commercial airplane flight to play four nights in New York City, chronicling the adventure in his song "Went to New York." His occasional trips to California included an appearance on Dennis Miller's talk show. NRBQ made him the subject of their song "Boozoo, That's Who," and Devo's Mark Mothersbaugh once listed "Paper in My Shoe" as his favorite song.

Still, Chavis has yet to receive the acclaim that both he and his Louisiana fans feel he's due. He was denied his chance at movie soundtracks when a scene from the movie *Twelve Monkeys* featuring "Zydeco Hee Haw" was cut. He has yet to accept an offer to travel overseas.

"The music is good and the people love it, but I should have been out on the East Coast thirty years ago," Chavis says. "If I'd have been out there, man, I'd have a mansion. When I go on tour, the people say, 'You must be Boozoo, nice to have you out here, and blah-blah-blah.' Sometimes they say, 'You never thought you'd be out here,' and I say, 'No, I sure didn't,' you know? 'Did you ever think you was going to be as famous as you are now?' Sometimes I says, 'No, because in them days I was as famous as I am now, but the people just hadn't recognized it.'"

Yet at home, Chavis's reputation is secure. "There are a lot of Boozoo prototypes coming out," says Paul Scott, of the Zydeco Festival. "They may be smoother than Boozoo, but they try to get his hard accordion, that rough, raw style, and his sore-throat type of singing." Young accordionist Jo Jo Reed had a local hit with his tribute song "I Got It from Boo." Reed starts by telling all the young players that they know they got their songs from Chavis, and then sings the chorus: "I got it from Boo / Big Daddy Boozoo." Then he continues with this story:

"You know, I made a mistake and I played this song over in Lake Charles, and I seen a little short man in a cowboy hat, comes running to the stage. He says, 'Hey boy, give me that accordion here, you're playing that wrong.' So I gave Boozoo the accordion, he took the accordion and he said, 'Let me show you how it's done.' He said, 'You follow me. If I'm wrong, you're wrong too.'"

Chavis's relationship with his followers is a complicated mix of friendship, respect, and competition. "I've helped Zydeco Force and Beau Jocque," he says. "They look at my fingers and I tell them when to pull and when to push. I don't get mad if they play my music. But I get mad if they mess it up."

Chavis and Beau Jocque staged a series of "showdown" concerts that were essentially good-natured publicity stunts, but Chavis has little patience when he hears one of his melodies in someone else's song. He acknowledges his debt to the older house-dance players for such songs as "Paper in My Shoe" and "Forty-One Days," but the turnaround rate for his tunes is unprecedented. In 1996, within weeks of the first time he played "You're Gonna Look Like a Monkey," it seemed to him that every band in South Louisiana was covering the song.

This is a subject that concerns him greatly this day on Dog Hill. Sometime this morning, before he went out to work on the barn, he turned on the radio and caught a new Keith Frank song, "Let Me Be," that owes its melody to Chavis's "Suzy-Q." Charges Chavis: "I heard Keith Frank made my record 'Suzy-Q.' But he sings, 'Let me be, the place to be.' Now you ask him, 'What you mean with where you ought to be?' What's he going to tell you?

He doesn't know where you ought to be. He can't tell you. If I make a record, I can tell you. I say, 'I ought to be in the movies,' or 'I ought to be in heaven.' But they can't explain what they're saying.

"I don't want them to wipe my face," he continues. "I'm just saying, they don't have history. They don't know about the cows and chickens and ducks.

"I tell it to the people on the mike. I say, everybody's trying to play Clifton's music, but there wasn't but one. And there ain't but one Boozoo. They ain't got two, they got one. Boozoo. One. Before me there was none. After me there ain't going to be no more like him. There's going to be some more, but not like Boozoo."

Standing around the kitchen table, his sons nod. In the kitchen, Leona Chavis laughs. "Not like Boozoo," she calls out.

Each Labor Day, the two Dog Hills — the musical and the geographical — come together for a day-long music festival that Boozoo Chavis holds in his carport. Leona makes hundreds of links of boudin, and Do-Right takes money at the door. Motor Dude and Camel stand in their stalls, watching as tourists lean over the fence, calling to them by name.

This year, as the sun beats down on the concrete drive, Charles Chavis sits under a green and white canopy next to a row of purple, yellow, and peach lights, mopping his forehead and announcing the bands. "If there's anybody in the back lot that needs to be pulled out, we have a tractor ready," he calls out. Moving on the road behind him can be seen the figure of Boozoo Chavis, driving the tractor to the back lot.

Boozoo is everywhere at once. Chugging from one end of the carport to the next, he folds a sheriff's badge over his shirt pocket, directs traffic, welcomes guests, checks on the food. He passes me and sees a tape recorder in my hand. I know what he's thinking, and tell him that it's for interviews, not to steal his music. But he waves away any explanation. "You can record all them other bands, but not me," he says quickly, and walks off.

He checks on his granddaughters, who are currently raffling a fifty-dollar prize. He dances with his sister while Lawrence Ardoin plays "Eunice Two-Step." As it gets dark, two drunk men start yelling at each other. Chavis throws a towel over his shoulder and storms to the scene. "Get him out," he says, and then goes inside. "Where's Boozoo at?" someone calls. "He went in the kitchen to get a gun!" shouts another. Charles's voice comes over the microphone: "You're on Dog Hill now, where Boozoo Chavis is the boss man!"

There are as many bands booked here as at the big Zydeco Festival in Plaisance, and by the end of the night, only about fifty aching and tired

*Boozoo Chavis feeding his chickens.*

people are left of the crowd; most are collapsed in plastic molded chairs. Then Boozoo Chavis takes the stage. He ceremoniously takes off his sheriff badge and calls for a Budweiser, then lights a cigarette with hands that are trembling from exhaustion. He talks into the microphone, his words tumbling out at a fast gallop. "You know, this past year we played in Alexandria, Shreveport, this way." He points behind him. "We played in Atlanta and New York, this way." He points over his right shoulder. "And in Beaumont and Port Arthur, this way." He points over his left shoulder. "And everywhere we play, we play last. And when we play here, we play last too."

Charles offers a weary "Yeah, you right," and Boozoo leans into his accordion. Hearing the notes, Charles says, "We're going to take it to you now with a little 'Don't Worry about Boozoo.'" The carport fills with dancers.

When I ask Chavis later about the song, he explains that his doctor keeps telling him to take it slow. "And I used to be a fool way over yonder," he says. "I was a fool then. But I ain't no fool now."

The next morning, like every morning, Chavis will fold a copy of the Lake Charles newspaper between his socks and his cowboy boots. He doesn't have to anymore, he explains, but it fits him.

"Shit," he says. "I got paper in my boot now."

Then he'll spend the day in the barn, and eat when it gets dark. Next weekend he'll load up four accordions, choose a Stetson, and take his band to Houston, Opelousas, or New Orleans. Because he's still on his comeback, and you can't let all the jokers get away with your songs.

So he goes, and the rest follow him. And if he's wrong, they're wrong too, night after night.

# 14

# TRAIL NOUVEAU

---

SUNDAY AFTERNOON ON A DIRT ROAD a few miles outside of Church Point. The sky is cloudless, and the road wet from water spilling off flooded rice fields. All is quiet. Suddenly, a yellow and white panel truck lurches around the bend, sinking into watery chuckholes, loudspeakers blasting the theme from *Shaft*. Following the truck are rows of slow-moving horses, steam rising from their flanks, carrying riders in starched, brightly colored shirts. Next are two hay wagons, filled with women and children, and finally a flatbed holding portable toilets. The music fades, and a booming voice comes over the speakers: "Come on, trail riders, get up front! Lawtell, Opelousas, Lebeau, get on up there! Uh-oh, I see a skip in the beat!"

In the truck, Frank Malbrough puts a new tape in the cassette player, and an accordion starts off the Keith Frank song "Only the Strong Survive." Malbrough's converted 1975 Bunny Bread delivery truck — now outfitted with audio equipment, green and blue shag carpet samples, and a painted cowboy hat on the old bunny logo — vibrates with the music. Malbrough switches off his microphone and turns around. His truck is filled with those of us who arrived at the trail ride without a horse. He gets everyone up to dance.

A horse sidles up to the window and a rider hands Malbrough a note. He turns the mike back on.

*Jeffery and Delton Broussard.*

"Somebody ain't got an extra girth from the saddle," he says in a sonorous voice.

He looks back in his truck, confused.

"A girth is to hold the saddle," explains a woman dressed in cowboy boots, tight jeans, and a striped Western shirt.

"A girth is to hold the saddle," announces Malbrough.

The woman laughs. "They know what it is!"

"Yeah, you know what it is!" Malbrough repeats. "Can't hold up the saddle without the girth, y'all!" He shrugs, then turns the dial and finishes the Keith Frank song. The horses continue to trudge forward into the zydeco.

Over the past decade, the trail ride has become the movable focal point of the current revival in zydeco. A weekend of back-road horseback trips that culminates in a big dance on Sunday, this mix of horses, music, and outdoor dancing has effectively redirected the modern zydeco scene out of the cities and back into the fields. "A lot of these youngsters, they've probably never been around a horse before," says Brian Gallow, president of the Rainbow Trail Riders Association. "Then they come out there to one of the trail rides and start dancing and fall in love with zydeco. The first time they come they have short pants and Nikes, next time they have a pair of Wranglers and boots and a hat."

The trail ride is a revival movement: it took its current shape over the past twenty years, but its roots can be found in the neighborhood *boucherie*, a nineteenth- and early twentieth-century social tradition that was once even more important to the survival of the community than the weekly house dance. On winter Saturdays, a designated farmer would get up in the middle of the night to boil a giant kettle of cooking water. He would kill perhaps a half dozen hogs, clean the intestines to make boudin casings, and remove the skin to fry into hog cracklin'. At daybreak his neighbors would arrive, and he would pass out bundles of food. The next week was somebody else's turn.

In the winter, whiskey and an accordion might help people warm up. "The trail ride brings a lot of memory back," says Wilbert Guillory. "Every Saturday, they would look for the smoke from the big fire. I was one of the persons who would go on and help kill a lot of the hogs with my machete, because they liked the way I did it."

In the spring and summer, *le bloc de boucherie* — block butchery — provided beef for the community. "They would draw numbers from a hat, and everyone would get on horseback, or they would walk, or they would go in a wagon, and get their ten or fifteen pounds of meat," Guillory recalls. "Now, if I'm killing today, I got the inside of the beef, the liver, the milt, the mery gut and all of that stuff, and we make a *bouilli*. Today they call that the cowboy stew, and they make it at the trail rides on Friday. It went like this all around Southwest Louisiana. We didn't know the word 'cooperative' at the time, but that's what it was. You couldn't survive without something like that."

Meat was kept fresh in a gallon jug tied to a rope and dropped down the well. As electricity and refrigerators started to reach even the most remote areas, the need for *boucheries* diminished. Yet there remained a desire for the weekly gathering, and by the late 1960s, country people had begun meeting on horseback, retracing the routes to the *boucherie* that was no longer there, in general agreement that the trail itself was worth the ride.

The first few excursions weren't much more than a group of friends picking up a cooler of beer and going out on their horses, and perhaps playing music over a truck radio. The contemporary trail ride has become a highly structured affair. The president leads the ride and sets the pace. Flagmen direct traffic. The trail ride boss keeps everyone in line. A code of conduct is strictly enforced. For example, if a horse kicks, a red ribbon is tied to its tail and it's sent to the back of the line. This is among the more embarrassing things that can happen to a person on a trail ride.

The most important rule covers attendance, for this secures the survival of the new tradition. Associations such as Gallow's Rainbow Trail Riders are composed of about forty organizations, ranging in size from a family of four to a group of a hundred. The trail ride is a social trade-off: you attend other rides to ensure attendance at yours. There is also a significant financial investment, with quarter horses starting at six hundred dollars apiece, and a Tennessee Walker at a thousand. Plus, as regular riders are quick to point out, a truck ride from Lake Charles to Opelousas with a two-horse trailer adds another fifty dollars in gas.

Trail rides typically welcome new visitors but don't advertise for them, and you have to know where to look. Publicity is generated by word of mouth or over zydeco radio shows, and maps are handed out at rides or in dance clubs. Sets of knee-high signs with hand-painted arrows appear alongside state highways and country roads. Some trail rides are held near popular clubs like Richard's and Slim's Y-Ki-Ki, but many venues are lesser known. The Henderson Rodeo dances take place in a red plywood barn where white extension cords running through ceiling beams power the band's instruments as well as two giant industrial fans. There is no cooling system in outdoor pavilions like the Southern Cross Ranch in Church Point, or King's Ranch in Carencro, where musicians and dancers meet on a slab of white concrete, and thousands of dancers show up as the trail ride season peaks during the most brutal days of the Louisiana summer.

\*       \*       \*

Brian Gallow, wearing a pressed red shirt and a wide-brimmed white cowboy hat, brings his Appaloosa up to the truck driver and gives him instructions.

"That's the leader over there," shouts a man over the music, pointing to
Gallow. "A very good man. We all stick to him, and he's behind us, too." The
line of horses moves into the ditch, and a rice truck passes. The trail ride
starts up again.

Malbrough continues exhorting the riders to stay in line. The passen-
gers in his truck are sitting across from each other on wooden benches.
"Everybody you see was mostly raised around here, and they kind of split
up," the man continues shouting. "When the trail ride got started, everybody started meeting each other again."

"We're all one family and every weekend we meet someone else," shouts
a woman on the other side. "It's an ongoing thing."

Across the truck, a heated conversation is under way.

"The board members are supposed to put up the signs," a woman
charges.

"I did," emphasizes a man sitting next to her.

She shoots him a look. "Well, you did a good job. Except coming from
my home."

"I did it from Lawtell, coming all the way down."

"I live in Lebeau," she says. "That's twenty-three miles north of Opelousas.
If I wouldn't have known how to get to Church Point — "

"So you couldn't see the signs."

"No, because you have to know how to get to Church Point in order to
find Church Point."

She glares at him. He laughs. Malbrough gets everyone dancing again.

After four hours of this, the trail ride pulls into the Southern Cross
Ranch, and Malbrough parks his truck. While a few teenagers pace their
horses backwards, showing off their skills, most of the crowd has gathered
at an outdoor pavilion to watch T-Broussard, a twenty-three-year-old college
student and zydeco band leader, set up his equipment. He's dressed in an
orange golf shirt and pressed green pants, and carries a cellular phone in
his pocket; he's staring nervously at a wasp nest above his head. "We've been
closer to them than that," he decides. "When you play the trail rides, you
have dust, moths, horse bites, everything. Last night in Kinder, we were way
out in the woods. We were getting ready to play, and all of a sudden, four
big ol' goats come from behind the bandstand and rammed all of us. It's a
different scene from the clubs, man."

A native of Tyrone, Louisiana, Broussard has only been performing for
three years, but he grew up hearing his mother, Mary Jane Broussard, play

accordion at private parties and festivals. He also learned French from listening to his grandmother and mother talk, and he plays more traditional two-steps and waltzes than his cousin, Keith Frank. This makes him a favorite of the trail rides.

Cars and pickups roll into the clearing, bringing fresh recruits to the dance. Broussard starts out his set, and his quick beats rattle the pavilion's corrugated metal roof and roll over the fields. Kids play on horses and climb on trailers. Cowboy boots begin clacking on the concrete floor. The dance is packed, the red sun burning just over the tree line, and many of the riders — both horse and bread truck — are standing on the sideline in various stages of heat exhaustion. A refrigerator is turned on its side and filled with ice, and a line has formed for beer.

Next to the line, two men in white aprons are deep-frying turkey wings in forty-eight-gallon cast-iron pots set over propane heaters, stirring the meat with shovels.

I watch the older man put his face in the steam and check on the wings. "That's Walter Joubert Senior," the younger man says. "I'm Walter Junior. He and I have been getting on good. He always did want to show me how to cook. Everywhere in Texas and Louisiana, they call him the fried turkey man. I've been following him for fifteen years. I'm in that track."

Behind us, two men are drinking cans of beer. "I used to ride mules," says one with a laugh.

"I ain't never rode no mules."

"Instead of walking behind that ol' mule pulling that doggone hair, I used to get on that ol' mule and ride him!"

T-Broussard starts a waltz, and the men leave. Walter Joubert Sr. comes over, and his son takes over stirring duties. "I went out of Opelousas in the late fifties, and went to Texas," Joubert says. "When I came back to Louisiana, I met everybody I grew up with, and that's when the trail rides started. Now I'm with the Ponderosa Riders, and I make forty-three rides every year.

"I think people are trying to get back to the country way of living," he continues. "When I was a young man, I left from Louisiana and went to Houston and Beaumont, and I was driving truck for a motor rebuilding company. They didn't have any of the things they used to have out in the country. Horseback riding, fields, hay. Now we have all that on the trail rides."

Joubert looks over his son's shoulders at the foaming wings. "That's all lard," he explains. "You can use it over and over." Then he finishes his story. "I remember when I went back to Louisiana, it was 'sixty-five. I couldn't put up with Texas anymore. One day I came back from work, this guy was walking down the street with a gun in his hand, just shooting it up in the air. That was a Thursday. When I got off work that next evening, I cashed my check, and I went to the U-Haul place and we packed our dishes and clothes and TVs, and I didn't stop until I got to Louisiana."

Beside me, a barrel-chested man named Junior Thomas is singing along in French with T-Broussard. He rode his horse today, and hosts his own trail ride later this year. He holds one hand to his chest and extends his other arm out, wiggling his fingers, as if teasing an accordion. He looks up. "I bought one twenty years ago," he says. "I thought I could learn to play. If I could play one note, I could make you dance."

He looks at T-Broussard and laughs. "But I can't," he says.


In the 1980s Boozoo Chavis became the leading musician on the trail rides, taking one of his own horses out for the day, and playing accordion for the dancers at night. "When the trail rides started, man, Boozoo was like the hot band at the time," Geno Delafose remembers. "Them people would flock out there with the horses, and it was just like hair on the head. Boozoo's a horseman, he's a real horseman, and that and his music all kind of went hand in hand."

By the end of the decade, Chavis started raising his fee, and the trail ride clubs began hiring younger bands to play his songs. The young bands began attracting young crowds, who responded — or perhaps led the way — by inventing new dance styles, showing off deeper bends, faster turns, and bodies more tightly coupled. The trail rides kept growing, and the new style — occasionally called *nouveau zydeco* — became the latest rage among young crowds.

Among zydeco fans the term "nouveau zydeco," like the music it describes, has become a source of controversy. First used in print in 1991 by *Rolling Stone* to describe Terrance Simien's contemporary take on traditional button-accordion zydeco, the phrase reemerged in 1994 when nineteen-year-old dance instructor Isaiah Reed used it to describe his moves while leading summer classes at University of Southwestern Louisiana. Today it refers to the sound of dozens of young zydeco bands in Louisiana and Texas. But like the term "bubblegum" in pop music, it is now a pejorative. Today's young players will usually use "nouveau zydeco" only to describe what they're not.

Yet if the name is out of favor, the sound — hypnotic single-row accordion riffs coupled with bass and drums amplified to the point of distortion — is pervasive. The style dates to the mid-1980s, when bass players like Classie

Ballou Jr., and Robby "Mann" Robinson began incorporating modern R&B licks into their playing. In the summer of 1986, Buckwheat Zydeco's reggae-style "Ya Ya," featuring bassist Lee Allen Zeno, became a major regional hit. "It was a conscious attempt to do something sonically different, to draw out zydeco's parallels with other African-Caribbean sounds," remembers Scott Billington, who produced the "Ya Ya" sessions. "This led us in the direction of shaping the low end of the record, and for better or worse, that's still the prevalent approach in recording zydeco."

Indeed, young bands today frequently perform zydeco versions of reggae tunes, and Keith Frank has been featured in local reggae festivals. But the primary innovation of nouveau zydeco has been the embrace of a beat called "double-kicking" or "double-clutching." Harking back to the syncopation of *juré* clappers and Clifton Chenier's "double shuffle," the rhythm is now propelled by two kicks on the bass drum, resulting in a stuttering heartbeat sound enormously popular with dancers.

Today the leading proponent of the style is Keith Frank, but the first notes were played by Zydeco Force and danced by their loyal following — composed primarily of relatives of the band. "It was Zydeco Force that appealed to us younger people," says Frank. "It's just that their relatives are really, really good dancers, and the way they would dance would fit real well to what they played. Watching them just originated a new style of dancing."

Zydeco Force leader Jeffery Broussard came by his nimble, syncopated accordion style and soulful vocals as one of eleven children of Delton Broussard, a sharecropper and head of the renowned Lawtell Playboys, which also featured Calvin Carrière on fiddle and J. C. Gallow on rubboard. When he turned eight, Jeffery began to play drums behind his father on such Lawtell Playboys signature songs as "Baby, Please Don't Go," "Colinda," and even "Ye Tou' Mande pou' Toi," a zydeco version of the Meters' "They All Asked for You."

"It was a lot of waltzes then," recalls Jeffery, sitting down in his Lawtell living room one Sunday after playing a trail ride. "The equipment we were playing on wasn't really powerful like the equipment they have now, and Daddy always played on a little bandstand, but he had a big sound."

The Broussard family had been making music for as long as Jeffery can recall. The children grew up singing in a local Catholic church choir, and Delton and Jeffery would bring their accordion to play at prayer meetings in Opelousas. "A lot of times when I was younger, my mama used to be up in the house singing and clapping hands and stuff, and she would call it *juré*," he remembers. The extended family often met for accordion jamborees and dances, but Jeffery admits he wasn't always interested in the old sounds. "My Daddy'd come in from the field, and if I was doing nothing he'd take his accordion down and play, but I was too busy running around learning how to kill chickens and shoot hogs, and stuff like that."

Like many of his generation, Jeffery was interested in soul, rock, and reggae, until Boozoo Chavis caught his ear. "My idol always was Boozoo, and what made me was that I was playing his type of music," he acknowledges. "But I discovered that I could take one of Boozoo's songs, and try to play it identical to what he's doing, but I couldn't. I would always feel myself doing certain things that I heard when I was growing up. For example, I never knew my Daddy to play a single-note accordion single, note for note, one at a time. He was always holding that two or three notes. That's a big difference, it makes it fuller. And he would play with a lot of chops, instead of playing it straight. And that's all in the style that I have now."

After leaving his father's band, Broussard played drums with Terrance Simien and then switched to bass for Roy Carrier, often leading the band when Carrier worked offshore. Then he joined with bass player Robby "Mann" Robinson to form Zydeco Force, and with Robinson acting as leader, the band began recording for Maison de Soul. The impact on local zydeco was immediate.

The popularity of Zydeco Force ensured that the single-row accordion would be the instrument of choice for young bands to follow. A more rugged instrument than the piano-key, it could withstand the elements of the trail ride, and it brought to the music an old-time sound that seemed appropriate for a dance surrounded by horses. The instrument, first revived by John Delafose's 1980 hit "Joe Pitre a deux femmes," was also the instrument of Amédé Ardoin. Yet if Ardoin sang in high-pitched cries, young musicians such as Broussard use low, hoarse vocals. Broussard admits that the old style sounds foreign to his ears. "Musicians like Bois Sec Ardoin, for some reason, they sing in a trembling voice, like they're about to cry," he says. "I never could figure that out, and I always did want to ask, but I never had the chance."

The lower pitch is also carried through in the choice of accordion key. Ardoin was famous for playing a D, but Broussard celebrates the lower registers in his song "B-flat":

> *Je l'aime la musique*
> *La musique créole.*
> *Je l'aime la musique*
> *La musique créole.*

> I like to dance
> And I like to sing.

I like to play,
Watch me do my thing.

Oh B-flat,
Oh B-flat,
I ain't going to play my C no more!

The chorus, based on Chavis's "Tee Black," is often misheard by dancers as an imperative: "Be black." It's a telling interpretation. Today, Amédé Ardoin's soaring cries are understood by many young Creoles as sounding Cajun, or white. When zydeco players emphasize bass and drums, they are identifying themselves with larger trends in African-American music. "We were one of the first zydeco bands to have that deep sound," Broussard recalls. "That's when Beau Jocque came, and it left from Beau Jocque and went to Keith Frank."

The trail to the new zydeco was rough at first, he recalls. Zydeco Force took their first gig — a trail ride at Richard's Club — for no pay, just to get the exposure. The next week, the band played in Crowley and each member earned ten dollars. "I sat down that night and thought, damn, I've got to give this up." Broussard laughs. "During that time, John Delafose and Boozoo was the stuff, and a lot of club owners didn't want to give us the chance."

The change came with the band's first hit, "Zydeco Extravaganza," an up-tempo romp of several Boozoo Chavis–inspired licks that runs through a list of local dance clubs. The song became both the theme song and the title of a popular local television show, which featured live zydeco performances filmed at local clubs.

Over the next decade, trail rides continued to provide Zydeco Force's main stomping grounds. "It's a lot of people that like horses and zydeco," says Broussard. "Some horses will even dance to the zydeco beat. And if you go to a trail ride and they say they have a rock-and-roll band, the people is bored. But the moment somebody's going to come up with an accordion, they say, 'Go ahead.'"

Zydeco Force introduced choreographed soul steps into their sets, but the more important dancing was being done on the other side of the speakers. Farmers famously raise large families to work in the fields, and this proved to be an advantage in zydeco as well. Thanks to Jeffery Broussard's five brothers and five sisters — as well as the nine siblings of his cousin and rubboard player Herbert Broussard — there was a sizable supply of cousins and nephews to follow the band from trail ride to trail ride, creating new dances as they went along. "A lot of the stuff comes from within my family,"

Broussard says. "We were just out there having fun and dancing between us, and a lot of people just took it, and now they're doing what they want with it.

"For starters, there's this little rock dance they got now, we started that. We just gave it a name and called it 'the push' — it's just rocking back and forth, you push this person and this person pushes you back. And we had a dance called 'the dip.' You're having the woman riding on your leg, and whenever you go back, her body would follow on you. Once we started it, a lot of people picked it up, and they're still dipping now.

"A lot of the elderly people complain and say that they weren't brought up dancing that way, which is true," Broussard admits. "But when we started, it was in the eighties, and it was time to make a change. Everybody just took the dance and started doing what they want with it. And I've noticed we do have a few elderly people that come. My daddy told me I was crazy, but he really got a kick out of it."

When Broussard was ten, his father left farming for work at an Opelousas oil field service company. Many in the new crowd of zydeco bands and dancers also moved to town long ago, but the music continues to reflect a rural lifestyle. Among Zydeco Force's most popular songs is "Shine," which tells the story of an incorrigible mule. "People come up and say, 'How did you make that song when you ain't never plowed behind no mule?'" Broussard says. "But we heard so much about the mule from my dad. He used to say that you didn't need a watch when you had a mule, because at twelve o'clock that mule sit down and wouldn't budge." Other Zydeco Force songs include "Madeline," a Cajun standard that Broussard first heard from the Lawtell Playboys, and "I'm on My Way," which Herbert Sam recalls hearing his father play at house dances. But not every musical element of his father's band translates to his sound, Broussard believes. "I find a fiddle is nice for Cajun music, but if I was trying to make my driving sound with that fiddle dragging me down, I'd probably catch a headache," he says.

Delton Broussard died in 1994; Jeffery played accordion at his funeral, and led a band of family members in a tribute concert for that year's Jazz Fest. After several years of enjoying its position as the hottest young band in the region, Zydeco Force started to see its audiences dwindle, and Robinson left to play with Keith Frank. But Broussard remains one of the most talented young accordionists and vocalists in zydeco, and he continues to work the trail ride circuit, hoping for a comeback.

"At one time, we had all the trail rides," he remembers. "Anytime they had a trail ride, we was there. It was hot, a lot of dust, dirt in the accordion, my mouth, and everything. But it was fun being around different kinds of people and seeing a lot of kids enjoy themselves. We played a trail ride in Henderson, I'll never forget it, they had so much people, and it was so dusty.

You couldn't see nothing, you couldn't open your mouth. We could play one song and we had to stop for the dust to go down until we could play again.

"I'm not very well educated," he concludes. "Just like my father — he never could read and he couldn't write. But I could sit down here in an hour and make up a song. And if I hear something one time I can play it right back. And for nine years, no matter where I played or where I went, I carried the people."

# 15

# RIDING LOW AND
# ROLLING HIGH

*The Hi-Rollers play a little harder,*
*The Hi-Rollers take zydeco farther,*
*But you gotta take a trip,*
*Now when you take that trip*
*You're gonna see . . .*

— *Beau Jocque, "Hi-Roller Theme/Low Rider"*

S OMETIME AFTER THREE on a Sunday morning in March, an oversize midnight blue Ford pickup storms through the prairie towns on
Highway 190 from Baton Rouge to Port Barre. Beau Jocque is near-
ing the tail end of another three-night weekend zydeco blitz. Lake
Charles and New Orleans are behind him. Port Arthur, Texas, is later today.

Michelle, Beau's wife, has just shut her eyes. A couple of the band members are snoring in the backseat. The whole truck has a feeling of peace and
tranquility. Beau Jocque can't stand it. "Everybody is waiting for me to be
quiet so they can go to sleep!" he bellows in the kind of voice you might find
at the top of a beanstalk. *"But I won't do it!"*

In 1992 Beau Jocque was a six-foot-six zydeco colossus who roared his
song "Mon Nom C'est Beau Jocque" and quickly began pummeling dance
halls with a thunderous sound. First was an eponymous debut for Lanor

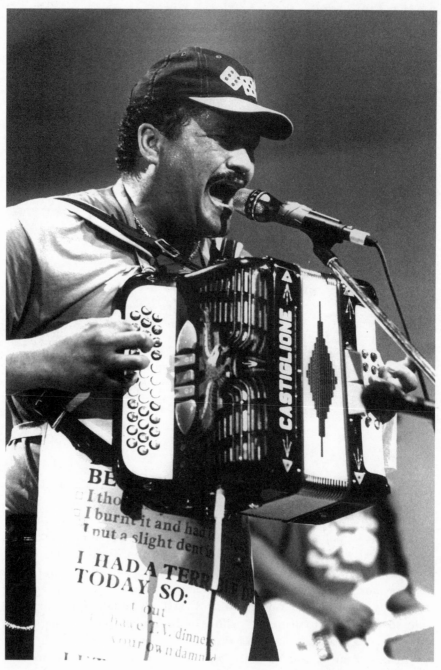

*Beau Jocque at the Habibi Temple, Lake Charles, Louisiana.*

Records, and then *Beau Jocque Boogie* launched a series of top-selling albums for Rounder. The first became a benchmark for local zydeco hit recordings, largely because of the song "Give Him Cornbread."

The song is rooted in Louisiana life and culture. Although Clifton Chenier, Huddie "Leadbelly" Ledbetter, and Bee Fontenot had previously recorded accordion songs about cornbread — called *pain maïs* and served for breakfast in Creole households as *couche-couche* — Beau Jocque based his version on Willis Prudhomme's "Cornbread Two-Step," recorded two years earlier. Prudhomme explains how he wrote the song: "My mom used to sing this little song to us all the time, 'Mama's little baby wants shortnin' bread.' She'd be singing while she was cooking — we were twelve in the family, she had a bunch to cook for. And I'd whistle that song going down in the cotton fields. So I took it and changed it to cornbread, because she was always making cornbread."

Like "Zydeco Sont Pas Salé" and "Paper in My Shoe," "Give Him Cornbread" makes a dance by evoking hard times. Indeed, having no money for corn flour is the subject of Bee Fontenot's song "Pain de mais," just as the lack of salt meat provides the title for Chenier's "Zydeco Sont Pas Salé." Beau Jocque's version combined the old folk melody with a rap number by FM called "Gimme What You Got (for a Porkchop)" and added a contemporary double-kick rhythm. Response was both immediate and, at times, overwhelming. At the 1993 Zydeco Festival nearly every band performed "Give Him Cornbread." When Beau Jocque played it — twice — the audience pelted him with pieces of the yellow food. Beau Jocque celebrated by buying two horses and naming them Cornbread and Porkchop.

Crowds began building for Beau Jocque, eventually making him the circuit's top draw. At his dances, rows of cars and trucks lined the shoulders of state highways in all directions. For the first time in history, Hamilton's Place had to move cows out of a neighboring pasture to create extra parking space.

At first Beau Jocque stuck to the interstate between New Orleans and Houston, following Boozoo Chavis's route in Louisiana and Texas. Later he began to tour internationally. But on this weekend, he is scheduled for Prime Time II in Lake Charles for the second time, and in Port Arthur he'll be at Raymond's Community Hall, another regular stop. "If I can stretch out between New Orleans and Austin, I'll be happy," says Beau Jocque, staring across his front hood, watching his truck eat up the Louisiana flatland.

\*        \*        \*

"I hope I don't forget my accordion tonight," Beau Jocque growls in irritation. "I can't find it anywhere. *Shell-eeee!*"

He is pacing across his Kinder home, his large feet sinking deeply into plush sky-blue carpet. The living room is dominated by a giant-screen TV and a horseshoe-shaped sofa, and a wall is filled with a mirror in which a large statue of a brass peacock is regarding himself. Beau Jocque reaches into a closet and closes a hand on an accordion. He calls for Michelle again and goes outside where his truck is waiting, preloaded and pointing westward toward the sunset and Lake Charles.

Since Beau Jocque began playing, his wife — who receives tribute in the song "Shelly Shelly" — has missed few shows. One Mother's Day a baby-sitter didn't show up, and Beau offered to "have the van break down." Only at Michelle's insistence did he make the gig. "We made a pact," he explains. "Whenever she wouldn't be able to go to a concert, I wouldn't go. And that way there wouldn't be any rumors — because a lot of marriages get broken up just from people talking. This is sacred to me. At one time I saw myself as being doomed. There were a lot of things I had to get over. Michelle's helped me get over them."

It was Michelle and her twelve sisters who teamed up to give Beau Jocque his first accordion, which he played in public for the first time in October 1991. But the musical birth of Beau Jocque really began four years earlier, on a date he says he'll never forget: September 4, 1987.

"It's hard to talk about," admits Beau Jocque, sitting down for a couple minutes Friday before leaving for Lake Charles. "It leads to a lot of depressing things." He was working as a hired electrician, and was trying to attach a monitor to a container for chemicals. Then his pipe wrench slipped. He fell about twenty feet and landed in a sitting position on a floor of concrete.

At first there was no pain. "My lower back just got real hot, like I fell on a hot blanket. Then I got scared and thought I was bleeding, but I wasn't bleeding at all. I knew something wrong had happened."

The fall shattered a disc and tore a muscle in his back. He underwent a series of operations and was told that he wouldn't be able to walk again. But he did get on his feet eventually, and he began visiting his parents' house. One day he picked up an old accordion that was lying around, and his father told him not to touch it. "That's how my daddy conned me into learning the accordion, by telling me I couldn't do it," he says now, laughing. "He just told me it works every time."

Beau Jocque was born Andrus Espre, a name few people today know or use. His father, Sandrus "Tee Toe" Espre, was a well-regarded accordion player for the house dances. "He speaks Cajun French and plays Cajun music as well, but then he'll get into this other thing, a bluesy style like

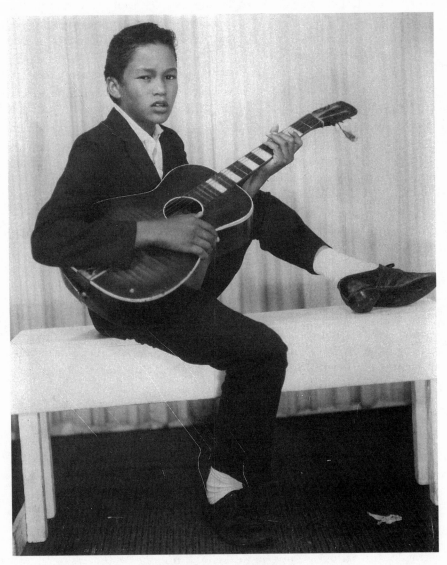

*Beau Jocque at around fourteen.*

Amédé Ardoin," Beau Jocque says. "It's so pretty when it's done well, and he does it well. But he'd like to clown around with his buddies when he played, and they'd always have too much to drink, and Mama wouldn't like that. When my oldest brother was born, he put the accordion away. And he left it alone, and the first time I really heard him play was the day I got married. It made me cry, because he could play that well, and I could see in his face that he loved it so much.

"I used to try to get him to show me how to play, but he's hell to learn from," Beau Jocque continues. "He's very, very strict, and nothing is ever right with him. You know, Kermon Richard and I talk a lot, and my daddy came to my wife's birthday party at Richard's Club, and Kermon stopped him at the door. He said, 'Well, what do you think of your boy now?' And my daddy said, 'He's coming along.' Kermon said, 'Coming along? Look at the place, it's packed!' My daddy said, 'Yeah, but maybe they didn't have nowhere else to go.' But you know, that's just how he is."

Beau Jocque had always picked up music quickly. In high school, class-mate Warren Ceasar nicknamed him Juke Jake for his speed at learning new songs. Beau Jocque admits that he was a bit of a troublemaker in those days, and on one ill-fated day, the two stole Ceasar's father's truck. "All I can re-member is seeing that old man standing against the sunset with a rope in his hands, and he said to me, 'Go home, boy,'" Beau Jocque recalls. "After that, I shot out of there." The pair also performed together in an R&B combo that was an offshoot of their high school band, with Beau Jocque playing tuba. But he left music alone until his recovery, when he began fig-uring out French tunes on his accordion. Then he and Michelle set out into the clubs.

"We started doing some professional surveying, for about five years," says Beau Jocque. "We'd check the crowd out, seeing what keeps them pumped up — that was during the whole time I was going through therapy and surgery. We'd go home and take notes. Then I had a few friends to tell me about Boozoo Chavis. I went to listen, and the strength of that accordion, and the effect that it had on the crowd, sort of fascinated me."

In Chavis's music, Beau Jocque found the steady dance rhythm that would eventually underpin his own sound. He listened closely to Chavis's couplets about life on Dog Hill, and he tried to imitate his voice. He began sitting in with various groups on weekends, until one of Chavis's nephews, bass player Retell Chavis, called him on the phone. His band, the Night Rockers, needed an accordion player. Beau met with them. "I said, 'Well, you guys are going to be called the Hi-Rollers if you want to work for me.'"

West of Kinder, the falling sun is turning wet rice fields into fiery red-orange pools. Beau Jocque hurtles down State Highway 383 to Lake Charles and describes how bleak everything once looked for him, when he was crippled and out of work. And then, he says, he started playing accordion. Zydeco music, he explains softly, was his "back door."

A silver disco ball, multicolored track lighting, and red and blue police lights illuminate the painted cinderblock and fibreboard interior of Lake Charles's Prime Time II. Usually the club features rap and R&B, but when Beau Jocque first played here, the place packed with dancers and had its best night ever. "Look at this," says co-owner Dr. Stephen Ayers happily, pointing to the wooden dance floor, which is coming apart at the base. "See how it's splitting? Beau Jocque did this."

The Hi-Rollers are setting up for the night. Chuck Bush is sitting on the stage, stringing six strings on the new bass that Beau Jocque bought him to play. Wilfred "Caveman" Pierre is bending his rubboard into a C-shape. Drummer Steve Charlot finishes a game of pool, then comes to the stage and picks up an accordion.

"Get away from my accordion," snaps Beau Jocque, playfully slapping at his wrist.

"*Owwww!*" yelps Charlot. "You bruised my hand!"

Onstage as well as off, the two are engaged in a constant comic dialogue. Twenty years Beau Jocque's junior, Charlot plays Robin to Beau Jocque's Batman. His squeaky vocals punctuate the bandleader's minor-key growls, and the two engage in friendly dozens on tunes like "Beau Jocque's Nursery Rhyme." Charlot is also a primary source of the band's rap influences.

The night starts, and the two begin trading lines. "Ah ya ya yaaaaa," starts Beau Jocque.

"Pump it up, pump it up!" shouts Charlot, his voice cracking.

"Yeah, yeah."

"K-k-k-k-k-kick it!"

"Oooomph!"

"G-g-g-g-g-give me some!"

"Work with it, work with it."

"Don't you quit it, don't you quit it."

"Rock awhile!"

"Do it again, do it again!"

Tonight Charlot has a present: a new rap about "imitators in zydeco music" which he inserts into a song called "Shaggy Dog." Beau Jocque likes it, and by the end of the weekend he's breaking down the song in the middle, letting the drums and rubboard take the lead, and calling to Charlot: "I hear your dog can rap! I'm going to give you a chance to let your dog express what he can do!" Later, Beau Jocque will base a new song on Char-lot's lines.

The crowd at the Prime Time — mostly McNeese State students — follow zydeco club customs. When the song starts, couples fill the floor. As soon as the song ends, they return to their tables. Nobody claps; nobody needs to.

Michelle takes a table at the side of the stage, and is joined by several other wives and girlfriends of the band. At one point a smoke machine is turned on, engulfing their table in a thick gray cloud. They move. "We're going to get our own smoke machine," decides Michelle.

Lake Charles is also home to Boozoo Chavis, and it's in this city's Habibi Temple that the two have occasionally engaged in zydeco battles. In the early days of the rivalry, Chavis was known to stand at the side of the stage when Beau Jocque played, drinking a beer and hurling insults. The next day, he would call up the younger player and offer advice on his songs.

Soon the accordionists began singing about each other. Beau Jocque wouldn't play his song when Chavis was at the dance, but the older accordionist eventually heard about the lines

*I don't know but it's been said*
*Boozoo Chavis has a leg up in the bed.*
*Doctor told him to take a rest,*
*Let the Hi-Rollers do the rest.*

On his 1993 record *Boozoo, That's Who,* Chavis offered this reply in his song "Boozoo's Payback":

*They play my music and they do me wrong*
*But they can't sing my song.*

The battles have taken unusual forms. At the 1995 Zydeco Festival, Beau Jocque asked Chavis to join him onstage. He thanked him for his songs, especially "Zydeco Hee Haw," and he gave him a wrapped gift and told him to open it on the drive back to Lake Charles. Chavis looked at the box, then at the audience. "I'm kind of curious to open it now," he said. But Beau Jocque made him wait, and the crowd never learned the odd contents: a pair of slippers that made flatulating sounds, and underwear that read OLD FART.

Then in New Orleans in 1997, Mid-City Lanes owner John Blancher staged a one-frame bowling tournament between the two players. Chavis had never bowled before, but he went first. He walked quickly to the foul line in his boots and Stetson, disadvantaged by the recent loss of the tips of two fingers. Then he bowled a strike. Beau Jocque gracefully conceded.

When all is said and done, Beau Jocque and Boozoo Chavis share both the same sense of humor and many of the same values. During a set break at the Prime Time, when Beau Jocque and Michelle go out to the truck to take a rest, they're quietly joined by Poncho Chavis, Boozoo's son. The two discuss an upcoming benefit for Boozoo's wife, Leona, who had recently undergone surgery. Beau Jocque promises to do anything he can. When the two camps are found in the truck together, Beau Jocque laughs about the rivalry. "We're fakes," he admits. "Just like professional wrestlers."


After a couple hours of sleep Saturday morning, Beau Jocque wakes at seven-thirty to super-glue a button that popped off his accordion the night before. "They're not supposed to do that," he mutters nervously. Then he cleans his truck and finds his blue suit. He's playing the House of Blues in New Orleans tonight — one of the first zydeco artists to appear at the new entertainment complex — and he wants to look his best. His band members meet at a truck stop in Port Barre and convoy to New Orleans.

Piloting his truck through the French Quarter, Beau Jocque looks at Bourbon Street and remembers aloud when he first saw the strip. He was a teenager, and had just enlisted in the Air Force. During his service, he made the rank of sergeant, received top security clearance, and was stationed in London and Germany. He escorted Kissinger once, and he says he guarded things that people still don't know about. And that's all he wants to say, except to add that he saw and experienced many accidents while in the military. This included his first near-death experience, when an explosion left him lying in the hospital with amnesia.

His second accident was the fall at work that eventually resulted in his zydeco career. Then, one hot day in 1996, Beau Jocque had his third near-death experience. He was playing an outdoor show in Austin, Texas, when he collapsed from heart strain and was rushed to the hospital. He canceled a cross-country tour and returned to Kinder. The following week, his Rounder producer, Scott Billington, drove to meet him, hoping to teach low-fat cooking techniques. He arrived to witness a strange scene. Remembers Billington: "They had been on the road for two and a half weeks, and we found out that two local radio stations were announcing all day that Beau Jocque had died of a heart attack. So there we were walking through the supermarket, buying mustard greens and turkey sausage, and every time somebody saw Beau Jocque, they turned white and dropped, figuring they saw a ghost. Somebody had even called the mayor of Kinder, who rushed down and just kept pumping Beau Jocque's hand."

"Accidents have played a big part of my life," Beau Jocque explains, parking by the House of Blues. "And me getting into zydeco — that was an accident."

Beau Jocque walks into the French Quarter club, looking for his dressing room. The bar staff is huddled in a meeting. "His name is Beau Jocque and he plays zydeco, that's all I know," says a man, reading off a notepad. When Beau Jocque hears his name, he looks up. Puzzled, he continues on.

Sound check was scheduled for four in the afternoon, but nobody seems to know why the band is so early. Then the Hi-Rollers discover one of the perks of playing the House of Blues, and they begin ordering supper. Beau Jocque and Michelle can't eat yet. They forgot his black dress shoes, so they walk to Canal Street to buy a new pair. Beau Jocque doesn't want to wear tennis shoes at the House of Blues.

It takes a couple of tries before Beau Jocque can find anything in a 12E, but he makes it back to the House of Blues in time to shower and change into his suit, as accordionist Lynn August plays the first set. Beau Jocque is waiting at the side of the stage, and when August finishes, he goes up to greet him. Then August drops something — whatever it was, he doesn't seem to need it anymore. But August is blind, so Beau Jocque bends down to pick up the object. When he does, his Italian suit pants split open, seam to seam. Never more appreciated, Michelle stands behind her husband and ushers him back to the dressing room. He glumly takes off his new shoes and his now shredded pants, puts his sweat suit and tennis shoes back on, and returns to the stage.

On the drive home later that evening, Beau Jocque tries to figure the House of Blues. He heard a lot of compliments, and there were small groups of people dancing like they do at Richard's Club and Prime Time II. But there were a lot more people that were just standing, nodding their heads and applauding. For Beau Jocque, who thinks about a dancing beat every time he writes a song, it was a disturbing sight. "I got them cranked up, but they just looked at me," he says with concern in his voice.

The surveying continues: Michelle brought her camcorder to the show tonight, and she made tapes of both the dancers and the stage. They'll study the tapes later to see what happened. "When I zoom in on Beau Jocque," she says, "I can tell exactly what he's thinking. I can tell exactly what he thinks about a solo by the way he nods his head."

The sky starts to lighten on the road to Kinder. Michelle falls asleep, and so does guitarist Cookie Chavis, playing with the band tonight. "Cookie is so cool," Beau Jocque says quietly. "I watch him when he takes a solo, and you can't even tell from his expression that he's playing. I would have to practice to do that. Me, I got to always freak out."

Driving time is used to "plan stuff," he says. Like the new song with Charlot's rap. Like the FM station and recording studio he wants to own. Like Beau Jocque's Place. "Yeah, my own club," he says, building his dream out of elements from all his favorite places in Louisiana and Texas. "It would be a nice roomy place with a bowling alley, a restaurant, and a nice wooden dance floor with suspension — a concrete floor can hurt your ankles and ruin your shoes. And the seats would be all padded and cushioned, just like J. B.'s Entertainment Center in Houston."

The road passes under him and Beau Jocque continues to build his new club until he reaches the truck stop in Port Barre.

One Halloween, the Hi-Rollers were resting in their hotel room during their first tour to California. There was a knock at the door. Chuck Bush answered it and saw something horrible. Whatever or whoever, it was over six feet tall, with glowing eyes and bushy hair. The bass player froze. Rubboard player Wilfred "Caveman" Pierre was on the bed watching TV. He couldn't move either.

Beau Jocque thought his joke was pretty funny.

Halloween pranks notwithstanding, Beau Jocque is a strict leader who'll dock someone's pay if he's late to a gig. Tonight in Port Arthur, a guitar player misses a string in his F chord. Beau Jocque turns around in the middle of the song and says, "I heard that."

The relationship between the players, however, extends beyond music. "If you don't like somebody, you can't play with them," says Bush. "I don't care how good you are, you're not going to get that groove."

"You're looking at them all the time, thinking, well, you did me wrong, I'm not going to join what you're playing," agrees Pierre.

The members of this band are also some of their own biggest fans. Bush will rave about the steadiness of Pierre's rubboard, and Charlot will talk about how nobody plays the bass like Bush, who started off as lead guitarist and still fills the air with jazzy riffs and countermelodies. And in Port Arthur, Bush points to Charlot and says admiringly, "There's the little shit that comes up with all the stuff."

They're leaders in its new sound, but most of the band didn't grow up on zydeco. Beau Jocque would hear his father play the accordion at home, but became more excited when he heard ZZ Top and War. Echoes of both are heard in his band's expanded line-up, which features Michael Lockett on Hammond B-3 organ and guitarist Russell "Sly" Dorion, who is also heard on a Peter Frampton–style voice box. Pierre remembers that he would turn off the radio when zydeco came on. So would Bush. "I didn't want to hear that old stuff," he remembers. "It sounded crazy-like. They'd have these French dances at the church hall, but there was just old people there all the time, so I didn't want to go."

The influences meld in Beau Jocque zydeco, which includes everything from a cover of "Cisco Kid" to a hip-hop mix called "Make It Stank." At Raymond's Community Hall in Port Arthur, it was Beau Jocque who started drawing the younger crowd, says owner Raymond McClain. And on this last night of the weekend, the green concrete floor is packed with dancers of all ages. Older couples hold each other in a more traditional two-step, and young couples work on moves they've just invented. "There's also a hundred-year-old man who comes here, who says that zydeco is good for his arthritis," says McClain.

By late Sunday night, the long weekend is finally over. The band members stand in a circle in the dark parking lot, and their leader hands each his pay. "I think that zydeco music is strong now, and the zydeco music that is strong is different from what's been done," says Beau Jocque, pulling his truck out of the lot. "Clifton was very popular, because he did Clifton's music. And Boozoo did things his way. But now I'm doing it my way, and I figure if I do that, I'll always have a road to travel on."

On the drive east, the Hi-Rollers get into a conversation about double-kicking, debating just who started playing the rhythmic skip of two pounds on the bass drum. Bush is talking about all the bands that are copying Beau Jocque — a favorite topic on these drives. Sometimes, they say, they catch other musicians with handheld tape recorders in their pockets.

So far, Charlot has been dozing in the backseat. He stirs and suddenly joins the conversation. "Before I started whistling and rapping, nobody was doing that," he says quickly. "Before Beau Jocque started going into the low keys, nobody was doing that. Before Chuck got on that five-string bass, nobody was doing that. And now they're all trying to do it. But Beau Jocque will keep doing what nobody has done before."

As quickly as he awoke, the exhausted drummer closes his eyes and sinks his chin on his hand. Chuck Bush switches on the radio and a Beau Jocque song comes on and most everyone sleeps until Church Point.

# 16

# IT TAKES A WHOLE LOT
# OF CLIMBING

---

KEITH FRANK'S FACE IS HALF HIDDEN INSIDE HIS RAINCOAT; he's standing in a large puddle of water, staring at the padlock on the front door to Slim's Y-Ki-Ki. He's agreed to meet me here early, and Tony Gradney, the owner, hasn't yet arrived. "We're not going to get too many people tonight," he says under his breath. Because of the rain? He shakes his head. "Lent," he says.

He's being modest. A generation ago, the community would have indeed stayed home, honoring the religious holidays. But by ten o'clock tonight, every chair and all the available standing room at the Opelousas club will be occupied, and the dance floor will be packed — as it is every time he plays.

Tony Gradney arrives to open the doors, and he leads the way into the cavernous room centered by a stage decorated with a string of colored lights. Tony's father, Arnold "Slim" Gradney, bought the building in 1949, and his famous love for Hawaii is reflected in the decor: yellow walls emblazoned with rows of palm trees that stretch across the room. Tony Gradney took over operations when his father died in 1994.

Recent years have seen an increase in attendance for all the local zydeco clubs. Slim's, Richard's Club in nearby Lawtell, and Hamilton's Place in Lafayette are the scene called "down east" by zydeco fans in Lake Charles

*Keith Frank.*

and Texas. The down-east crowd is notorious for following only one player at a time. Being the leader, then, is a precarious thing, but for the past several years the position has been held by Keith Frank. Many who come to Slim's tonight were with him at Richard's Club the night before, and will show up tomorrow for a trail ride at King's Ranch. On a busy four-day weekend, Frank might play ten dances, and his popularity is so high that dance promoters often hire him as a defensive maneuver. "You almost have to handle it like a business," Brian Gallow explains. "If I have a trail ride dance at Richard's and Keith is playing at Slim's, I'm going to have to close the door, because we won't have enough dancers."

Frank knows the dance crowd because he's one of them: predominantly black Creoles in their twenties. A minority speak French, although some may emphasize a statement with a French phrase or two. They heard about house dances from their grandparents, and from their parents they learned about Clifton Chenier. But they first became interested in zydeco on hearing Boozoo Chavis and Zydeco Force, and then Beau Jocque, and now Keith Frank.

"I think the thing that I enjoy the most about zydeco is that if people enjoy it, I enjoy it," Frank says. Watching him work a dance, it is evident he is a performer with a deep appreciation of why his audience is with him. He delivers his songs in short, clipped segments, and usually has little to say between the numbers. When he plays, the double-kick rhythm gives his music an intense, metronomic quality that sets a steady marathon pace for dancers. Perhaps most important, his music interprets the hip-hop aesthetic for a zydeco crowd — even though he specifically denies it. "To tell you the truth, I think Beau Jocque — in my personal opinion — is trying to play rap with the accordion," he says. "Some people like it, but I'm not a big fan of it, I never have been. I just didn't take a liking to it, like I did Zydeco Force and Boozoo."

Yet his body of work indicates otherwise. The title of his early hit "What's His Name" was inspired by Snoop Doggy Dogg, and his lyrics are a hip-hop-style pastiche of popular culture references. During a Zydeco Festival appearance, he played his local hit "Get On Boy" with added accordion licks from "The Star Spangled Banner" and the themes to *The Woody Woodpecker Show, The Andy Griffith Show*, and *The Good, the Bad and the Ugly*. Other riffs include the chorus to Sonny & Cher's "The Beat Goes On," the *Beverly Hillbillies* theme, and a commercial jingle for Chia Pets. One of Frank's biggest hits is "Movin' On Up," in which he plays the theme to *The Jeffersons* in its entirety; anyone with a television knows the words, and his whole crowd frequently sings along:

Beans don't burn in the kitchen,
Meat don't burn on the grill.
Took a whole lot of climbing
Just to get up this hill.

In Frank's hands, zydeco has also moved sonically closer to hip-hop, becoming younger, louder, and deeper. A graduate in electronics from McNeese State University in Lake Charles, he is meticulous about his technology, and frequently leaves the bandstand during a song to listen to the mix and adjust the sound levels himself. Following the lead of Zydeco Force and especially Beau Jocque, he has expanded his bass and drums — to the breaking point, some musicians fear. "What I'm hearing now is nothing but bass drum, where I feel I want to hear that accordion," says Jeffery Broussard. "A lot of younger people that's getting into zydeco, they're looking for that bottom, and if it doesn't have that punch, now the first thing they're going to tell you is that you sound weak. They don't know what that old-time French sounds like."

In fact, many of the old zydeco clubs have been rewired to accommodate the demands of Frank's zydeco. "You know, when I was coming up, you bring one amplifier for guitar, bass, and accordion, and you had your drums," Tony Gradney says. "With Keith Frank, I have to sit there after the dance for two hours for him to load up his equipment in the trailer. But he takes so much pride in his music, and he's got to have everything right. So I hired another electrician, and now I have a special circuit that I switch on just for him."

This night in Slim's, three hours before dancers begin to arrive, Frank is helping his band members haul in his sound equipment. Despite the tropical decor, Slim's Y-Ki-Ki is chilly. Frank slaps water from his coat and, seeing that his jobs are finished, takes a chair off a table and sits down to talk about the changes in music he's both witnessed and set in motion. Did he imagine that he would be such a success in his early twenties? He laughs at the question. "To be honest," he says, "I didn't think it would take this long."

Keith Frank, like most young zydeco players today, grew up in a musical family. The Preston Frank Swallow Band — which included Keith's father, Preston, on accordion, his great-uncle Carlton Frank on fiddle, and another great-uncle, Hampton Frank, on guitar — was best known for the song "Why Do You Want to Make Me Cry?" composed by Preston with drummer Leo "the Bull" Thomas, and adapted from Bois Sec Ardoin and Canray

Fontenot's bluesy "'Tit monde." The song is played by nearly every zydeco band today, including Willis Prudhomme and Nathan Williams, who recast it as "Why You Wanna Make Poor Cha Cha Cry?"

Despite their popular song, the Frank family believe they never quite received their due. "Where we grew up in the town of Soileau, it's mostly a lot of fields," remembers Preston Frank. "They'd call us the Soileau birds when we would go to Oberlin High School. Oberlin always did say that Soileau wasn't nothing. In them days, it was kind of embarrassing to be from the country."

"The band started around 'seventy-seven, when I started playing with Carlton," Preston continues. "I worked hard to try to get the Frank name recognized as musicians. About five or six years ago, my job at a plywood plant wasn't giving me much time with the music, so I told Keith to do what he needs to do."

Preston Frank's great-grandfather Joseph Frank Jr. was an accordion player, and his great-great-grandfather Joseph Frank Sr. was known to be a fiddler. But they never recorded. "He would play a fiddle real good, my daddy and them told me," he recalls. "But he was never recognized, they never had anything said about him. He was there at the time when Dennis McGee and Amédé Ardoin were playing. Maybe there was some kind of way they got it from him and he didn't get the recognition."

Today the Frank name in music largely rests on Keith's shoulders. "I fought so hard to keep playing, and once Keith got himself established, then I kind of backed off," Preston explains. "When Keith started playing on his own, they thought I'd died. I'm not dead yet, I'm still here. They want to kill me a little bit too fast.

"I started Keith young, him. He played my style at first, then he changed to Boozoo's style, then he went to another style, then he went to his own style. But there's still some of me in there. When I'm determined to do something and make something, I don't give it up until I accomplish what I want. Keith's like that. We've come a long ways. We're recognized now, but we sure worked like hell to get that recognition."

Keith Frank was four years old when he first played drums behind his father, and he became his full-time drummer when he turned nine. But zydeco was not his first love. "I hated it," Keith says, laughing. "I swear, I hated it. I could not stand playing music. I hated zydeco, I hated the whole thing. My old man would make me practice, and I could always find something better to be doing. Then as things moved on, my dad started playing less and less. Then I realized it's a part of my life, and I couldn't stand being without it."

By the time he started in Oberlin High School, Frank had his own band

and was entering talent contests. On marching band trips, when other students brought radios, Frank brought his accordion. "On the way there, I would play on the bus, play in the band room. People would laugh, say it was hilarious. I didn't think it was funny. But back then, if you played accordions, they laughed at you and called it country music. A lot of the people spoke French, but they didn't want anybody to know it. In fact, if I went back and played in Oberlin, I'd get no support at all. But I don't let it bother me."

Early on, Frank was inspired when he saw Chavis on the comeback trail. "Sometimes we were the only young ones in the place, me and my sister," he says. "Boozoo became my idol — well, my daddy is my idol, but Boozoo was up there. And then Zydeco Force started coming on the scene."

When Preston Frank began performing less frequently, Keith started playing guitar in Jo Jo Reed's band. With his father's approval, he switched to accordion and began fronting the family band, which included his sister Jennifer on bass and his brother Brad on drums. "I didn't really take it over," he says. "We had two separate groups with the same people, but two totally different styles. My dad plays the real zydeco, traditional — he does some Clifton, his own stuff, and the stuff that's been handed down in French."

In 1982 Preston Frank and Classie Ballou Sr. went to Church Point to meet with Lee Lavergne, who'd recently built a music studio behind his Sound Center music store. The visit resulted in an album released on Lavergne's Lanor label. The next time Frank returned, he brought his children. The Preston Frank Family Band released a series of records, ending with *Let's Dance* in 1991. "They were good little kids, because the mama and the daddy, they raised them very strict," Lavergne recalls. "They would always come around, and I told Keith one day, 'You kids ought to get together and do something.' They played a little bit different than their daddy, and they were doing jobs without their daddy, because Preston worked shift work and was tied down."

Keith Frank and the Soileau Zydeco Band recorded one cassette for Lanor, *On the Bandstand.* The tape included a new version of Amédé Ardoin's "Two Step de Prairie Soileau," as well as songs influenced by Boozoo Chavis and Zydeco Force. "They were searching for something different," remembers Lavergne. The relationship between the producer and the young bandleader quickly broke down, however, and they never worked together again. "It never could be loud enough on the drum for him," Lavergne explains. "He wanted the drums to be heavy, and I like them heavy, too. But you don't send those needles into the red and distort. I'm concerned about the quality of the sound. But he wanted to do things his way, and we didn't get along about that, and he went and did his thing with somebody else. And he done good, you know."

In 1993 Keith Frank searched for a place where he could do it his way, and he launched a long-standing partnership with Eunice-based producer Fred Charlie and sound engineer Scott Ardoin. He took an active role in every stage of the production, resulting in *Get On Boy!* The album showcased Frank's new sound, and the title became his nickname. He reworked Boozoo Chavis's "Zydeco Hee Haw" into his own "Murdock," and D. L. Menard's Cajun classic "The Back Door" into an instrumental called "Huh." He was most inventive in songs like "Going to McDonald's," in which he chose to portray modern Creole life as he knew it. "I wrote that song at a trail ride," he remembers. "I hadn't had a thing to eat all day, and they had this cowboy stew or something like that, and then somebody came in with a bag of burgers from Checkers. And that's what I wanted, because I always eat at Checkers and McDonald's at McNeese."

Some of the songs on *Get On Boy!* featured the same minor chord vamps and classic rock riffs used by another performer who lived just a few miles down Highway 165 from Soileau, and who had also gone to Lanor to make his debut record: Beau Jocque. By this time, Beau Jocque and "Give Him Cornbread" had become the top draw on the local zydeco circuit. "Keith saw where Beau Jocque was getting the attention of the young ones, and how he was going into that rap beat," Lavergne believes. "I think he kind of copied Beau Jocque to some extent, because he changed his style completely after he left me."

It wasn't long before a feud began to develop between the two musicians. Frank believes the dispute began when he was sitting in with Beau Jocque's band on guitar and drums, and some sound equipment broke. Whatever the cause, the two found themselves locked in perhaps the most bitter rivalry in zydeco history. They hurled gauntlets at each other from stages and over local radio shows. There were charges — and counter-charges — that one performer was trying to stop a club or festival from booking the other. When the two would run into each other in public, they either kept their distance or looked like they might break into a fight. Stories of the feud were recounted over dinner tables throughout Louisiana, and promoters shook their heads in disgust, wondering why the two players didn't take advantage of the attention to stage joint appearances called zydeco battles. But this was no longer the friendly rivalry once seen between Beau Jocque and Boozoo Chavis.

The first major battle erupted over a song — or two songs. In 1993, *Get*

*On Boy!* featured a bouncy tune called "Went Out Last Night," also known as "Hamilton's Club." It was an immediate hit at the dances. Also in 1993, Beau Jocque recorded the song "Yesterday," released the following year on his disc *Pick Up on This!* It was also a hit. Many zydeco songs share rhythms and melodies, but "Yesterday" and "Went Out Last Night" were, without a doubt, the same song. On their respective albums, each performer was credited as songwriter. Then the two songs began competing with each other for the top position on local zydeco radio shows.

The dispute brought up larger questions of originality in songwriting. In zydeco, matters of "authenticity" and "originality" are often set aside in the immediacy of crowd response. Families may debate the origins of particular songs, but when contemporary musicians tap the deep vein of shared songs and styles, they establish continuity both in the current scene and between generations. Today's greater emphasis on recorded music, however, raises issues involved not only with pride of authorship but with royalties. The current debate on originality in zydeco parallels larger discussions in contemporary rap and hip-hop.

The jury is still out, most observers believe. "There's no town hall meeting to discuss these things amongst the musicians, you know," says Floyd Soileau, whose Maison de Soul distributes Frank's records. "Now, if one of these songs should suddenly make a lot of money, then you'll see the problems start."

Every musician has a tale about outright song-rustling. "One night at Richard's Club, a guy was parked right in the back where I usually leave my trailer," recalls Beau Jocque. "Jeffery Broussard of Zydeco Force was in the house, so I had him come up to the stage and take my place. So he started playing, and Michelle and I decided to walk outside and go in the back of the club. So we made the corner, and there was a black Dodge van, and these guys had the sliding door wide open with the tape player on the floor. So I went up there, and they all jumped up and reached for the cassette player. But I didn't make a scene."

Other times, the original source of a song is harder to trace. "Sometimes, you sit down and you're thinking about something, and then another guy is sitting four or five miles down the road, he's thinking of the same thing," says Jeffery Broussard. "You don't know how it happens, but sometimes it happens. You sit down and you think you hear something out the window. Maybe you're watching TV, and somebody is watching the same thing. But the same idea keeps falling at the same time."

Complicating matters is the collaborative spirit between musicians and dancers, which means that zydeco songs are rarely composed in isolation.

"It's like cookies," explains Frank. "You got to take it out, and test if it's done yet. Now if I play it out, and another musician takes it, well, it's my fault, because I shouldn't play it out. I've played new stuff out and other people have played it before I recorded it, and that kind of got to me, but I shouldn't have played it in the first place."

When asked directly about "Went Out Last Night," Frank grows serious. "I think my reputation speaks for itself," he says, now speaking of Beau Jocque directly. "He's borrowed a lot of stuff from a lot of people in the past, I think a lot of people know that. And every now and then, I do some other people's stuff, but I don't make a habit out of it."

For his part, Beau Jocque is clear that he originated the song in question. "If somebody's going to be creative, that's fine, that's good," he says. "But not if you're just going to rip somebody off and race to the studio with something you know that's not yours."

The relatively small amounts of money at stake seemed to keep the matter from spilling into the courts, but pride and reputation are priceless commodities. Fans took sides over "Yesterday" and "Went Out Last Night." The matter was finally resolved to nobody's satisfaction: it was determined that both songs derived from "I Got Loaded," a popular R&B song by Little Bob and the Lollipops.

But bad blood was just starting to flow between Frank and Beau Jocque. "He made comments about me on the mike," says Frank, "saying that the next time I steal one of his songs, to play it right." In this case, no velvet crowns were introduced to lighten — or at least focus — the tension, and the rivalry took on the gloves-off nastiness of a bitter political campaign. The next volley was a song on Keith Frank's *What's His Name?* that everyone knew was about Beau Jocque. Against a minimalist background of accordion and double-kicking drum, he sang:

> One lick from my get-on boy, the pork chop got sick.
> Two licks from my get-on boy, the pork chop ain't —

A cymbal crash finished the thought.

The recording was one of Frank's most effective performances, but the song's belligerent tone set it apart from the more playful cutting tunes that Chavis, Beau Jocque, and other bandleaders had been offering up. It was apparent to all that a line had been crossed; indeed, a teenaged contestant at a Lafayette accordion contest was immediately disqualified when he performed the song and completed the final line. Chavis could get away with "Deacon Jones" and "Uncle Bud," but by even hinting at obscenity, Frank seemed to be moving closer to rap. In fact, "One Shot" seemed less a zydeco tune than the kind of attack in rhyme that was heard after Los Angeles rapper Eazy-E broke with N.W.A.

Beau Jocque didn't record a response, but he picked up the bait with a tune called "What's Wrong with the Get-On Boy?" which he played in the clubs. The general congeniality of the zydeco scene was sorely tested when a series of events led to this counterattack receiving regular play over the Washington, Louisiana, radio station KNEK. Deejay Luke Collins recounts the story, which was readily confirmed by station manager Don Wilson:

"It began when Don Wilson claimed that Keith was trying to tell him how to run his radio station. He said that Keith came in here one day and said that we were playing too much Beau Jocque. And that's when he and Don started cussing in the office. One time they were on the phone, and I was on the air. All of a sudden, Don bust the door open. He said, 'Mr. Luke, where's Keith Frank?' I said, 'Right there,' and I pointed to a CD. 'Where's the other one?' I said, 'Right there.' Then he said, 'I want the daddy, too.' Preston Frank had a few cassettes, and I gave him the handful. You know what he did? He opened that door, he went and threw them on the highway.

"Then, Don went to El Sid O's, and Beau Jocque was singing 'What's Wrong with the Get-On Boy?' Beau Jocque didn't want to put that on record, but Don taped it. Man, every day Don had us play that song. Every hour. So we did. But the trouble is that the people get mad at the deejay, and Keith Frank got mad, too. So one day I was coming back from Gilton's club, I saw that Keith Frank was playing at Richard's. The dance was over, and Keith Frank was getting his stuff off the bandstand when he saw me walk in. I said, 'Keith, I want to tell you something, I'm glad you're doing a good job, you're one of the best zydeco musicians, but whatever you and Don have, don't bring it in the public.'

"After I talked with Keith at Richard's, he shook hands with me. His mama was sitting in the corner. I said, 'I know your mama ain't going to shake hands with me.' I looked at his mama and I waved my hands. And we used to be real good friends, but she just turned. We didn't make up until one day when I was introducing Keith Frank at a festival, and I was talking good about him, and I made her smile."

Some social rifts may have healed, but the story of Keith Frank reveals the inherent shakiness of being at the top of the current zydeco field. "This success couldn't happen to a nicer guy," Soileau says. "But I do think he worries too much. He's really concerned about his craft, and pleasing the fans, and staying on top of the hill." Frank expresses this anxiety in his music, especially on his 1996 disc *Only the Strong Survive.* The title track includes an oblique shot at Jeffery Broussard, recorded after bass player Robby "Mann" Robinson left Zydeco Force to join his band. On other songs, Keith Frank struck a defensive note, as on "Everywhere I Be":

> Everywhere I be
> They're always picking on me.
> Why can't they see
> I just got to be me?

But perhaps the most remarkable song on the disc is "Good Old Days," in which Frank became nostalgic for the days before he dominated the contemporary zydeco scene. In his lyrics, he pays homage to some of the bands that preceded him:

> I want to go back to the good old days,
> Back to the music Boozoo and the Force played,
> When the Force was rising to the top,
> But Boozoo just couldn't be stopped.

Of course, Frank did not introduce a sense of competition into zydeco. Rivalry stories date back to the legends that Amédé Ardoin was shot by another accordion player through a church window. Even Clifton Chenier was not immune to charges of underhandedness. "Clifton came here to Houston, and he tried to get into different places where I play," Anderson Moss recalls. "A woman came running over to me, she said, 'I got a man, Mr. Moss, he said he's your friend. But see, Mr. Moss, he's not your friend, he's trying to get your place to play, for nothing.'"

But the rivalry between Keith Frank and Beau Jocque brought a mean-spirited streak into the community that remains to this day. It appears, however, that the war of words has begun to cool down. Beau Jocque started to tour more frequently, and the younger player became the undisputed ruler of the local scene. In 1996, Beau Jocque took zydeco one step further into hip-hop when he released a studio-created dance mix of the song "Make It Stank," which seemed to position itself somewhere between a homage and a parody of Keith Frank's "What's His Name."

Still a young player, Frank has already honed an effective sound, combining double-kicking zydeco, anachronistic but pleasing classic R&B and doo-wop, and accordion-powered reggae. He has demonstrated just how far an artist can go while rarely leaving the state, and is now Maison de Soul's top-selling zydeco player. His releases fill the bins in the local Wal-Marts, and in some neighborhoods in Houston, gas stations stock cardboard boxes of bootleg Keith Frank tapes. Frank reached another career high-point when he put on a suit and tie and performed for President Clinton in Baton Rouge; he later marveled that Clinton pronounced "Soileau" correctly.

The lasting effects of Frank's popularity are still being debated. Some observers wonder how much of his crowd will become lifelong zydeco fans. Many older Creoles express hope that Frank and his followers will introduce more French songs and waltzes to their crowds. Frank may be facing a long and unpredictable career, but those who try to make a preservationist out of him will probably be disappointed, at least for now. "I get criticized because I don't play a lot of waltzes," he acknowledges. "I know a thousand waltzes, but I just don't like to play them."

Others wonder if Frank will be able to translate his phenomenal regional success onto a national scale. For a time, Soileau thought "Movin' On Up" could become the next "My Toot-Toot," but he thinks the song's chances were hurt by changing times in the record industry. "Back in the old days, if you had sold as much product as Keith has, you'd have had a major label on their knees begging to take over that product," he explains. "But the industry today is not interested in a regional performer unless they think they can multiply that into a half million sales nationally."

For now, Keith Frank seems content with his own reasons for coming to the dance. On this Saturday night in Lent, Slim's Y-Ki-Ki has erupted in a bustle of activity. A woman is marking tables with strips of masking tape, reserving them for the night. Her brother stacks bowls for liquor setups behind the bar, and spaces ashtrays on the Formica counter. Tony Gradney circles the room, plugging in signs for Kool cigarettes and Miller and Silver Bullet beer. The green and blue neon flickers on, and Keith Frank looks around. "I knew it was dark in here," he says.

He pushes back from the table. Brad and Jennifer Frank are on the stage, waiting to check sound levels. The rain has stopped; the crowd is arriving, and the temperature in the club is rising. "My dad gave me some advice," he says with a final laugh. "Enjoy it while it lasts." Then he stops for one last story. "I remember one time we went to a trail ride in Carencro. Beau Jocque was just coming onto the scene, and a woman came up to the van and asked for my card, and she said, 'Oh, I love the way y'all play, y'all sound good.' And I gave her my card and she looked at it and said, 'Are you Beau Jocque?' I said, 'No, ma'am,' and she gave my card back and closed the door and walked away.

"You see, they saw me, and my little brother and my sister, and they didn't think we'd be able to play. But we had a chance to prove them wrong, you know? It's about being underestimated, and then proving people wrong. It's a good feeling to be able to show people that we can play a little something."

*Jermaine Jack and Gerard and John Delafose.*

*Geno Delafose.*

# 17

# RUNNING AGAINST
# THE FIELD

---

*I want to go home but I can't get back.*
*I want to get back but I can't go home.*

— *John Delafose, "Hold That Tiger"*

GENO DELAFOSE'S HIGH-PITCHED CRIES carry across early morning rice fields and cattle pastures as he gently leads his favorite horse, King, down the quiet road to his house. With his nephew Gerard Delafose hanging on to his shirt for balance, Geno is making up a song:

> My dog is blind
> But he don't mind.

As he sings, a cream-colored labrador named Chino happily bounds through tall brush, making occasional clanging noises when he runs into mailbox posts. He rarely breaks stride, until he veers into a patch of woods and howls for Delafose to ride through the tall grass and lead him out.

> My dog is blind,
> My dog is mine.

Geno approaches a white frame farmhouse with green trim. The Delafose family moved from this farm to the town of Eunice on Geno's nineteenth birthday. Two years later he moved back, and he's been here since. "My house is like my own little corner of the world," he says. "No traffic back here. By the time I come home from the tour, there's even some grass on the road.

"It's kind of strange," he continues, his words measured by his horse's easy pace. "Everything always leaves when I go out on tour. I have some chickens, they leave. Some cats, a couple dogs, they leave. It's like, 'Damn, when I left, I had some dogs here.' The only one that stays is Chino, because he's got to stick around."

The son of renowned accordionist John Delafose, Geno — like many young bandleaders — grew up playing drums for his father. But among young Creole musicians today, Delafose rides alone. He ignores the latest zydeco trends, preferring to play all three accordions: single-row, triple, and piano. He still performs his father's songs — and not too differently from how his father once played them. He does versions of Amédé Ardoin and Iry LeJeune tunes, and he even composes new songs in French. "I just like the accordion work on the older songs," he explains. "And you don't have to get really really excited to play them. I'm not the type of person who gets wild and out of it, except every now and then."

Writing in the *New Orleans Times-Picayune*, music critic Keith Spera described Delafose as the zydeco equivalent of what in country music is called a new traditionalist — a young player who embraces forms of the past. Except that in Delafose's case, it's a movement of one, for Keith Frank's crowd considers him an anomaly, when they consider him at all. "You know, I get a lot of complaints from some of the young people that do come out and hear me, and they say, 'Oh, you play too many waltzes,'" he says, his voice sparking with a rare display of anger. "You know what? I'm happy people don't appreciate my music around here like they do elsewhere. I really enjoy the road, and I'm making a good living, and I'm not ready to be popular at home."

Indeed, in the years since he started his own band, Delafose has moved into the top echelon of touring zydeco musicians. Just back from playing fifty-two shows in forty-seven days, he estimates he was on the road seven months out of the last year, playing seated auditoriums, art centers, festivals, an occasional cruise, and week-long music and dance instruction camps. His versatility has made him the most in-demand player for dance crowds around the country.

So on a Sunday like today, when most twenty-five-year-old accordionists would be hustling trail rides, Delafose can afford a day off. He wakes up early to ride King, and goes to the races to hang out with the horsemen. Tonight he's playing the small Assumption Catholic Hall in the town of Basile, because it's one of the places his father played, and the old crowd will be there. "To sing for older people in French, and to know what I'm singing, and then go back and just kind of shoot the breeze with them — that's something I really like a lot," he says.

The horses quicken when they realize they're taking the familiar path back to their stalls. Delafose hums a Boozoo Chavis song to himself. "Going to *ma maison*," he sings quietly. *"Mo tout seule."* Going to my house, all alone.

The Delafose world was not so tranquil when I first visited their Eunice home. It was 1993, and I'd arrived to interview Geno's father, John Delafose, for the liner notes for what would be his last record, *Blues Stay Away from Me.* The Saturday afternoon kitchen could have been a small train station: Geno and his brother Tony were sitting at the kitchen counter eating gumbo while their mother, JoAnn, was passing out more bowls to daughters, cousins, and a line of friends streaming in from the front yard. The dinner seemed to be a ritual practiced every weekend that John Delafose and the Eunice Playboys went to play a dance.

This time was different, though, for John himself had to stay home and recuperate from recent heart surgery. The family carried on busily, but it was hard to see him sidelined. A gregarious and warm man, John Delafose characterized the zydeco spirit.

Born in Duralde in 1939, he began playing on a homemade fiddle, and as a teenager he performed on harmonica for dances. He quit "playing out" after he married, and busied himself working and raising seven children. Then, when he reached his early thirties, he bought an accordion. "I started practicing at home by myself, and my little boys would hit on a cardboard box like it was a drum," he once told Ann Savoy. "I decided I was going to go all the way, no stopping."

John Delafose backed his single-row accordion with a strong rhythm section, featuring Charles and Slim Prudhomme on guitar and bass, and his sons John Jr. and Tony on rubboard and drums. His local success was ensured in 1980 with his popular new version of Canray Fontenot and Bois Sec Ardoin's bluesy "Joe Pitre a deux femmes." He also traveled extensively, including a forty-day tour to Africa in the early 1980s. When Geno turned eight, he began playing rubboard, soon advancing to drums. John turned the rubboard over to his young nephew, Jermaine Jack. Each time the band had a personnel change, John introduced crowds to a new member of the family.

John Delafose and his band were still going strong in 1993 when, on the way to a festival in Rhode Island, he suffered a heart attack. Tony steered the van off the road and the family pulled John onto the side of the highway. A doctor was driving three cars behind, and he stopped and performed CPR, restoring his pulse. After bringing their leader to a nearby hospital, the Eunice Playboys climbed back in the van and made the festival. Geno took over accordion duties. Gerard, then eight years old, flew out to play rubboard for the rest of the tour. John couldn't have been more proud. "I've always told them that if I'm sick, that they have a mission to carry the show," he said.

On this night in Eunice, after the band pulled out of the driveway, JoAnn led the way down a hallway papered with get-well cards and letters from around the world. Inside his bedroom, John was watching a Western on TV, and at first he seemed too tired to talk. But when asked some tentative questions about the songs on his record, he quickly became animated and soon brought up other topics.

He spoke about an upcoming local festival and how he'd like to play it, except that the previous year he had been switched to the last position of the day. He'd told them, he said, to stick the festival up their ass. It was a matter of professional pride. "I know when they can switch a smaller band to fit a bigger band," he said.

He talked about the many players he used to let sit on his bandstand. "There was Terrance Simien, Chubby Carrier, even Beau Jocque," he said. "You know, most of the bands played with me, and they'd catch a few of my numbers, and watch me play, and catch some notes. Some people don't like that, but I didn't mind. I can't have all the music for myself."

Then he brought up a story about an accordion player who had lost his following in Houston five years earlier. The musician had gone before his crowd and told them that his wife would never come to the dance, because she doesn't mix with poor people. John stared at the TV in disgust. "He said that poor people are messy! Is that something to tell the people? On stage! So when I went to Houston, the people were telling me this stuff, and I got on the mike and said that it makes me mad. I said, 'I don't think that his wife is any more than mine, and my wife is down here with you people dancing and cutting up and having fun.' Shit. That was stupid. No more Houston for him.

"I try to teach the young ones that you have to have the respect for the people," he explained. "That when you walk into a place, people are happy to see you, and they want to shake hands with you. A lot of them young musicians, after a while their head busts. Then they're out of business. Thinking that because they're up there, that they're more than anybody that's down there. So I tell them, don't be too big to talk to the smallest man in the place.

"I taught that to Geno," he continued. "I'm very, very proud of that boy. And everybody that I talk with says how nice those boys are, how nice they present themself, how they're good with people. You see, the average father and son don't get along in music. The average band doesn't get along. People be fighting amongst themselves, relatives, kinfolks. But they respect me. I always say, if I tell you something, it's because I know of that. If I didn't know, I wouldn't tell you.

"Like I told Geno a long time ago, do some touching music. That's what counts. The music you're playing gets to the people, that's what you want. When you're doing music like that, you have to be thinking deep love-emotion or trouble-emotion to have it be played correctly. You got to have that feeling about it, to bring it out. And when you see people dancing to that, all their emotions in it, the excitement, the feeling, it makes you put more effort into the song. And when you're playing the music, it makes everyone better with their feelings. Because you're doing something with it. Singing about it. Screaming about it. It's not just thinking about it. And then while you're playing, you got people screaming at you, waving at you, winking at you, hollering at you, so it makes it exciting."

Those were the types of lessons that John Delafose taught his sons.

In time, he recovered from his surgery to make a triumphant return to the stage at the Zydeco Festival in Plaisance, an event he helped originate. That night, he was greeted with loud cheers. He clearly did not want to quit playing. When he later appeared at Richard's Club, even Boozoo Chavis could be seen dancing at the side of the stage, stopping only to catch his breath. "I don't usually dance anymore," Chavis said. "But John Delafose plays the real zydeco."

Yet around this same time, the pressures seemed to become too much for both the family band and the family. John Delafose moved to Lake Charles. He moved in with another woman, and started working with other musicians. Geno took over the Eunice Playboys. In September 1994 Delafose was at Richard's Club when he complained of fatigue, and suggested that another accordion player take his place. His heart gave out shortly after he left the bandstand.

Claude Johnwell, a soft-spoken man with short silver hair, removes a ten-dollar bill from his billfold and carefully puts it in his front pocket. Geno introduces him to me with admiration in his voice: he's the man who cares for his twenty-seven cows and five horses. He's a real horseman.

Delafose steers his shiny black '93 Chevy truck — the most visible marker of his recent success — onto a dirt driveway that leads to the Rayne

Quarter Pole Training Center. The equivalent of a bush league in baseball, this "bush track" is a place for horse people who wish to informally meet and bet amongst themselves. Every town used to have a bush track. Rayne is one of the last ones left.

"Mr. Claude," Geno Delafose asks in French, "have you ever seen Boozoo over here?"

"Boozoo's not over here," Johnwell replies. "He's at the big track, him."

Did Geno ever receive any advice about music from Chavis? "Well, Mr. Claude and I went over to his house a while back," he recalls. "They got talking about a horse, then all of a sudden Boozoo was saying, 'You see me, when I was younger, I could take off running.' And then he took off running from his back door to where his butane tank is at, which is about fifteen yards. And he's just running, he had his cowboy hat on, and some slippers, and he said, 'You see, I'm here at the tank. I'm burned out, I'm finished. My ankles can't take the pressure.' I couldn't believe it. But you see, I respect Boozoo a lot. I wish a lot of musicians could be the way my dad and Boozoo were. There was no animosity between them."

He and Johnwell continue their conversation in French. In the backseat next to me, Gerard, now thirteen, is counting his change. He looks up. "I'm going to race a horse for Geno," he announces.

"Which horse?" asks Johnwell, switching to English.

"Lee."

"No, he's too old," says Johnwell with a laugh. "He's just like me."

"He can still run, can't he?"

We park the truck on a hot gravel lot, and Johnwell walks quickly to the paddock, a low-lying collection of wooden horse stalls. "Mr. Claude, he's in his eighties, he saw my dad raised," Delafose says, following behind him. "Then he moved to Lake Charles and he has a suitcase full of pictures from when his horses won races. When I was a kid, we would play over at Thibodeaux's in Lake Charles, it was called Walker's then. He and his wife would always come to the dance, and they would always have that bottle of VO. And then we got together and started talking.

"I leaned on his shoulder a lot, just to know that my dad was so close to him. When my dad moved to Lake Charles, Mr. Claude and I were both hurt a whole lot. Because every morning he'd pick him up and come to my house. I was staying alone like I am now. Seven-thirty, eight in the morning, I would hear somebody blowing the horn, and a lot of times they would just come and pull up under the tree, and sit down and talk and look at the cows. And then when I get out of the house, they'd tease me: 'You waiting on the sun to heat your stomach up for you to get up, man?' Stuff like that.

And it just went on and on, and then he was the next closest thing to my dad that I had."

Gerard leads me to a pale cinderblock building to buy drinks and hamburgers. Outside, people are sitting in folding chairs along the wall, fanning themselves. A new race is about to begin, and hands go up in the air, offering wagers. A man next to me gives me the field against his horse. I take the bet. After a quick thunder of hooves, I hand him his money. Gerard looks at me. "Let's find Geno," he says.

When we reach the paddock, Delafose and Johnwell are sitting on coolers, looking at a brown horse. The owner of the horse is standing on the gate, a sixty-year-old man in Western clothes. He's shouting in French at two young men wearing T-shirts and shorts.

"I'll bet you fifty dollars he's going to win right now!" he calls out. "Look at his legs! Look at his eyes! Fuck them all!"

Delafose laughs and translates for me. Johnwell stands up and pulls his friend down. "Quit before you get your ass whipped," he hisses at him.

"I'm the kingpin!" his friend shouts merrily. "I'm going to come over there and kick your asses!"

The argument isn't picked up, possibly because the two young men don't seem to speak French. They laugh and walk away.

"I won a race a while back," says the owner, opening a beer. "Now everything I touch turns to mashed potatoes."

Johnwell laughs.

"You can get closer to everything at the small tracks," Delafose explains to me. "You'd have to have a license to be back here at Evangeline Downs."

On the way back to the truck, I ask Geno about a gesture I often see used in zydeco to ask a person to dance. It looks like a move a jockey might make to pull on the reins. He nods. "Same thing. If you go to a track, the jockey is always holding on the rein like that. And if you go to the dance, you take your hands like that. It's kind of like being in control." He demonstrates the move. "When you're dancing, you're in control. When you're holding the accordion and pulling on it, same thing. And if you're pulling on the horse, you're sure letting him know that you're in control. You better be, because if you're not, you're in trouble."

For the drive back to Eunice, Gerard keeps to himself in the backseat, rehearsing how he will tell his mother why he had to go to tonight's dance. "I tried to get a ride back, but nobody was able to take me," he repeats to himself, trying to sound believable.

When Geno walks into his mother's house, he launches into a throaty impression of his father's voice. "We're late!" he bellows. "Goddamn, now I'm going to have to drive like a bat out of hell!" Everyone laughs. Outside, the van is loading with members of the Delafose family. "If they're not ready, I get in the van and I'm gone," Geno says, getting in the driver's seat. "When I have a job to do, I have a job to do. That's what he always told me. A man that is always on time is better than the best musician in the world.

"People may think that I'm kind of mean," he continues. "They say, 'You better be ready, because if you ain't, Geno's going to leave you.' But somebody's got to play the daddy role around here. And nobody else does it, so I do it."

A twenty-minute drive from the Delafose's house, the Assumption Catholic Church in the tiny town of Basile is composed of twin buildings separated by a statue of the Virgin Mary. The first room is lined with pews and an altar; the other is for dancing. We go in, and the band sets up in a small corner by the front door, and the rest of the Delafoses set up their places on a bench in front of the speakers. JoAnn places a Winn-Dixie grocery bag on a folding table and lifts out a bag of pretzels, two bags of peanuts, two cartons of orange juice, two apple juices, two liters of Sprite, and a bottle of brandy. She fills Styrofoam bowls with ice and begins cajoling people into eating and drinking. Claude Johnwell and his wife sit across from her. Next to the Delafoses, Morris Ardoin and his family take their positions. The rest of the hall is filled with couples and families from the area, along with a few Delafose fans from Lafayette.

As the band sets up, Gerard stands by the speakers, his arms folded across his red sleeveless T-shirt. Before the music starts, he walks through the room and politely shakes everyone's hand. Then he goes back to his original place. Geno kicks off the night with "Eunice Two-Step" and follows with a waltz he's recently penned, "La valse à Pop":

> *Mourir, c'est mauvais.*
> *Tu m'as quitté pour t'en aller.*
> *Et que c'est mauvais pour perdre mon vieux pop.*

> *Tu m'as montré comment chanter.*
> *Tu m'as montré comment danser.*
> *Et c'est mauvais pour perdre mon vieux pop.*

> To die, it's hard.
> You left me to go away.
> And it's so hard to lose my old pop.

> You taught me to sing.
> You taught me to dance.
> And it's hard to lose my old pop.

Then Geno launches into the two-step "The Back Door" and nods at Gerard, lifting his hands as he plays, exposing how he's using his little finger for the grace notes. Gerard peers around the speakers and watches closely.

A few songs later, Geno covers the Arthur Conley classic "Sweet Soul Music," a recent hit for Keith Frank, and the teenaged dancers that have come here with their parents fill the floor. They shrink back to the walls as Leo "the Bull" Thomas, wearing a spangled vest and striped tie, is introduced. The Bull goes behind the drums and pulls the mike to his mouth. "I want to thank Geno," he says in a smooth voice, hitting the tom-toms. "We're like a little team together, you know." Then, with Geno playing piano accordion, Thomas crashes his sticks down on his cymbals and points them at various women in the room, flashing a gold-toothed smile. After the band plays "Why Do You Want to Make Me Cry?" and a string of other Thomas classics, the drummer leaves the stage to loud cheering.

By the end of the evening, the ice in the Styrofoam bowls has melted to pools of water. Geno has one song remaining: a tribute he wrote to his mother called "JoAnn, JoAnn." When the song starts, she climbs on the bench and waves the plastic Winn-Dixie bag in the air with a shy smile while her daughters shout their approval. Then Geno plays one last waltz, and the Sunday dance is ended.

Geno helps break down the bandstand and returns to Eunice. The rest of the family is already sleeping. He pours two Cokes, then he sits at the kitchen counter. I ask him about Gerard walking to the tables to shake people's hands. He nods in approval. "With my dad, when we would go on the road, we would just sit and talk. He would always tell me to go out and talk with the people, because if there's nobody at your dance, then you have no dance."

He laughs. "You know, I played in Washington, D.C., the other day, and when I took a break, I just went around and talked with everybody. People sit along the walls in the dance halls up around Washington, there aren't tables in the middle like we have here, and you can pretty much get a chance to tell everybody 'hi' as you go around. And they were all like, 'Man, you need to be a politician the way you go around the room.' I just died laughing when they told me that."

At the dance, JoAnn Delafose had described her son as "an old man in

*Geno Delafose's ninth-grade school picture.*

a young man's body." He smiles; he's heard it before. "Yeah, and that's the main thing I want to teach Gerard," he says. "Respect old people, respect everybody. And if you respect yourself, and you got manners, people are going to respect you, and you're going to go a long way. Because I'm not — and I'm not ashamed to say this to anybody — I'm not a supereducated young man. I finished high school and all that, but there are so many new things going on these days that I don't know anything about. I don't watch the news that much, I don't watch television."

He remembers that his first lessons in music were all in endurance. "My daddy was rough when you played drums behind him," he says. "Many nights it'd be, 'Goddamn it, you got to whup them damn drums. Hit them! If they bust, I'm going to buy you some more!' Especially some nights I would be tired and, man, I swear to God, there were some nights I was sleeping on those drums. I am not lying, I was literally sleeping. And he would laugh at me afterwards. I was about fourteen, and I was so sleepy, I would miss the drums and hit my hand on the rims, man. When I'd wake up, sticks would be flying."

By the time Delafose started high school in Mamou, he was dressing differently from most of the other students. "Ever since I was a kid I wanted to be a cowboy," he explains. "Always had big cowboy boots on and cap down over my ears and stuff, just try to have the rough look." He played in a school band with Cajun accordionist Steve Riley, but originally intended to study nursing. Those plans eventually changed. "I was one of the few kids in high school that was making eight hundred dollars a month," he says. "So when I got out, I just stayed playing music."

At that time, he expected that he would be playing in his father's band for many years to come. "Me and my dad, we were like two brothers," he says. "You end up being a team after so long, kind of like Bois Sec and Canray." But he had long known that his father's health was failing. "A lot of times we would go out on the road, and he'd tell us, 'I don't know what I'm doing here. I need to be back home. I'm a sick dad.'" Geno recalls once seeing his father laugh so hard he became sick from the strain. Other nights, the two shared a hotel room, and he witnessed how the only way John could rest comfortably was by kneeling at the foot of the bed.

Yet the most difficult time came after his father moved to Lake Charles and it looked like the family band could split up for good. He never lost respect for his father, and he says that whenever they parted, it was on good terms. But the twenty-one-year-old also knew that the time had come to make a decision about the future. "The music business was just kind of going to nothing, and it was either sink or swim," he says. "The choice that I gave him, I said, 'Daddy, whatever you want to do is fine, but if you move back with Mama, I'll play in your band. And if you don't move back, I'm going to go my own way and get my new band.' I knew how Daddy was and what he was going through, but it was something I had to do."

Joined by his brother Tony and cousin Jermaine Jack, Geno took charge of the Eunice Playboys. John Delafose started a new band for local shows, continuing to play with his family for occasional festivals. But steady touring meant that Geno began to see less of his father. "We kind of went our separate ways, and I was starting to be gone a whole lot," he says. "Then I remember I just came back home from a tour to Washington, and my brother and my sister were in from Lake Charles. It was a Sunday night and all the lights were on, and I pulled up and I was like, 'Man, something ain't right.'" John Delafose was buried the following Saturday, and Geno played "I'm Coming Home" at the funeral. The next Tuesday, he left home for a thirty-day tour.

Today Geno's band, French Rockin' Boogie, includes only drummer Jermaine Jack from the Eunice Playboys days. His brother Tony now tours regularly with his own band. Although Geno says that the music he plays is something his father would recognize, he acknowledges that there are differences. He recalls how John could come up with melodies on the bandstand, and improvise a song even when he hadn't learned it. "One thing about my dad, he was never scared to try a song," he says. "We were so used to him, and we knew how he played, we could just fall in anytime behind him. But I'm not that way, you know, and my music is a little bit more professional. But he could get up there and sing it with a voice that I don't think I'll ever have."

There are also differences in lifestyle. "You know, if I would have bought that truck and he would still have been living, he probably would have passed out," Geno says with a laugh. "He would have been like, 'Who's over here in that truck? Who's over here in that truck?' But the one thing I always tried to do was make my dad proud of me. If my dad was happy and he give me a compliment, and said, 'Well, that's good that you're on time,' or 'You got your van looking good,' that done me all the good in the world. He was my dad, but he was always also my boss, you know.

"Sometimes he told me things that I didn't agree with. Because my dad was from the old school, he would sometimes play a song off time. But he'd say, 'Don't worry about it, just beat them drums like I tell you.' And that was my dad. 'If I tell you something, it's because I know it.' That was it."

When off the road, Geno Delafose continues to play at local church halls and clubs, and each year he throws a free dance in Eunice, attracting fans from around the country. But he admits that he sometimes feels like a stranger in his old haunts. "I walked in Richard's Club awhile back, it was

Step Rideau playing, and I didn't hardly know anybody," he says. "There's so many younger people in there." By "younger," he explains, he means people his own age, with different tastes. The road remains the only place where Delafose can make a good living playing waltzes and singing in French. Someday, he thinks, that may change. "All it boils down to is everybody's got their time, that's just the way it is. It used to be the Ardoin Brothers, and then my dad, and Boozoo, and Zydeco Force, and Beau Jocque, and Keith Frank. And it goes on and on.

"One of the things that a lot of older people tell me when I really play my heart out, 'You need to be the king of zydeco, and we're going to give you a crown.' But that is the last thing I would ever want. And I tell them, 'Whatever y'all do, don't ever offer that to me.' I would not take that. I know when I go to play a dance, you got to be nice and respect the people. I play some dance music and give them what they want. That's really all that I know, and people look up to me for that. And that's what I'm trying to show Gerard."

*Aaron Laws on rubboard and Jimmy "Li'l Pookie" Seraile Jr., on accordion.*

# 18

# THIS IS
# THE SOUND

---

I N LAFAYETTE'S BLACKHAM COLISEUM, the cheers are nearly deafening. For the first time today, the crowd of thousands has stopped dancing on the oversize plywood floor. Two teenaged accordionists are sharing the stage, engaged in a cutting contest of Boozoo Chavis songs. The first, looking preppy in a golf shirt and khakis, offers a riff from "Dog Hill." He's greeted by a roar of approval. Then the second player launches into "Zydeco Hee Haw." His lanky frame is draped by a navy blue work shirt, and a brimmed cap covers his eyes. He lifts his knees and bobs his head, and steps back in a youthful imitation of how Chavis dances on stage.

The crowd doesn't hold back. In a wash of shouts and applause, State Senator Don Cravins crowns the second player with a cash prize of one hundred dollars. At the front of the crowd, Willis Prudhomme is yelling and pointing at the stage. "Don't they look good up there!" he says. "That last one that sounded so good, his name's Shine. That's my accordion. He told me, 'Mr. Willis, I know I can win.' I never heard him play. He said, 'I'm going to give you twenty-five dollars if you let me play your accordion.' I said, 'Take it, go.' And now look at him. He's putting on a show!"

Each Sunday before Memorial Day, a new class of young accordion players enters the contest at the day-long Zydeco Extravaganza. At the end of the day, in addition to the prize money, the winner is awarded an invaluable amount of community esteem. "It's one way for these young folks to express themselves," says Cravins, who started the festival in 1987 with his brother Charles. "A kid comes up and performs exceptionally well, and the crowd dictates who wins. And they build their confidence from that, and now some of them have a band behind them."

The event is one indication of just how popular zydeco has become among young Creoles. The new wave that started during Chavis's comeback and surged for Zydeco Force and Beau Jocque is today a deluge. Every weekend, Keith Frank demonstrates the command a young player can exert over zydeco. In his wake, between fifty and seventy-five active zydeco bands are now working in Louisiana and Texas, many of them headed by accordion players in their teens or early twenties. "We got accordion players falling out the trees," says Jeffery Broussard. "They're going to sit down and learn one song and, next week: 'Look out, man, I got a band.'"

It's a dancer's market. Despite the proliferation of trail rides and festivals, there are still limited places to play. The hub of the current scene remains the "down east" dance clubs of Richard's, Slim's Y-Ki-Ki, and Hamilton's Place, and even younger players are grumbling about the glut of bands. "Back in the late seventies, early eighties, you could make between six and a thousand a gig," says Sean Ardoin. "Then around the mid-eighties, zydeco started becoming popular, and all these young guys started getting interested in it, and they started going and playing places for a hundred fifty, two hundred fifty dollars. That whole bunch of small bands took the price and just slammed it down."

The popularity of single-row accordions — thousands of dollars cheaper than the piano-keys — makes it easier for a young musician to obtain his first instrument. "This guy I know, he wants to play music so bad and have his band," Broussard says, laughing. "He has two accordions, and a while back he called me. He bought himself a truck. I said, 'You got your band together?' 'No, not yet.' Two weeks later, he called me again. 'Man, I bought me a trailer.' I said, 'Now you have your truck and your trailer, but you still don't have anybody to play with.' But he's ready to roll."

Success in this new scene involves factors beyond musical ability. "The zydeco community is like a close-knit family," explains Floyd Soileau. "The fans got to love you personally, and they got to love what you're doing. They got to enjoy dancing to your music, and feel like you're one of the family. Word of mouth can be for you or against you, and if it's against you, you can forget it. You can hang up your accordion and take another profession."

Most young players started out in musical families, where both instruction and equipment are readily available. Li'l Malcolm Walker recalls that when he was eight, he first tested a triple-row accordion that belonged to his grandfather, Melvin Walker. He then began to follow his father, musician Percy Walker. "He used to play at old clubs and trail rides in Mamou," he remembers. "The whole family used to go out when I was young. Mom would always tell me and my sisters to go dance, saying, 'That's how you learn.' I was the only one that built up enough guts to get on the floor."

Like most young players, Walker started on rubboard. With his father, he toured weeknights to New Orleans to play at the Maple Leaf, and he still remembers having to wake up for school the next morning. "Man, I used to be one to fall asleep on the bandstand, rubbing the rubboard. I was young, in the club at twelve, one at night. So I would get into the music, start moving and dancing, that's how I kept awake."

Today Walker leads his own band, which includes his father on guitar. He knows he is in a field crowded by other young accordionists, the most talented among them including Li'l Pookie and JaVon Chambers of Creole Junction. "I like Chris Ardoin, Corey Arceneaux — I like all of them. Us younger people, we boost ourselves up. If Chris plays, I compliment him, tell him it's jamming, and I dance on his. It ain't no use for one of us to sit down and try to be big-timing and better than the other."

But not everyone agrees that the current extravaganza of voices is sounding so harmonious.


Senator Don Cravins — state senator, restaurateur, insurance salesman, and zydeco promoter — is finishing a conversation on the phone. "I don't want his ribs showing," he is saying. "I have a saddle ready, and I want my horse to be ready. The saddle is not going to look better than the horse. Good-bye."

He hangs up the phone and laces his fingers behind his head. "I've been having a horse, but I'm just getting him broken to ride at a trail ride in Lebeau," he explains. "You know, you certainly want a nice animal to ride. You don't want to be out on a scrub. It's a thing of pride."

Don Cravins could be called zydeco's first politician. He is head of the congressional black caucus, one of the most powerful entities in state politics. But in Southwest Louisiana, he is still better known as the originator — with his brother, Charles — of a popular zydeco radio show, television program, and festival, all called Zydeco Extravaganza.

His two careers are inextricably linked, he says. "The radio show played a very important part in my decision to run for public office. The district I ran in was the listening area for the radio program, from New Iberia through St. Landry Parish. I would go into different areas, and people would say, 'That's the zydeco man.' It is one of the reasons why I've been very successful politically.

"When I was elected back in 1991, it was the first time that someone of color had represented this area since Reconstruction," he explains. "I guess I went in with a sense of difference, in the fact that *je parle français* and that's part of my lineage. And I've brought zydeco to Baton Rouge, because we bring a band or two to Baton Rouge every year to play for the rest of the state — I call them *les Américains*. We even had Keith Frank play for the president on his last visit."

His zydeco career began in 1988, when Charles Cravins was managing an FM radio station in Maurice. "We started a program which became very, very popular, because we would really talk about everything and everybody," he recalls. "We would talk about the music, of course. But if we knew something about our friends, we would tell about it on the air, and we would kind of poke a little fun at them. There was this friend of mine, I believe I might have caused him a little problem at home, because somebody told me he had bought two microwave ovens for Christmas. And we were trying to figure out how the hell he could have bought two. It turned out he had bought one for his wife, and one for his girlfriend. That's why people liked to listen to us."

The Cravins brothers started taking the program on the road, doing remotes from trail rides and nursing homes. They launched the first zydeco television program, taping segments in local clubs, and then the Zydeco Extravaganza festival.

But Cravins has one more goal he'd like to attain: he hopes to use his political skills to smooth the differences between zydeco players. "This sense of competition between bands is unfortunate," he says. "It's not been healthy competition at all. I think it has done a lot to diminish the value of those people. I really believe that. I've seen even in our own festival where I had to step in and actually put my foot down, because one band would not play behind the other. That kind of foolishness. And then their public gets involved, and starts choosing sides.

"I went to a trail ride yesterday in Carencro, they had at least two or three thousand people," he continues. "There are enough people to go around to keep a lot of bands playing. But there's a mindset that if one band's good, that's the only band I want to listen to. And that's the one thing I find most hard to understand in zydeco music. For example, Keith Frank has risen as the leader in the music in the course of six months to a year. Next year it could be Li'l Pookie or Chris Ardoin or T-Broussard. But there seems never to be enough room for two or three bands to do well at the same time locally."

The senator folds his hands. "How do we change that?" he considers, for now unable to come up with the answer.

\* \* \*

From his post at the door of Richard's Club, owner Kermon Richard has also been trying to make sense of the new scene. "Things have changed so much since the early eighties," he says. "Back then, you could pretty much get any one of these zydeco musicians like Hiram Sampy, Fernest Arceneaux, Rockin' Dopsie, and have a respectable crowd. Now, the older people want to come to the dance, but it's the younger people that's taken over. It's just a mess, really. The older ones complain because the youngsters are there, and if the youngsters aren't there, it's not a crowd, and the old folks won't come! It's a very aggravating business, really."

Playing a Saturday night at Kermon Richard's Lawtell club is usually the first step for a young band making a name for itself. Today called zydeco's answer to the Grand Ole Opry, Richard's Club was built by Kermon's father, Eddie Richard, in 1947. At first, the club booked touring R&B and blues acts, as well as an occasional boxing match. Eddie Richard initially hired Clifton Chenier because his price — forty dollars a night — was lower than acts like Jimmy Reed and Smiley Lewis. Soon Chenier's dances became so popular that Richard's was booking only zydeco, sending drivers into neighboring towns to shuttle dancers. "School buses would leave from Church Point full of people for the dance," Kermon Richard recalls. "Nobody wanted to be the first one picked up. All the little old gals would have the new dresses, and they wanted to come in the club after the crowd had gotten kind of big. They would raise hell if there was nobody in the club, and they couldn't make their grand appearance."

Lately, Richard says he has been investigating the reasons for the popularity of artists like Keith Frank. "I've asked a couple of them why they only follow a certain musician, and they say, 'Well, we've learned how to dance a certain way behind him, and then we can't dance to nobody else.' When they try to dance to somebody else's music, they get all confused.

"And I'll tell you another thing, too, that's very interesting," he continues. "If I was to get on that bandstand with a damn old foot tub and a stick, and if I packed the club, they wouldn't ask no question, they'd pay their money at the door and come in and look at me beat on that washtub all night long. Because the damn place is full up of people. No matter how good you are, they're going to peek in the door, and if the people ain't there, they're going to ride around until they see a crowd come in. If they don't see the crowd, they're not coming in. That's right. They want to be jam-packed. And then they complain that it's too full.

"But what I was telling somebody the other day, it's not that the crowd is getting younger," Richard concludes. "Hell, we're getting older, that's what it is."


For new bands who can't yet draw a Saturday night crowd, there is another option: Roy's Offshore Lounge, located in Lawtell across the track from Richard's Club and down a road of small farms and chicken coops.

Once the grandest dance club in town, the building had fallen into disrepair when accordionist Roy Carrier bought it in 1980. Today Carrier cheerfully admits that it's the ricketiest zydeco club in operation, and that he frequently has to crawl under the floor to prop up the dance floor with bricks. "In zydeco, they tell me if the floor don't rock, it ain't no dance floor," he says. "Shit, you get five hundred people in here, if you rock it too much, you're going to break something."

Carrier's introduction to music began when his father, Warren, bought an accordion from Cajun musician Nathan Abshire after a meeting at the Yambilee building in Opelousas. "They would bring the potatoes there and see who had the best potato," he says. "And my dad was one of the top men. Nathan Abshire, he was next to him, and they started talking.

"Man, after he got that accordion, every night I had to be the one to beat the scrubboard. Every night, every night. I'd go to bed at seven o'clock with the chickens, and he'd wake me up, and we'd play until two o'clock in the morning. And then I'd go to bed and get up when the sun got up. We were ten in the family, and I was the one who was beating the scrubboard. If I wobbled a little in the daytime, he would understand that, because I was tired. The next night, he was ready again, and I had to get up and scrub the board. He was playing 'Baby, Please Don't Go,' and my favorite song he'd play was 'Black Gal.' He had about ten songs, and he'd play them every night.

"I was getting bored, but I was listening to what he was doing. I liked the accordion. And I started stealing his accordion, and started playing it. I'd take it and go up to the barnyard. I guess I'd done better if I'd stayed in the house and play it. Because, man, in them days back, if a train was blowing in Lawtell, you could hear it in Church Point. I'm talking about ten miles. So when I'd go play accordion in that barnyard, you could hear it a long ways. He caught me, he whipped me one time. After that he saw I wanted to learn, so he let me play it."

When Carrier started his own band, he brought his sons Chubby and Troy into the fold, as well as his nephew Dwight. Then in 1987 he began to

*Roy and Troy Carrier.*

host the Thursday soirée that continues to this day. "I gave up the oil field in 'eighty-seven and started doing jam sessions every Thursday night," he says. "When I got started doing this, I could have counted the musicians I had playing. Now, I can't count the people that came and learned in this place and left, and did a lot of things.

"Beau Jocque, Jo Jo Reed, Dwight Carrier, John T., Corey Arceneaux, Zydeco Force, they would all come with their group, and each one played for a half an hour. If we have a lot of bands, we get them set for next Thursday. We charge two dollars, and we just get together and jam. It's a big, quiet place back here, and you can do what you want.

"And that's how it started. Wherever I go, I announce where I'll be. People know about the jam session now. When they have festivals in Lafayette or Plaisance, people come from New York, Washington, Chicago, Canada, and the big night over here is Thursday night."

For young accordion players, the first stop is often radio. On weekends between New Orleans and Houston, a turn around the radio dials will usually produce several programs featuring the latest zydeco hits. But only one station broadcasts a steady diet: the low-wattage KNEK, in Washington, best known as the current home of zydeco radio pioneer Luke Collins.

"I started working in the fields when I was sixteen years old," remembers Collins, speaking between songs one afternoon at the station. "I was forty when I first got into radio. At first, I wanted to be a rock-and-roll deejay. I wrote letters to the big stations in New Orleans and Houston, and sent them audition tapes. They said my accent was holding me back, but they sent me back nice letters. Now the other day a woman from Wisconsin called, and she said, 'You have a beautiful accent.' I said, 'Thank you.'"

Collins pauses his story. He pushes in a promotional tape, and a deep voice issues from the speakers: *"Foot-stomping zydeco music with Luke, Luke, Luke — the Godfather of Zydeco."* He cues a Keith Frank song and returns to his story.

"So what I did, I took a correspondence course," he remembers. "It was from Boston, and for six months they sent me lessons about what a deejay is supposed to talk about. I'd seen the class advertised in a rock-and-roll magazine. It had pictures of Little Richard and Fats Domino, and it said, 'How would you like to be a deejay? Meet people, have fun, and have famous stars calling you by your own name.' Man, that got to my head. The course was twenty-seven dollars. Some people would say that's just wasting money, but it really did help me out.

*Luke Collins, the "Godfather of Radio Zydeco."*

*Richard's Club, Lawtell, Louisiana.*

"Then one day around 1980 I went to Floyd Soileau's record shop, and I bought an album by Clifton Chenier. It had 'Oh, My Lucille' and 'Shake It, Don't Break It.' I was listening to that album, and I was thinking, 'That's some good songs, and I'm the only one hearing it.' And that got me going."

The next week, Collins was hunting doves with Carl Dowan, then the manager of KEUN in Eunice. Collins told Dowan about the new batch of zydeco records available by John Delafose, Rockin' Dopsie, and Bois Sec Ardoin. "So I started going into the station to practice, and he kept straightening me out with my English," he recalls. "Then he said, 'I'll give you an hour show, but you're going to have to talk French.' And that's the way it went."

Soon Collins began to receive on-air visits from players such as John Delafose and Rockin' Sidney. He also learned the unique type of anonymity that comes with being a deejay. "Now, this is going to make you laugh," he recalls. "One time, John Delafose came on my show and advertised that he was going to be at Richard's Club. And I told him I was going to be there. The next day, I went to a café over in Eunice, and the owners there were talking about that. The woman turned to her husband and said, 'Now you know that white man's lying, he ain't going to go around them black people.' They didn't think a deejay could be black."

Collins stops to play another promotion. The booming voice returns: *"Throw a little salt on the beans and let's zydeco, cher — with Luke, Luke, Luke, the Godfather of Zydeco."* He finds a Boozoo Chavis song and marks it on his playlist. "Now you know why they call me the Godfather of Zydeco?" he asks. "I'm the original. One time, Todd Ortego was giving away free Zydeco Festival tickets to callers who could name the Godfather of Zydeco. That made me feel good. I was the first out there. If not for that, I'd just be a face in the crowd."

Thanks to deejays such as Collins, the Cravins brothers, Lester and Paul Thibeaux, and J. J. Caillier, radio is now an essential component of the zydeco scene. In Houston, zydeco has even carved out air time on major FM rap and contemporary R&B stations. In Southwest Louisiana, current weekly shows include Melvin Caesar and John Broussard's *Zydeco Est Pas Salé,* a six-hour broadcast that precedes afternoon opera on public radio affiliate KRVS. On country station KBAZ in Eunice, Sunday afternoons bring the *Front Porch Zydeco* show, hosted by Todd Ortego and Joe Burge. (Ortego's connections to zydeco include his own record shop/snow-cone café, as well as teaming up with music veteran Mike Lachney to produce the John Delafose hit "Ka-wann" and other recordings.)

But as Luke Collins goes into his third decade of broadcasting, he remains the steadiest voice in zydeco radio. Being at the microphone has given him the opportunity to witness the changes in the music. "Today, they just want to give the credit to one or two players. Look at Roy Carrier. You couldn't ask for a better accordion player. And Geno — that son of a gun can play. But they're not at the top of the hill, so they don't draw a crowd.

"I like them all," he explains. "When I was a young kid, I remember people making zydeco in the front yard. They'd say, 'We sold some cotton today, let's make a little la-la.' And it was just *chaque à leur* — some fooling around on the accordion. They weren't concerned about who's the man pulling the accordion, if it's James or John or Joe. They knew that whoever had that accordion was going to make them dance. But they don't look at it that way no more. That's what we call *longtemps passé.*"

Today only a handful of players continue to play the piano-key accordion of Clifton Chenier. Many in this cadre are older players who came to zydeco after establishing themselves in blues and R&B, including Joe Walker and Jude Taylor. In Houston, Li'l Willie Davis received his first accordion after he retired, and he credits Chenier with getting him started on the right path. "That New Year's Eve, Clifton was playing at St. Francis, and we talked," he recalls. "I said, 'Cliff, man, I done got an accordion. But I don't know nothing about accordion.' And Cliff showed me middle C."

One of the best in this field is Lynn August, who was forty when he bought his first piano accordion. By then, his already eventful career in music included drumming for Stanley Dural Jr. (before he became Buck-wheat Zydeco) as well as for the flamboyant entertainer Esquerita, an early influence on Little Richard. A versatile player, August now leads his own band in an eclectic range of material, from R&B obscurities to new versions of the *juré* songs first recorded by Alan Lomax.

But there are only a handful of young players on the piano-key, including Malcolm Walker, Geno Delafose, Brian Terry, J. J. Caillier Jr., and Corey Arceneaux. "Really and truly, Clifton brought the black Creole Frenchmen zydeco music back with a piano-note," says Terry. "But it seemed that when Clifton Chenier died, the piano notes were wiped out for a while."

Among the youngest on the instrument is Corey Arceneaux. "When Clifton Chenier died, I was an altar boy at Immaculate Heart, and I served at his funeral," he recalls. "That was the year I started playing." Among his first teachers were Clayton Sampy and his uncle Fernest Arceneaux, and he first took the stage when Nathan Williams let him sit in at El Sid O's. Plus, he adds, his neighbor Buckwheat Zydeco occasionally helps him with accordion repairs.

But it was two bands that emerged from Houston — one in the 1970s and the other in the 1990s — that really answered Clifton Chenier's call to put new hinges on the old French music and update it for a new generation. First came the Sam Brothers Five, a family band that initially reminded many of the Jackson Five with an accordion. Their repertoire ranged from blues to disco, including a reworking of Chic's "Le Freak" that became their signature "S.A.M." In the center of this swirl of seventies influences stood preteen accordionist Leon Sam, wearing a headband around processed hair, sounding so much like Chenier that dancers would peer around the stage for a tape player.

"I would go in front of the bandstand and just watch Clifton," Leon recalls of his role model. "I would go to sleep listening to his music, so I could play it exactly like that."

The band started when Herbert Sam was playing around Houston with his oldest son Ronnie, billed as Good Rockin' Sam and Son. "My daddy did shows," recounts Glenn Sam proudly. "He'd sit on the table, make the accordion come all the way out, and then make it come back in like a snake. That showmanship is what rubbed in our blood." Herbert worked as a roofer during the day, and his sons would set up his instruments and play in the garage. "The whole neighborhood would go and watch," recalls Herbert Sam. "And I'm not knowing nothing, and my wife wouldn't tell me."

Sporting flared pants and Afros, the Sam Brothers toured to California, where they recorded for Arhoolie Records. "We played a Catholic church in Los Angeles, and the people were there like hair on your head," remembers Herbert. "When we got through that night, they went up with us all the way to the highway. Then we went to San Francisco, and we did some shows at a TV studio with Queen Ida. The next morning it came out in the paper that Clifton Chenier had shrunk."

With young Leon on accordion, the band took Houston by storm, playing bars, pizza restaurants, talent shows, and church dances. They opened shows for Gatemouth Brown and the Houston soul group Archie Bell and the Drells, and even brought the accordion into the hippest venue in town: the roller skating rink. "I was about nine when we played the biggest rink in Texas," remembers Calvin Sam. "We played in the center, and they skated around us. Then they'd cut the lights out, except for the little lights everyone had on their skates. It was a beautiful thing."

"We were kicking in the seventies," adds Glenn Sam proudly. "We'd change uniforms three times a night. We had a tailor lady out of Cecilia, she made some hell of a uniform for us. Orange, black pin-stripe, loud colors. White turtlenecks with little green waistcoats. And we wouldn't wear our bell bottoms unless they covered our shoes. And we had great big hair and little faces. I had the biggest Afro in the family, and nobody could even come around me and talk about a haircut, or I'd cry."

Clifton Chenier stayed in touch with his musical protégés, repeatedly telling Herbert Sam not to work the boys too hard. Today, the family members are scattered through Louisiana and Texas; no longer the Sam Brothers Five, they are now billed as Leon Sam and the Sam Brothers. "Just before he died, I played to his club," Leon remembers. "And he told me, 'Don't stop playing my music.' He said, 'You got it. It's there, but just take your time with it. It'll all come right there to you.' Because if you know what to do with a piano-note accordion, you can get anything you want out of it."

In the 1990s, nobody tested this theory more than a Crosby, Texas-based accordionist named Li'l Brian Terry. Although players such as Beau Jocque and Keith Frank have selectively absorbed some hip-hop influences, rap and zydeco still draw two different followings in Louisiana and Texas. For a zydeco musician, crossing the line is considered a risk. Then in 1995 Terry released his first Rounder album, *Fresh*, as an attempt to forge a musical link between the two sounds.

"I was raised with zydeco, it was practically a meal at my table," Terry explains. "But you know, I'm a young man, and I started liking Snoop Dogg rap, and Tupac. So I started to feel if they can do it, man, why can't I do it — but just do it with zydeco music, something I was brought up with?"

Although Terry grew up in the city, he received his first zydeco lessons when he turned ten and spent a summer in Eunice visiting his cousin Geno Delafose. "There was a lot of the stuff I didn't know about," he says, laughing. "One time, Jermaine and Geno got together and decided they were going to treat me, a city boy, to a lesson. I was kind of scared of those horses, so they decided they were going to make me ride. They were stronger than me, because they'd been picking up on that horse feed every day. So they wrestled me down, and they'd already had the horse saddled up, and John was out there, just laughing. And they threw me on that horse, man, and kind of gave him a little slap, and he took off.

"I can remember another time when Geno was teaching me a song on the accordion, 'Good for the Goose.' And I just couldn't get it. And, man, he put his accordion down and he gave me an old-fashioned whipping. He got down, boy, he was beating me up real bad. And I was in there hollering, 'Miss JoAnn, Miss JoAnn!' And she used to come in there and make him leave me alone, man. But right now, I can honestly say, I appreciate those whippings. Because they're sure paying off now, man."

Just a year later, Terry got onstage for the first time, with Leo Thomas's band. "I only knew one song, and it was 'Turn On Your Lovelight.' And the people started screaming and hollering, and that was the greatest feeling. I can remember going back to school Monday and telling all my little friends. But at that time there was nobody into zydeco like they are now, and they didn't understand what I was talking about."

By the time Terry was fifteen, he was holding down a weekly gig at Houston's famed zydeco dance hall, the Continental Ballroom. Then, during a lunchtime show in his high school cafeteria, he looked out at his crowd and decided to try a new style. He went to a Houston tattoo parlor and had a picture of Buckwheat Zydeco's accordion inked into his right arm. He secured jobs opening for Boyz II Men and Luther Vandross. And on his second Rounder album, *Z-Funk*, he delivered his mission statement to the easy cadence of West Coast–style rap:

> Believe it, you know that I'm here,
> Grew up on that blues and that Clifton Chenier. . . .
> It appears that a lot of the zydeco bands have lost the juice
> But Li'l Brian and the Travellers, you know we're getting loose

Managed by Buckwheat Zydeco's bass player Lee Allen Zeno, Terry considers his eclecticism to be in the best tradition of zydeco. "Cliff did country into zydeco, and blues into zydeco," he states. "Just because I got an accordion and a scrubboard doesn't mean I can't play hip-hop and rap. You know, music changes every six months, and you got to change with the times. How can you draw a line and say, 'This is going overboard with it?' It's music. How can you go overboard with music?"

If there are only a few young piano-key players, there are even fewer women currently taking the zydeco stage. First to follow Queen Ida's path was the talented Ann Goodly, who started out in the mid-eighties at Papa Paul's, a Mamou zydeco club owned by her grandfather. The newest arrivals on the scene include the Houston-based Diane Lady "D" Weatherall, who gained fame by winning the Zydeco Extravaganza accordion contest. And one of the biggest hits on Louisiana zydeco radio shows in 1998 was "Old Man's Sweetheart," a tribute to Boozoo Chavis by new bandleader Donna Angelle.

But next to Queen Ida, the largest impact on the zydeco scene has been made by Rosie Ledet, a soft-spoken woman who began performing in her mid-twenties, circled by a family band that includes her husband, Morris, on bass, her father-in-law, Lanice, on rubboard, and her nephew Corey Ledet

*Rosie Ledet.*

*Sam Brothers Five at Jazz Fest, 1978.*

on drums. In the center of this clan, Ledet often startles her crowd with songs like "The Mardi Gras," in which she turns the annual holiday into a girl's coming-of-age story:

> Mardi Gras coming down the road,
> Painted faces and colored clothes,
> 'Mama, run' — 'No, child, no' —
> Do the Mardi Gras, baby, watch 'em roll.

By the end of the song she's conquered her fear, singing:

> Mardi Gras man dance with me,
> I ain't scared like I used to be.

Other lyrics include "My Joy Box," a double entendre about her accordion. Her most popular song is "I'm Gonna Take Care of Your Dog." Since Boozoo Chavis first offered canine howls in his comeback recording "Dog Hill," both dogs and dog noises have been a recurring image in modern zydeco lyrics. In 1995 Ledet offered a dog song to end all dog songs:

> You better keep your dog
> On a real short leash.
> He comes back to my yard,
> He's going to belong to me.
> Bow wow.

Explains Ledet: "Every one of their songs is either about a dog or a no-good woman. They're fun to listen to, but I really don't get the meaning of it. I hear about the no-good women, but I meet the wives, and they don't seem no-good. That's not right. Give the girl a chance."

Her musical personality came as a shock to her parents, Ledet recalls. "When I was coming up, I was always holding on to my mother's leg. I didn't want to talk to some of my own family. So my mom was really surprised to see me get onstage." She was sixteen when she went to her first zydeco dance. "My uncle dragged me over there. I sat down, and everybody was dancing around, and I was surprised that there were some young people there. Boozoo was jamming, playing 'Zydeco Lady,' which was 'Disco Lady' done zydeco-style. I really liked that." Then she gestures to her husband. "And then this thing right here, he sat in for a while, and I thought, 'That's all right.'"

Morris Ledet picks up the story. "At the time I was learning to play, and nobody wanted to give me a break," he remembers. "Then I asked Boozoo, and he said, 'Can you play any songs?' and I said, 'I can play about four or five songs.' And he said, 'Can you play them well?' And I said, 'Good enough.' So I was sitting at the table and he hollered at me and said, 'I have a young man out there and nobody wants to give him a break, and I'm going to give him a break right here and right now.' So I went up and started playing Amédé Ardoin's 'Eunice Two-Step' and Boozoo's 'Dog Hill,' and it went on from there." The next week, the couple went to hear Chavis play at Richard's Club; they were married within the year.

What next happened in the Ledet house is another variation on a familiar story: When Morris went to work, he asked his new wife not to open his accordion case. After he left, she would unsnap the case, take the accordion out, and practice; at the end of the day, she'd return it to the case. One day, she opened the case and played her song for Morris. Soon she was sitting in with his band. She finally took on accordion duties full-time, and Morris switched to bass.

Rosie Ledet and the Zydeco Playboys started on the Louisiana and Texas circuit; with help from Morris's second cousin Terrance Simien, they have started to tour more frequently. On a trip to California, Ledet had the opportunity to meet her idol, Queen Ida. She also has an eye on the next generation: her young daughter, Kasaundra, is currently in elementary school, and Rosie occasionally goes over to her classroom and plays for the students. She hopes that more women will continue to pick up the accordion — including her daughter. "I can't really tell which way Kasaundra's going to go now," she says. "But I hope she plays."

Vidrine's grocery store and recording studio sits off a state highway between Plaisance and Frilot Cove. In the 1970s and 1980s, the dusty room behind the shelves of canned goods and cellophane-wrapped pies was called the Hideaway Club; now it's the control center of Ron Vidrine's record company. Bluesman Roscoe Chenier — cousin to Clifton—recorded here, and Corey Arceneaux made his 1995 CD here. Tonight, Jimmy "Li'l Pookie" Seraile Jr. has come to Vidrine's to mix his second tape.

The studio is heated by a foot-high flame shooting up from a cast iron stove. In the summer, songs are recorded one at a time and the air conditioner is switched on between takes to cool off the studio. Seated behind a mixing board, engineer Sammy Coon takes a sip from a Grape Crush. From the speakers issues Li'l Pookie's isolated voice, repeating the same lines.

> Where the people go
> They come to see me!

The engineer adjusts some knobs on the board and adds the double-bass drum beat to the voice. Li'l Pookie stands in the doorway and frowns. "There's something about that kick I don't like," he says.

It's not Vidrine's policy to bring artists in for mixing. "But Pookie insisted," Vidrine explains. "And Pookie's got a better idea of what the people he's playing for want to hear." Plus, Vidrine admits that he quit guessing just what makes a hit song in zydeco. "The one I usually like the best —" He makes a thumbs-down sign. "The album that I think is going to do great —" He repeats it.

Li'l Pookie's mother is one of Delton Broussard's eleven children. His uncle Jeffery Broussard named Pookie's band the Zydeco Heartbreakers, after a band in the movie *Howard the Duck*. Recalls Jeffery Broussard about Pookie's early training: "Sometimes we used to sit up in the yard, it would be me, Pookie, John Broussard, my dad, and my older brother Clinton, and we'd all sit down with accordions and just come up with some stuff." Three days after his grandfather's death, Li'l Pookie joined his uncles to play a tribute to his grandfather at the 1994 Jazz Fest in New Orleans, and they formed an accordion trio to play "I'm Coming Home" and "Will the Circle Be Unbroken" at his funeral.

It's not surprising that Li'l Pookie, given his family tradition, should be the most successful alumnus of the Zydeco Extravaganza accordion contest, which he won when he was sixteen. Since then, he's toured with swamp-rocker C. C. Adcock, and he's frequently cited as an up-and-coming player by zydeco club owners.

And at Vidrine's, hours pass until the first song is finally mixed. "It's got enough bass now?" Coon asks.

"That's how I want it."

"That's a lot of bass."

"I know," Li'l Pookie says.

A few minutes later the two men go to the parking lot, where Li'l Pookie wants to give the tape the final test: play it in his bass-enhanced car stereo. When he hears the heavy beats, Li'l Pookie nods. "This is the sound." Ron Vidrine turns off the flame and locks the store. Li'l Pookie gets in his car, slips in the tape, and drives home to Opelousas.

# 19

# CONQUERED AND
# CONVERTED

*"Now didn't they dance where you come from?"*

— *Remy McSwain to Anne Osborne,* The Big Easy

THE MALLET PLAYBOYS ARE MEETING IN THEIR TOUR VAN, currently resting on its 180,000th mile in the musicians' parking lot at the New Orleans Jazz and Heritage Festival. Sitting in the front seat is Terrance Simien, wearing a purple and orange tie-dyed T-shirt and Converse shorts. He pulls a note from a red triple-row accordion. "Will I ever le-e-earn?" he sings. "Le-e-earn?" his band harmonizes.

As they rehearse, crowd noises and music drift from the other side of the dirt horse track that circles the Jazz Fest: rock drums and guitar chords collide with the shouts of a gospel choir. Simien looks at his watch, then squeezes his accordion once more, his voice cascading in a Sam Cooke–style melisma. Then he passes out a small stack of set lists. "At the end of 'Zydeco sont pas salé,' hold that D a little longer until you see that I've got my accordion," he instructs. "Keep your eye on Danny for the stage dive." He looks up and grins. "We've got Phish kids out there?"

"Last night the hippies were packed on Bourbon Street!" says rubboard player Ralph Fontenot with a laugh.

"Phi-i-ish kids!" Simien leans back and drums out a tattoo on the

*Terrance Simien, Paul Simon, and C. J. Chenier.*

*Terrance Simien at Jazz Fest.*

dashboard. Then he turns serious. "We only have fifty minutes," he reminds his band. "The whole energy level has to be faster. 'Uncle Bud' has to be faster. 'Zydeco sont pas salé' has to be —"

"Snappy," his drummer finishes.

One hour later Simien is standing on the side of one of the festival's main stages. Since its humble beginnings in a local park in 1970, the New Orleans Jazz and Heritage Festival has grown into the world's primary showcase for Louisiana music. With annual ticket sales for the two-weekend event numbering a half million, the organizers are in a unique position to expose Louisiana bands to fans of top national acts. Next weekend, C. J. Chenier will precede the Dave Matthews Band. Today Simien is looking over a sea of thirty thousand young faces; most of the attendees have been camped under the hot sun since morning, waiting to see Phish, a young New England band with a loyal Grateful Dead–style following. He is hopeful. "The alternative crowd is getting into all kinds of music, and zydeco connects with so many things," he says. "You put an accordion and a rubboard combination in reggae, in rock and roll, and you got some new shit."

At exactly 1:40 in the afternoon, Simien kicks off his Birkenstocks and hoists his accordion around his shoulders. "All right, here we go," he says to his wife and young daughter, and walks to the center of the stage. He plays a line on the accordion, then bends down and shakes his head, and his ponytail dissolves into a spray of loose hair. The band launches into a few lines of "Zydeco Boogaloo" and quickly segues into the Jackson Five's "I Want You Back." Simien offers a short moonwalk, then he lifts up his long curls and cups his hand around his ears. "Are you ready to zydeco?" he sings out. A few sun-dazed fans of Phish stand up, and some Simien fans on the side cheer. But the accordionist finds no unified response from the crowd.

Undaunted, he sings the time-honored French lines about the snap beans, and creeps along the lip of the stage, going into a fast spin and slowly stretching his accordion to full length. Then he drops the accordion, leaving the extended bellows dangling raunchily at his side. He arches his back. "Oh Jazz Fest," he calls out, "I want to know if it would be all right if I told you a Creole story about a man named Uncle Bud?"

The crowd is beginning to respond, but the set is already more than half over. Just a few songs later, Simien is into the finale, climbing off the stage and onto metal fencing, now singing into a tiny mike built onto his accordion. He falls from the fence onto a bed of outstretched hands, which pass the accordionist to the center of the crowd and then back to the stage, where he sings "Iko-Iko." He shouts, "Give it up for the late great brother Jerry Garcia," eliciting the heartiest cheer of the day. Then, as the crowd

328 • KINGDOM OF ZYDECO

finally warms up, the short set is over. On his way offstage, he passes Trey Anastasio, lead singer for Phish, who has been sitting on some stage equipment and nodding his head at the show.

For all of Simien's hard work, he's elicited stronger reactions at previous Jazz Fests, when the crowd was mainly there to see him. Back in the van, he is mostly occupied with his daughter, but he addresses the show on the way back to Lafayette. "You saw we had a long way to go," he says cheerfully.


Today, zydeco is on a never-ending tour.

After "Toot-Toot," *Graceland,* and the movie *The Big Easy,* the national appetite was piqued, and zydeco bands began to travel more frequently. Among the first out of the gate was Simien. As Buckwheat Zydeco was testing the boundaries of zydeco on his piano accordion, Simien did the same on the single- and triple-rows. "I'm trying to follow the path of Clifton Chenier and Queen Ida and Buckwheat Zydeco," he explains. "They took the music and went in their own direction with it. Clifton incorporated the blues, Buckwheat incorporated soul and R&B, and Queen Ida put Tex-Mex into the music. And each one of them made their own sound."

The early innovators in zydeco developed their styles when they were away from the Louisiana zydeco circuit. Chenier started out in Texas, Queen Ida in California, and Buckwheat Zydeco in the R&B clubs. But Simien began in the proving grounds of clubs and church halls surrounding his hometown of Mallet, located between Opelousas and Eunice. His introduction to music came when he was a child, following his parents to dances at St. Ann's Catholic Church in Mallet, where he watched the older people dancing to the Lawtell Playboys and Nolton Simien. He also remembers family gatherings — his father, Matthew, was one of sixteen children — and his uncle Lyman Leduke's collection of Chenier records. "They'd listen to that, and he'd clown around and grab his wife and dance," he says. "They'd go to laughing, and that's how we passed the time."

At fifteen, Simien received his first accordion from his father. "Every Saturday I listened to Luke Collins's zydeco show on KEUN in Eunice. I'd tape it and I'd take my little Hohner accordion in my room. I did some Amédé and Bois Sec Ardoin, and Clifton Chenier. And I did a lot of John Delafose songs, because he was the man that would draw the crowd." Simien also credits Delafose with helping him take the next step to the bandstand. "John Delafose was a big inspiration to me. When I was growing up, he used to let me sit in with him onstage, and let me get exposed to his crowd. I'd play about two or three numbers, and he'd walk around and tell people,

'Hey, check this kid out, he's a young musician, coming up.' He just did that all on his own."

Yet not everyone who heard Simien was so encouraging. His first gig — a Christmas party at a National Guard post in Oakdale — was a success. A church dance in Mallet was another story. "Here I am at sixteen," he recounts. "And they're complaining about it being too loud and too fast, and that it's not sounding right. It was mostly older people, and some of them were trying to be nice about it. But some were just coming up right in front of me and holding their hands over their ears."

Later, Simien's accelerated accordion on songs like "Zydeco sont pas salé" would become widely imitated, launching a sort of breakneck "party zydeco" style. In 1994 a *Rolling Stone* profile would say that he "delivers soul worthy of the Stax greats and makes aural confetti of straight zydeco." But he admits that many of his innovations really started because he was young and making mistakes. "Speeding it up, playing it rough, it's not like I did it on purpose," he says. "Sometimes the drummer would kick the beat off fast, and you just had to go with it, or sometimes I'd kick it off too fast. It was just a matter of putting your face in the dirt and looking ugly until you get better."

At home, meanwhile, the dance crowds remained unforgiving. "They're real vocal," he says. "Sometimes I couldn't believe they would say some of the things they said. They had some old people, they'd stop dancing and come up and yell at me." After a couple of empty nights at Richard's Club, Simien began to notice that the farther he was from home, the better it went. In church halls in Raywood, Texas, or even up the road in Leonville, crowds responded to his new style, and crowded around the stage to watch the way he clowned around with his rubboard player, Earl Sally.

Simien's first break came in 1984, when Philip Broussard, who was drumming with the Lawtell Playboys, passed his name to the organizers of the World's Fair being held that year in New Orleans. Not long after, Simien and his band boarded a Greyhound for the fair, where they played a total of three weeks, doing several shows daily. It was there, he recalls, that he discovered a new audience, and where he first became a show band.

"They had us on a stage called the Wonder Wall," he says. "The first day, the sound man told us, 'OK, guys, this is what's happening. The gates are going to open, and then there will be probably about two or three thousand people coming through. When you see the whites of their eyes, man, then go for it.' Next thing you know, all these people were just rushing in, and we had to get them to stop and check us out. And we got a reaction from the crowd. For the first time in my life, I heard people applaud. Because when you're playing a dance, you're pretty much just in the corner making music — whether it's you or the jukebox doesn't make much difference. But then we got a taste of the applause, and we started doing things a little differently."

Before long, all doors would seem to be flinging wide open. Simien had dreamed of going on the road ever since he watched Willie Nelson in the movie *Honeysuckle Rose*. He booked his first show in New York at the Lone Star Cafe. But before he could take that trip, he was playing a dance at a restaurant in Breaux Bridge and was asked by a man in the crowd if he'd like to record with Paul Simon. And before the year was out, he would be in front of the cameras in *The Big Easy*. "Man, I was flipping," Simien remembers with a laugh. "I come from out of high school, ready to live my whole life playing Slim's Y-Ki-Ki and Richard's Club and whatever church hall I can get, and lay bricks during the week. That was my life, that's what I wanted to do, I had made up my mind, fuck it. Then all of a sudden all that stuff started happening. A movie, and Paul Simon, I'm going to meet him? No, I'm going in the studio and *record* with him."

The local conduit for both *Graceland* and *The Big Easy* was Dicky Landry, the composer and saxophonist with one foot on New York concrete and the other in his home in Cecilia, Louisiana. In the 1970s Landry began sitting in with Clifton Chenier, and it was he who once introduced Chenier to Mick Jagger at a Los Angeles church dance. In the 1980s Landry found himself in the center of what was promising to be a new national craze for zydeco.

He recalls that his involvement in *Graceland* started when he met Paul Simon at a BeauSoleil concert at the Carnegie Recital Hall. "I said, 'Have you heard the black music of Louisiana?' He said, 'Zy-DECO?' I said, 'No, ZY-deco.' He said, 'Yeah, I know. Clifton Chenier.'"

At the time, Simon was searching for an American connection to the African accordion music he'd been recording for *Graceland*. He was disappointed that Chenier was too sick to record. Landry suggested he go hear Buckwheat Zydeco, who was playing a show at Tramps. Simon went, and the next night he asked Landry to set up two more bands in a studio in Louisiana. During this time, Landry first met Simien. "The owner of Mulatte's, Kerry Boutte, calls me," he remembers. "He says, 'You just got to hear this young group.' And I get there, and Terrance Simien has the place jumping. He was a wild man from the very beginning, and Earl Sally had a real presence on stage."

In addition to Simien and Buckwheat Zydeco, Landry picked Rockin' Dopsie and the Cajun Twisters for the sessions in Crowley's Master-Trak studios. After Simon recorded all three bands, he chose Dopsie's instrumental version of "Josephine c'est pas ma femme" — originally recorded by Clifton Chenier for Arhoolie Records in 1969 — as the basis for his song "That Was Your Mother." His trip to Louisiana turned out to be his final session for *Graceland,* which went on to win the 1986 Grammy for Album of the Year and become Simon's best-selling solo album.

Not all participants were pleased with the results, however. After mixing and editing Dopsie's performance into a three-minute song, Simon took credit for both words and music. At first, it looked like the matter might end up in the courts. However, any claim that Rockin' Dopsie ever had to the material was dropped when it was determined that the melody dated to the Cajun fiddle duet "Adieu Rosa," first recorded by Dennis McGee and Sady Courville in 1929, and possibly based on an old *juré* song.

If Rockin' Dopsie was left with ambivalent feelings about his participation in *Graceland,* the project nonetheless gave him a career resurgence. In 1991 he made his major-label debut, *Louisiana Music,* produced by Ahmet Ertegun and Shane Keister for Atlantic Records. The album was nominated for a Grammy, and Rockin' Dopsie was invited into the studio to play on sessions for Bob Dylan's *Oh Mercy.* (His work was not used in the final product.) But the veteran accordionist seemed less interested in his new fame than in keeping to his familiar circuit, a fact Landry learned the hard way when he received a call from *Saturday Night Live* producer Lorne Michaels. "Paul Simon said that once the record comes out, he'd help get him on *Saturday Night Live,*" Landry recalls. "So I get a call from Lorne, offering to put Dopsie on in a couple weeks. So I call Dopsie, he says, 'Oh no, man, I can't do that. I got a job at a church dance in Houston.' Unbelievable. I'd have dropped everything." Rockin' Dopsie, however, would not be persuaded. He continued to keep to his regular schedule until his untimely death in 1993 at the age of sixty-one. His son David "Rockin' Dopsie Jr." Rubin now leads the band.

Rockin' Dopsie may have had a mixed reaction to his new success, but Terrance Simien was a young accordionist looking for a break. He found it in the *Graceland* sessions. Before he left the Crowley studio, Simon offered to sing backup vocals for Simien on the Clifton Chenier waltz "You Used To Call Me." He then handed Landry the tape, suggesting that he release a single and become Simien's manager.

For Simien, the life of a touring zydeco musician kept getting better. In the summer of 1985, shortly after the *Graceland* sessions, he left for the scheduled trip to New York. "We drove out of Louisiana in a rented van, but it broke down in Knoxville, Tennessee," he recalls. "So we stopped at the rental place in Knoxville, but they didn't have a van. Instead, they have two

Chrysler Fifth Avenue New Yorkers. So now we're going in style, we're going to play a club on Fifth Avenue, New York, in two Fifth Avenue New Yorkers. I mean, the vibe was right."

When he arrived at the club, Simien learned that he happened to be playing in New York on the night of the Live Aid benefit. "So we got to the place and did our first set. Then Paul Simon comes in there with Penny Marshall, and we got us something to eat at the bar, and there we were, eating and talking and laughing with Paul Simon and Penny Marshall. We had just come out of the studio together, so we knew Paul, but now he had Penny Marshall with him! And I'm calling her 'Laverne' and being all stupid. But I was a kid from here, man!

"And so we went on, and then Paul Simon said, 'This is going to be an interesting night. I met quite a few people that said they were coming.' So I thought nothing of it, and all of a sudden Mick Jagger walks in the dressing room. 'Hey, guys, what's happening?' I said, 'Damn, can I get your autograph?' He said, 'What type of music you play?' I said, 'Man, I play zydeco.' He said, 'Clifton Chenier.' And then he told me all about hearing him at Verbum Dei. And then Keith Richards and Ron Woods got onstage that night, and Dylan was there. Now, this is our first time in New York, and we're starting to think that maybe this is all normal."

The magical night even appeared in Simon's song on *Graceland*. Before going to the Lone Star, Simon had been at a dinner party that included both Landry and Marshall, at a restaurant on Lafayette Street, across the street from Joseph Papp's Public Theatre. After eating, the three went to the club. Simon concludes his song with these lines:

> Well, I'm standing on the corner of Lafayette
> Across the street from The Public
> Heading down to the Lone Star Café
> Maybe get a little conversation
> Drink a little red wine
> Standing in the shadow of Clifton Chenier
> Dancing the night away.

After five years of working together, Terrance Simien and Dick Landry parted ways. Simien is now managed by his wife, Cynthia. Landry continues to develop plans to popularize zydeco. Not all have been winners: an attempted Armani fashion shoot at the Zydeco Festival in Plaisance fell through. But during the time he was still working with Simien, Landry played a role in one of the biggest commercial boosts that zydeco — and Louisiana music in general — has ever received.

It all started when director Jim McBride was attending a wedding in Louisiana, and he visited Landry in Cecilia. He had been planning to shoot a movie in Chicago about a corrupt Italian policeman, and he asked Landry what he thought about changing the location to New Orleans. Landry suggested he make the cop a Cajun. "And a lightbulb went off in his head," Landry says. "He stayed two extra weeks, rewrote the script, changed all the names to Cajun names, and then we started going through all the bands."

The movie opened with a tracking shot that led directly from the Louisiana bayous to downtown New Orleans, accompanied by a Beausoleil song, "Zydeco Gris-Gris," based on an old Canray Fontenot fiddle tune. Final credits were accompanied by Buckwheat Zydeco singing "Jolie blonde." The only scene of live zydeco in *The Big Easy* had Dennis Quaid's Remy McSwain give a dance lesson to Ellen Barkin's Anne Osborne. As the two leads fumble with their feet, Simien is on accordion; the scene culminates when Earl Sally leaps into the crowd with his rubboard.

Simien's performance in *The Big Easy* meant a new audience for both zydeco and the young accordion player from Mallet. He was soon logging 250 dates annually, and in 1987 was voted one of *Billboard*'s Top Ten Performance Acts. Remembers Chubby Carrier, who was then drumming in the Mallet Playboys: "Wherever we'd go, they'd say, 'Straight from the movie *The Big Easy,* Terrance Simien and the Mallet Playboys.' Everybody was going, 'Wow, we saw y'all in the movie.' We'd be packing joints with no record deal, no T-shirts, nothing. The movies can do a lot for you, man."

Simien was setting himself apart from other zydeco players in look as well as sound. He was described in one 1989 review as the "wild-haired, barefoot man playing accordion, wearing a sleeveless Guardian Angels T-shirt and beat-up jeans." (He had been performing barefoot since the beginning; he says it gives him better balance.) He took his first stage dive — a rock-and-roll commonplace, but a novelty for a zydeco accordionist — at the Ann Arbor Blues and Jazz Festival. But nothing was quite so unusual to people back home as the sight of Simien's custom-built accordion, which he ordered from Cajun musician and accordion builder Marc Savoy. "When I bought my first handmade accordion from Marc, I started breaking the bellows," he remembers. "Marc said, 'Man, you're going through a lot of bellows.' I said, 'What if we put two together?' He laughed and said, 'I'll do it if that's what you want me to do.' Then when I went to pick it up, it was this big huge long thing, and there were a few people in the store that were kind of making a joke about it. What they were saying behind my back I'm sure was something I don't want to have to even think about."

He also kept stretching his music into new forms. He recorded with the New Orleans funk band the Meters, and even added an electric sitar to his version of "Dog Hill." He was featured in numerous television commercials, including a national campaign for Chevrolet. Today, in an era when Irish stepdancers can become an international phenomenon, he wonders about the potential for his culture's music and dance. "I look at reggae music, I look at blues and how it all evolved," he says. "It all started from the house, and now it's all over the world. And I think it's just a matter of time for zydeco music to get like that. What if you did a full, rounded show, with dancers and scenes of trail rides, and lasers and flashpots going off? When it's right, it can work."

Purists may cringe, but other young zydeco players are sharing Simien's dreams of a zydeco crossover success. Musicians such as Buckwheat Zydeco have already demonstrated that you can aim above the dance floor and connect with a mass audience. In the late 1990s, commercials and soundtracks continue to use zydeco rhythms, and rocker John Mellencamp even included a zydeco rubboard in a popular video. Today, bands around the world blend zydeco and rock, including New York's Loup Garou, which features Lafayette-born accordionist Jimmy Macdonell, playing Southern-style rock along with tunes by Rockin' Sidney Simien. Perhaps the most unusual recording has been *Rock the Zydeco* by Chris Jagger, Mick Jagger's younger brother. Backup singers included both Mick and 1970s pop star Leo Sayer.

Other innovations have emerged from unlikely sources. Massachusetts-based Rounder Records is primarily a home of blues, folk, bluegrass, and other traditional sounds, including zydeco artists such as Boozoo Chavis and John Delafose. But beginning with Buckwheat Zydeco's album *Waitin' for My Ya Ya*, the label has also led the current drive to explore new sounds — including studio-generated dance mixes with artists such as Beau Jocque and Chris Ardoin, and accordion-driven rap songs by Houston's Li'l Brian and the Zydeco Travellers. "It's a little scary to be part of that process," admits Rounder producer Scott Billington. "Sometimes I worry that all music is just moving toward this universal commercial standard, where everyone is aspiring to be a pop artist based on something they see on MTV or BET, and letting that be the direction of their music, instead of following something more personal or tied to their culture. But at the same time, I have to admit it's fun to fuse these different styles, to try production techniques you would associate with rap or hip-hop, or turn a zydeco musician on to ska or reggae."

Today, touring zydeco musicians have more choices than ever before. Many are trying to stake their positions in the shifting musical mainstream, looking at the example set by the Dave Matthews Band, which features

African-American violinist Boyd Tinsley. For young musicians who grew up hearing Creole fiddlers Canray Fontenot and Bébé and Calvin Carrière, nothing could be more encouraging. "A black fiddle player, that's what gets me," says Chubby Carrier. "At one time we would never put that fiddle with rock and roll. And I'm thinking if Dave Matthews can go over with the fiddle, maybe a black guy with the accordion can get over too. You never know."

Carrier is a good representative of the new generation of zydeco popularizers. He grew up surrounded by zydeco; when he was twelve, he started drumming for his father, Roy Carrier. At fifteen, Chubby played his first show as accordionist at the American Legion in Church Point. Now, as leader of his own Bayou Swamp Band, he seeks both a different sound and a different dance floor. "Enough 'Jolie blonde,' enough 'Back Door,' enough two-step, enough of the same 'Toot-Toot,'" he states. "My daddy's traditional, but I'm blues, R&B, soul, rock-and-roll, I'm everything."

"I love to hear the old players, they're from the heart," Carrier continues. "They got it from being there when it wasn't accepted, before its time. But now they've been playing the same songs for over thirty years, the same waltzes I've been hearing since I was born. It's like they're afraid to learn something new. Now, if you listen to Beau Jocque, and especially that guitar work, he's adding a different vibe to it. That's what I'm doing, looking for a new sound. When my crowds come out, they don't expect to two-step, they just come out and say, 'Man, let's just dance.' And they just get together and get on the dance floor in the middle, and everybody's just bobbing heads, man. It's a big party going on."

In the last half of the 1990s, the shape of zydeco outside of Louisiana began to shift again. This time, it wasn't a result of touring zydeco bands conquering new territory. Instead, the lands were being converted from within. Cities around the world began to boast their own accordion and rubboard combos, as well as their own packed dance floors.

Today, it is hard to find a city without its own band. In New Orleans a former pro football linebacker and blues harp player named Bruce "Sunpie" Barnes picked up the accordion, learned Creole French, and became a devoted student of Hiram Sampy; he now leads his popular band, the Sunspots. From Pennsylvania came Zydecoal, from Colorado the Zukes of Zydeco, and from Minnesota the Swamp Sextet and Zolo Go. In Baltimore, Maryland, a group of Peabody Institute graduates formed Gumbo Junkyard. Overseas, Queen Bee and the Zydeco Amigos were based in Sweden, and Denmark has three bands: the Bayous, Alfa and Bodega, and Captain Crawfish and the Jumping Zydeco. Psycho Zydeco performs in Sydney, Australia. British bands include Joe Le Taxi and R. Cajun and the Zydeco Brothers. Around the world, new zydeco groups are forming each year.

As in the folk and blues revivals, the current explosion of zydeco has sparked new debates over cultural authenticity. Is a zydeco band composed of Minnesotans or Pennsylvanians a true *zydeco* band? There are as many answers to that question as there are musicians and dancers. "When music goes beyond here, a lot of people mess it up," Michael Levier, an organizer of a new Louisiana-based zydeco preservation society, told the *Opelousas Daily World.* Others believe the future of zydeco may be in the hands of musicians outside of the state. Suggests Thomas Fields: "They're doing it right, because they're learning French and studying the culture that we were raised in."

For many, authenticity turns on the meanings of the word *zydeco*. In its home communities, *zydeco* has always referred to dancing as much as music. Today, fans around the world are eager to apply both definitions to their weekend nights. Today, in nearly any major city in the United States, there is probably at least one floor filled with couples holding, stepping, stomping, and spinning in moves that would be more or less familiar to dancers at Richard's Club or Slim's Y-Ki-Ki.

In Louisiana, zydeco dancing is usually a habit acquired at an early age. The right and wrong ways to move to music are learned and relearned over a lifetime of church dances, trail rides, and weekends in the clubs. But now there is a new way to learn: classes. Some of the first formal instruction took place in New Orleans, where a dancer named Peggy Usner formed her Cajun Dance Troupe in 1981; among Usner's choreographing jobs were a scene in *The Big Easy* and a Rockin' Dopsie dance for a televised Dolly Parton special. Outside Louisiana, one of the earliest zydeco classes happened by accident, when Opelousas native Millie Ortego was teaching Cajun dance at the Escoheag Bluegrass and Cajun festival in Rhode Island, and she noticed Lawtell Playboys rubboard player J. C. Gallow on the dance floor. The pair began offering workshops in a variety of settings, including Buffalo Gap and Augusta Heritage Center, two folk culture centers located in West Virginia.

The newest star among zydeco dance teachers is a financial analyst for Texaco named Mona Wilson. The daughter of a club owner in the tiny town of Cade, south of Lafayette, Wilson first attracted attention when she entered a series of zydeco dance contests in Texas and Louisiana in the early 1990s. The biggest match of all was a set of five semifinals that culminated in a final dance-off at Richard's Club. Wilson and her partner were awarded a six-and-a-half-foot trophy naming them "World's Best Zydeco Dance Couple."

Her secret to winning was knowing both new and old dance moves. "Sometimes you couldn't see the floor for the number of people," Wilson recalls. "The way they got rid of a lot of contestants was by making them waltz.

You might have a hundred couples on the floor, and when they finish with that waltz, you were down to ten." Following the Richard's Club contest, Wilson appeared on radio with zydeco deejay Lester Thibeaux, who introduced her as the Zydeco Queen after a song by Willis Prudhomme. She began to use the title when she started teaching.

As one of the few black Creoles teaching zydeco dance, she turns her classes into literal exercises in cross-cultural contact. Explains Wilson: "When I teach, I tell people: 'You don't get this opportunity often. If you want candid answers about the culture, you need to ask me here and now.' So I was at Augusta, and a man asked, 'Why won't the black women dance with me when I'm in Louisiana?' I told him, 'Let's dance.' And he started jumping around and doing all kinds of things, and I said, 'That's why.' And his explanation to me was, 'But I like to have fun.' I said, 'That's fine, but you think having fun when you go to Louisiana would be dancing with black women. If the people in Louisiana don't dance that way, why should you?'"

At first, she admits, not everyone back home supported her decision to teach the moves. "Some of the Creole people looked at it as people invading our culture. My thing is, clubs are integrated now, and you can not stop people from coming. I prefer for tourists to come in and do the dance as close to right as possible. After I first taught people in 'ninety-five, they came down for the Zydeco Extravaganza, and I had some people from the Creole community who came up to me and said, 'We can tell who you taught.' So that made me feel good. I wish more people from the community would get out here and try to do the same thing."

The first zydeco dance video, *Learn to Zydeco Dance Tonite!,* was produced in 1995 by a Washington, D.C., medical entomologist and zydeco dance instructor named Ben Pagac. In 1997 Pagac took his first tour to England to teach zydeco dancing, where he met a committed group of learners. "They weren't like, 'Let's have a few beers and try this step.' They were really focusing, they really wanted to get it."

In addition to footwork, zydeco initiates also attempt to reproduce a Creole style. "The way I see it, the dance has a real controlled dignity to it," New Orleans–based teacher Michael Seider explains. "Most people maintain an erect upper body with a lot of hip movement. A lot of the dancers will not crack a smile, and the woman's look has got to be sort of disinterested. It can also get to be kind of competitive, with someone stomping off a footwork, and someone who's adjacent kind of stomping off a reply."

The scene continues to grow. In 1998 a zydeco cruise to Jamaica featured Geno Delafose and dance classes with five instructors. The growth of zydeco dance crowds has meant greater demand for touring bands. "If you put chairs on the dance floor and bring in the Louisiana bands and don't allow dancing, the people wouldn't return," says Gary Hayman, a retired hypnotherapist and current dance instructor in Washington, D.C. In addition to giving dance lessons, Hayman also devotes forty hours a week to maintaining a schedule of Cajun and zydeco dances around the country, as well as volumes of zydeco articles, which he regularly e-mails to thousands of subscribers. "The Internet helps a lot," he says. "We all get to know each other nationwide, and we all meet down in Louisiana."

This dance community states a preference for steady dance rhythms, favoring bands such as Geno Delafose, the Creole Zydeco Farmers, Willis Prudhomme, and Roy Carrier. More Louisiana musicians are seeing a market for traditional two-steps and waltzes. Such is the case with one of the newest players on the dance scene, Thomas Fields and the Foot Stompin' Zydeco Band. As a child, Fields played rubboard behind Claude Faulk, but he didn't pick up his first accordion until he was forty-three. "The road was my intention when I first got started," he explains. "I think right now it's just too many clubs in Louisiana for the amount of people." Steady jobs include appearances at the Orleans Casino in Las Vegas, a Louisiana-themed casino that presents nightly zydeco in its lounge. But it's the dancers that really keep him going, he says. "You go to Seattle, Portland, New Orleans, all parts of California, that's where the dancing people are. And in Atlanta, Washington D.C., they all want to jump."

Of course, dance fads are regularly embraced and discarded: this year's macarena soon becomes last year's lambada. So far, zydeco dancing is holding its ground. In Washington, D.C., up to a thousand dancers now show up in the peeling grandeur of the Spanish Ballroom in Glen Echo Park; near the door, a table is stocked with color xeroxes listing other area dances. In Berkeley, at the Ashkanaz Music & Dance Community Center, zydeco bands perform on a stage decorated in vintage protest posters. Perhaps no scene inspires such reverence as the Mid-City Lanes Rock 'n' Bowl, a New Orleans bowling alley that books zydeco bands each Wednesday and Thursday. "There are only two places where I have experienced that certain feeling of magic," says Hayman. "One is driving into Paris, and the other is walking up the stairs into the Rock 'n' Bowl."

Hayman believes that interest in zydeco dancing is still growing. "It is a tremendous communication device," he explains. "You can have a little contest or you can do things in sync. And the community is very unique. Outside of Louisiana, people do not refuse dances."

Wilson recalls a dance in Atlanta at which forty people were expected and exactly 206 showed up. "I hope it continues," she says. "Right now it's still growing, and it's growing at a fast pace. But even if something else comes along and it dies down around the United States, it's always going to be here in Louisiana and Texas. Because the churches use it at least one weekend a month, and that's how they make money. And at Richard's and Slim's and Hamilton's, it's lasted a long time, and the dances are still full."


A few weeks following his Jazz Fest show, Terrance Simien has returned to his home in Lafayette. He opens the door to a tasteful suburban living room, where the only signs of a musician's life are a few rock biographies on the bookshelf. He is going through his mail, and he smiles when he sees a check for his work in *The Big Easy* a decade earlier. Then he looks up. "Let's take a drive to Mallet," he says.

His car is in the shop, so he climbs in a rental. After a stop at a Checkers drive-through to pick up hamburgers, he heads north from town and reaches cruising speed. "My thoughts get rolling when I'm traveling," he says.

The road to Mallet is the same one that leads to Richard's Club. Does Simien ever think of going back to the club and playing a dance?

"I have sense enough to know not to do that," he replies. "Kermon assures me that I'm wrong, that the people are going to like what I'm doing, that they're ready for me and all this and all that. Might be, but I don't know. I could change my set and do something I did six, seven years ago. I could play John Delafose songs note for note. But for me, that would be just like telling a lie. I'd rather leave that for the younger kids, or for whoever is hot in the area.

"There's only so many people around here, you know," he continues. "And that's the way it is. But when you leave, you realize so many things. One thing you realize is that there's a big world out there. A big-ass world, and with a lot of different kinds of people. That, to me, is what every zydeco musician — every musician — needs to realize. Hey, if something is not working for you in one place, don't get discouraged. Move on. Try somewhere else."

Simien gives a quick tour of Mallet, pointing out St. Ann's Catholic Church, where he once sang in the choir and where he played his first miserable church dance when he was a teenager. He stops at a brick house that his father built by hand, and introduces his parents. He keeps moving down a network of winding roads that finally ends at a gated clearing. This is his family's camp. He leads the way to the door of a small patched-together structure, and opens the door. "Something died," he announces, closing the door and taking the bag of hamburgers to a nearby picnic table.

Across the road, the sun is wavering over a steamy crawfish pond.

Simien was raised in a religious family, he says. One brother is in the seminary, and two aunts are nuns. Then, when he was young, he used to go to visit an old man he named Baisse, whose photograph he now keeps in his studio. "He was a cowboy, then he worked around here castrating horses," he says. "He was a storyteller. I'd stop at his house and we'd sit on his porch and he'd talk for probably five hours without stopping. Some would be true, some not so true. He told me some stuff about Amédé Ardoin. He told about going to the four corners. He talked about somebody that had done him wrong and how he had got back at him. How when he was a kid they had Indians that used to live around here, and they'd do certain dances in the winter."

Simien goes into the bag and pulls out another burger. "Yeah, zydeco music," he says. "Your father's a bricklayer, out in the sun. You come from a place, you think you're so out of touch with the rest of the world. And sometimes when you're in a big city, you feel inferior. When I first went to New York City, I was scared shitless. But to see people from all over the world admiring something that's so common for us, it just puts it all into place.

"You know, I see more people coming out to the dances, and I see a lot of people that come down to hear the music and learn how to dance. You know, the band in Sydney, Australia, Psycho Zydeco. I mean, this cat is playing the accordion and the guy's real good. He's playing some complicated Clifton Chenier stuff that I probably can't play. Even in Japan you got a band full of Japanese cats that's playing zydeco music. It's all over the world. So if there are people clean on the other side of Mallet and Mamou and these little towns where this shit come from, if it could come a time where it can go that far, anything is possible."

The sun has dropped, the birds have quieted. Across the field, two horses are batting their tails at mosquitoes. A car drives by, and Simien throws up his hand in a wave. "Yeah, man, I tell you what," he concludes. "I just hope I can always have this place to come to."

# 20

# A NEW STAGE

CHRIS ARDOIN SPINS OUT OF HIS ROOM and lands in the hall, bending his knees in a quick, personal dance. "Uh-oh, I'm on the radio," he says, going to the living room stereo and turning up the volume. He's wearing his school clothes, pressed white pants and a mall shirt, and a clean blue washrag is folded over his belt. A fresh part zig-zags through his hair.

He listens as the announcer introduces his song: "This is the zydeco weekend, now, so enjoy yourself in the zydeco way. This is for the gentleman who called me up and asked me to play something to entertain his employees planting sugarcane."

Chris slaps the kitchen wall. "I'm going to bust open an apron today," he says. "Just like Beau Jocque." He goes outside to the carport, where a van is loaded with accordions, metal rubboards, and sound equipment, prepared to take the family to the annual Southwest Louisiana Zydeco Festival in Plaisance.

Sitting at the kitchen table, Lawrence Ardoin watches his son breeze past. A black accordion is snapped shut and resting in his lap. "I don't know why I feel this way," he says, his usual smile not playing beneath his thin moustache. "I've gone before crowds and I've never been nervous. I'm

*Chris Ardoin at Carnegie Hall, 1990.*

nervous this morning." He moves the accordion to the floor and finishes packing the van.

Much has changed in the hundred years since Amédé Ardoin was born into a sharecropping family in Southwest Louisiana. Today young Creoles speak English and play zydeco, and dancers do moves that even Canray Fontenot and Bois Sec Ardoin didn't foresee when they snuck the blues into a house dance. Modern bands play at local clubs, trail rides, and festivals, or they can leave the state. In the 1930s Ardoin's first recordings began to appear in Southwest Louisiana. Today young players are well advised to put their music on CD before playing it in clubs.

Yet one thing remains the same: there is still an Ardoin at the accordion. Bois Sec Ardoin continues to play the music he once learned from his cousin Amédé. His son Lawrence plays the old songs with fiddlers such as his brother Morris and Edward Poullard. But the most active player in the family today is Chris, who was four years old when he first picked up the accordion in public, to perform "My Toot-Toot" at a gumbo cookoff in Texas. "His little stomach was in a knot — hard, hard, hard," recalls Lawrence of that day. "He was sitting on top of a truck bed, and they had about three thousand people there. He picked up money that day."

Growing up, Lawrence Ardoin's sons always knew they were born into a unique family. "We always played a packed house," recalls Sean, who began drumming with his father's band when he was four. "At first they didn't have any zydeco festivals, and so we'd go and play a Cajun festival, where we were the only black band. And when my dad and them would play, dust would just be kicking up everywhere, they'd really turn the crowd out. That made me proud. Friday and Saturday, it was just guaranteed that the band was gone. Guaranteed gone. And they were always making money, too."

In 1990 Chris and Sean performed in Carnegie Hall with their father, grandfather, and uncles. That same year, Chris joined his father's band, sharing accordion duties on his first record. But Lawrence soon realized his son was changing his sound. "I tried to get Chris to go with the music we were doing, but he wasn't interested in doing that," he says. "My daughter, Erica, and my son Sean, they would play everything just like I played it. I'd get off the stage and one of them could come on, and you couldn't tell I'd left. But Chris was different. So one day I said, 'Well, this here is not working anymore.'"

The family met at the kitchen table. Lawrence told Chris and Sean if they didn't want to keep playing, he was going to sell all of the equipment, and get out of music. They replied that they wanted to play. "I just decided that the Ardoin family has been doing this now for a century, and things are changing," says Lawrence. "So I might as well let them go with the flow.

People can walk up to the stage and ask Chris to play the old songs, and he'll play it. But if they don't ask, he's not going to play it."

As Chris was working out the new accordion style, Sean began learning the new double kick on drums. He credits his sister, Erica, for teaching him the secret: first learn how to dance. "I had already drummed through three changes in the music," he says. "The way I learned this style was by dancing it. Before Beau Jocque, you really didn't move your shoulders. Now, it's shoulders, chest, all that. So now when I'm playing, I always check my shoulders to see if I'm doing it right."

Today, when Chris Ardoin and Double Clutchin' play Slim's Y-Ki-Ki and Richard's Club, they are starting to draw a crowd — even when Keith Frank is playing the same night. Their style combines traditional Ardoin melodies with contemporary R&B stylings, along with new compositions about young love and trail rides. Recently, Sean has learned to sing the waltz "Dimanche après midi," first recorded by his grandfather. "Anybody who hears that high-pitched voice will know that the Ardoins are still alive and well," says Lawrence proudly.

"The music is changing a lot, but it's not going to stop," Sean believes. "Zydeco isn't going anywhere. My grandfather's always had two wallets since he started playing in the late twenties. He had one wallet for twenties and one wallet for hundreds. And he was doing European tours in the nineteen-sixties, a black man right outside of Mamou. Most people hadn't made it to New Orleans, much less to Paris and London. That was the thing that set us apart. And until he retired, he was playing every weekend. Then my dad was playing every weekend, and now it's us."

The Ardoins assume their family positions in the van: Lawrence driving, Chris in the backseat with a Walkman. Sean is meeting them from Baton Rouge. Lawrence steers the van out of Lake Charles on Interstate 10. Chris clicks off his tape player when he hears his name.

"Chris still won't talk onstage," Lawrence is saying. "He needs to talk to his fans. That's going to make all the difference in the world. All he would have to do is get up there some time and say, 'Well, how's everybody doing?' 'Are you having a good time here?' 'I'm going to send this song out to everybody in the house, this is from me to you.'"

But Chris says that it doesn't feel natural to him. "It feels stupid." He shrugs.

"It might feel stupid, but there's a big reward behind that," Lawrence emphasizes. After a brief silence, father and son debate the latest fluctuations on the zydeco market: who's up, who's down.

"Keith is kind of dropping right now," Chris says.

Lawrence looks unconvinced.

"Oh, he's dropping," Chris maintains. "I think the only real competition we got now is Step Rideau."

The conversation returns to the subject of stage presence. Lawrence tries a new approach. "You have to work your crowd. That's one of the things Keith does now. He talks to them. And Step is doing that."

Chris nods, and switches his Walkman back on. Lawrence turns onto Highway 165. The van picks up speed. Suddenly, Lawrence slows down. He points to an intersection of two roads and a railroad track. "This is where my brother Gus was killed," he tells me. "He always was a fast driver."

Until his death in 1974, Gustave Ardoin had been leading the Ardoin Brothers band. He was considered one of the finest players the family had ever produced. "The weekend that he got killed, we played at the Four Corners club between Basile and Iota," Lawrence remembers. "That was me, Morris, Gustave, and Russell, my baby brother. Five of us, we called ourselves the Ardoin brothers. Let me tell you we were hot, and we never, never, never rehearsed. Get out there and play. We played 'Mon chapeau,' 'Jolie catin,' 'Bosco Stomp.' And we had Canray on the fiddle, and he'd always be a little drunk, but there were certain songs like 'Mamou Hot Step' that we could play to sober him up.

"We just played from the heart and soul, and we played it to the best of our ability. You know, we could get a white musician to play with us, and step for step, note for note, he was right with us. But when he played with his own band it was different. And the song was the same. I never could figure out why.

"After my brother was killed it wasn't until two years later that we started playing again," he remembers. "Then one weekend in 1976, in October, we had played a dance at the Sacred Heart Church in Lake Charles. Morris called Raymond Latour to come up and play. That made me very angry, because he had to go outside the family. So I took that accordion home that weekend, and two weeks later we came back and I started playing two or three songs a night.

"But that Gus — " Lawrence's voice trails off. "Talk about a musician. I was the drummer. If I didn't play, he didn't play." He holds up two finger pressed together. "We were close."

The end of this drive is the Southwest Louisiana Zydeco Festival in Plaisance. More than any other event, the Zydeco Festival is the annual showcase for the new crop of zydeco players. Since its inception in 1982, this famously hot and shadeless Saturday event before Labor Day has seen numerous milestone events in zydeco: Clifton Chenier playing "I'm Coming Home"; John Delafose triumphantly returning after a heart attack; Beau Jocque ensuring his local celebrity status in a storm of cornbread; Boozoo Chavis releasing into the crowd a tent-sized pair of embossed underwear.

The festival began when a group of parishioners of the Holy Ghost Catholic Church formed an organization called Treasures of Opelousas to help raise money for an education fund. "French la-la, or zydeco, was always in the area, but a festival hadn't been done," recalls Wilbert Levier, an original member of the group. "Putting a number of bands together all on a little flat stage outside, that was something new." Levier credits Vanessa Green, who had previously been involved with the Mace Blues Festival in Greenville, Mississippi, for making the initial suggestion and applying for federal grant money to launch the event.

For land, the organization decided on a soybean field owned by the Southern Development Foundation, a black farmers' cooperative whose president, the Reverend A. J. McKnight, was a priest at Holy Ghost. To help promote the event, they turned to a foundation organizer named Wilbert Guillory. Explains Levier: "Wil was a Creole-speaking person, and we decided we needed a Frenchman to help get people involved."

In Wilbert Guillory, the festival had found a person with two passions: his Creole culture and political activism. "I never played music, I hardly dance," Guillory admits. "But in the music, I could see something so great that was going away." By the time he started with the festival, Guillory was already a veteran of the civil rights movement, having worked with the NAACP in the 1960s to integrate both churches and dances. "I remember a night when I was about seventeen years old and we went to a dance in a schoolhouse they had in Mallet, going towards Eunice," he says. "When we got there, they told me and another guy, Calvin Citizen, that we were invited, but the two dark-skinned guys that were with us were not. And we liked that. It was a struggle, but it was also fun. So we went in, we bullied our way in. And they stopped the musicians from playing. We actually broke the dance, and everyone just went home."

Another time, he recalls, he asked the local priest if he could organize a zydeco dance for his church. The priest took a look at Guillory's beard and his wife's cowboy boots, and gave a sermon the following Sunday about why he wouldn't work with hippies.

Guillory's work with the Southern Development Foundation began when he helped organize a co-op of black sweet-potato growers who he says were being denied crates during harvest time. He set up a few benefit zydeco dances, but he remembers that he was skeptical when he first met Green. "She came by and said we can do the festival at the farm, and to me

*Wilbert Guillory.*

it should have been done inside a building," he recalls. "'No,' she said. 'We did the blues festival, and if y'all want to do a festival here it needs to be done in a big field.'"

So in June 1982 a team of workers attached a bush hog to the back of a tractor and cleared five acres in the soybeans. Grass was raked and hauled away. Wooden pallets were stacked together, and a large piece of plywood was nailed on top. A microphone was attached to an extension cord that ran out to a single vegetable shed. The stage was set. "People thought we were crazy to do a festival in a vegetable field in the middle of nowhere," Guillory recalls, laughing. About four hundred people arrived to hear the three bands: John Delafose, the Sam Brothers Five, and Terrance Simien (who also brought Ann Goodly onstage to sit in). When four thousand people showed up the second year, the organizers knew they had a hit. "The second year surprised everybody, because we were not ready," Guillory admits. "We had a line of cars on the highway from Plaisance almost to Opelousas."

With his brother Morris beside him on the fiddle, Lawrence Ardoin looks across the faces at the Zydeco Festival. Children stand in groups on the hard-packed dirt in front of him; behind them their parents and grandparents sit beneath tarps on folding chairs. Cradling his accordion, Ardoin gives a short talk about la-la music and house dances. "This is a little indication of what it was in the nineteen twenties, what Amédé was doing," he says. "So bear with us, don't get disgusted."

His soaring French vocals are both earthy and delicate. The fiddle and steady clang of an iron triangle contrast with the chugging zydeco rhythms heard the rest of the day. "I don't know why the young blacks don't want to do that," Morris will later say, looking consolingly at his fiddle. "That's a good instrument."

Much else will happen this day, onstage and off. Backstage after Chris Ardoin's performance, Scott Billington will talk to Lawrence Ardoin about putting the band on Rounder Records. Then Fred Charlie, who worked with Keith Frank, will counsel Ardoin to resist the other company, saying they should build an "iron fence" around Louisiana music. Ardoin will pocket both business cards.

Keith Frank will pass them, surrounded by fans. "Hey, you ain't through here yet, get that baby autographed," one woman demands. "I want Keith Frank's name on her." Frank will oblige. Later on, he will start off his show with a short waltz. "That dude is cocky," Lawrence will say, shaking his head.

*Zydeco Music Festival, Plaisance, Louisiana.*

Zydeco bands never start with a waltz. Then Frank will play "Get On Boy": *The pork chop ain't* —.

In the musicians' parking area, at the periphery of the sound, Beau Jocque and his wife will be in the cab of a large pickup, listening to the song and planning his entrance to the stage: clouds of smoke, a billowing red cape, and the theme to *Rocky*. Boozoo Chavis will walk through the metal gate into the backstage area, surrounded by men in cowboy hats. "Take me and any of them and put us in the field," he will insist. "We can play side by side, and you tell us who's best." Around him, the cowboy hats will nod.

This all happens later in the evening, as crowds of dancers kick up a light mist of dust, and the sun shimmers and sets over cleared fields. But right now, Chris Ardoin has taken the stage, wiping his hands on a towel. He looks back to his brother and forward at the crowd.

"Y'all ready?" he says, and grins. "Y'all hot?"

*Irene Hebert, Lafayette, Louisiana.*

*Arnold "Slim" Gradney, Slim's Y-Ki-Ki, Opelousas, Louisiana.*

# KEYS TO THE
# KINGDOM:

## FURTHER LISTENING, READING,

## VIEWING, DANCING

### Recommended Recordings

Hopefully, zydeco recordings will be available at your better local stores. If not, in Louisiana try Floyd's Record Shop in Ville Platte, at (800) 738-8668, Music Machine & Video in Eunice, at (318) 457-4846 and Louisiana Music Factory in New Orleans at (504) 586-1094; and in San Francisco Down Home Music Store, at (510) 525-2129. Each of these stores takes phone orders. Floyd also offers a catalogue featuring music, books, videos, rubboards, shotglasses, and rosaries. Another recommended source for zydeco discs, films, and merchandise is Louisiana Catalogue in Larose, at (800) 375-4100. When in Lafayette, be sure to stop by House Rocker Records, phone (318) 234-6231.

Here, by chapter, is the music I most listened to during the writing of this book. Unless otherwise noted, all music is available on CD.

**Chapter One**

At this writing, *Louisiana Cajun and Creole Music 1934* is being prepared for reissue as a CD on Swallow records. Produced by Barry Ancelet and Michael

Doucet, this two-disc set features Alan Lomax's best Louisiana field record-ings, including Jimmy Peters's and Wilfred Charles's *juré* songs, and selec-tions by Paul Junius Malveaux and Ernest Lafitte, and Cleveland Benoit and Darby Hicks. The only Creole accordionist represented is Oakdale Carrière, whom the Lomaxes met in Angola State Penitentiary. Lomax's introduction and Ancelet's notes and translations give the context of many of these mys-terious songs. Highly recommended.

Lomax's field recordings have proved the Holy Grail for Cajun revival bands, and BeauSoleil has refashioned some of the *juré* material into new songs. Only one zydeco performer has been moved to rerecord this mate-rial: Lynn August. His versions of the *juré* songs can be heard on the rec-ommended discs *Creole Cruiser* and *Sauce Piquante* (Black Top). The other songs reveal August to be one of the best singers and blues accordionists in zydeco. By the way, Rounder Records is currently reissuing the massive bulk of Lomax's recordings under the series title *The Alan Lomax Collection*.

A live version of Willis Prudhomme's "My Woman Is a Salty Dog" is on *Zydeco Live!* (Rounder), which includes Richard's Club dance sets by Prud-homme and John Delafose. Lightnin' Hopkins's "Zolo Go" is on *The Gold Star Sessions, Vol. 1* (Arhoolie). The most complete collection of Clarence "Bon Ton" Garlow can be found on *Louisiana Swamp Blues* (Capitol). The reissue of Clifton Chenier's first Arhoolie album, *Louisiana Blues and Zydeco*, has "Zydeco Sont Pas Salé." But Mack McCormick's *A Treasury of Field Record-ings* (77 Records) has not yet been reissued on CD. Its eclectic selection of Houston-based musicians and informative notes would make it a treasure indeed.

**Chapter Two**

Few of the house dance players went on to make records. The only available CD sampling of the old styles is *Zydeco — The Early Years (1961 – 1962)*. These were the first zydeco recordings made by Chris Strachwitz for his new Arhoolie label. Performers include Paul McZiel at a Lafayette house dance party, and Houston club players Albert Chevalier and Willie Green. Also on the disc is the only recording of Boozoo Chavis's great-uncle Sidney "Blind" Babineaux, as well as Clarence Garlow's original "Bon Ton Roula." A special nod to Herbert "Good Rockin'" Sam, who storms through just one tune here: his signature "They Call Me Good Rockin'." Herbert Sam's brother Ambrose comprises one-half of Arhoolie's wonderful *Zydeco Volume 2,* not on CD. Finally, such house-dance players as Freeman and Bee Fontenot are included on the wonderful *Les Haricots Sont Pas Salés* (Cing Planetos).

**Chapter Three**

This chapter's namesake is Nathan Williams's *Creole Crossroads*, available on Rounder. Clifton Chenier's "Black Snake Blues" has been reissued on *Bon Ton Roulet* (Arhoolie), and Beau Jocque sings "Damballah" on his first Rounder disc, *Beau Jocque Boogie*. For another haunting zydeco tune, seek out Bruce "Sunpie" Barnes's excellent *Loup Garou* (D.L.R.).

Fans of the accordion will want to take a guided world tour of the instrument on *Planet Squeezebox* (Ellipses Arts). Zydeco, polka, juju, conjunto, tango, and dozens more styles are represented on three discs, and the accompanying book gives a detailed history of the accordion. The biggest surprises come on selections like that of Cape Verde accordionist Antonio Sanches, who performs a *funana* accompanied only by Tshota Suari on the ridged metal *ferro*. Distant cousins to zydeco, perhaps, but the resemblance is certainly audible.

**Chapter Four**

Amédé Ardoin recorded his music in four sessions. Nearly all the songs of the final three — New Orleans in 1930, and San Antonio and New York City in 1934 — have been collected on *I'm Never Comin' Back* (Arhoolie); the package includes transcriptions and translations, essays by Michael Doucet and Jared Snyder, and my first writing about Ardoin. Unfortunately, the collection is not complete: two songs from San Antonio have yet to be reissued. Also, the songs from Ardoin and Dennis McGee's 1929 session in New Orleans are currently available only on the collection *Cajun Dance Party: Fais Do-Do* (Columbia). It's well worth getting for landmark tunes such as "La Valse à Abe," "Two Step de Eunice," and "Two Step de Prairie Soileau." Interestingly, one of the more well-traveled Cajun tunes on *Cajun Dance Party: Fais Do-Do* is the Breaux Frères' "Le blues du petit chien." Probably influenced by Blind Lemon Jefferson, this rollicking Cajun blues anticipates Cajun accordionist Nathan Abshire's "Pine Grove Blues," which decades later would cross color lines once more as Buckwheat Zydeco's "Ma 'Tit Fille."

For more music by Ardoin's only recording partner, there's *The Complete Early Recordings of Dennis McGee* (Shanachie), a highly recommended disc with informative notes by coproducer Ann Savoy. To hear how Ardoin was interpreted by the influential Cajun accordionist Iry LeJeune, look for *Iry LeJeune, Cajun's Greatest: The Definitive Collection* (Ace), the best of available compilations, also thanks to Savoy's notations.

**Chapter Five**

The finest collection of the Ardoin family's music is *La Musique Creole* (Arhoolie). This reissue includes the complete album *Les Blues du Bayou,* produced by Dick Spottswood during Bois Sec Ardoin and Canray Fontenot's journey home from the 1966 Newport Folk Festival. Also included on the disc are recordings made in the early 1970s at the Ardoins' home with Bois Sec's sons Morris, Gustave, and Lawrence. The companion disc to this set is the excellent *Louisiana Hot Sauce Creole Style* (Arhoolie), a two-decade survey of Canray Fontenot's career. More Bois Sec Ardoin and Canray Fontenot can be heard on *Cajun and Creole Masters* (Music of the World) and *Louisiana Cajun French Music: From the Southwest Prairies, Recorded 1964–1967, Volume Two* (Rounder).

*Louisiana Creole Music* (Smithsonian Folkways) has Gerard Dole's interviews and recordings of Eraste Carrière, Inez Catalon, Freeman Fontenot, Bee Fontenot, and more. Two other wonderful recordings of old-style Creole music were produced by folklorist Nicholas Spitzer in 1976. The Carrière family are given their due on *La La: Louisiana Black French Music* (Maison de Soul): the first side features Bébé and Eraste Carrière, and side two has the Lawtell Playboys featuring Eraste's son, fiddler Calvin Carrière. Spitzer's *Zodico: Louisiana Creole Music* presents the widest spectrum of Creole music collected on one record, including the Carrière brothers, Freeman Fontenot, ballad singer Inez Catalon, the Ardoin family (leading a Mardi Gras chant!), and Hiram Sampy and the Bad Habits. Creole ballad singers Inez Catalon and Alma Barthelemy can also be heard on *La Musique de la Maison* (Smithsonian Folkways), to be issued early 1999. Both Dole's and Spitzer's work are currently available only on cassette, although there are plans to reissue *Zodico* on CD. Its liner notes constitute one of the most complete treatments of Creole music in print.

The Carrière brothers also recorded for *Cajun Fiddle Styles Vol. 1: The Creole Tradition,* unavailable on CD. And except for the selection on *Zodico,* Hiram Sampy's recordings are currently out of print, as are any made by Anderson Moss and Walter Polite. Early work of two of Moss's Houston contemporaries, Lonnie Mitchell and Vincent Frank, is found on the compilation *Texas Zydeco Greats* (Collectables). One can only imagine the possible benefits to modern zydeco if other recordings of early Creole pioneers would be made more readily available.

**Chapter Six**

Not surprisingly, Clifton Chenier is the most recorded zydeco artist in the music's history. In general, you can't go wrong with a Chenier disc, although his first and last recordings don't quite hold up to the rest. Recorded in 1975, *Bogalusa Boogie* (Arhoolie) is rightly lauded as Chenier's best studio album; it earned a five-star rating from the *Rolling Stone Record Guide*, and features the core of the Red Hot Louisiana Band: Cleveland Chenier, John Hart, Little Buck Senegal, Jumpin' Joe Morris, and Robert St. Judy. Great accordion work abounds, and the predominantly Creole French songs range from the unusual protest waltz "Je suis en recolteur" ("I'm a Farmer") to the bawdy "Take Off Your Dress," which is the song recalled in these pages by Claude Boudreaux. The remake of "Sa m'appel fou" ("They Call Me Crazy") settles any dispute of how the musician pronounced his last name: shen-YAY.

Yet Chenier's 1960s Arhoolie sessions shouldn't be overlooked, and they have all been repackaged (and re-repackaged) into various greatest-hits collections. The best are his first session, *Louisiana Blues and Zydeco*, along with *Bon Ton Roulet*, *King of the Bayous*, and *Clifton Sings the Blues*, which adds seven songs from 1977 with Buckwheat Zydeco on piano and organ. *Out West* was recorded in San Francisco in 1973 with guests Elvin Bishop on guitar and Steve Miller on piano. My favorite recording of a zydeco dance is Chenier's *Live at St. Mark's*, made in 1971 in a church in Richmond, California.

In 1993 Rhino released the attractive two-disc set *Zydeco Dynamite: The Clifton Chenier Anthology*. For my taste, this collection leans too heavily on Chenier's early R&B work — there is, for example, not a single waltz. And although material from his last sessions may be necessary for a complete portrait, it also sadly demonstrates the eventual decline of his abilities. Yet *Zydeco Dynamite* is well worth the purchase, especially for the hard-to-find Chess nugget "My Soul." Also included is the Rod Bernard collaboration "My Babe," which comes from *Boogie in Black & White*; regrettably, other tracks from this session have only been reissued on various editions of Jin's *Swamp Gold* series.

Chenier's 1954 recordings with J. R. Fulbright are now available on *Louisiana Swamp Blues* (Capitol). His rocking Specialty material is found on the excellent *Zodico Blues & Boogie*, which includes alternate takes of most songs. Of his later work, the best is *Frenchin' the Boogie* (Verve), a unique set that includes a French version of Ray Charles's "I Got A Woman" called "Moi, j'ai une p'tite femme," and the odd "Goin' Down Slow (In Paris)," a musical dialogue in which Clifton and Cleveland discuss sickness, mortality, and the ways in which people in France are different from everyone else.

THE OLD HOUSE OF MUSIC for COMMERCIAL USE

Elko

J. R. M&F Pub. Co.
(226)

LOUISIANA STOMP

CLISTON CHANIER
King of the South

920-A

823 EAST ADAMS BLVD. L.A., CALIF.

Folk-Star

RECORDS

★ ★ ★ ★

Vocal By
Boozoo

PAPER IN MY SHOE
(Shuler-Chavis)

BOOZOO CHAVIS
and
His Orchestra

GF-1197-B

Chenier won a Grammy for his 1982 album *I'm Here!*; produced by Sam Charters, it's good but not great, with an expanded horn section taking on a greater musical burden. Finally, *Zydeco Legend* (Maison de Soul) is a mixed bag, a combination of the hot *Boogie 'N' Zydeco* album, which produced the hits "Oh My Lucille" and "Hot Tamale Baby," and the inferior *Country Boy/Now Grammy Award Winner 1984!*

**Chapter Seven**

C. J. Chenier's recorded work reveals the imprint of two quite different producers. On *My Baby Don't Wear No Shoes* (Arhoolie) and *Hot Rod* (Slash), the influence of Chris Strachwitz means even louder echoes of Clifton Chenier's work — not a bad thing. My favorite is the former, recorded just a year after Clifton's passing; songs like "Blue Flame Blues" show C. J.'s accordion first opening to full throttle. This was also the last recording made by Cleveland Chenier. In addition to *Hot Rod*, C. J. Chenier made *I Ain't No Playboy* for Slash; both are good but currently difficult to find. Today Chenier records for Alligator; his partnership with producer Bruce Iglauer has encouraged the accordionist to branch out a bit on two accomplished discs, *Too Much Fun* and *The Big Squeeze*. My favorite of the two is *Too Much Fun*, which includes the Memphis Horns and great zydeco versions of "Man Smart, Woman Smarter" and "Got You on My Mind." The sole remaining member of Clifton Chenier's Red Hot Louisiana Band is the blues guitarist Harry Hypolite, whose vocals range in influence from B. B. King to Barry White.

**Chapter Eight**

The best of Buckwheat Zydeco's albums for Blues Unlimited is collected on the CD *The Best of Louisiana Zydeco* (AVI). French blues, two-steps, and waltzes include Buckwheat's first version of "Ma 'Tit Fille," "Madame Coco Bo," and "I Bought a Raccoon." His soul hit "Take Me to the Mountain Top" — always a favorite at El Sid O's — is on *100% Fortified Zydeco* (Black Top). The best representation of mid-1980s Buckwheat Zydeco is the generous *Buckwheat's Zydeco Party* (Rounder). Included is most of his excellent Rounder discs *Turning Point* and *Waitin' for My Ya Ya*.

Buckwheat Zydeco's Island debut, *On a Night Like This*, is perhaps the most consistently pleasing zydeco album since Clifton Chenier's *Bogalusa*

*Boogie*. The Bob Dylan title track makes it clear that this was a play for commercial market, but it equally succeeds on aesthetic levels. The best of the rest can be found on *Menagerie: The Essential Zydeco Collection*, including appearances by David Hidalgo, Dwight Yoakam, and the Dirty Dozen Brass Band. Recent work includes the recommended *Trouble* (Mesa) and *Choo Choo Boogaloo* (Music For Little People), the first zydeco children's album. (I tested this last one on my daughter Cecilia, but she seemed just as happy with *On a Night Like This*.) As one might suspect, Buckwheat Zydeco has led the charge into cyberspace: reach his website at www.buckwheatzydeco.com.

## Chapter Nine

Nathan Williams's songwriting talents make for especially satisfying recordings. My favorite studio effort is his first, *Steady Rock*. However, *Your Mama Don't Know* and *Follow Me Chicken* — with the funky saxophone on the title track and a French version of Stevie Wonder's "Isn't She Lovely" — are also excellent. *Creole Crossroads* is atypical but worthwhile: several songs are picked from the Clifton Chenier songbook, and Williams's vocals are at their most soulful on "Black Snake Blues." But my favorite Williams disc is a live one: *I'm a Zydeco Hog*, recorded at Mid-City Lanes Rock 'n' Bowl for an enthusiastic crowd from around the country. Included on this tour-de-force dance set are many of his best compositions, such as "Zydeco Hog," "Slow Horses and Fast Women," "Everything on the Hog," and the anthemic "Zydeco Road."

## Chapter Ten

Ironically, zydeco's hitmaker has the most neglected catalogue of the genre. The best Rockin' Sidney album, *Boogie Blues 'n' Zydeco* (Maison de Soul), is currently available only on cassette. Fronting an ace band that includes pianist Katie Webster and legendary swamp pop drummer Warren Storm, Rockin' Sidney has fun with a variety of styles, including a bluesy tribute to "Slim's Y-Kee-Kee" [sic]. To hear Rockin' Sidney's 1960s swamp pop gems for the Jin and Fame labels, check out the import *My Toot Toot* (Ace), the best Rockin' Sidney collection available, featuring recordings from 1959–1984, and notes by author John Broven. "My Toot-Toot" itself is available on dozens of compilations, but be warned: newer versions add a third verse and extra instrumentation. Somehow the extra baggage upsets the cart. Other performers' "toot toots" and "cu cus" are found on various compilations (except for John Fogerty's version, which was never released on an album). Rockin' Sidney's later zydeco discs continued the same mix of humorous songs and home-studio production; the best is *Mais Yeah Chere!* and its bovine motorcycle tune "Moo Cow-A-Sockee."

## Chapter Eleven

It's not her slickest production, but Queen Ida's 1976 debut *Play the Zydeco* is still my favorite of her many GNP/Crescendo releases. Heard two decades later, it still captures the flush of a hot zydeco/Tex-Mex band with something to prove. It deserves reissue on CD. The Grammy-winning *On Tour* is an exuberant live set recorded in an uncredited foreign land, and offers the best versions of tunes such as "Frisco Zydeco" and "Capitaine Gumbo." Another fine live set — and closer to home — is *Caught in the Act,* recorded at the Great American Music Hall in San Francisco. The fine 1994 studio album *Mardi Gras* includes Queen Ida's son Myrick "Freeze" Guillory.

Al Rapone went on to record albums for a number of labels, including *Zydeco to Go* (Blind Pig). My favorite is *Plays Tribute* (Atomic Theory); backed by the Minneapolis bar band the Butanes, Rapone gives homage to Clifton Chenier on classics such as "Tu Le Ton Son Ton" and "It's My Soul."

Other California artists include accordionist Danny Poullard, who can be heard with fiddler Michael Doucet on the cassette *Cajun Jam Session* (Arhoolie), as well as with the adept California Cajun Orchestra on two Arhoolie discs, *Nonc Adam Two-Step* and *Not Lonesome Anymore.* Lisa Haley and the Zydekats' most recent recording is *Waiting for the Sky . . .* (Blue Fiddle). T-Lou and his Zydeco Band are on *Super Hot* (Maison de Soul), Zydeco Slim is on a self-titled debut (A-2-Fay), and Bon Ton St. Mary can be heard on *Highway Zydeco* (Goldband). A treasure worth unearthing is the disc *Joe Simien Special* (Blue Fiddle). The patron saint of the California zydeco scene teams with fiddler Lisa Haley for a lovely collection of Cajun and Creole waltzes and two-steps. To order a copy, call (310) 549-4884 or visit Haley's website at www.zydecomusic.com.

## Chapter Twelve

Rockin' Dopsie can best be heard on *Louisiana Music* (Atlantic); coproduced by legendary record man Ahmet Ertegun, the album features wonderful saxophone breaks by John Hart and accordion versions of classic R&B material such as Little Richard's "Keep A-Knockin'" and Guitar Slim's "The Things I Used to Do." Rockin' Dopsie also includes his version of

Clifton Chenier's "Josephine c'est pas ma femme," possibly as a reminder of just where Paul Simon's "That Was Your Mother" began.

Two other zydeco princes that deserve listening are Jabo (a/k/a Donald Glenn), who recorded the blues-heavy zydeco album *Texas Prince of Zydeco* (Maison de Soul), currently available on cassette. Fernest Arceneaux also stakes his sounds on the shifting boundaries of zydeco, blues, and R&B. His most recent disc, *Zydeco Blues Party* (Mardi Gras), features stellar backing by alumni of the old Red Hot Louisiana Band, including John Hart and Little Buck Senegal. Other great Arceneaux recordings are harder to find, including the imports *Zydeco Stomp* (JSP) and *Rockin' Pneumonia* (Ornament/CMA). Look for his good 1979 Blues Unlimited LP *Fernest and the Thunders,* which includes his original "Zydeco Boogoloo." Arceneaux's former backup band has regrouped as the Creole Zydeco Farmers, whose *Come to Party* (Lanor) is also recommended.

**Chapter Thirteen**

Boozoo Chavis's first "Paper in My Shoe" is included on *Louisiana Swamp Blues,* and other Goldband material has been reissued on *The Lake Charles Atomic Bomb* (Rounder). These early recordings, alas, are of historical interest only. To find an enjoyable Chavis disc, it is necessary to skip up thirty years. One of my favorite zydeco records is Chavis's self-titled major label appearance on Elektra Nonesuch's American Explorer series; definitive versions of Goldband classics "Forty-One Days" are joined by newer hits such as "Dog Hill" and "Zydeco Hee Haw." Most welcome are three accordion-only tunes, "Bernadette," "Oh Yae Yae," and "Johnnie Billie Goat." And "I'm Ready Me" is a classic slice of Dog Hill life, a re-creation of early morning conversations between Boozoo, Leona, and their sons.

All of Chavis's 1980s and 1990s recordings come well recommended. *Zydeco Trail Ride* and *Zydeco Homebrew* both provide excellent selections from his Maison de Soul albums. *Boozoo, That's Who!* (Rounder) is produced by the same team that did the Elektra release. His most recent *Hey Do Right!* launched yet another comeback tune: "You're Gonna Look Like a Monkey." Chavis has two live discs. *Live! At the Habibi Temple, Lake Charles, Louisiana* was recorded in the midst of a staged "battle" with Beau Jocque, and his performance is especially fiery. Chavis also appears as one-half of *Zydeco Live! Direct from Richard's Club, Lawtell, Louisiana* (Rounder). The recording quality of this show is comparatively poor, but the thrilling performance includes a five-minute version of "Deacon Jones" in which Chavis spontaneously rhymes new verses with the names of everyone in the club.

**Chapter Fourteen**

Jeffery Broussard's soulful vocals and skilled accordion work are the main reason to look for Zydeco Force's Maison de Soul recordings. Of the three currently available on CD, *Shaggy Dog Two-Step* has the better song selection, including "B-flat," the rap-influenced "Pop That Zydeco Coochie," and their biggest hit, "Zydeco Extravaganza." Other highlights are accordion versions of Clifton Chenier's "I'm a Farmer" and "Oh My Lucille." *The Zydeco Push* opens with an unusual song that pays homage to food stamps and plaid suits, and the title track describes a step in the nouveau zydeco dance craze. Standouts on *It's La La Time* are new versions of "Why You Wanna Make Me Cry?" and John Delafose's "Broken-Hearted." Coincidentally, Jeffery's father, Delton Broussard, is heard leading the Lawtell Playboys on the similarly titled album *La La Louisiana Black French Music*. Selections include "Baby, Please Don't Go," the song that Jeffery played for Delton's funeral.

**Chapter Fifteen**

Thundering vocals, punchy accordion work, exciting arrangements, and a remarkable band are the hallmarks of all Beau Jocque recordings, but the superior song content distinguishes *Beau Jocque Boogie* (Rounder). In addition to original homages to his favorite dance hall ("Richard's Club") and to his wife ("Shelly Shelly"), Beau Jocque grabs the Cajun/Creole tradition by the collar on his versions of "I Went to the Dance Last Night" and "Oh Bye Moreau." This album also marked the debut of "Give Him Cornbread." Also on Rounder are the well-recommended *Pick Up on This!*, *Gonna Take You Downtown*, and *Git It, Beau Jocque!* Beau Jocque released his own twenty-five-minute maxisingle *Beau Jocque's Nursery Rhyme;* the title track is a lively cutting contest between the accordionist and his drummer Steve Charlot. The absence of the Hi-Rollers — especially secret weapons Chuck Bush on bass and Wilfred "Caveman" Pierre on rubboard — is felt on the debut *My Name Is Beau Jocque* (Paula), but songs such as "Don't Sell That Monkey," "When You Think about Me," and "Tee Toe Hot Step" (named for Beau Jocque's father) make it recommended.

**Chapter Sixteen**

Given the sales of his Maison de Soul discs, it is odd that Keith Frank's early recordings *On the Bandstand* (Lanor) and *Get On Boy!* (Zydeco Hound) are still only available on cassette. Especially appealing on the Lanor tape are sister Jennifer Frank's introduction on "Going to McDonald's" and her charming vocals on "Going Back to Big Mamou." The lean sound of *What's His Name?* is heard on songs such as "One Shot," which combines vitriolic lyrics and a gritty performance. Of his other Maison de Soul discs, *Only the Strong Survive* is his most consistent work, although the title track of *Movin' On Up!* has its television-generation charms. (Every zydeco generation has its song about overcoming poverty. That Frank's contribution comes from the theme to the television show *The Jeffersons* symbolizes either his capitulation to mass culture or his deftness at reworking its raw material into a unique cultural statement. I take the latter view.) Meanwhile, Preston Frank is currently available on the cassettes *Let's Dance* (Lanor) and the recommended *Zydeco Volume Two* (Arhoolie).

**Chapter Seventeen**

The Delafose family is well represented on record. John Delafose's Arhoolie work is compiled in *Joe Pitre Got Two Women*, which includes "I Just Want to Be Your Lovin' Man," and the mournful "Crying in the Streets." *Heartaches and Hot Steps* has his modern classic "Broken-Hearted," as well as "Ka-wann," his answer song to "My Toot-Toot." His only live recording was one-half of *Zydeco Live! Direct from Richard's Club, Lawtell, Louisiana.*

Beginning in the early 1990s, John Delafose began trading accordion lead with Geno. My favorite of this era is *Père et Garçon Zydeco* (Rounder), but father and son also teamed up for *Blues Stay Away from Me*, which includes "Joe Simien Special," named for the legendary California accordionist. Geno Delafose's solo recordings for Rounder include *French Rockin' Boogie, That's What I'm Talking About,* and *The Lost Song*, which features Cajun artists Steve Riley and Christine Balfa.

John Delafose was honored in *A Tribute to John Delafose* (Deep South), a recommended collection of performances by Terrance Simien, Willis Prudhomme, C. J. Chenier, Buckwheat Zydeco, Geno Delafose, and more. The project was spearheaded by John's son Tony, who played bass for the Eunice Playboys and now leads his own band.

**Chapter Eighteen**

One of the most promising players in the current extravaganza of young musicians is Li'l Malcolm Walker. His self-titled debut on Maison de Soul boasts a sound more varied than most of his contemporaries, in part because his father, Percy Walker Sr., plays guitar and takes the lead for a couple tunes. Other promising young lions are J. Paul Jr. & the Zydeco Newbreeds (*Taking Over* on Maison de Soul), Gregg Chambers and Creole Junction (a self-titled debut and *Don't Need a Ticket to Ride*, both on Maison de Soul), Li'l Pookie and the Zydeco Heartbreakers (a self-titled debut on Vidrine), Corey and the Hot Peppers (*Hit and Run* on Vidrine), and Jo Jo Reed, whose *Funky Zydeco* includes his wonderful tribute to Boozoo Chavis, "Got It from Boo."

Troy Carrier leads Dikki Du and the Zydeco Crew, which had their debut on Lanor in 1997 with *The Way It Is*. Meanwhile Troy's father, Roy Carrier, recorded several cassettes for Lanor; the highlights have been reissued on the recommended disc *At His Best* (Zane). Carrier's own versions of "Tequila" and "Strokin'" are here, along with the satisfying "Backbone Zydeco" and "Leaving Lawtell." Carrier's 1997 disc *Nasty Girls* (Right On Rhythm) is a collection of live appearances in the Washington, D.C., area.

After years of silence, the Sam Brothers reemerged in the late 1990s with the excellent *Leon's Boogie Is Back!* (MTE) which immediately became impossible to find. Their early recordings for Maison de Soul and Arhoolie are also recommended. Li'l Brian and the Zydeco Travellers combine driving Buckwheat Zydeco–inspired zydeco with rap on their Rounder discs *Fresh* and *Z-Funk*. Other suggested piano-key recordings include Joe Walker's *Zydeco Fever* (Zane) and Jude Taylor's *Best of Zydeco* (Mardi Gras).

Ann Goodly is a zydeco artist most deserving of a comeback; her Maison de Soul outing *Miss Ann Goodly and the Zydeco Bros.* features warm vocals and talented accordion work on tunes such as "Don't Let the Green Grass Fool You" and John Delafose's "I Got a Broken Heart." Of Rosie Ledet's work for Maison de Soul, *Sweet Brown Sugar* has the best songs, including "Should've Been Mine" and "The Mardi Gras." *Zesty Zydeco* is also recommended, especially for "I'm Gonna Take Care of Your Dog."

**Chapter Nineteen**

Terrance Simien's 1990 debut disc *Zydeco on the Bayou* (Restless) gave the young accordionist rein to make a personal statement with his inherited tradition, as well as to explore the hybrid possibilities of pop and reggae. Commendably, Simien makes a greater effort than most to acknowledge the original sources of his new tunes, crediting Preston Frank's "Why Do You Want to Make Me Cry?" for his "The Love We Shared." Simien has fresh versions of tunes by Fernest Arceneaux and Boozoo Chavis on his 1993 Black Top release *There's Room for Us All.* He also explores the connection between zydeco and New Orleans funk by bringing in the Meters for a faithful reading of King Floyd's "Groove Me." He made a 1998 debut on the Tone-Cool label and is planning a zydeco-themed children's project. Fans will also want to look for *A Tribute to John Delafose* (Deep South), which includes five Simien tracks.

Chubby Carrier's recordings include *Boogie Woogie Zydeco* (Flying Fish) and *Dance All Night* (Blind Pig), but I prefer his *Who Stole the Hot Sauce?* (Blind Pig), which has a selection of bubbly new compositions to showcase the accordionist's talent. It also has zydeco versions of Pete Townshend's "Squeeze Box" and a guest turn on harmonica by Billy Branch on "The Cisco Kid." Thomas Fields offers a very different sound with the two-steps, waltzes, and zydeco stomps on *Come to Louisiana* and the better *Louisiana Is the Place to See!,* both on Lanor.

## Chapter Twenty

My favorite Lawrence Ardoin recording is *Lawrence "Black" Ardoin and his French Zydeco Band* (Arhoolie), available only on cassette. This traditional set includes great fiddle accompaniment by Edward Poullard on tunes such as "Midland Two-Step," the bluesy "Walking down the Interstate," and a country-tinged "Haunted House." Chris Ardoin first joined his father for *Lawrence Ardoin and Lagniappe* (Maison de Soul), which also has Sean Ardoin on drums. Chris Ardoin and Double Clutchin' made their debut on *That's Da Lick* (Maison de Soul), and continued this theme on *Lick It Up!* Both discs are enjoyable, but Double Clutchin' really began to come into its own on *Gon' Be Jus' Fine* (Rounder), blending more contemporary R&B stylings into their family's traditional music. The band is still taking its first steps, and many fans hope that these talented players will be moved to further explore the wealth of tunes and styles from Amédé and Bois Sec Ardoin.

## Zydeco Compilations

Allow me a moment of self-promotion: I am currently in production with Rounder Records on a compilation of zydeco to complement this book. It will feature both historic and contemporary zydeco styles culled from a variety of labels. Its intentions are threefold: to highlight the variety of styles in zydeco, to demonstrate the links between the music's past and present, and to make a great dance mix. Here are other compilations I like: *Let's Go Zydeco* (Ace), *Zydeco Festival* (Maison de Soul), *Stomp Down Zydeco* (Rounder), *The Royal Family of Zydeco* (Rock 'n' Bowl), *101 Proof Zydeco* (Maison de Soul), *J'ai Eté au Bal, Vol. 2* (Arhoolie), *Rockin' Zydeco Party* (Maison de Soul), *Zydeco Shootout At El Sid O's* (Rounder), and *Cajun Music and Zydeco* and *More Cajun Music and Zydeco* (Rounder). Rhino's *Alligator Stomp* series is also good.

# A Select Bibliography

The following works have been helpful in understanding and appreciating the richness of the music and culture of Southwest Louisiana and East Texas.

## Books About Zydeco and Related Music

Abernathy, Francis Edward, ed. *What's Going On? (In Modern Texas Folklore)*. Austin, Tex.: The Encino Press, 1976. The chapter by Joseph Lomax titled "Zydeco — Must Live On!" has information about and photographs of early Texas accordionists, including Anderson Moss.

Allan, Johnnie. *Memories: A Pictorial History of South Louisiana Music, Volumes 1 & 2 Combined, 1910s–1990s*. Lafayette, La.: Johnnie Allan/JADFEL Publishing, 1995. Includes rare home, live, and publicity photographs of zydeco players.

Ancelet, Barry Jean, Jay D. Edwards, and Glen Pitre. *Cajun Country*. Jackson: University Press of Mississippi, 1991. The most comprehensive treatment of Cajun culture in print.

Ancelet, Barry Jean, and Elemore Morgan Jr. *The Makers of Cajun Music*. Austin: University of Texas Press, 1984. Morgan's distinctive photography illustrates Ancelet's bilingual oral histories of Bois Sec Ardoin, Canray Fontenot, and Freeman Fontenot, as well as a profile of Clifton Chenier.

Bernard, Shane K. *Swamp Pop: Cajun and Creole Rhythm and Blues*. Jackson: University Press of Mississippi, 1996. A thorough account of a cousin genre to zydeco. Of particular interest is the chapter "Cajun and Black Creole Elements in Swamp Pop Music."

Broven, John. *South to Louisiana: The Music of the Cajun Bayous*. Gretna, La.: Pelican, 1987. A rollicking portrait of Cajun, zydeco, and swamp pop, with useful information on Clifton Chenier, Clarence Garlow, Rockin' Sidney, Boozoo Chavis, and more.

Daigle, Pierre V. *Tears, Love and Laughter: The Story of the Cajuns and Their Music.* Ville Platte, La.: Swallow Publications, 1972. This pioneering work is still a pleasure to read.

Dormon, James H., ed. *Creoles of Color of the Gulf South.* Knoxville: University of Tennessee Press, 1996. An essential book for anyone hoping to grasp the intricacies of calling oneself Creole in Louisiana. Of particular interest are Carl Brasseaux's history "Creoles of Color in Louisiana's Bayou Country, 1776 – 1877," Nicholas Spitzer's "Mardi Gras in L'Anse de 'Prien Noir: A Creole Community Performance in Rural French Louisiana," and Barry Ancelet's "Zydeco/Zarico: The Term and the Tradition."

Francois, Raymond E. *Yé Yaille, Chère! Traditional Cajun Dance Music.* Lafayette, La.: Thunderstone Press, 1990. Song lyrics, translations, and transcriptions.

Fry, Macon, and Julie Posner. *Cajun Country Guide.* Gretna, La.: Pelican, 1992. A unique travel guide that emphasizes music and dance clubs in Southwest Louisiana.

Fusilier, Freida Marie, and Jolene M. Adams. *Hé Là-Bas! A History of Louisiana Cajun and Zydeco Music in California.* Self-published, 1994. Available by calling (916) 451-9618 or (318) 461-2216.

Gould, Philip; introduction by Barry Ancelet. *Cajun Music and Zydeco.* Baton Rouge: Louisiana State University Press, 1992. Of Gould's several grand photographic treatments of South Louisiana life, this one is devoted to musicians. Ancelet's essay is both elegant and informative.

Govenar, Alan. *Meeting the Blues: The Rise of the Texas Sound.* Dallas, Tex.: Taylor Publishing, 1988. Especially useful for understanding the Texas impact on zydeco. Includes brief interviews with L. C. Donatto Jr. and Sr., Clifton Chenier, and church dance promoter Clarence Gallien.

Guillory, Queen Ida, and Naomi Wise. *Cookin' with Queen Ida.* Rocklin, Cal.: Prima Publishing, 1996. A good cookbook is made even better with an extended oral history that covers Queen Ida's childhood experiences in Lake Charles.

Lichtenstein, Grace, and Laura Dankner. *Musical Gumbo: The Music of New Orleans.* New York: W. W. Norton, 1993. Includes information about Clifton and C. J. Chenier, Rockin' Sidney, Buckwheat Zydeco, and other contemporary zydeco players.

Murray, Albert. *Stomping the Blues.* New York: McGraw-Hill, 1976. Murray's classic extended essay on the spirit of jazz provokes new ways of hearing zydeco as well.

Nyhan, Pat, Brian Rollins, and David Babb. *Let the Good Times Roll! A Guide to Cajun and Zydeco Music.* Portland, Me.: Upbeat Books, 1997. A well-researched guide with informed and opinionated ratings of most available recordings of Cajun and zydeco music.

Orlean, Susan. *Saturday Night.* New York: Alfred A. Knopf, 1990. This series of profiles of American communities celebrating Saturday night includes a wonderful chapter on Houston church dances. Orlean captures the spirit and the details of a zydeco night, and even has an unforgettable cameo appearance by Boozoo Chavis.

Savoy, Ann Allen, ed. *Cajun Music: A Reflection of a People, Volume I.* Eunice, La.: Bluebird Press, 1984. This indispensable collection of profiles, interviews, photographs, and song transcriptions is like an extended family scrapbook. Creole and zydeco artists included: Amédé Ardoin, Canray Fontenot, Marceline Ardoin, Bois Sec Ardoin, Freeman Fontenot, Claude Faulk, Bébé Carrière, John Delafose, Rockin' Dopsie, and Clifton Chenier.

## South Louisiana Culture and History

Ancelet, Barry. *Cajun and Creole Folktales: The French Oral Tradition of South Louisiana.* Jackson: University Press of Mississippi, 1994. Informed and entertaining. Includes stories by Creole ballad singer Inez Catalon.

Brasseaux, Carl A., Keith P. Fontenot, and Claude F. Oubre. *Creoles of Color in the Bayou Country.* Jackson: University Press of Mississippi, 1994. An examination of the documented roots of Creole life in Southwest Louisiana.

Hall, Gwendolyn Midlo. *Africans in Colonial Louisiana: The Development of Afro-Creole Culture in the Eighteenth Century.* Baton Rouge: Louisiana State University Press, 1992. A ground-breaking overview of the first stages in the development of African-American and Creole culture in Louisiana.

Lindahl, Carl, Maida Owens, and C. Renee Harvison, eds. *Swapping Stories: Folktales from Louisiana.* This collection features several tales spun about musicians. A great way to understand the inner life of the people of Louisiana.

Macdonald, Robert R., John R. Kemp, and Edward F. Haas, eds. *Louisiana's Black Heritage.* New Orleans: Louisiana State Museum, 1979. Scholarly essays about the history of black cultures in the state.

McDonald, Roderick A. *The Economy and Material Culture of Slaves.* Baton Rouge: Louisiana State University Press, 1993. A study that emphasizes the resourcefulness of slaves on sugar plantations in building their own economies and ways of living.

Saxon, Lyle, Edward Dreyer, and Robert Tallant. *Gumbo Ya-Ya: A Collection of Louisiana Folk Tales.* Gretna, La.: Pelican, 1987. A lively classic in Louisiana lore first written as part of the WPA Louisiana Writers' Project.

Tallant, Robert. *Voodoo in New Orleans.* Gretna, La.: Pelican, 1990. Too colorfully rendered, this book, first published in 1946, is nonetheless useful for understanding the roots of current Louisiana spiritual and musical activity.

Wall, Bennett H., ed. *Louisiana: A History.* Arlington Heights, Ill.: Forum Press, 1990. General textbook.

## Reference Works Consulted

Donald Clarke, ed. *The Penguin Encyclopedia of Popular Music.* New York: Viking, 1989.

Wilson, Charles Reagan, and William Ferris, eds. *Encyclopedia of Southern Culture.* Chapel Hill: University of North Carolina Press, 1989. Includes essays by Nicholas Spitzer and Barry Ancelet.

*World Music: The Rough Guide.* London: Rough Guides, 1994. Includes zydeco musicians and useful information about African music.

## Related Works of Fiction

Chopin, Kate. *The Awakening and Selected Stories.* New York: Random House, 1984.

Proulx, E. Annie. *Accordion Crimes.* New York: Scribner, 1996.

## Articles and Liner Notes

Zydeco — especially reviews and profiles of zydeco players — is frequently covered in the popular music press. Some specific articles are cited in the text. Many more articles and liner notes were used for general background, especially work by Herman Fuselier, Geoffrey Himes, Ben Sandmel, Todd Mouton, Nicholas Spitzer, Arsenio Orteza, and Keith Spera. The following articles were especially helpful:

Ancelet, Barry. Liner notes for *Louisiana Cajun and Creole Music 1934: The Lomax Recordings.* Swallow, 1987.

Bernard, Shane, and Julia Girouard. "'Colinda': Mysterious Origins of a Cajun Folksong." *Journal of Folklore Research,* vol. 29, no. 1, 1992.

Minton, John. "Houston Creoles and Zydeco: The Emergence of an African American Urban Popular Style." *American Music,* winter 1996, pp. 480 – 526.

Snyder, Jared. "Squeezebox: The Legacy of the Afro-Mississippi Accordionists." *Black Music Research Journal,* vol. 17, no. 1, spring 1997, pp. 37 – 58.

Spitzer, Nicholas. Liner notes for *Zodico.* Rounder, 1979.

Toureille, Pierre. Liner notes for *Ile Maurice: Hommage à Ti Frère.* Radio France, 1991.

Wagner, Christoph, Jared Snyder, et al. Liner notes for *Planet Squeezebox.* Ellipses Arts, 1995.

## A Selected Filmography

Most of the following films are available on videocassette through the record shops and catalogues listed above.

*Big Easy, The,* dir. Jim McBride. 1987. The soundtrack of this Hollywood detective movie did for Louisiana music what Paul Prudhomme did for Cajun cooking. Terrance Simien appears.

*Buckwheat Zydeco: Taking It Home,* dir. Bob Portway. Island, 1990. Filmed concert.

*Cajun Visits/Les Blues de Balfa,* dir. Yasha Aginsky. Flower Films, 1983. Includes a visit with Canray Fontenot and footage of Rockin' Dopsie and Dewey Balfa touring Louisiana schools.

*Clifton Chenier: The King of Zydeco,* prod. Chris Strachwitz. Arhoolie, 1987. The live footage of the 1982 San Francisco Blues Festival doesn't present the King at his mightiest, but it's still good. Rare interviews and footage from appearances on Lafayette television make this more than worthwhile, but watch *Hot Pepper* first.

*Dedans le Sud de la Louisiane (In the South of Louisiana),* dir. Jean-Pierre Bruneau. Cote Blanche, 1983. Wonderful scenes of Cajun and zydeco players, including Bois Sec Ardoin, Clifton and Cleveland Chenier (including the only recorded interview with Cleveland), and Canray and Bee Fontenot.

*Dry Wood,* dir. Les Blank. Flower Films, 1979. This loving portrait of Bois Sec Ardoin includes a scene of a *boucherie* that may require intestinal fortitude for some viewers.

*Hot Pepper,* dir. Les Blank. Flower Films, 1973. In the peak years of his career, Clifton Chenier spent a couple weeks leading filmmaker Blank through his Louisiana haunts. Incredible scenes of Chenier playing dances and making music with friends and family.

*J'ai Eté au Bal (I Went to the Dance),* dir. Les Blank. Brazos Films, 1989. The best overview available of zydeco and Cajun music origins and the modern (circa 1989) scene. Live footage of Queen Ida, Boozoo Chavis, Canray Fontenot, Rockin' Sidney, and many more.

*Kingdom of Zydeco, The,* dir. Robert Mugge. BMG Video, 1994. Along with a lively showdown concert between Boozoo Chavis and Beau Jocque, this music documentary features an unforgettable interview with Chavis, visits with Sid and Nathan Williams, and one of the final performances of John Delafose.

*Learn to Zydeco Dance Tonite!* Insectefex, 1995. The only commercially available zydeco dance instructional video features explanations by Washington, D.C., instructor Ben Pagac and music by Roy Carrier.

*Les Creoles,* dirs. André Gladu and Michel Brault. 1983. Includes scenes of Delton Broussard, Bébé Carrière, and Inez Catalon. (In French without subtitles.)

*Passion Fish,* dir. John Sayles. 1992. The writer/director turns his talents to a fiction set in Southwest Louisiana that includes black Creole characters, zydeco dance settings, and a performance by John Delafose.

*True Believers,* dir. Robert Mugge. BMG Video, 1995. Profile of Rounder Records includes performance footage of Beau Jocque and an interview with Kermon Richard.

*Zarico,* dir. André Gladu. Montreal, National Film Board of Canada, 1994. Wonderful scenes include Luke Collins and Morris Ardoin broadcasting on KEUN in Eunice, a dance at Ardoin's Cowboy Club, and interviews with and performances by Bois Sec Ardoin, Canray Fontenot, Ambrose Sam, Rockin' Dopsie, and a very young Ann Goodly.

*Zydeco,* dirs. Nicholas Spitzer and Steven Duplantier. Flower Films, 1984. Documentary includes music and interviews with Bois Sec Ardoin and Bébé Carrière, and rare footage of *juré* performers. Highly recommended.

*Zydeco Gumbo,* dir. Dan Hildebrandt. Rhapsody Films, 1990. Includes Clifton Chenier's final performance of "I'm Coming Home" at the Zydeco Festival, as well as unusual early footage of Beau Jocque.

*Zydeco Nite 'n' Day,* prods. Karen Anderson and Robert Dowling. Island, 1991. Festival performances by Clifton Chenier, Boozoo Chavis, Rockin' Dopsie, and more.


# Where It's At


Finally, Clarence Garlow's advice still rings true. If you want to have fun, you go way out to the country to the zydeco. Whether you're at a day-long festival or a night-long dance, there is simply no substitute for hours of prolonged exposure for discovering the music and its appeal. In Louisiana, zydeco club owners and crowds are generally very welcoming of out-of-towners. Venues for zydeco are also springing up around the world.

The flagship zydeco clubs are located within a thirty-mile radius in Southwest Louisiana. In Lawtell are Richard's Club and Roy's Offshore Lounge. Slim's Y-Ki-Ki is in Opelousas. El Sid O's and Hamilton's Place are in Lafayette. Dances — held on Fridays and Saturdays except for Roy's Thursday jam sessions — are announced on signboards outside the clubs. When there, keep your ears open for announcements about trail rides and other dances.

In Houston, only two of the great Frenchtown zydeco hubs remain open. The Silver Slipper is a smaller club with illuminated multicolored tiles on the dance floor. The barnlike Continental Ballroom Zydeco dates to the 1940s, when it was known as Johnson's Cafe and was the center of Creole life in Houston. Its future, however, is in question following the 1998 death of owner Doris McClendon. Today, popular Houston bands Step Rideau and J. Paul Jr. hold weekly dances at R&B clubs around the city. The church dances are announced in the "Around the Diocese" section of the *Weekly Catholic Herald,* available in many churches or at the Chancery. Another popular venue is Pe-Te's Cajun Barbecue, which has zydeco dances on Saturday afternoons.

The closest stop for touring zydeco bands is New Orleans, just a two-hour drive from Southwest Louisiana. With dances on Wednesdays, Thursdays, and some weekends, the Mid-City Lanes Rock 'n' Bowl has the busiest zydeco schedule found anywhere. Zydeco bands also regularly perform at the Maple Leaf Bar and several other New Orleans clubs and restaurants. Major cities around the country with zydeco venues include: Chicago area (Fitzgerald's Club and Crawdaddy Bayou), Seattle (Tractor Tavern), San Francisco Bay Area (Ashkenaz, Eagle's Hall, Bobby's Back Door, DeMarco's 23 Club, and many churches), Los Angeles (the War Memorial Hall), Washington, D.C. (Twist and Shout, the Spanish Ballroom in Glen Echo Park, and the Barns of Wolf Trap), Las Vegas (Orleans Hotel and Casino), and New York (Tramps and Louisiana Community Bar and Grill). Information about venues in the South is available by contacting the Atlanta Cajun Dance Association at (770) 451-5365. Cajun/zydeco hotlines on the West Coast include (213) 344-4044 and (626) 793-4333 in Southern California and (415) 467-7630 in San Francisco.

The Southwest Louisiana Zydeco Festival takes place annually in Plaisance, Louisiana, on the Saturday before Labor Day. Richard's Club holds a festival the following Sunday, and Boozoo Chavis opens the gates to Dog Hill each Labor Day. Call the Lafayette Visitors Center at (800) 346-1958 for more information on the Plaisance event as well as the Zydeco Extravaganza, which takes place each Memorial Day weekend in Lafayette. The New Orleans Jazz and Heritage Festival is on the last weekend of April and the first weekend of May. Among the other major festivals in Louisiana and Texas that feature zydeco music are the Breaux Bridge Crawfish Festival, Lafayette's Festivals Internationals and Festivals Acadiens, the Houston International Festival, and the Swamp Festival in New Orleans. Zydeco is featured in hundreds of other smaller events annually that celebrate shrimp, petroleum, and other local passions.

Here is a list of just some of the major events that regularly present zydeco outside of Louisiana: the Cajun Zydeco Crawfish Festival in Fort Lauderdale, Florida; City Stages in Birmingham, Alabama; the Beale Street

Zydeco Festival in Memphis; the Escoheag Americana Roots Music Festival in Rhode Island; the American Music Festival at Fitzgerald's in the Chicago area; the American Roots Fourth of July Festival and the Louisiana Swamp Romp in the Washington, D.C., area; New Orleans by the Bay in the San Francisco Bay Area; the Simi Valley Cajun Zydeco Festival near Los Angeles; the San Diego Street Scene; the Cajun/Creole week at Augusta Heritage Center at Davis and Elkins College in West Virginia; Jam on the River in Philadelphia; the Bayou Boogaloo in Norfolk, Virginia; Bumpershoot in Seattle; Summerfest in Milwaukee; the Preston Cajun Zydeco Festival in Connecticut. There are also Cajun and zydeco festivals in England, Holland, Belgium, and new countries each year. These are all large events, and local tourist bureaus will have more information.

The above represent just a fraction of the opportunities to hear live zydeco. In Louisiana, the Louisiana Association of Fairs and Festivals (504/342-8119) offers a listing of statewide events; also, New Orleans author Julie Posner publishes the comprehensive *Huli's Calendar of Louisiana Festivals and Events,* available for sale at (504) 733-5923. The best source for national and international zydeco schedules — even directions to zydeco clubs — is Gary Hayman's ZydE-Magic Cajun/Zydeco Web Page (http://www.nmaa.org/member/ghayman). This site provides links to regions throughout the country, and to the United Kingdom Cajun and Zydeco Resources Page, as well as information on how to receive e-mail listings of zydeco dances.

Regular coverage of zydeco can be found in *OffBeat* magazine, published in New Orleans, which also staffs a recommended website (http://www.offbeat.com). I write a column about zydeco for *Living Blues,* and zydeco is also regularly featured in Lafayette's *In Tune* newspaper. Finally, when in Louisiana, turn your radio dial to WWOZ 88.7 in New Orleans, KRVS 88.7 in Lafayette, KNEK 1190 AM in Washington, and KEUN 1330 AM in Eunice.

# PHOTO CREDITS

# LYRICS CREDITS

# INDEX OF NAMES

Note: page numbers in boldface denote photographs